Annals of St. Louis in its Early Days under the French and Spanish Dominations

Frederic L. Billon

HERITAGE BOOKS
2008

HERITAGE BOOKS
AN IMPRINT OF HERITAGE BOOKS, INC.

Books, CDs, and more—Worldwide

For our listing of thousands of titles see our website at
www.HeritageBooks.com

Published 2008 by
HERITAGE BOOKS, INC.
Publishing Division
100 Railroad Ave. #104
Westminster, Maryland 21157

Copyright © 1886 Frederic L. Billon

Other books by the author:
Annals of St. Louis in its Territorial Days From 1804 to 1821

All rights reserved. No part of this book may be reproduced or transmitted in any form or by any means, electronic or mechanical, including photocopying, recording or by any information storage and retrieval system without written permission from the author, except for the inclusion of brief quotations in a review.

International Standard Book Numbers
Paperbound: 978-0-7884-0690-4
Clothbound: 978-0-7884-7032-5

Fredc. L. Billon

Oct. 1886

PREFACE.

To my Readers:

It has been frequently urged upon me, by perhaps too partial friends, that "my long residence of exceeding sixty years in the place," (coming here when it was yet almost in its infancy, when there were yet still living a goodly number of its original settlers, with many of whom, from my familiarity with their language and customs, being descended from the same nationality, I had soon become on intimate terms) gave me facilities not, perhaps, possessed by any other one to the same extent, to prepare, so far as it could be done with the scant materials at command for the purpose, what had long been a *desideratum* not easily supplied, viz., an authentic history of St. Louis during its French and Spanish days, its origin and progress.

In compliance with that oft preferred request, and in furtherance of my own views on the subject, I submit to you, as the result of my long researches and investigations in that field, the following pages, with the simple observation that however deficient they may prove as a literary effort, they will at least possess the merit of authenticity and reliability; and, I flatter myself, will establish beyond controversy many facts heretofore vague and obscure, connected with the early history of our place.

I am well aware of the difficulty of eradicating from the minds of the majority of mankind their preconceived ideas, however erroneous, upon any subject-matter whatsoever — ideas that they have perhaps imbibed from their childhood, coming down to them with the authority and prestige of parents to children, particularly of occurrences that transpired before their day, and which have reached them through tradition alone, with its manifold errors and exaggerations; and the almost useless task one undertakes in endeavoring to correct these erroneous impressions. This I shall not endeavor to do, but will simply present the facts in all cases as I found them, derived from the original official Spanish and French documents, most of them translated by myself, some of them yet in the archives, and others placed in my possession by descendants of the original participants therein.

Much of the information I have gathered relating to St. Louis I have obtained from certain works on Illinois and Indiana, the materials for a reliable history of the early days of the settlement of this upper country on the other side of the river, now Illinois, Indiana, etc., being much more abundant and authentic than those of this side.

From the time the English received possession of that side in 1765, during the thirteen years they held it, and subsequently when taken by Clark for the Virginians in 1778, down to the date of the transfer of the country on the west side of the river to the United States in 1804, a period of nearly forty years, courts had been established and records kept, from which a reliable, although but a brief, history could be produced. But not so with the country on this side, which dates its settlement only from the time of that transfer to the British, and to which circumstance mainly it owes its sudden growth. For whatever documents there might have been, if any, in the so-called Spanish archives of St. Louis of a political or historical nature, calculated to furnish materials for history, were carried away with the cannon and munitions of war at the evacuation by De Lassus in 1804. As by the terms of the treaty of purchase, and his instructions from the governor-general at New Orleans, he was directed to leave only such papers as related to the private affairs of individuals, such as deeds, concessions, etc., affording but little information of a historical nature, and throwing but little light upon matters of public interest, consequently much of what we have hitherto regarded as *history* of those early days had come down to us through oral tradition alone, with the manifold exaggerations and misstatements to which all unrecorded history is liable in transmission.

Many facts connected with the abandonment of Fort Chartres, St. Phillippe and Kaskaskia have been brought to light in works on these two States and Kentucky that cannot be found in any work on Upper Louisiana.

Major Amos Stoddard, United States army, was the first who ever wrote anything in the shape of a sketch of St. Louis, and here is all he has to say of it in 1804, from his own observation: —

"In 1764 St. Louis was founded by Pierre Laclede, Maxan & Co., as a trading post. In 1766 the village received an accession of inhabitants from the other side of the river, who preferred the Spanish to the English government. It contains about 180 houses, the best of them of stone. A small sloping hill extends along the rear of the town, on the summit of which is a garrison, and beyond it is an extensive prairie which affords plenty of hay.

"After the Indian attack on St. Louis in 1780, the government deemed it necessary to fortify the town. It was immediately stockaded and the stone bastion and the demilune at the upper end of it were constructed. The succeeding peace of 1783 lessened the danger and the works were suspended. In 1794, the garrison on the hill in the rear of the town and government house was completed. In 1797, when an unfriendly visit was expected from Canada, four stone towers were erected at nearly equal distances in a circular direction around the town, as also a wooden block house near the lower end of it. It was contemplated to enclose the town by a regular chain of works, and the towers were intended to answer the purposes of bastions. But as the times grew more auspicious the design was abandoned, and the works left in an unfinished state."

In his "Sketches of Louisiana," Phila., 1812, Stoddard says in his preface:

"It fell to my lot in the month of March, 1804, to take possession of Upper Louisiana under the treaty of cession. * * * The records and other public documents were open to my inspection; and, as it was my fortune to be stationed about five years on various parts of the Lower Mississippi, and nearly six months on Red river, my inquiries gradually extended to Louisiana in general.

"That country, even at that day, was less known than any other (inhabited by a civilized people), of the same extent on the globe. While it was in possession of France and Spain, at least till near the close of the American Revolution, it was almost inaccessible to us; nor were we influenced by motives of interest or curiosity to visit it. The entrance of our vessels into its ports was either interdicted, or its commerce too unimportant to incite maritime adventures, and the mountains and uninhabited wilderness on our frontiers presented strong barriers to enterprise overland. The Spanish government, in particular, was always actuated by a dark and intricate policy; it was careful to exclude strangers from its dominions * * * No wonder, then, that Louisiana at the time of the cession was so little known to the United States * * * I, therefore, indulge the hope that my sketches, however imperfect may not prove unacceptable, particularly as no one before me, to my knowledge, has attempted an history and description of this territory.

AMOS STODDARD.,
Major U. S. Artillery."[1]

"FORT COLUMBUS, 1812."

Stoddard further says: " The causes that led the Americans to cross from the east to the west side, were : *First*, the Ordinance of 1787, accepting by the United States the country on the east side from Virginia, which prohibited slavery ; and *secondly*, the rupture of 1797, when an attack from Canada was apprehended on the Spanish possessions of the Mississippi, to strengthen which they held out inducements to the Americans to come over and settle."

---

[1] Stoddard was in the United States Army from 1794 to his death in 1814, twenty years.

PREFACE.

The incidents narrated in these pages, are derived largely from original manuscripts of the day, all in the French and Spanish languages: the French being that of the inhabitants of the country, nearly all of whom were descendants of that nationality, and the Spanish, the official language of the government from the year 1770. For the use of many of these documents I am indebted to my friend Augustus De Lassus, the only son of the last of the Spanish lieutenant-governors of this upper portion of Louisiana, residing, as he has for many years past, in St. Francois County, who sent me a large mass of his father's official and private papers; to my old friend G. S. Chouteau, the last surviving son of the original Col. Augte. Chouteau, who had much to do with the founding of the place, and who lived with us a period of sixty-five years until his death in 1829, at the ripe old age of seventy-nine; to Dr. Charles Gratiot and sister, of Cheltenham, in this city, grand children of the first Charles Gratiot, a prominent personage of the little village from the year 1780 until his death at the age of sixty-five years in 1817, and others to whom I am largely indebted for the invaluable aid I derived from the use of their documents.

FRED'C L. BILLON.

ST. LOUIS, 1886.

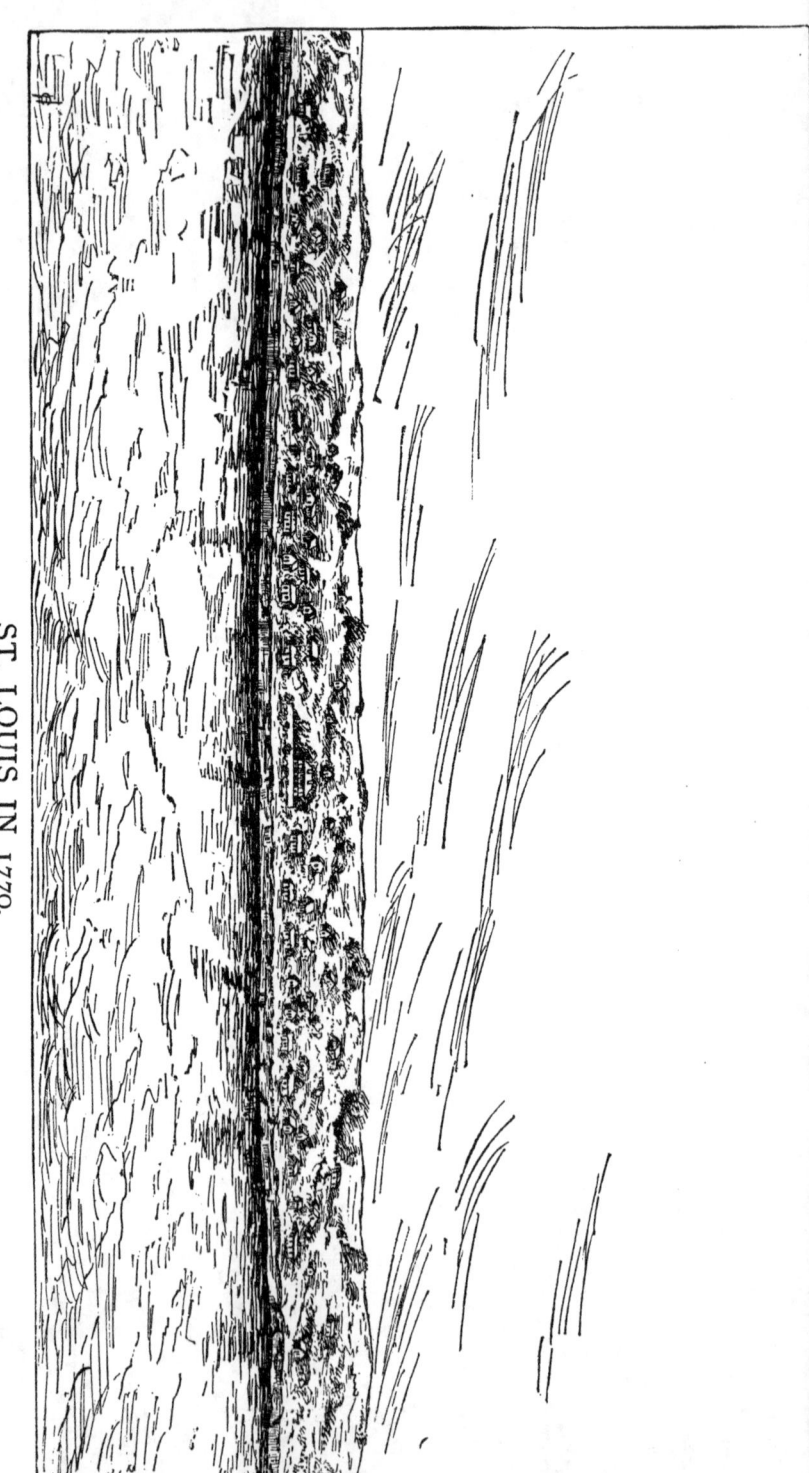

ST. LOUIS IN 1770.
AS SEEN FROM ILLINOIS SIDE.
[*Drawn by C. Heberer under direction of F. L. Billon.*]

INTRODUCTORY CHRONOLOGY.

DISCOVERY AND DESCENT OF THE MISSISSIPPI RIVER.

(*From Father Marquette's Journal, published by Thevenot, Paris, 1682.*)

Prior to the year 1668, Michilimackinac was the extreme point of trade of the Canadians with the Indian tribes of the Northwest. In that year the Jesuit Missionaries, Fathers Claude Allouez, Claude Dablon and James Marquette, reached the western extremity of Lake Superior.

1673, May 13th. — The Sieur Joliet of Quebec, a Canadian trader, and Father Marquette, a missionary priest, with five French hands, seven in the party, embarked in two bark canoes at Mackinaw, to seek the great river of the west, of which they had frequently heard through the Indians of that region. The first nation they met was the Folle Avoines (Menominees). They next arrived at the Pottawatomies at Green Bay. Entering Fox River they arrived on June 7th at the villages of the Maskoutens and Miamies. June 10th, taking with them two Indian guides, they ascended the Fox River, crossed the portage of one and a half miles, carrying their canoes,

(1)

which they launched in the Meskonsing (Ouisconsin), dismissed their guides and descended that river.

June 17th, they entered the Mississippi River at about the forty-second degree of north latitude, and commenced its descent. 25th. Found tracks of men which led to their village, two leagues inland; they were of the Indians called the Illinois.

Passed the mouth of the Pekitanoui (Missouri) on their right, then the Ouabouskigou (Ouabache), Indian name of the Ohio, coming in from the east in latitude north about thirty-six. Below here they met Indians, the Chicachas (Chicasaws), descended to near the thirty-third degree and passed on their right the village of the Michigamias, and ten leagues below the large village called Akamsca (Arkansas).

Here, being within one and a half degrees, or two or three days' journey to the Gulf of Florida, after a day's rest, they left this village of Akamsca on July 17th, on their return up the Mississippi, being one month in descending that river from the forty-second degree to below the thirty-fourth. On arriving at the thirty-ninth degree they left the Mississippi to enter another river of the east side (the Illinois) which shortened their return to the lake of the Illinois Indians (Lake Michigan), and reached Green Bay at the close of September, having been over four months on their voyage.

1675, May 13. — Louis, the fourteenth king of France, made to Robert Cavalier de La Salle a grant of lands at Frontenac, Canada.

1678, May 12. — Another grant from the king, confirming and extending the first, with instructions to prosecute the discoveries in New France — the name given the country on the Mississippi.

1681, December. — La Salle and Lieut. Tonty left Chekagou, on Lake Michigan, with twenty-two Frenchmen and eighteen Indians, Hurons, etc., descended the Illinois and Mississippi Rivers, and on April 6, 1682, arrived at the three outlets of the river into the Gulf, and having selected a suitable spot they, on the 9th, planted a column with a cross bearing the Arms of France and this inscription:

LOUIS THE GRAND,
KING OF FRANCE AND NAVARRE.
APRIL 9, 1682.

The *Te Deum, Exaudiat* and the *Domine Salvum fac Regem* were chanted by the whole party, and after a salute of fire-arms and shouts of "Long live the king," M. de La Salle delivered an address and proclaimed the country taken possession of in the name of the king of France, and then buried at the foot of the cross a metallic plate on which was engraved the arms of France and an appropriate inscription.

A verbal process was drawn up by Jacques La Metairie, and signatures affixed: —

De La Salle,
Father Zenobé Membré, recollet missionary,
Henri de Tonty,
Francois de Boisrondet,
Jean Bourdon,
Sieur d'Autray,
Jacques Cauchois,
Pierre You,
Gilles Meucret,
Jean Michel, surgeon,
Jean Mas,
Jean Dulignon,
Nicholas De La Salle,
La Metairie, notary.

1683. — Further instructions were issued to La Salle to open a communication to New France by the Gulf of Mexico.

FROM CAPT. D'IBERVILLE'S REPORT, JULY 3, 1699.

1698, Oct. 24. — M. Capt. d' Iberville sailed from Brest in his flagship "La Badine," with the frigate "Le Marin," Capt. de Surgeres, to take possession of Louisiana, cast anchor at the Chandeleur Islands early in February, 1699, and on the 21st, with his brothers, Sauvolle and Bienville and others, and fifty-three men, left the vessels in two boats and some canoes, found the mouth of the Mississippi, and entered the river on March 2d, which he ascended as far up as the Natchez tribe of Indians, then returned down the river to the Bayou Manchac. Here leaving the large boats to descend the river, he passed in a canoe through the Bayou, the Amitié River and the lakes Maurepas, Pontchartrain and Borgne, which he so named, and reached his ships on the 31st.

1699, April — Commenced the erection of a fort (Maurepas) at Biloxi, on the main land, and on its completion he sailed for France May 3, 1699, leaving M. De Sauvolle in command with Lieut. De Bienville of the navy, a chaplain, a major, two captains, two cannoniers, four sailors, eighteen filibusters, ten mechanics, six masons, thirteen Canadians and twenty sub-officers and privates — eighty in all — to commence the colony.

1699, December 7. — The second arrival of Iberville from France. Sauvolle had been appointed by the king the first governor of Louisiana.

1700, Jan. 17. — Iberville and Bienville went up the Mississippi and selected a site for a fort fifty-four miles from the mouth. On May 3d, Iberville sailed again for France.

1701, July 22. — Death of Sauvolle, the first governor.

1702, March 18. — Capt. Iberville's third arrival with two ships from France and return there in June.

1703. — War declared between Great Britain and France and Spain. August 15, arrival of Chateauguay, another brother of Bienville.

1707. — Death of Iberville at San Domingo. Bienville acting governor *ad interim*.

1708. — Population 279 French and 60 Canadians.

1712, Sept. 14. — The king granted to M. Crozat a charter of the colony.

1713, May 17. — Arrival of Lamothe Cadillac, new governor for Crozat.

1716. — Recall of Cadillac and resumption by Bienville.

1717, March 9. — Arrival of the new governor M. De L' Epinay. August 13, Crozat surrendered his charter to the King, and Jno. Laws' India Company was established to succeed him in the proprietorship.

1718. — De l' Epinay recalled to France and Bienville reappointed governor; Bienville selected a site for a new capital on the Mississippi, and New Orleans was commenced.

1723. — Seat of government transferred to the new city New Orleans.

1724, Jan. 16. — Gov. Bienville was called to France; he sailed in

1725 — And Boisbriant succeeded him *ad interim*.

1726, Aug. 9. — M. Perier appointed governor.

1731, Jan. 23. — The India Company surrendered their charter to the king.

1733. — Gov. Bienville reappointed and returned after eight years' absence.

1742. — Gov. Bienville requested to be recalled.

1743, May 10. — The Marquis De Vaudreuil, his successor, arrived, and Bienville left the country for France forever.

1753. — The Marquis De Vaudreuil was appointed governor-general of Canada. February 9, he was succeeded in Louisiana by Capt. Kerlerec of the navy.

1760, Dec. 21. — The fortifications of New Orleans were completed.

1762, Nov. 3. — By a treaty at Fontainebleau France ceded to Spain all of Louisiana, which was accepted by the Spanish king November 13. This treaty was kept secret for a time.

1763, Feb. 10. — Final treaty of peace at Paris between France and Spain and Great Britain, by which France ceded to Great Britain all her possessions east of the Mississippi River and north of the Iberville, which excluded the Island of New Orleans, also her pretensions to Nova Scotia and the Canadas, and Spain her claims to Florida.

All North America then belonged only to Spain and Great Britain.

Arrival at Pensacola of Mr. George Johnson, the new English governor of Florida, who received possession, accompanied by the British Major Loftus to ascend the Mississippi and take command of the Illinois country.

June 29. — Arrival at New Orleans of Mr. D'Abadie from Paris, appointed by the king of France Director General, to relieve Gov. Kerlerec, *ad interim*, and turn over the country to the Spanish authorities when they would arrive to receive it.

In October the British Capt. Farmer was in possession of Mobile, and Capt. Ford at Tombeckbee.

Capt. Kerlerec was the last French governor of Louisiana, which he had been for the ten years preceding the arrival of Mr. D'Abadie in June, 1763, when Kerlerec was recalled to France to render an account of the mal-administration of the affairs of the colony under his governorship, consequently the license to Maxent, Laclede & Co., to establish Indian trade on the upper Missouri, if issued in 1762, as Chouteau states in his narrative, came from Kerlerec, the then governor, and not from D'Abadie, who never was governor, but called director-general, appointed by Louis XV. after the country was no longer his own, but belonged to England and Spain, between whom he had divided it, consequently could no longer appoint a governor for it.

He named D'Abadie "director-general" and sent him over from France as soon as he had parted with the country, to relieve Kerlerec, gather together the French troops scattered at the various posts throughout the country, and send them all back to France but four companies, which he was to retain with him until he should turn over the country to the new owners so soon as they would arrive to receive possession. This the English did without delay, they being already at hand in Florida, but the Spanish were so dilatory in the matter that poor D'Abadie was compelled to remain until he fell a victim to the effects of the climate.

Letter of Louis XV. to Mr. D'Abadie.
(*From State Papers, Vol. 17, page 240*):—

"By a special act executed at Fontainebleau November 13, 1762, having ceded of my own free will to my well beloved cousin, the King of Spain, and to his successors and heirs, without any reservation, all the country known under the name of Louisiana, including New Orleans, and the island on which that city is situated, and by another act executed at the Escurial, signed by the King of Spain the 13th of November of the same year, his Catholic Majesty having accepted the cession of the said country of Louisiana and the city and island of New Orleans, in conformity with the said cession which you will find herewith, I make you this letter to say to you that my intention is at the receipt of the present, let it come to you by officers of his Catholic Majesty, or directly by French vessels charged with it, you will at once place in the hands of the governor, or the officer appointed for the purpose by the King of Spain, the said country and colony of Louisiana and dependant posts, with the city and island of New Orleans, as it was on the day of the cession, so that in the future it may belong to his Catholic Majesty, to be governed by his officers as belonging to him in full right, without any reservation. I therefore direct you, that so soon as the Governor and troops of his Catholic Majesty will have arrived in said colonies, you will place them in possession, and withdraw all the officers, soldiers and employes in my service that may yet be there in garrison, to be sent to France, or to my other colonies in America, those who may not think proper to remain under the Spanish domination.

"I desire further that after the complete evacuation of said posts and city of New Orleans, you gather all the papers and documents relating to the finances and administration of the colony of Louisiana and come to France to settle them; my intention is, nevertheless, that you hand over to said Governor, or his proper officer, all the papers and documents that especially concern the government of said colony in relation to the country and its boundaries, to the Indians and various posts, taking proper receipts for them for your safety; and that you give said governor all the information in your power to enable him to govern said colony to the satisfaction of his Catholic Majesty; to the end that said cession be reciprocally satisfactory to the two nations; my will is that an inventory be made in duplicate between you and the commissioner of his Catholic Majesty of all artillery, arms, munitions, effects, stores, buildings, vessels, etc., which belong to me in said colony, and duly appraised, so that after having put the Spanish commissioner in possession of the buildings, etc., an appraisement be made of the value of what may be left to be paid for by his Catholic Majesty.

"I hope, for the advantage and tranquillity of the inhabitants of the colony of Louisiana, and I promise in consequence of the friendship and affection of his Catholic Majesty that he will give orders to his Governor, and all others in his service in said city and colony, that the clergy and religious establishments who deserve protection, may continue their functions, and enjoy the rights, privileges and exceptions now enjoyed by them; that the civil magistrates be continued, as also the Superior Council, to render justice according to the laws, forms and usages of the colony, that the inhabitants be protected and maintained in their possessions, and their lands be confirmed according to the concessions that have been made them by the former governors, etc., of the colony—that said concessions be confirmed by his Catholic Majesty, although they have not yet been so by myself, hoping above all things that his Catholic Majesty will give to his new subjects of Louisiana the same marks of good will and protection that they had found under my domination, and which the misfortunes of war alone prevented them enjoying to a greater extent.

"You will have these letters made of record in the Superior Council of New Orleans, so that the various districts of the colony be informed of its contents, and if necessary can have recourse to them, having no other object.

"I pray God, Mr. D'Abadie, to have you in his holy keeping.
"[Signed] "LOUIS,
"THE DUC DE CHOISEUL."
"VERSAILLES, April 21, 1764."

CONDENSATION OF PRECEDING FACTS.

In 1762, Maxent, Laclede & Co., merchants at New Orleans, obtained from Gov. Kerlerec a license to trade with the Indians on the Upper Mississippi and Missouri, and commenced making their preparations for that trade by procuring their goods from Cuba at once.

On November 13 of that year, 1762, France ceded to Spain by a secret treaty at Fontainebleau all her possessions on the Mississippi River, and by another treaty at Paris, February 10, 1763, France and Spain conjointly conceded to Great Britain all the country on the east bank with the Canadas.

1763.— The king of France then appointed Mons. D'Abadie, not to be governor but director-general, to come over to Louisiana relieve Gov.

Kerlerec, who was recalled to France to give an account of his ten years' administration, to collect the French troops in Louisiana at New Orleans, to be sent to France, all but four companies, and to remain there in charge *ad interim*, until the Spanish should arrive to receive possession of the country. Mr. D'Abadie arrived in New Orleans June 29th, five weeks before Laclede's departure for the Upper Mississippi on August 3, 1763. Of course the fact of the cession of the country to Spain could hardly have been a secret then, although the king's official letter proclaiming the cession was not promulgated until the following year, 1764. Consequently, when Laclede arrived and established himself here, the country no longer belonged to France, and he was in some sense, perhaps unwittingly, a trespasser on the soil of another sovereignty, as were also all those who followed him from the other side, until after the establishment of the Spanish authority; they became subjects of that power by remaining in the country and taking the oath of allegiance to the new authorities.

And here let us take a retrospective glance and look back in our history to some of the remote causes that led to the cession of the Louisianas to Spain and England. We gather from Charles Gayarre's works on Louisiana, that down to the treaty of cession to Spain, November 3, 1762, the long continued efforts of France to colonize the lower province, so far from proving a source of great revenue to the French exchequer, as had been fondly anticipated from the exaggerated misrepresentations of its early enthusiastic and sanguine explorers of the unlimited richness of the country, even in the precious metals, etc., had not only caused the bankruptcy of the early companies of adventurers, but had also been a constant drain on the finances of France, to so great an extent that she herself was on the verge of bankruptcy and would willingly have parted with it before this period had she known in what manner to get rid of it.

The treaty between the three powers which put an end to the seven years' war, afforded the French king an excellent occasion to part with his "elephant," by generously bestowing it upon his royal cousin of Spain, who, it appears, not appreciating it so highly as the generous donor of the princely gift, was in no hurry to take immediate possession of it, as he suffered seven years to elapse before he sent O'Reilly to enforce his authority in his new acquisition.

1763, Aug. 3. — Laclede left New Orleans with his boat, arrived at Ste. Genevieve, and proceeded on to Fort Chartres where he arrived November 3. In December with a small party he proceeded by land as far as the mouth of the Missouri River, selected and marked the spot for his trading post and returned to Fort Chartres, where he passed the winter of 1763-64, awaiting the opening of the river in the spring to come up and establish his new trading post at the point selected. During this period orders were received by Lieut.-Gov. Neyon de Villiers, the French commandant at that fort, from Mr. D'Abadie at New Orleans to "collect his men together from the few French posts then in this upper country, turn over possession to the British, then daily expected, when they should appear, and with his men come down to New Orleans."

The receipt of the news of the transfer to Great Britain, produced great excitement and indignation in the minds of the inhabitants of the Upper Illinois. To be thus transferred body and soul, without their consent, and compelled to live as the subjects of a nation that for long ages back they had regarded in the light of hereditary enemies and heretics in religion, was an outrage on their feelings not to be silently acquiesced in. So, as in the case of their fellow-countrymen below, they gave free expression to their discontent and disgust, many resolving not to remain in the country.

From this circumstance Laclede imbibed the idea of establishing a village immediately around his contemplated "trading post," and cordially invited all those dissatisfied with the transfer of that side of the country to the British, to come over with him and establish themselves on this side. Hence, the almost immediate springing up of the new village.

(In the meantime the British being detained by unforeseen circumstances, from appearing at Fort Chartres as early as expected, to be placed in possession, De Villiers, disgusted with the turn in affairs, became impatient to be gone. So after waiting until the 15th of June, and still no appearance of the British, his patience being completely exhausted, he left on that day and arrived at New Orleans on July 2d, with six officers and sixty-three men in his command — seventy in all — accompanied by eighty inhabitants, including women and children, whom he had induced to go below with assurances that they would receive land there from the authorities in lieu of that they had abandoned up here.

He left at Fort Chartres Capt. St. Ange De Bellerive with some twenty officers and men expecting to follow him in a few days, but who were detained there for sixteen months longer. The British Highlanders, under Capt. Sterling, finally reaching there, October 10, 1765, when Capt. St. Ange delivered him possession of the fort, and with it the country, and crossed over to St. Louis, then all life and bustle in building up.)

On the opening of navigation in the spring, Laclede dispatched his boat in charge of Chouteau, on which were thirty men and boys, with the following instructions to C.: "You will proceed and land where we marked the trees, commence to have the place cleared, build a large shed to protect the provisions and tools, and some cabins to shelter the men. I give you two men on whom you can depend to aid you, and I will join you before long."

Chouteau then proceeds: "I landed at the place designated on the 14th of March, and on the morning of the next day (March 15th) I put the men to work."

ANNALS OF ST. LOUIS.

PART FIRST.

THE FRENCH DOMINATION.
1764–1770.

I commence these Annals with the names of those thirty worthies who, conducted by Laclede, were the pioneers that led the way in opening up to settlement a boundless territory then inhabited but by a few roving savages and the wild animals of the forest, but now after a lapse of one hundred and twenty years the flourishing homes of so many thousands of happy human beings.

I head the list with the name of —

Antoine Riviere, Sr., the patriarch of the colony, who born in 1706, was fifty-eight years of age in 1764, when he drove up the cart with Mrs. Chouteau and children from Fort Chartres to Cahokia, and died at St. Ferdinand in 1816, having attained the age of one hundred and ten years, the oldest person we have any knowledge of to that day.

August Chouteau, born in 1750 was fourteen years old, and died in 1829 at seventy-nine years of age.

Joseph Taillon, miller, born in 1715 was forty-nine years old, and died in 1807 at ninety-two years of age.

Roger Taillon, miller.

Joseph Mainville, carpenter, born in 1740 was twenty-four years old, and died in 1795 at fifty-five years of age.

Jno. B. Martigny, trader, born in 1712 was fifty-two years old, and died in 1792 at eighty years of age.

Jos. L. Martigny.

Nicholas Beaugenou, farmer, born in 1719 was forty-five years old, and died in 1771 at fifty-two years of age.

Alexis Cotté, farmer, born in 1743, was twenty-one years old.

Gabriel Dodier, Jr., farmer, born in 1735 was twenty-nine years old, and died in 1805 at seventy years of age.

Jno. B. Hervieux, gunsmith, died in 1775.

Jno. B. Riviere, boy, born in 1752 was twelve years old.

René Kiersereau, church chorister, born in 1730 was thirty-four years old, and died in 1798 at sixty-nine years of age.

Alexis Picard, farmer, born in 1711 was fifty-three years old, and died in 1781 at seventy years of age.

Francis Delin, carpenter, died in 1781.

Joseph Labrosse, trader, died in 1798.

Theodore Labrosse.

Joseph Chancellier, farmer, born in 1750 was fourteen years old, and died in 1784 at thirty-four years of age.

Louis Chancellier, farmer, born in 1752 was twelve years old, and died in 1785 at thirty-three years of age.

Jno. B. Gamache, farmer, born in 1733 was thirty-one years old, and died in 1805 at seventy-two years of age.

Louis Ride, farmer, died in 1787.

Julien Le Roy, trader.

Jean Sallé Lajoie, trader, born in 1741 was twenty-three years old.

Jno. B. Becquet, blacksmith.

Jno. B. Becquet, miller.

Antoine Pothier, trader.

Antoine Valliere Pichet, carpenter.

Beauchamp, farmer.

Marcereau.

Legrain, died in 1766.

La Garrosse.

Immediately after Laclede had dispatched his boat with Chouteau and party from Fort Chartres, he set out from there by land for Cahokia, bringing with him Mrs. Chouteau and her four young children in a French cart driven by Antoine Riviere, senior, and escorted by Laclede *in propria persona*, as bodyguard, mounted on a French pony, a natural pacer, a peculiar institution of those primitive days in these parts. Chouteau says in his narrative: "Early in April Laclede came over, selected the spot for his house, and then returned to Fort Chartres to remove his goods from there to Cahokia before the English would arrive to take possession of the country. A party of Missouri Indians came to our camp to beg and steal; they remained about fifteen days, Chouteau employing the women and children in digging out the cellar for Laclede's house, carrying out the earth in wooden platters and baskets on their heads."

The summer of this year Laclede spent in the erection of his temporary buildings, and providing for his permanent removal to this side. In the month of September, his house being completed, he brought over his family from Cahokia, where they had spent the summer, and established himself in his new house, the first finished on the place, which became the nucleus around which the village was in time built up. In the meantime, Laclede had been busily engaged in preparing and laying down the plan of his prospective new village, and in assigning lots on which to build their houses to these first arrivals, all of whom had come to stay. Their selections were generally along the river front to be near water, as they soon ascertained that the whole place was underlaid by a deep bed of lime stone, and there were but few springs found.

The first thirty who came in the boat with Chouteau were followed soon after (Laclede had taken possession of his house in September) by some six or eight more the same fall of 1764. They were —

Gabriel Decarry, an Indian interpreter from Fort Chartres.
Michel Rolette, a former French soldier from Fort Chartres.
Louis Tesson Honoré, a trader from Kaskaskia.
Jno. B. Cardinal, a farmer from St. Phillippe.
Louis Deshetres, from Cahokia.
Alexander Langlois, trader from Cahokia.
Jean B. Provenché, wheelwright from Cahokia.
René Buet, trader from Cahokia.

Making a total of about forty who located here in this first year, 1764.

As was the case with all the other villages in this western region at that early day of our history, they originated either through trading posts or missionary establishments.

In the following year, 1765, so large a number came over from the east side, with several families from Ste. Genevieve and New Orleans, and built their houses on lots assigned them verbally by Laclede, that the village seemed to spring into existence, as it were, all at once, in this and the following year; but the greatest progress in building up the village was made in this year. Many of those coming over from the other side brought with them not only all they possessed that was movable, but in numerous instances even dismantling their houses and bringing the doors and windows, planking, in fact everything that could be removed, leaving but the logs and chimneys.

So anxious did these simple people seem to fly from their new English masters, that they acted as if panic stricken in their haste to get away. The little village of Ste. Phillippe, about four miles north of Fort Chartres, containing some ten or twelve families was completely deserted, all but one family leaving it to come to this side, and he owning a mill and other property which he could not dispose of, was compelled to remain. As he was the captain of the militia of the village, he was left alone in all his glory. All traces of the village have long since disappeared.

The three first and most essential steps to be taken by each new comer on this side, were:

First. To procure a village lot and put up a house or temporary cabin for the shelter of his family.

Second. To provide a commons for the joint security of their live stock. For this purpose a large tract of land lying southwest of the new village, well timbered and watered, with good pasturage, was set apart, and a portion of it enclosed at once by the united labor of those to be benefited by the use of it.

Third. To set aside another suitable tract for cultivation as common fields the next year, their breadstuffs for the present year being brought over from the other side; this common field tract lay northwest of the village, the land in that direction being better adapted for cultivation, and largely prairie land.

The settlement was called for some time "Laclede's Village."

The cession from France to Spain dates from November 13, 1762, and the arrival of Count Ulloa at New Orleans, to receive possession March 5, 1766, three years and four months after the cession. Why this long delay of the Spanish King? It would appear as if he was in no hurry to accept the munificent gift of his cousin of France. It was naturally supposed that the Spanish, imitating the example of the British, who lost no time in taking possession of their portion of the ceded country below, and were only prevented by the hostility of the Natchez tribe of Indians from ascending the river to receive their portion of this upper region, would take early possession of New Orleans, and the district of country ceded them below, but it seems they were in no hurry to do so.

While awaiting their arrival, Mr. D'Abadie, an European Frenchman, fell a victim to the climate, and died on February 4, 1765, after a residence in the place of but twenty months, and Capt. Aubry, of the French regular service, the senior officer in the place, succeeded to the command.

In the meantime the delay of the Spanish in taking possession tended largely to strengthen the popular belief of the French inhabitants below, that the cession to Spain was but a temporary measure for political reasons, and that before long they would be retroceded to France, and when eventually after exceeding three years' delay, Ulloa did appear there, although no opposition was made to his landing with his two companies, yet the French there declined to make to him a formal transfer of the place as is usual in these cases, and Ulloa would not assume the responsibility of endeavoring to take a forcible possession. This delay led to the subsequent troubles below, which resulted so disastrously for the French population of the place.

Among the first of those who came over from Fort Chartres, were Joseph D'Inglebert, Debruisseau, and Joseph Labusciere.

Debruisseau had been a prominent man there in his day, a native of France, he had come to New Orleans with Gov. De Vaudreuil in 1743, and up to Fort Chartres in 1744, with a license from him for the exclusive trade for five years with the Indians of the Illinois country, and for a number of years afterwards had filled the office of judge at Fort Chartres.

Joseph Labusciere was a lawyer and a notary, styling himself the king's procureur (attorney) and appears to have been a very important personage in the incipiency of the village, discharging the various functions of secretary, notary, scribe, etc.

After several unsuccessful attempts of the British to reach the Illinois country by way of the Mississippi and otherwise, Capt. Sterling, of the Highlanders, with a hundred men of that regiment, had finally succeeded by crossing the Allegheny Mountains from Philadelphia and descending the Ohio to reach Fort Chartres, and on the 10th of October of this year, Capt. St. Ange, who had been awaiting his arrival, gave him possession of the country and brought over his men, numbering some twenty, to St. Louis.

Up to this time, the winter of 1765–66, Laclede, by virtue of the license from the French governor at

New Orleans, to select his own point for his Indian trade, was considered by all who came to settle around him, as the legal proprietor of the new place, and all grants of lots in the place were made by him verbally, and he had exercised the only authority in the place, but it having now become a village of several hundred souls from its rapid increase, it became essentially necessary for the protection and welfare of the inhabitants, while awaiting the coming of the new authorities of the country, that there should be established a temporary government of some nature, to frame such regulations as might be necessary for the village. For this purpose Capt. St. Ange, with the unanimous approbation of the inhabitants, was vested with the functions of temporary governor, but not choosing to assume the sole responsibility of making concessions to individuals of lots and lands, now the possessions of their new sovereign, Lefebvre, who had been judge on the other side, was associated with him for that purpose in the temporary civil government of the place, and Joseph Labusciere, a man of legal knowledge, who had filled the position of the king's attorney, was assigned to the position of acting secretary and executed all the official writings of the temporary government.

Under this arrangement the temporary administration of Acting-Gov. St. Ange and his colleagues went into operation on January 21, 1766, that being the date of the first recorded document on file in the archives.

It is stated in some of the early annals of the Illinois side, that after the death of Capt. Sterling, within three months after he was placed in possession at Fort Chartres, that St. Ange, at the request of the people there, went over and took temporary command in December, 1765, until the new British commandant, Maj. Frazer, should arrive.

There is no reason to doubt the correctness of this statement, for the reason that although many crossed over to this side in 1765 as stated, yet a much larger number yet inhabited the other side, and as St. Ange had been for so long a period their military commandant, they entertained for him kindly feelings of affection and great respect for his authority. Again, St. Ange's name does not appear on any document, as commandant, for some time after the "government" on this side was set in motion in January, 1766. Lefebvre, who styles himself judge in St. Louis, having been such at Fort Chartres, and Labusciere who had been the royal notary and attorney, on the other side, appear to have taken charge of the civil affairs of the new place, as all the early papers found in the archives appear to have been executed in the presence of one or the other of these last two parties. Labusciere appears to have been the custodian of the public papers during this temporary government under St. Ange, and he delivered them over to the first Spanish governor, Piernas. St. Ange contenting himself with simply affixing his signature to the land grants as commandant.

Capt. Louis St. Ange de Bellerive was a Canadian by birth, was well advanced in years at the date of the transfer to Capt. Sterling at Fort Chartres, October 10, 1765, and had been in the military service of France in the Canadas and the Illinois country from his youth, and had only attained the rank of captain, promotion in these western wilds being at that early day but very slow.

After having placed Capt. Sterling in possession of Fort Chartres, and with it the upper portion of the country on the east side of the Mississippi River, St. Ange came over to St. Louis with his few soldiers, numbering some twenty, bringing with them, as instructed, the arms, stores and munitions of war belonging to the king of France, which had been left there the previous year when abandoned by Gov. De Villiers, finally abandoning altogether the east side of the river.

Shortly afterwards the people of the new place, after having waited patiently for exceeding a year in the constant expectation of the new authorities of the country making their appearance, as had been done by the English on the east side, the rapid and sudden growth of the village, and above all the necessity for some authority to grant lands for cultivation, compelled the people to assume the responsibility of vesting this authority temporarily in some person for that purpose; hence the establishment, by the people themselves collectively, of the temporary government, and the assumption by St. Ange and associates, with the approbation of the inhabitants, of the positions they had filled on the other side of the river. True, it was nothing more than a self-constituted government of the whole people of the place, adopted, under the circumstances in which they found themselves placed, for their safety and protection until the new owners of the country should appear and receive possession, which from the example of their new neighbors, the English on the other side, who had already been in possession for a considerable time, they naturally expected as soon to occur, never for a moment dreaming that through the ill-advised action of their misguided countrymen below (and for which they subsequently paid so severe a penalty) so long a period as four years would elapse before the authority of their new sovereign would be established.

This temporary government of the people of the place then went into operation with the first recorded concession in April, 1766. Previously to this date a few papers of a private nature executed

JOSEPH LABUSCIERE. 29

before Labusciere in his quality as notary; the first, on January 21, 1776, were entered by him in the archives; this is the oldest document of the place.

Joseph Labusciere came from Canada to the Illinois country, and was married at the little village of St. Phillippe on the other side, now extinct, to Catherine Vifvarenne, who was born in that village of Canadian parents; possessing some education, he claimed to be the deputy of the king's attorney, and acted in the capacity of notary and writer. He was among the first to come over to the west side in 1765, and participated with Laclede, St. Ange and Lefebvre in setting in operation the temporary government in January, 1766, of which he did nearly all the writing during its existence of over four years. The land grant books and nearly all the original documents in the early archives are in his handwriting; his first official document on record is of date January 21, 1766, and his last in May, 1770. The concession to him of block No. 13 in the village is the first on record in the *Livre Terrien*, April 27, 1766. St. Ange was associated with Judge Lefebvre in the first fifteen of these concessions, and afterwards Labusciere with Gov. St. Ange until the close of the French administration. After the establishment of the Spanish authority by Capt. Pedro

Piernas May 10, 1770, he had nothing further to do with the management of public affairs, but continued to exercise the calling of notary and scrivener in the place for many years. He died elsewhere, I think at New Madrid, and left three sons, — Joseph, Jr., Louis and Francis.

Joseph Lefebvre, D'Inglebert Debruisseau, was a native of France, and came to Louisiana with his wife and infant son in 1743, with the new governor-general, De Vaudreuil. In 1744 he came up from New Orleans with a license from the governor granting him "the exclusive privilege of the Indian trade in the upper country, or Illinois district, for five years," and settled at Fort Chartres, where in after years he officiated as judge of that district. Judge Lefebvre was among the first in 1765 to come to this side, and in conjunction with Joseph Labusciere, were the two parties that first assumed to set the *civil* government of St. Louis in operation, while awaiting the arrival of the Spanish officials to take possession of the country. He received from Laclede in 1765 a verbal grant of the north half of block No. 11, where he built a small house of posts at the southeast corner of Main and Locust.

When the system of *Livre Terriens*, or "Land Books" was commenced in April, 1766, Lefebvre was associated with Capt. St. Ange in the grants of lots and lands; this position he filled for a few months and was then appointed by Acting Governor St. Ange to the office of the king's military storekeeper. He died on April 3, 1767, one of the earliest deaths in the new village of less than two years' existence.

His son, Pierre Francois Brunot Joseph D'Inglebert Lefebvre, was married November 10, 1768, to Miss Margaret, daughter of Bardet de la Ferne, surgeon in the king's service. Lieut. Lefebvre died in New Orleans in 1770, at the age of twenty-seven years, leaving no children. His widow became subsequently the wife of Joseph Segond, a merchant of the early day from France. She died there in 1844, at exceeding ninety years of age, leaving a numerous posterity.

Pierre Ignace Bardet de la Ferne, a surgeon-major in the French service at Fort Chartres, was the husband of Marie Anne Barrois. They had two daughters, the oldest, Marie Anne, who was married to Dr. Auguste Condé, also a surgeon in the French service at Fort Chartres, July 16, 1763, and a younger one, Marguerite, then about ten years of age. Dr. Bardet de la Ferne died, whether before or after the marriage of his eldest daughter to Dr. Condé, we have not found on record. Subsequently his widow also died and named Mr. Henry Carpentier, of Ste. Genevieve, her executor and guardian for her minor daughter Marguerite.

In the year 1766, Dr. Condé being about to remove to St. Louis; for the convenience of all parties, with the consent of the court, Dr. Condé was appointed guardian to the minor daughter, Miss Marguerite, then about twelve and a half years of age, and received from Mr. Carpentier all the property, real and personal as mentioned in the inventory of the widow, Madame Bardet de la Ferne. This was done at Ste. Genevieve in presence of Francois Duchouquet and Pierre Fauché, November 12, 1766. Two years thereafter, on November 10, 1768, when the young lady had attained the age of fourteen and a half years, as stated above, she was married to Pierre Francois Brunot Joseph D' Inglebert Lefebvre.

The first document recorded in the archives of St. Louis was a sale January 21, 1766, by James Denis, a joiner, to Antoine Hubert, merchant, of a half lot of ground, sixty feet front by one hundred and fifty deep at the southeast corner of Walnut and Second, with a house of posts on the same built by himself, the lot having been granted him by the commander verbally, the sale made for $220 (the house $200, the ground $20).

Another sale by the said Denis to the same Hubert on March 15, 1766, of the other half lot, adjoining the first, 60 by 150, for $20 and six quarts of rum, the whole being 120 feet on Second by 150 on Walnut, opposite the lot where Barnum's Hotel now stands.

The "*Livres Terriens,*" or register of grants of lots in the village of St. Louis, commenced on April 27, 1766, with a grant to Labusciere of the present block No. 13, 300 feet French from Vine to Washington Avenue by 150 from Main to the river.

The document that follows is one of the earliest inventories and is introduced as a specimen: —

AN EARLY INVENTORY.

"In the year 1766, March 15, at nine o'clock, a. m., we, Joseph Lefebvre d' Inglebert, Deputy of the Orderer of Louisiana, and Judge in the Royal Jurisdiction of the Illinois, on the request of Mr. Joseph Labusciere, attorney for the vacant localities in this said jurisdiction, who represented to us in his petition of the 12th instant, that he had been informed of the capture of Mr. Cazeau by Indians on the Mississippi in ascending from New Orleans, said Mr. Cazeau having goods on the boat of Mr. Lambert, which arrived with the said goods at the post of Ste. Genevieve, and requested us to repair to said post of Ste. Genevieve to take cognizance of the same, and place our seals on the goods belonging to the said Mr. Cazeau; to preserve his rights, and that of others to whom they may belong, and in consequence of our ordinance, affixed to the bottom of the petition of the said attorney for vacant localities, dated the same day, we repaired to the said Ste. Genevieve, twenty-one leagues distant from our post, accompanied by the said attorney for vacant places, and by Mr. Cabazie, writer at said Ste. Genevieve, where on our arrival, we went to the house of Mr. Lambert, and after summoning him to show us the effects, trunks and bales belonging to Mr. Cazeau, and after having sworn him in the usual manner, gave us in evidence what follows, where we found the seals already applied by Mr. Du Breuil, du Rieu and Larralde, and which we found whole and perfect, said merchandise consisting, viz.:

"A cloth portmanteau on which we found the seals affixed at three places on the covering, after removing it in the presence of Messrs. Rocheblave, Lambert, Datchurut, Vallé, Blondeau, Bloin, Leclerc and Fagot, all merchants at said place of Ste. Genevieve, we found the following articles:—

Two silver spoons, no mark,
Twelve linen shirts,
One polonaise skirt,
Three pair stockings, much worn,
Three vests,
One cloak,
One pair shoes,
One blue cloth vest,
A jacket, in pocket a small knife and gloves.

Two Beaufort sheets,
Four small cotton handkerchiefs,
One large cotton breeches,
Four towels,
One cotton vest,
One large linen breeches,
Nine pair of socks,
One cotton cap,
A shoe brush.

"Opened a trunk and found in it—

A white hat and two black ones,
Six rolls of chocolate,
A shaving cup,
A row of pins,
An ell of black ribbon,
Six silver forks,
Four silver spoons,
Two Ragout spoons,
One soup spoon,

A gilt hunting knife scabbard,
A gray linen vest,
A piece of cloth,
A coat and vest of green camlet and breeches,
A seersucker vest,
A black velvet breeches,
Two small diaries and a box of tea,

AN OLD INVENTORY.

Five knives,
A small silver candlestick,
Three packs of cards,
Fifteen clasp knives,
A pack of pins,
Two bunches of thread,
A piece of black ribbon,
A handkerchief,
A red canlet breeches,
A pair of black wool stockings,
A brush,
A piece of crape,
Six red handkerchiefs, silk and cotton,
A calico petticoat and dress,
A toilet mirror,
A black velvet breeches,
A gray linen breeches,
A red camlet cloak (a volant),
A damask robe de chambre for man
A volant of blue silk, same as breeches,
A vest and breeches of gray linen,
A green camlet breeches,
A linen combing cloth,
Four sheets and two table cloths,
A pack of pins and strings.
A silver handled sword and scabbard,
Two packages indigo and an old hair bag,
A gold dragonne and vial of laudanum,
Twenty-six old towels,
Twenty-two collars, white and black,
Three linen jackets,
Fourteen cotton handkerchiefs,
Two dimity vests,
Thirty-three linen shirts, partly used,
Ten pair stockings, thread, silk and cotton,
A purse, seven linen night caps, towels,
Four pair linen knee bands,
Nineteen cotton handkerchiefs,
A small pack of gold and silver twist,
A pack of thread,
Three pair gloves, a wash-bale,
A pocket-book we did not open,
Several papers and two small books, put back in trunk,
A small casket in which there was a gold watch in a snuff-box,
A paper of pins,
A mother of pearl snuff-box,
Three shell-handled razors,
Several letters put back in the boxes,
A gold cross with gold buckles, claimed by Mr. Lagrange's negress, handed to Mr. Lambert.

"The foregoing articles were put back in the portmanteau, as also in the said trunk, each in its place, and after shutting up the said goods, we placed on them our seals, and gave them into the hands of Mr. Lambert to produce them when found necessary, and after maturely considering the circumstances, and that Mr. Cazeau might have partners interested at New Orleans, the attorney of the vacant places required us to have a meeting of the most prominent merchants of this post, to consider the most advisable steps to take for the interests of the said Cazeau and others interested, and in consequence of his request we assembled, Messrs. Rocheblave, Lambert, Datchurut, Vallé, Blondeau,

Blouin, Leclerc and Fagot, who, after maturely considering, concluded that all the merchandise and things of said Mr. Cazeau shall be left in custody of Mr. Lambert, until information was given to Mr. Devaugine, relative of said Mr. Cazeau, and those in interest with him, which is to be done in a statement in the shape of an inventory of the bales by numbers and marks, barrels, boxes and other things which may be found shut up, without opening them, for all is to be put in the care of Mr. Lambert, who has voluntarily taken charge of them, saving all unforeseen risks, accidents and dangers, and we proceed as follows: —

Four boxes which appeared to contain drinkables marked C B,
Four ankers of brandy, C B,
A small box, fastened with lock and key, C B,
Four kegs powder, two of 50 lbs, two of 30 lbs, C B,
Two pieces of Beaufort marked C B
Five barrels Taffia (Rum) marked L B on a cross,
Five bales, marked C B,

Two baskets with two decanters each of cordials,
One box of 22 bottles of wine,
One quarter of sugar,
Six guns, half stocks, 3 axes, a piece of rope,
A large green blanket, a white one, bad, two hatchets,
A mattress and pillow, a piece of coarse brin, marked C B,

"Two negroes, one named Samson, and the other Larose, which were turned over this day to Mr. Fagot to be sent to Mr. Vaugine, at New Orleans, and of which we relieved Mr. Lambert. The above mentioned articles, are all that said Mr. Lambert says he had any knowledge of as belonging to Mr. Cazeau and which we have entrusted to him, to be produced when called for, as in the hands of the court.

"LEFEBVRE D' INGLEBERT, *Judge.*"

LACLEDE'S VERBAL GRANTS OF VILLAGE LOTS.

Laclede made verbal grants in 1765 to various parties of a lot each upon which to build his house, as soon as it was possible to accomplish it. The largest portion of them, of upright posts set in the

VERBAL GRANTS BY LACLEDE.

ground, were put up the same year, a few of stone, were built soon afterwards : —

BLOCK No. 1, north half to Gilles Chemin, house 20 x 17 feet
No. 2, south half to Charles Parent, do. 20 x 25 feet.
No. 2, north half to Alexis Cotté, first post, then stone do., in 1774.
No. 3, south half to Louis Laroche, post do., 23 x 20.
No. 3, north half to Louis Marcheteau, post do., 20 x 30.
No. 4, south half to Constantine Quirigoust, post do., 20 x 20.
No. 4, north half to Louis Marcheteau, post do., 15 x 20.
No. 5, south half to Julien Leroy, post, 23 x 23, post in a wall do.
No. 5, north half to Amable Guion, first a small post, then a stone do.
No. 6, south half to Louis Ride, Sr., post do.
No. 6, north half to John B. Martigny, first post, then a stone do.
No. 7, reserved for Place d'Armes.
No. 8, south half to Alexander Langlois, post and stone do.
No. 8, north half to Francis Bissonet, stone do.
No. 9, south half to Joseph Dubé, small cabin.
No. 9, north half to René Kiersereau, 20 x 25 do.
No. 10, south half to Charles Routier, mason, 35 x 20 do.
No. 10, north half to Alexis Picard, 25 x 20 do.
No. 11, south half to John B. Bayet, 25 x 20 do.
No. 11, north half to Judge Joseph Lefebvre, 40 x 22 do.
No. 12, south half to John B. Hervieux, gunsmith, 30 x 16 do.
No. 29, southeast quarter to John B. Jacquemin, 15 x 18 do.
No. 29, southwest quarter to Isidor Peltier, 15 x 20 do.
No. 30, northwest quarter to Francis Larche, 15 x 20 do.
No. 30, southeast quarter to John B. Bidet, 15 x 20 do.
No. 31, southeast quarter to John B. Gamache, 20 x 25 do.
No. 31, northwest quarter to Francis Thibaut, carpenter, 15 x 20 do.
No. 32, northeast quarter to Louis Deshetres, stone do.
No. 32, northwest quarter to Paul G. Kiersereau, 25 x 20 do.
No. 32, southeast quarter to Nicholas Marechal, 20 x 25 do.
No. 32, southwest quarter to Joseph Denoyer Marcheteau, 15 x 18 do.
No. 33, northeast quarter to Laclede for Mrs. Chouteau, stone do.

BLOCK No. 33, northwest quarter to Joseph Labrosse, stone house.
No. 33, south half to Joseph Taillon, stone do.
No. 34, Laclede's Block for Maxent & Co., stone do.
No. 35, northeast quarter to Lambert Bonvarlet, cabin.
No. 35, northwest quarter to Jacques Denis, carpenter, cabin.
No. 35, southeast quarter to John B. Deschamps, 20 x 25 do.
No. 35, southwest quarter to Marcereau.
No. 36, northeast quarter to Kiery Desnoyers, 20 x 25 do.
No. 36, southeast quarter to John B. Becquet, 20 x 16 do.
No. 36, northwest quarter to Gabriel Dodier, Jr., 21 x 22 do.
No. 36, southwest quarter to Gabriel Dodier's, Sr., widow, 20 x 22 do.
No. 37, southeast quarter to Jacques Noise du Labbé, 22 x 30 do.
No. 37, southwest quarter to Antoine Riviere, Sr., stone do.
No. 38, northeast quarter to Rougeau & Desfonds, posts, 15 x 15 do.
No. 38, northwest quarter to Pierre Montardy, posts, 20 x 18 do.
No. 38, south half to Ignace Hebert's widow, stone do.
No. 39, north half to Nicholas Beaugenou, Sr., 35 x 25 do.
No. 39, southeast quarter to Joseph Hebert, 25 x 15 do.
No. 40, southeast quarter to Francis Marcheteau, 15 x 16 do.
No. 40, northeast quarter to Charles Carrier, 20 x 25 do.
No. 41, northeast one-sixth to Toussaint Hunaud, 20 x 25 do.
No. 41, center one-sixth to Joseph L. Martigny, 20 x 18 do.
No. 41, northwest one-sixth to Pierre Berger, 20 x 25 do.
No. 41, southwest one-sixth to Gilles Chemin, 12 x 15 do.
No. 44, north half to Gabriel Descary, 22 x 20 do.
No. 52, center one-sixth to Claude Tinon, 22 x 16 do.
No. 53, south half to John B. Durand, 20 x 18 do.
No. 54, northeast quarter to Joseph Turgeon, 20 x 18 do.
No. 57, southeast quarter to Legrain.
No. 57, northeast quarter to Marie Juannette, 25 x 20 do.
No. 58, northeast quarter to Michel Rollet, 25 x 20 do.
No. 62, south half to Francis Moreau, 25 x 22 do.
No. 62, north half to Julien Leroy, 12 x 15 do.
No. 63, northeast quarter to Ignace Laroche, 16 x 16 do.
No. 64, south half to Louis Robert, 15 x 15 do.
No. 82, southeast quarter to Pierre Montardy, soldier, 20 x 19 do.
No. 82, northeast quarter to Pierre Montardy, soldier, 40 x 22 do.

As the site of the village was then thickly covered with timber and each one had to do, or have done, his own clearing, the only landmark to guide him in finding the location assigned him by Laclede, was the spot on which Laclede was then building his trading post, which was the initial point of the village, from which all the others were ascertained by admeasurement, etc.

THE FIRST MANUMISSION.

[*Extract from the rolls of the Registry of the Royal Jurisdiction of the Illinois.*]

" *To Messrs. De Neyon de Villiers, Major Commandant, and Bobé Desclauseaux, Acting Commissioner and Judge in Illinois:*

" The Abbé Forget, vicar-general, and superior of the missions, requests that it may please you, to authorize granting freedom to the negro slaves of this mission, for the care and good services they rendered my predecessors and to myself, to wit: a negro named Appollo, aged about sixty years, his wife, Jeannette, thirty-eight, and his youngest child, Anselmo, three years and a half.

"At Fort Chartres, Nov. 4, 1763.

" Forget,
" *Miss'y Priest, Vicar-General.*"

" Considering the above request of the Abbé Forget, we grant full and entire liberty to the above named Appollo, Jeannette his wife, and Anselmo their child; to enjoy all the rights granted to the enfranchised, with the injunction to pursue an irreproachable conduct, and to hold in respect Mr. Forget, as well as all others worthy of respect, under penalty of being punished according to the laws of the realm.

"ILLINOIS, Nov. 12, 1763.

"NEYON DE VILLIERS,
"BOBÉ.

"Copy conforming to the original.   LABUSCIERE, *Notary*.

"I, John Arnold Valentine Bobé Desclauseaux, Orderer and Judge in the Royal Jurisdiction of Illinois, certify to whom it may concern, that the signature at the bottom of the act of emancipation on the previous page is that of Mr. Labusciere, and that he is notary and register in this jurisdiction, and that full faith may be put in his official acts as such.

"In testimony we have affixed the seals of our office.
"In ILLINOIS, Nov. 11, 1763.

"BOBÉ."

"I certify having sold, in advance of her dowry, to Madame De Volsay, the daughter of Madelon, named Juannette, for the sum of five hundred livres, which she is to account for to her brother and sister, when you will make partition after my death.

"NATCHITOCHES, July 16, 1768.

"DE VILLIERS, *Knight*."

STE. GENEVIEVE.

Daniel Blouin was a son-in-law of the original Joseph Chauvin *dit* Charleville, and his home was at Kaskaskia, although he had operated largely in lead at the mine Lamothe, and salt at the works on the Saline, as would appear from the following: —

"Daniel Blouin, merchant of Kaskaskia, put on record in the archives of St. Louis, December 17, 1766, an inventory of the property he possessed on that day in the District of Ste. Gene-

AN EARLY SALE.

vieve, and which he had disposed of to Mr. John Datchurut on that date at Mine Lamothe and the Salines:

"A negro man named Cæsar, and wife Jeanetton.
" Four negro men, Marthurin, Batiste, Noyos and Jasmin.
" Half a house and three negro cabins.
" A piece of ground from Labastille and Picart.
" A piece of ground from each, Laroze, Tassin and Moreau.
" Two lots of mineral, one in partnership with Mr. Beauvais.
" Two hundred and eighty-four pigs of lead, ten horses, and the necessary tools.
" A house in Ste. Genevieve acquired from the minors of Lin, and at the Saline, 50 pigs of lead, a pump, a shed and pig-sty, 2 leaden kettles for salt and 150 cedar stakes.
" All which I have sold to Mr. Datchurut, who has this day taken possession of the whole, except the ground in suit with Mr. Catalan until after the decision of the suit before the council which will be Datchurut's if decided in my favor.
" The whole for the sum of forty-nine thousand six hundred livres (49,600) in genuine money, which I have received in cash, for which I hold the said Datchurut released.
" The deed to be executed with the same date.

"DATCHURUT — BLOUIN."

The deed for the above was executed in St. Louis, January 17, 1767.

Isidor Peltier sold to Louis Blouin, both of Ste. Genevieve, October 7, 1767, a negro man, and house and lot in that place for one thousand two hundred and fifty livres, and gave his note for the amount, upon which he paid April 23, 1768, nine hundred livres. (Archives.)

MADAME STE. ANGE — FORT CHARTRES.

The following receipt is found on record in the earliest archives of St. Louis: —

I, the undersigned, acknowledge to have received from Mr. De Volsay the sum of three thousand three hundred and forty livres, accruing to my wife, Joachina De Villiers from the estate of Madame Ste. Ange, her grandmother, with which I am satisfied in regard to said estate, and release the said M. De Volsay and all others, for which this is a general release.

Moreover, I acknowledge the receipt of my brother-in-law's portion, the Chevallier de Villiers, of three thousand, three hundred and forty livres, which I will deliver to him when he comes of age. Done at Fort Chartres the 10th of May, 1765.

PICOTÉ BELESTRE,

ST. ANGE, witness, LEFEBVRE, *Judge.*

This statement was made by De Volsay about a year after De Villiers had abandoned Fort Chartres and gone below. Mrs. St. Ange, the old lady, mother of Capt. St. Ange and his sister Mrs. De Villiers, and grandmother of De Villiers' three children, had died some years previously. Judge Lefebvre was still there that summer.

[*Extract from the Registry of Ste. Genevieve, of the 24th of December, 1769.*]

"This day December 24, 1769, personally appeared at the Register's office in Ste. Genevieve, one Chatal, a lead miner, who affirmed that he has never presented an application to prospect, or had extracted any lead mineral from the Mine Lamothe; that the commandants had never been importuned by him nor by Gaignon, his associate, to which deposition he adheres as veritable.

"Done at Ste. Genevieve the day and year above written.
"A true copy. "CABAZIE, *Register*.
"In presence of Messrs. Deguirre and Girard Langlois, witnesses."

"Having full knowledge that Mr. Picar did not work, nor extract mineral from the hole of Mr. Larose, having full knowledge is why we have given him this certificate.
"Done at Mine Lamothe the 21st November, 1770.
"Mr. Pepin's X mark, "MENAGER,
"FONBLON, *Witness*."

Immediately after Captain Sterling had received possession of Fort Chartres, and with it the Illinois country in 1765, Capt. Philip Pitman, of the British Engineer Corps, a man in every way competent, was sent out by General Gage to make a survey of the forts, and report on the condition of the villages and settlements of the country; this he did in 1766.

His report, a very complete one of one hundred and eight pages, was published in London in 1770. In it he gives a full and minute description of the Fort Chartres and the various buildings in it, and concludes his description by saying that "it was generally considered the most convenient and best built fort in North America."

KASKASKIA.

Then he proceeds with the villages, commencing with Kaskaskia, the most important, which he thus describes: —

"'Cascasquias' is by far the most considerable settlement in the Illinois country. It has a church and Jesuit's house, which with a few other houses are of stone. There are sixty-five families in the village, with a few merchants and traders. A Mr. Paget built the first water mill in the country, on the Kaskaskia, about a mile above the village, where he was killed with his two negroes by the Cherokees in 1764. The Jesuits had a plantation of 240 arpents in cultivation, with a stock of cattle and a brewery, all of which was sold by the French commander after the cession to the English, the order being suppressed; a Mr. Beauvais, the richest man here, possessing eighty slaves, was the purchaser. The fort on the bluffs across the Kaskaskia River, of wooden timbers, was burnt down in October, 1766. An officer and twenty soldiers are now quartered in the village."

Pitman does not give the number of houses in the village nor its population, but allowing each of the sixty-five families a house to itself, there could not have been more than seventy, and the population, say five hundred whites and slaves, a very large estimate.

"CAHOKIA.

"The village 'Kaokias,' twenty leagues from Kaskaskia, was the first settlement in the country by a few French Canadians; it is the next in size to Kaskaskia, and contains forty-five dwellings and a church. A house in the village where a few soldiers were kept was called the 'garrison.' "

Pitman did not give its population — it was but a few hundred.

"PRAIRIE DU ROCHER

"Fourteen miles north of Kaskaskia is a village of twenty-two houses and the same number of families, with a little chapel."

"SAINT PHILLIPPE,

"Five miles north from Fort Chartres on the road to Cahokia, has " about sixteen deserted houses and a small church still standing, all having been deserted in 1765, the inhabitants crossing over to the French side, leaving only the captain of the militia, who was compelled to remain, having a grist and saw mill which he could not dispose of."

"FORT CHARTRES VILLAGE

"Was the seat of government, and in the year 1764 contained forty families in the village adjoining the fort, and a parish church."

"In the next year, 1765, when the English received possession of the country, they all, with the exception of three or four families, abandoned their houses and removed over to the west side of the Mississippi, choosing to continue under the French government."

"The first fort was built in 1720; rebuilt as now in 1756." (In 1772 the inundation caused the fall of the west wall and two bastions; the fort was then abandoned, and the British garrison removed to Fort Gage at Kaskaskia, which then became the seat of government.)

Capt. Pitman was a man of ability, for which reason he was selected by Gen'l Gage for his mission, in which it so happened he was engaged at the very moment that St. Louis had just sprung into existence. His report, therefore, furnishes conclusive proof that St. Louis, then in her infancy of barely two years, was already in every respect, — size, population, etc., — in advance of what Kaskaskia had ever attained in her most prosperous period, and that the old traditions of large population, great wealth, etc., etc., so freely bestowed upon her in her early days, were neither more nor less than the gratuitous exaggerations of visionaries.

Judge Lefebvre acted in his official capacity as the colleague of St. Ange in the first few land concessions but for a few months, as we find his last official act as such on August 15, 1766, when he was appointed keeper of the king's warehouse, St. Ange having brought over from Fort Chartres with his men the military stores left there by Capt. Neyon de Villiers. Labusciere then assumed Lefebvre's place as the associate in the government with Capt. St. Ange, and appears to have discharged the functions of that office almost exclusively until the assumption of the Spanish authority in May, 1770, as all the official documents are in his handwriting or executed in his presence, the signature of St. Ange appearing but rarely.

From the following document found in the archives we learn that Judge Lefebvre Desbruisseau died on April 3, 1767.

"In the year one thousand, seven hundred and sixty-seven, the seventh of April at 8 o'clock, a. m., before Joseph Labusciere, Deputy of the Attorney-General of the King in Illinois, acting as judge in the place of Judge Lefebvre, deceased; in presence of Mr. St. Ange de Bellerive, Captain, commanding on the French side of the Illinois, of Mr. De Bergueville, officer of infantry of this garrison, and Mr. Laclede Liguest, merchant, all residing at the post of St. Louis.

"In virtue of our act of placing the seals on the king's warehouse on the third of this month, in consequence of the death on that day of Mr. Lefebvre, we repaired this day to the house of Laclede, accompanied by Mr. Peri, scrivener of this place, to remove our seals from the door of the store, which we had left in the charge and care of Mr. Lefebvre Desbruisseau, where being arrived and summoning the said Desbruisseau, Louis Deshetres, Indian interpreter and Louis Chancellier, inhabitant, as witnesses, we caused the door to be opened with the key which had been sent us by Mr. St. Ange, and immediately proceeded to the description of the effects and merchandise which we found in said store, shown and placed before us by said Lefebvre Desbruisseau as follows, and which we signed on the same day and year, said Deshetres saying he could not sign it."

"First: —
6131 pounds of wool.
  14 grenadiers' guns.
  16 half axes.
  27 tomahawks.
  14 lbs. damaged powder.
    A block of copper to press paper.
  15 minots of corn.
  40 minots more.
 844 lbs. of balls.
1000 lbs. of bar lead.
   2 pairs small copper scales.
 616 dog-head knives.
  13½ dozen butchers' knives.
    A case of surgeons' instruments.
  59 blankets, two and a half point.
   9 three point do.
   6 do. cazernée.
   2 old uniform coats.
  10 shirts, gingham.
   4 boxes with handles to draw.
 106 shirts of Morley.
  26 white do. damaged.
   5 necklaces.
   2 boat-sails with their ropes.
   3 augurs.
  21 pickaxes.
   3 beef tongues.
    An old chafing dish.
   2 saw handles.
  13 lbs of sheet lead.
  25 lbs. nails assorted.
   2 Fleur de Lis stamps.
    A draw knife.
    A hand saw,
    A coil of rope.

   2 lbs. of vermillion.
 127 small bells.
   3 Calumet pipes.
   3 lbs. of steel.
   3 pairs of wooden scales.
    A flail.
  10 lbs. of thread.
   6 old pewter basins.
    A pewter dish.
   2 mortars and pestles.
    A copper quart measure.
   8 tin measures.
   2 padlocks, no keys.
   2 copper stew-pans and old coffee-pot.
   2 tin funnels.
    An old lantern.
   2 small copper kettles.
   1 brass quoit.
   6 pair iron shackles and bars.
   2 pair handcuffs and bars.
   7 spades.
   8 chisels.
  13½ pair andirons, good and bad.
1500 gun flints.
    A tackle.
    A chimney crane and hooks.
  11 cannon balls.
   3 boxes of screws.
   2 hammers.
   2 pair tongs.
   6 fire shovels.
    A ladle.
    A pair of pincers.
   2 hatchets and 3 tomahawks.
    A poor tripod.
  16 pairs of hinges.

INVENTORY OF PUBLIC PROPERTY. 49

5 lbs. of iron wire.
20 ells Limbourg.
93¾ ells of same.
2 dozen dog-head knives.
13½ pieces red binding tape.
4½ groce of awls.
   A piece of red tape.
72 boxwood combs.
5 hooked knives.
2 hyde scrapers.
3 hyde needles.
5 gimlets.
437 gun screws.
13 files assorted.
16 pair scissors.
2½ lbs. candlewick.
597 fire steels.
31 awls.
½ lb. vermillion.
4 boat awnings.
   An ell measure.
2 bayonets and scabbards.
   An old sword for a sergeant.
324 lbs. of rope.
   A pair of oaken scales with iron beams.
322 large springs.
349 gun-pan covers.
340 small bells.
259 gun cocks.
11 old gun plates.
386 lbs. wrought iron in 22 parcels.
13½ lbs. weight of lead.
309 gun nuts.
22 weights.
   A tarpaulin.
7 tarred barrel covers.
49 bags, good and bad.
6 barrels rum, short 48 quarts.
   A grapnel.

7 small bolts.
70 lbs. of old iron.
2 copper kettles.
   A piece of Fuller's earth.
3 broad-axes.
9 small pick-axes.
52 lbs. fine beads.
   An axe.
   A broken padlock.
42 lbs. Spanish white.
80 lbs. of steel.
   A brass candlestick.
25 pewter candle moulds.
247 lbs. of bar iron.
   A stack for arms.
4 boat sails.

The following was at the guard-house:—

4 large couches.
1 middling do.
4 straw beds.
1 middling do.
   A table.
2 benches.
   A kneading trough.
   A bread-board.
   A brass candlestick.
   A table-cloth.
8 plates, knives and forks.
   A Sentinel's capot.
2 linen bread cloths.
2 iron kettles.
   A brass lamp.
   A large brass kettle and cover.
   A spade.
   A hatchet.
2 picks.
4348 beads of porcelain.

After diligent search we were told there was nothing more, and should anything more be found, said Mr. St. Ange promised to add it to the inventory, and everything was left in the care of Mr. St. Ange, to give an account of the same to the orderer of Louisiana and we signed it acccordingly.

St. Ange,
F. de Bergueville,
Lefebvre Dezruisseau,
Chancellier,
Labusciere,
Peri,
Laclede Liguest.

In the month of April, 1765, before the establishment of any government here, a boat loaded with merchandise for the Indian trade of the Missouri River, under the charge and management of one Joseph Calvé, a clerk of the owners, Messrs. John Datchurut and Louis Viviat, merchants of St. Genevieve, was seized by employes of the government, at the instance of Pierre Laclede, as violating the laws of the Indian trade, and more especially the claims of the firm of Maxent, Laclede & Co. to the exclusive trade with the Indians of the Missouri. She was brought to St. Louis, an inventory taken of her cargo, and the merchandise placed in the hands of Alexander Langlois for safe keeping. These gentlemen brought their case before the Superior Council at New Orleans, who decided it against Laclede and company, condemning them to pay for the goods, with costs, etc. This second inventory was then taken on April 30, 1767, to ascertain the amount to be paid by Maxent and Laclede, which amounted to 6,485 livres 8 sols, equal to $1,297.

"In the year seventeen hundred and sixty-seven, April 30, at 8 o'clock a. m., before Joseph Labusciere, the deputy of the attorney-general of the king, acting as judge in the royal jurisdiction of the Illinois, on the petition of Mr. Pierre Laclede Liguest, merchant on the French side of the country, as well in his own name as in that of Maxent and Company, desiring to have a re-examination in the shape of an inventory of the merchandise that had been seized on his petition, the — day of April, 1765, as having the exclusive control of the trade from Mr. D'Abbadie, Commissioner of Louisiana, with the purpose of ascertaining the deficit which may be found in said merchandise since the date of the seizure to this day, and their present actual value, and in conformity to our decree of yesterday, we have this day repaired to Mr. Tayon's, the custodian of the said goods, accompanied by Messrs. Joseph Papin, William Bissette and Alexander Rondeau (Langlois), all merchants * of St. Louis, arbitrators and referee officially appointed in this jurisdiction, where we summoned the said custodian to produce the goods that had been placed in his special care, which he immediately did, and before proceeding, having qualified the arbitrators to faithfully ascertain the waste and deficiency they may have sustained since the date of the seizure by their respective affirmations, they proceeded to the discharge of their duty, in the following manner, viz.: (here follows the valuation), which having completed is duly signed on the same day as above.

"Joseph Papin,
"William Bissette,
"Alexander $\times$ Langlois, *dit* Rondeau,
HIS CROSS

"In presence of Joseph Labusciere."

[*See Archives May 25, 1767, Vol. 4.*]

---

* Every man engaged in trading of any kind, a peddler with his pack on his back, or a couple of fellows swapping knives, styled themselves merchants.

Having now almost built up our primitive little village, and set on foot its temporary government, we will proceed in its annals by the recital, in their chronological order, of such events and occurrences as may be found of sufficient interest to be recorded.

The first event of this nature was the arrival, towards the close of the year 1767, of Capt. Francisco Rios (anglicised Rivers), of the Spanish service, with a company of some twenty-five men sent up from New Orleans by Count Ulloa to receive possession of and establish the Spanish authority on the west side of this upper region of the Mississippi.

His somewhat unexpected arrival was a source of much annoyance and dissatisfaction to the people of our new little place, who, from the tardiness of the Spanish in establishing their authority over their new acquisition, — so different from the example set them by their British neighbors on the east side of the river, who lost no time in taking immediate possession of their side after the treaty of cession, — were impressed with the idea that the cession was to be merely a nominal one for political reasons, not to be carried practically into effect, and that they would in a little time be retroceded to their legitimate sovereign, the French king.

Capt. Rios, finding his advent here inopportune and distasteful to the people of the place, who received them as unwelcome intruders, and finding no place in which to quarter his men (for bear it in mind that the village at that time contained but some seventy houses and cabins in which to shelter at least double that number of families, besides all the single stragglers that had flocked to the place from the other side to escape British rule), judiciously concluded, to avoid collision, to erect at some suitable point in its near vicinity a fort and garrison which would serve, not only as present quarters for his men, but as a future defense against any attempted inroad on the part of the Indian tribes of the country. With this view he selected an elevated rocky bluff on the south side of the Missouri River, at a short distance above its junction with the Mississippi, at the distance of fourteen miles directly north of the village.

To this point he proceeded at once to remove his men and to commence the erection of his fort, which was nearly completed in the course of the year 1768, and to which he gave the name of "Fort Prince Charles," in honor of the son of his sovereign, who, after the death of his father in 1788, succeeded him on the throne of Spain as Charles the Fourth.*

---

* The selection of this point by Capt. Rios, exhibited his judgment, as it was the same subsequently selected by Gen. James Wilkinson, United States army, in 1805, as the headquarters in the west of the United States troops, and so remained for many years, until the establishment of Jefferson Barracks in 1825.

Capt. Francis Rios brought up with him from New Orleans: —

Don Fernando de Gomez, his Lieut.
Don Joseph Barelas, a cadet engineer.
Doct. Jno. B. Valleau, surgeon.
Charles Covos, orderly sergeant.
Michael Piguera, corporal.
Manuel Martini,   do.
Benjn. Moureau,   do.
Lion,   do.
Carlos Herrara, drummer.
Jourdan, cook and baker.
Francis Tiendra,   soldier.
Jean Mignon,   do.
Gaspard Demarque,   do.
Dominic Auterre,   do.
Antonio Tagouais,   do.
Alex'r Pegnoles,   do.
Pierre Perez,   do.
Jos. Nich's Navarro, do.

And a few others whose names are not found in the archives.

During the period that Rios' company were at "Fort Charles the Prince," they were under the command of his Lieutenant Gomez, who from the testimony of witnesses in several trials that occurred there that summer, must have exercised great severity and oppression over the men, Rios spending much of his time in St. Louis.

A JUDICIAL INQUIRY.

"An inquiry made by me, Mr. Joseph Labusciere, king's attorney, acting as judge and deputy of the commander of Louisiana: —

"On the petition of Michael Trille, a stone mason, working at Fort Charles the Prince, near the mouth of the Missouri River, accused and held in irons in the prison at the French post of St. Louis, on the complaint brought against him by Monr. De Rive for Don Fernando de Gomez, Lieut. at the fort. Having repaired to the place this June 15, 1768, I proceeded on the following day to take the depositions of the following witnesses, through the interpretations of John Bap. Dehetres and William Boyer, as follows, viz. :

Francis Soliel, sailor, a Catholic.
Antoine de Thaguas, mason, do.
Charles Herrara, drummer, do.
Wm. Boyer his × cross, sailor, do.
Antoine × Dargaud, blacksmith.
Joseph × Segue, stonecutter.
Pierre × Perez, stonecutter.

"Being then about to proceed to take the depositions of the soldiers within the fort, I was unable to do so for want of an interpreter, after requesting Mr. Joseph Barelas, a cadet officer, Jno. B. Deshetres, Indian interpreter, the king's baker, and one Boyer, a sailor, who severally refused to interpret and retired into the fort, also declining to sign their refusal to act. Seeing this I withdrew, having finished the declaration at the fort, June 16, 1768.

"JOSEPH LABUSCIERE."

The substance of the testimony of the above witnesses was to the following effect : —

"Trille was a Spaniard, a stone mason, at work on the fort. One day he had a piece of fresh fish on the ground within the fort; a corporal, Lion, passing along, said the fish smelt bad, and ordered it to be thrown out. Trille objected, saying it smelt no worse than the salt meat issued to them in their rations, this provoked the corporal, hot words ensued, when another corporal, Moreau, attempted to knock Trille down with the butt of his musket; at this moment Lieutenant Gomez came on the ground, and without knowing anything of the cause of the fracas, ordered Trille to be handcuffed and sent a prisoner to St. Louis, at the same time kicking and striking him."

All the witnesses examined, testified to the good character of Trille, as a peaceable man and steady workman. One of the witnesses closely questioned as to the cause of the ill-will displayed by Gomez towards Trille, had no doubt it arose from the fact that Trille when he came to work at the fort, brought with him from St. Louis, a small keg of brandy, from which he occasionally gave his fellow-workmen a small dram; this was so much out of Gomez's pocket, who besides being the lieutenant-commandant was also purveyor (sutler).

Nothing further appears in regard to the affair, Trille being released from confinement.

"An inquiry made by me, Joseph Labusciere, acting as judge and deputy of the commander of Louisiana, and proxy of the king's attorney-general of the Illinois.

On the petition of Mr. Joseph Barelas, a cadet engineer of the garrison of "Fort Charles, the Prince," near the mouth of the Missouri, against Don Fernando de Gomez, lieutenant commanding at the fort, and Charles Covos, first sergeant of the garrison. By virtue of orders from Mr. De Rive, civil and military governor of the Missouri section, we repaired on said date to the fort

A JUDICIAL INQUIRY. 57

accompanied by M. Milony Duralde, to act as interpreter, I not understanding the Spanish language, where on my arrival, I caused to appear before me: —

1. Francis Soleil.
2. Carlos Herrara, drummer.
3. Ante. Victorine, blacksmith.
4. Michel Peguere, corporal.
5. Wm. Boyer, caulker.
6. Francois Tiendra, soldier.
7. Manuel Martine, corporal.
8. Joseph Marin, carpenter.
9. Jean Mignon, soldier.
10. Gaspard de Marqua, do.
11. Francisco Poutau.
12. Jean Marie Moulin.
13. Antoine Tagouais, mason.
14. Dominic Auterre, soldier.
15. Joseph Segue, stone-cutter.
16. Benito Maureau, corporal.
17. Francois Sespedes, carpenter.
18. Alex'r Pegnoles.
19. Pierre Perez, stone mason.
20. Man'l Aug'n Abréon, carpenter.
21. Jourdan, baker.
22. Nicholas Navarro.
23. Charles Covos, sergeant.

These witnesses being all sworn, testified successively to the same purport, that in their frequent disputes Gomez was in the habit of applying to Barelas offensive epithets, as horse, mule, animal, etc., which Barelas could not resent, Gomez being his superior officer. They all agreed that Barelas was faithful and trusty in the discharge of his official duties.

"AUGUST 3, 1768.

MILONY DURALDE,"
JOSEPH LABUSCIERE."

DOCT. JNO. B. VALLEAU.

This gentleman, a native of France from La Rochelle, in the Spanish service, came up to St. Louis from New Orleans with Capt. Rios, as surgeon of his company, arriving here late in the year 1767. Expecting to be stationed here for some time, and houses difficult to be obtained, immediately after his arrival he made application for a lot in the village upon which to build one for his family, whom he had left in France. Accordingly he received a grant from St. Ange, dated January 2, 1768, of the northeast quarter of our present block No. 61, being 120 French feet on the west side of Second by 150 deep west up the hill on the south side of Pine (the quarter block on which stood the Mechanics' Bank). After Valleau received the grant of his lot, it was several months before he found any one to undertake to build him a house, owing to the scarcity of workmen in that early day of the village, finally, he entered into an agreement on April 23, 1768, with one Peter Tousignan, a carpenter, "for a house of one story, eighteen feet long by fourteen wide on the outside, of posts set in the ground, with a partition of small square posts in the center to divide it into two rooms of 9 by 14 feet, house to be shingled, with a stone chimney in the center, with two doors, one outside and one between the rooms, a window in each room with shutters, floored and ceiled with hewn cottonwood, the whole to be completed by the 15th of July. For which Doct. Valleau is to pay, when completed, the sum of sixty silver dollars, and to furnish all the iron and nails necessary for the house, but nothing else."

The agreement drawn up by Labusciere is signed by Valleau and Tousignan's X mark, and witnessed by Labusciere.

The house was never built — why, does not appear. The lot of Joseph Calvé, adjoining Valleau's on the south, of the same size, 120 by 150 feet, with a small log house of 16 feet square, was purchased by Valleau September 26, 1768, at a public sale by the governor to pay the debts of Calvé, who had absconded, for the sum of six hundred livres — $120. Valleau then owned the front from Chestnut to Pine — 240 feet French measure.

Doct. Valleau, in the discharge of his duty as surgeon of the Spanish troops here, had to make frequent trips back and forth to the garrison on the Missouri, where the troops were then building the fort. Towards the close of November, being seriously ill, and finding his end approaching, in conformity to a custom almost universally followed by devout Catholics here at that day, he executed his will on November 23d, and expired on the following day, a young man scarcely in his prime, surviving but one short year his advent to the place. He was but one of numerous others who fell victims by exposure to the deleterious influences incidental to all newly settled countries in certain latitudes, particularly on water-courses.

So universally was it the custom at that day in these colonies for a sick person to execute his will and commend his soul to his Maker that the man who died without having done so was deemed to have neglected one of his most important religious duties. It mattered little whether he possessed much or no property whatever to dispose of, the will appeared to be essential to entitle him to sepulture, with all the solemnities of the Holy Mother Church, in *consecrated* ground.

The will of John B. Valleau was the first one executed in St. Louis. I introduce it *in extenso* to exhibit the usual form and style of such documents in those early times of the place:—

WILL OF DOCT. VALLEAU.

" Before the royal notary in the Illinois, province of Louisiana, in presence of the hereinafter named witnesses, was personally present, Mr. John B. Valleau, a senior surgeon of his Catholic Majesty in the Illinois, being now at the post of St. Louis, in the French part of the Illinois, lying sick in bed, in the house of Denoyers',* but sound of mind, memory, and understanding, as

---

* Just opposite Valleau's, at the northeast corner of Chestnut and Second.

appears to the undersigned notary and witnesses, who, considering there is nothing more certain than death, nor nothing so uncertain as its hour, fearing to be overtaken by it, without having disposed of the few goods which God has given him; the said Jno. B. Valleau has made and dictated to the notary, in the presence of the undersigned witnesses, his last will and testament, in the following manner: —

"First, as a Christian and a Catholic, he commends his soul to God the Father, Son and Holy Ghost, beseeching His divine bounty by the merits of His passion, and by the intercession of the Holy Virgin, of Holy St. John his guardian, and of all the saints of the celestial court, to receive it among the blessed.

"The said testator wishes and ordains that his debts should be paid, and the injuries occasioned by him, if there be any, shall be relieved by his executor hereinafter named.

"He declares, wishes and ordains that Duralde, employed in the Spanish service, residing in this post of St. Louis, whom he appoints his executor, shall take possession of all his effects, situated in this colony of the Illinois and at New Orleans, either personal or real property, goods, effects, money, or anything belonging to the said testator at the day of his death, in whatever part of this colony they may be situated, without any reservation, appointing the said Duralde as the executor of this will, and praying him to undertake the charge, as a last proof of friendship.

"The said Duralde shall make a good and exact inventory of the property belonging to said testator, shall make the sale thereof, and the money arising therefrom, shall be sent by him to Madame Valleau, or to her children, residing at *La Rochelle* in the house of Madame Cholet, Main Street. Revoking all other wills and codicils which I might have made before this present will, to which I adhere as being my last will.

"Thus made, dictated and declared by the said testator, by the said notary and witnesses, and to him read and reread, he declaring to have well understood it, and wishing the said last will to be executed according to its tenor.

"Done in the room in which the said testator keeps his bed, the year one thousand seven hundred and sixty-eight, the 23d of November, about six o'clock p. m. In the presence of De

Rive, civil and military Governor of the Missouri part, being at present in this post of St. Louis, and of Joseph Papin, trader, of the same place, witnesses summoned for the purpose, and who have with the notary and the testator, signed these presents, after the same was read, conformably to the ordinance.

        " FRANCISCO RIVE,
        " JOS. PAPIN,
        " LABUSCIERE, *Notary*.
        " VALLEAU."

After Valleau's death, Duralde, his executor, proceeded at once to carry out his behests. He sold at public sale on December 11, 1768, his lot of 240 feet front on Second with the house; it produced but 251 livres — $50.

If Duralde took an inventory of the personal property it is not on record; he may have sent them to New Orleans, where they would produce a larger sum.

AN EARLY AGREEMENT.

"Before the royal notary of the Illinois, province of Louisiana, in presence of the hereinafter named witnesses, was present in person, Alexander Langlais, a traveling trader, living at the post of St. Louis, who, by these presents, voluntarily binds himself to Mr. Antoine Hubert, merchant, residing at the post of St. Louis, to go up for him, as his clerk, to the post of the Little Osages, to trade at that place his goods to the Indians, and manage his business, and do all for the advantage of said Mr. Hubert. Said Mr. Langlais promises to conduct said boat, and bring her back after said trade is over, as also the peltries he may have acquired, and give all the care to avoid loss or damage to said Mr. Hubert; and will start from said port of St. Louis at the first requisition of Mr. Hubert.

"This agreement is made for the sum of eight hundred livres in peltries, deer skins, or beaver, at the current price of the same at this poste, which they will establish on the peltries of this trade at his arrival at St. Louis. It is also agreed that in case said Langlais will take a negro in place of the said sum of eight hundred livres in peltries, said Mr. Hubert obligates himself to deliver him one on the arrival of the convoy from New Orleans in the next spring, said negro to be sound and free from all disease, in which case the said Langlais will repay to Mr. Hubert said amount of eight hundred livres in the same manner in peltries.

"And said Langlais is free to manage the said Hubert's business as he may think best, promising the said Mr. Hubert to do the best he can for him. All the foregoing has been agreed to at the poste of St. Louis, in the house of Mr. Hubert, in the year one thousand seven hundred and sixty-eight, the fourteenth of August, in presence of Mr. Chauvin, merchant, and Joseph Blondeau, trader, witnesses, who have, with said Mr. Hubert and said notary, signed these presents, after being read, the said Langlais declaring he did not know how to write.

"BLONDEAU,
"LABUSCIERE, *Notary*,
"HUBERT,
"CHAUVIN."

Below these signatures, in the handwriting of Joseph Labusciere, is written: —

"Rondo was condemned by sentence of arbitration to lose his wages, not having carried out his agreement. LABUSCIERE."

AN EARLY BOND.

"Before the royal notary of Illinois, province of Louisiana, in presence of the undersigned witnesses, was personally present Joseph Pouillot, a trader, living at present in this poste of St. Louis, on the French side of the Illinois country, who acknowledges himself indebted to, and promises to pay Francis Duchouquet, merchant of poste of Ste. Genevieve, at present in St. Louis, and agreeing to the same, the sum of 472 livres and 5 sols in peltries, which the said Duchouquet now lends and delivers to said Pouillot, who borrows the same to liquidate the same amount he owes to Mr. Lambert.

"The said sum of 472 livres and 5 sols, said Pouillot promises to refund to said Duchouquet, or to his order of this date, in all the month of May next of this present year, under penalty of all costs, damages and interest. And to secure the same the said Pouillot now places in the possession of said Duchouquet, an Indian female slave named Angelique, aged about twenty years, pregnant and near her confinement, whom the said Duchouquet accepts, and is to hold as security until the complete payment of the aforesaid sum in beaver or deer skins, inspected and valued at the current rate. Said Duchouquet promises to take good care of the said slave, to have her well attended to in her confinement, or any other sicknesses, as if she was his own property, but all at the expense and risque of said Pouillot. And in default of payment by said Pouillot within the time specified, the said Indian slave to become the property of said Duchouquet, without any recourse on the part of the said Pouillot.

"Done in office at the post of St. Louis of Illinois, this March 28th, 1769, in presence of Messrs. Dubreuil and Condé, merchants of the place, who have, together with the said Duchouquet and the notary, signed the same after being read, the said Pouillot declaring that he could not write.

"Du Breuil,
"Du Chouquet,
"Augte Condé,
"Labusciere, <i>Notary.</i>"

1768, Nov. 1. — Count Ulloa sailed from New Orleans for Havana, where he arrived on December the 4th.

1768–69. — So soon as Capt. Rios learned of the

departure of Ulloa, he descended with his men to New Orleans, leaving "Fort Charles the Prince" in an unfinished condition.

Capt. Rios was, as were all the Spanish officers of the period, a well bred gentleman, and although in the discharge of his unpleasant duty he was considered somewhat in the light of an intruder, yet from his prudent course in quartering his men at a distance from the village to avoid possible collisions with the people, he acquired during his brief stay here the good-will and respect of the judicious, and made a favorable impression on them. In his few official acts he modestly styles himself, "*Commandant of the Missouri portion of the Illinois.*"

1769. — After the departure of Rios from St. Louis we find nothing in our archives deserving of especial notice.

1769, July 24. — Lieut.-Gen. Alexander O'Reilly, with 2,600 choice troops of Spain, in twenty-four ships arrived at the Balize, and proceeded up the river to New Orleans.

Aug. 18. — O'Reilly landed at five o'clock p. m.

Oct. 29. — O'Reilly, after a stay of fourteen months at New Orleans, during which he established the Spanish authority in the country and organized the new government, appointed Don Luis Unzaga his successor, and sailed for Spain, leaving 1,200 regulars. Capt. Pedro Piernas, with two companies of the Louisiana regiment, had been sent up to St. Louis by O'Reilly, and on his arrival here assumed authority in Upper Louisiana May 20, 1,770.

MILITARY MATTERS.

Many persons of the present day have but very erroneous and exaggerated ideas in regard to the numerical strength of the regular military forces maintained by the three powers, England, France and Spain, whose colonists then possessed the North American Continent. In the French and Spanish service a full company of regulars in times of peace numbered about forty men.

I append briefly a few of the most important military affairs in our early history, to exemplify how small the force that accomplished them: —

When, in 1763, the king of France ceded the east side of this Upper Louisiana to Great Britain and the west side to Spain, he appointed Mons. D'Abadie Director General (not Governor, as he has been erroneously called) to come over from France and hold the country until the arrival of the Spanish officials to receive it, with instructions to retain *four* companies, and send back to France all the rest of the regular troops.

MILITARY MATTERS. 67

When, in the winter of 1763-64, De Villiers at Fort Chartres received advices from New Orleans of the cession of the east side to England, and instructions to concentrate all his regulars in this upper country at that point, prepared to give them immediate possession, and then to evacuate the country and bring his men down to New Orleans, his whole force concentrated at that point from Cahokia, Vincennes, Fort Massac, added to those at Fort de Chartres, amounted to about one hundred men, of which he took with him to New Orleans in the early summer about eighty, leaving Capt. St. Ange with about twenty to await the arrival of the British.

In 1765, after the failure of the British to ascend the Mississippi from New Orleans in 1764, owing to the hostility of the Natchez and other Indian tribes on the Lower Mississippi who opposed their passage, General Gage, the British Commander-in-Chief in North America, sent out Capt. Sterling with *one hundred men* of the regiment of Scotch Highlanders to cross the Allegheny Mountains, build their boats at Fort Pitt, descend the Ohio, and ascend the Missippi to Fort Chartres, — a force he deemed fully equal to the dangerous nature of the service, and which was verified by its successful accomplishment.

In 1766, when Count Ulloa came from Cuba to receive possession of New Orleans from the French, he brought with him but two companies, numbering some eighty men, of which he distributed a portion east towards Mobile, west to the Arkansas and Red Rivers, sending Capt. Rios with some twenty or twenty-five men to St. Louis, and retaining with him about twenty men. When Ulloa landed, the whole French force there, under Capt. Aubrey, who had succeeded D'Abadie, did not exceed a hundred regulars.

In 1778, Clark surprised Kaskaskia with a force of but one hundred and fifty-three men all told, with which he had descended from Pittsburgh, made up entirely of volunteers from Virginia, Pennsylvania and Kentucky, but few, if any, ever having been soldiers.

In 1779, when the British Col. Hamilton, from Detroit, recaptured Vincennes from Capt. Held, he had but twenty regulars with him, the balance of his force being Canadians and Indians.

In 1797, a Col. Howard, of the Spanish service, came up to St. Louis from New Orleans with a force of about an hundred men, then almost an army, apprehending trouble with the Americans, growing out of the violation by the Spanish officials at New Orleans of the stipulations of the treaty of 1795, guaranteeing to the Americans the joint navigation of the Lower Mississippi.

In 1804, Capt. Stoddard, when he came to receive

possession of this Upper Louisiana, brought with him but a single company of artillerists, not exceeding forty men.

Finally, in the same year, 1804, Capts. Lewis and Clark's expedition from St. Louis to cross the Rocky Mountains to the Pacific Ocean, which had never yet been attempted by white men, comprised but thirty-one men all told, and which they successfully accomplished, returning, in 1806, after an absence of two and one-half years, with thirty of the party, having lost but one man, and he by an accident.

Capt. St. Ange brought over with him from Fort Chartres in October, 1765, the first soldiers that came to St. Louis:—

Pierre Francois DeVolsay, first lieutenant and brevet captain.
Picoté de Belestre and F. De Bergueville, lieutenants.
Joseph Bruno Lefebvre Desruisseau, a cadet lieutenant.
Pierre Montardy and Philibert Gagnon, sergeants in 1766.
Nicholas Auguste Vincent, a sergeant in 1767.
Jean De Lage, a corporal in 1767.
D'amours de Louvieres, Nicholas Royer, Michel Rollette, Claude Tinon, Jean Comparios, Lambert Bonvarlet, Blondin Pion, Ayot, St. Marie, Beauvais, Desjardins, Lamotte, Langlais and Marechal, soldiers.

These were French.

Capt. Francisco Rios brought up from New Orleans in 1767:—

Fernando de Gomez, first lieut.   Francis Tienda, private.
Joseph Barela, a cadet engineer.   Jean Mignon,   do.

Tomaso Covos, 1st sergeant, Gaspard De Marque, do.
Francis Soliel, sergeant, Dominico Auterre, do.
Miguel Piguera, corporal, Jno. M. Houlino, do.
Manuel Martini, do. Alex. Pegnoles do.
Benito Moureau, do. Joseph N. Navarre, do.
Carlos Herrera, drummer. —— Jourdan, the baker.

and a few others whose names are not of record. These were Spanish, and returned below with Rios in 1769. Dr. Valleau was their surgeon.

I append the names of some of the early soldiers found in the archives — who came up with Piernas in 1770, and his successors : —

Don Antonio De Oro, Piernas' first lieutenant, acted as commandant in Piernas' occasional absence.
Diego Blanco, sergeant, 1770, afterwards ensign and lieutenant.

Joseph A. Hortiz, corporal, Juan Purzada, sergeant 1780,
   Gonsales, do. Louis Richard, soldier,
Eugenio Alvarez, soldier, Fernando Lisoro, sergeant, 1781,
Benito Basquez, do. Joseph Bermio,
Manuel Escolera, do. Pedro de Santos,
Antonio Cutian, do. Lopez Godoy, officer, 1783,
Charles Ouilf, do. 1779, Manuel Gonzales Moro, sergeant, 1788.
Daniel Appleby, do.
Joachim Perrara, do.

French soldiers who came over with St. Ange, and received a grant of a lot each, and built for himself each a house : —

D'amours de Louvieres, in 1765; Pierre Montardy, 1766; Gagnon, Royer, Rollette, Tinon, Delage, Comparios and Bonvarlet, 9.

The following bought each a house: —

Lous. Jos. D'amours, 1773; Jean Olivier, 1776; Tropez Ricard, 1785; Pedro Torrico, 1785; Joseph Perez, 1788, and Pedro Gabino, 1790.

Soldiers interred in the cemetery, from the register: —

1771. Jan. 7. Jno. B. Olivier, private.
1773. Nov. 15. Nicholas Vincent, sergeant.
1773. Nov. 22. Jac Bonvarlet, corporal.
1778. July 27. Jean Comparios, soldier.
1778. Nov. 6. B. Damvier, do.
1779. June 28. Benoit de Meru, do., aged 45.
1786. Jan. 28. Joseph L. Crespo, do., aged 68.
1786. Aug. 11. Francois Barrié, private.
1789, May 19. Pedro Ruiz, do.
1794. March 17. Franco Ventura, private.
1797. July 30. Daniel Appleby, do.
1801. Dec. 30. Louis Dubois, do, aged 60.
1802. Nov. Franco Lorenzo, do., aged 44.
Francois Barrera.

THE STATIONARY REGIMENT OF LOUISIANA.

After the establishment of the Spanish authority in Louisiana in 1769, and the withdrawal of the last of the French troops from the country, General O'Reilly assigned one of the Spanish regular regiments of infantry to the permanent occupation of the country, and styled it the "Stationary Regiment of Louisiana." This regiment, with such changes in its *personnel* as time and casualties produce, remained in the country the whole of the thirty-five years of the Spanish domination, and they were the only Spanish regulars in the country during that long period. One company was stationed at St. Louis, with a small squad of its men at Ste. Genevieve and New Madrid, and the balance of the regiment at the various posts in the lower country at Baton Rouge, Natchitoches, etc., the largest portion at New Orleans, the headquarters of the regiment, and the commandants at these various posts were all attached to this regiment.

At the cession of the country to the United States in 1804, Governor De Lassus was lieutenant-colonel of the regiment, and became its full colonel after it had gone below. The principal service rendered by these soldiers was somewhat in the nature of a military police, to preserve peace and order in the community and maintain the sovereignty of the king, there being no enemy to contend with either at home or abroad, and for protection against possible inroads of Indian tribes.

THE FIRST BILLIARD TABLE IN ST. LOUIS.

"Before me, the royal notary of Illinois, Province of Louisiana, in presence of the hereafter named undersigned witnesses, was personally present Jean Bapte Vien, billiard table keeper at the post of St. Louis, on the Spanish side of the Illinois; who by these presents has leased for three full, consecutive, and completed years, commencing from to-day, the date of these presents, to-wit: A billiard table, furnished complete with its cloth, maces, and cues, and balls, such as they are at present, of which the parties did not think it necessary to make a fuller description, with the building in which it is constructed, situated at the said post of St. Louis, bounded by the ground of Cadien on one side, and on the other side by the lot of Isidor Peltier, and another side a cross street, separating it from Durcy's lot;* and it is understood that the building in which is the billiard table is not included in said lease, and will be taken away in the first days of May next, said lease being for the billiard table, etc., only. This lease is made to Mr. Louis Vigé, merchant, living at present in St. Louis, to keep the table running for his profit during the three years, and return it at the end of that time in good order.

"This present bargain, made for the sum of six hundred livres in peltries at current prices at this post of St. Louis, which said Mr. Vigé promises to pay to said Vien, or to the holder of the present, at the end of each year, and besides said Vigé is to have completed by the end of the three years a building, covered with shingles, floored below and ceiled above, with a stone chimney, for the billiard table at this post of St. Louis, when it will be placed by Mr. Vigé, ready to run, and Mr. Vigé will take it to the place where it will be built, when it will be delivered to Vien, with six feet of ground all around the billiard building.† All the above has been agreed between the parties, who, for the execution of the present lease, have bound and mortgaged all their property, present and future. Done and passed at the post of St. Louis, Feby. 7, 1770, in presence of Louis Dubreuil, merchant, and Francis Cotin, witnesses, who have signed the same with the notary, after being read, the parties not knowing how to write.

"LOUIS DUBREUIL and COTIN, witnesses.

"LABUSCIERE, *Notary.*"

FIRST INDENTURE.

"Personally present Francis Baribault, a free boy, living in this post of St. Louis, aged about 19 years, who by these pres-

---

* This billiard room was on the south side of Vine Street, at the east corner of the alley, between Main and Vine Streets. — F. L. B.

† An indorsement on it shows Vigé paid the first year's rent, two hundred livres.

ents voluntarily binds himself for two years and an half to James Denis, joiner, also of this place, as an apprentice to learn the trade and mystery of a joiner — commencing with this day, and to end, without discontinuance, at the close of the two and half years; said Denis binds himself to feed, clothe and maintain said apprentice, with proper medical attendance if sick, during the term of his apprenticeship, and to use his best endeavours, as a good citizen and master, to teach said apprentice his said business as a joiner; and in like manner said Baribault binds himself to work with all his ability and strength for the interest of his master in acquiring his trade, and to obey his proper commands in all things connected with the said business. Denis to have no claim on said apprentice's services beyond the expiration of his term, unless for loss of time through fault of said apprentice.

"In addition said Denis is to put up at his cost and expense, at the close of said apprenticeship, a small house of posts in the ground of 12 by 15 feet, with an earthern chimney and covered with shingles, on such lot of ground as Barribault may then have acquired, so that he may have a place to live in when he leaves said Denis.

Done at office in St. Louis, of Illinois, April 4, 1770, in presence of the undersigned witnesses and parties, who have signed the same, after being read, except Baribault, who knows not how to write.

JULIEN LEROY,
BEAU SOLIEL, } Witnesses.
HERVIEUX,

JACQUES DENIS,

LABUSCIERE, *Notary.*

EARLY FRENCH MERCHANTS.

Much of the early emigration to lower Louisiana came from the southwest part of France, bordering on Spain and along the shores of the Atlantic and Mediterranean, many of them well educated business men of the best families, from the principal towns

PLAT OF ST. LOUIS IN 1770.

SHOWING ALL THE HOUSES BUILT IN ITS FIRST SIX YEARS WHILE UNDER THE FRENCH ADMINISTRATION OF ST. ANGE AND HIS ASSOCIATES IN THE GOVERNMENT.

There were 100 Wood and 15 Stone Buildings. The wood are indicated in solid black; the stone in outline. No Church Building until 1776, prior to which date there was a small log Chapel at northeast corner of Church Block.

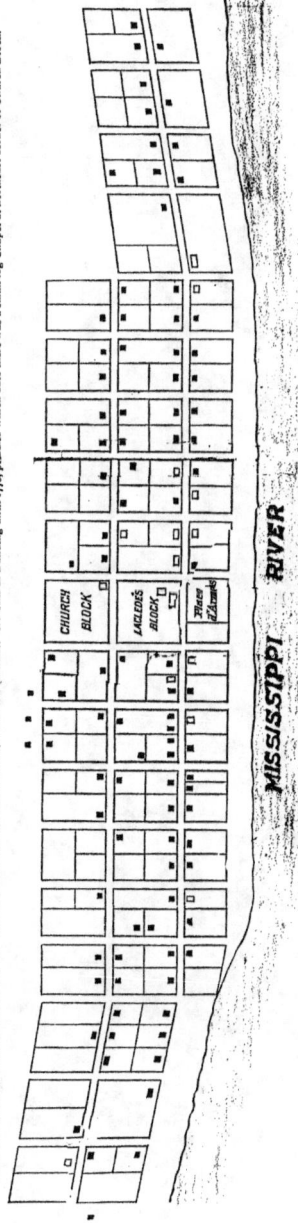

throughout this region of country, quite a number of them finding their way up to St. Louis: —

Laclede Liguest, Pierre
Bidet, Jno. B. Langoumois
Butaud, Jno. B. Brind'amour
Eloi, Francis
Dubreuil, Louis Chauvet
Barsalou, Nicholas
Thoulouse, Jno. M.
Hubert, Antoine
Durcy, Francis
Lambert, Louis
Fouche, Pierre
Dutillet, M.
Berard, Antoine, Bordeau
Lepage, Francois
Peri, Pierre
August Conde, Surgeon
Valeau, Jno. B., Sur.
Motard, J. A. J., Avignon
Sarpy, Jno. B., Funel
Segond, Joseph
Labbadie, Silvestre, Tarbes
Duralde, M. M.
Conand, Joseph
Duclos, Jno.
Barré, Etienne
Lagarciniere.

Papin, Jos. M.
Roubieux, Gaspard
Yosti, Emelien
Vigo, Francis
Bargas, Domingo
Pourcelly, John P.
Gratiot, Charles
Clamorgan, Jacques
Bouis, A. V., Marseilles
Sorin, Joseph, Larochelle
Collel, Bonaventura, Barcelona
Sarpy, Gregoire, Funel
Sarpy, Pierre Silvestre, Funel
Sarpy, Pierre Berald, Funel
Reilhe, Antoine
Marmillon, Francois
Fusilier de la Claire, Gabriel
Delorier, Louis Merlet
Barrouselle, Francois, St. Domingo.
Coignard, Louis, Chatillon
Cabanné, John P., Pau
Rutgers, Arend
Delaunay, David

By an examination of the plat of the village and tables, it will be seen that St. Louis contained in the year 1770, at the conclusion of her first and French administration, one hundred and fifteen houses — one hundred of wood and fifteen of stone — of which number seventy-five, about two-thirds of the whole, had been put up in her two first years — 1765 and 1766 — with a population of about 500 souls. And at the transfer of the country to the United States in 1804 they had increased to one hundred and thirty of wood and fifty-one of stone — one hundred and eighty-one in all; an increase in the thirty-four years under Spanish rule of sixty-six buildings; an average of barely two per annum, and this included stores, warehouses, kitchens and other buildings, etc., some twenty or so. The dwellings being about one hundred and sixty, and the population 925 souls — an average of less than six to a house.

St. Louis in her first five years of existence, with her one hundred and fifteen houses, had become larger than Kaskaskia ever had been in her best days, drawing the largest portion of her new comers from the Illinois side of the river, reducing somewhat the populations of Kaskaskia, Cahokia and Prairie du Rocher, and completely depopulating and annihilating the two villages of Fort Chartres and St. Phillippe, which ceased to exist.

During the thirty-four years of Spanish authority succeeding the first six years of French rule, the place continued to be French in every essential but the partial use of Spanish in a few official documents; the intercourse of the people with each other, and their governors, their commerce, trade, habits, customs, manners, amusements, marriages, funerals, services in church, parish registers, everything was French; the governors and officers all spoke French, it was a *sine qua non* in their appointment; the few Spaniards that settled in the country soon became Frenchmen, and all married French wives; no Frenchman became a Spaniard; two or three of the governors were Frenchmen by birth; the wives of Gov. Piernas and Trudeau were French ladies. Outside of the Spanish officials and soldiers not more than a dozen Spaniards came to the place during the domination of Spain; Governor Delassus was born in France and Trudeau of French stock, and nearly all the papers in the archives were in the French language. The country was only Spanish by possession, but practically French in all else.

THE EARLY PRIESTS.

Father I. L. Meurin, parish curate of our Lady of Cahokia, was the first, and after him Father Gibault, curate of the Immaculate Conception at Kaskaskia, and Vicar General of my Lord Bishop of Quebec, the second who came over occasionally from the other side, and officiated for a few years in a tent, and from the summer of 1768 in a small log chapel put up for temporary use on the northeast corner of the church square, which served until the erection of the first church in 1776.

The first public sale at the door of the chapel took place on Sunday, September 12, 1768, by Cottin, the first constable.*

During the French period prior to 1770, the churches in this province were under the ecclesiastical authority of the Bishopric of Quebec, after the establishment of the Spanish authority by Don Pedro Piernas May 20, 1770, they came under that of the Bishopric of Cuba.

The first book in which were registered the baptisms, marriages and deaths of this parish of St. Louis, was commenced on October 4, 1770, by Rene Kiersereau, the sexton of the church, there being then no parish priest as yet, who on that date interred the body of Gregory, a free negro man, and who continued, as sexton, to inter until March 25, 1772, up to which date he had interred thirty-four bodies, when Father Valentin, who had just been appointed the first curate of the parish of St. Louis, entered upon his duties, and took charge of the church register.

---

* Archives, vol. 2, page 24, No. 24.

FIRST PARISH REGISTER. 79

The first baptism in St. Louis was by Father Meurin in May, 1766, of Marie Deschamps, born in September, 1765, and his last one, of Marie Josepha Kiersereau, February 7, 1769 — numbering twenty-nine by him and three by Kiersereau — thirty-two in the three years. They were noted down at the time on loose sheets of paper, and afterwards, when the first register book was procured by Governor Piernas, copied therein, several of them imperfect, torn and mice-eaten.

1. Marie Deschamps, 1765, 1766.
2. Veronica Ride, May 9.
3. Antoine, a half-breed Panis, May 9.
4. Catherine Bissonnet, May 7, 1767.
5. Helen Hebert, May 7, 1767.
6. Pelagie Kiersereau " "
7. Marie Langevin, " "
8. Henry Francois Leroy " "
9. Joseph Guion, June 21, 1767.
10. Gabriel Dodier, Aug. 10, 1767.
11. Claude ———, Sept. 1, 1767.
12. Pad, a slave, Sept. 1, 1767.
13. Paul Gregory, a free negro, Sept. 1, 1767.
14. Catherine Rollet, Sept. 1, 1767.
15. Jno. B. Gamache, May 3, 1768.
16. Angelica Bissonnet, May 3, 1768.
17. Peter Berger, May 3, 1768.
18. Louis Denoyer, " "
19. Angelica Grammont, "
20. Elizabeth Hunand "
21. Constance Labusciere, "
22. Marie M. Robert, "
23. Louis Denoyer's daughter, 1769.
24. Marie Josa. Kiersereau, Feb. 7, 1769.

The last by Father Meurin, and eight others, slaves and Indians.

So, also, with the deaths during these five years, no register of them was kept, but through the archives, wills and inventories we have ascertained the most prominent of the men to the extent of ten or twelve.

1766. — Mr. Legrain, who came in the boat with Chouteau.

1767, April 3d. — Judge Joseph Lefebvre, Debruisseau.

1767, April 3d. — Mr. Francis Eloy, at New Orleans.

1768, Nov. 25. — Doc. Jno. B. Valleau, army surgeon.

1769, May. — Mr. Thos. Blondeau, son of Joseph Blondeau.

1769, Aug. — Paul Sigle, tanner, from the Island of Malta.

1769, Aug. — John Ante. D'Aunis, *alias* St. Vincent, merchant.

1769, Aug. — Mrs. Nicholas H. Beaugenou.

1769 or 1770. — Mr. Constantine Quirigou Phillip.

1770, Aug. 12. — Mr. Louis Deshetres, Indian interpreter.

1770. — Lieut. P. F. B. I. Debruisseau, son of Judge Lefebvre, at New Orleans.

1770, Sept. — Nicholas Marechal, native of France.

1771, Oct. 25. — Mr. Joseph Detailly, Indian interpreter.

As to the marriages, they are all preserved in the archives, as the law required all contracts to be executed in presence of the governor, for which a fee was exacted.

This first church register served for fifteen years, from 1766 to 1781, after which a separate book was used for marriages, baptisms and deaths.

EARLY HOUSES.

Until some years after the transfer in 1804, the houses were of but two materials, stone and timber. The stone was quarried with a crow-bar and sledge-hammer, from along the river bluffs in front of the village, and much of the timber for the first houses was cut on the ground and in the near vicinity.

The houses were uniformly of one style, such as prevails in the South, one story in height, with a loft above and a steep roof, the largest and best with galleries all around, some with galleries in front and sides, and a few of the poorer sort only in front, generally covered with clapboards, the best shingled.

About four-fifths of the houses were of posts set in the ground, the best of them hewed about nine inches square, the others of round posts set about three feet deep; a few of the best of these houses were of hewed posts set on a stone wall from four to five feet high above ground. The largest portion of these houses were from twenty to thirty feet in size, divided usually into two and some of them three rooms; some smaller, of fifteen to twenty feet square, a single room, which had to serve as parlor, bed and dining-room and kitchen; a few had a shed attached to the house for the latter purpose. A few of the larger houses were divided into three rooms, with a stone chimney in the center and a fire-place in each room; they were mostly floored with hewed puncheons, the ceilings from eight to ten feet high.

A few of the largest stone houses were divided into five rooms, a large one in the center extending from front to rear, and two small ones on each side, opening into the large center room; the floor some ten feet above ground, the lower part used for cellar or store-rooms; the flooring sawed with whip-saws, there being no saw-mill in the country, with ceilings about ten feet high, with from one to two windows in a room, opening, in the French style, on hinges, and glazed with 8 by 10 lights, a few with 10 by 12, the largest size used in the country for many years.

HOUSEHOLD FURNITURE.

It is plainly evident that in houses of the sizes as described there was but little room for furniture, however desirable it might have been to possess it; with many, a bedstead and bedding, table, a few chairs, with a cupboard for their few articles of table ware, and a chest or trunk for their apparel, constituted the sum total of their possessions in that line, with some few in larger houses, a bureau or clothes-press, with other necessary articles. Of course the few comparatively wealthy ones with larger houses had more and better furniture, and some of them a little silverware and plate, but floor carpets were not introduced into the country for many long years thereafter.

WATER.

For some years after the commencement of the village settlement there were no wells sunk, the underlying formation being limestone but a few feet below the surface and cropping out at various points, particularly on the edge of the bluffs, where the rock was bare along the whole front. With the exception of two or three springs, the inhabitants used the river water for all purposes, and for this reason the lots along the river front were first sought and built upon.

The water was hauled up from the river in a barrel laid across two sappling poles which served for shafts, called a "drag." After a time a few wells were sunk, back on the second and third streets, but as they had to bore through the limestone bed-rock of the village in their excavation they cost much money and but few undertook them.

Col. Chouteau, who lived on his block almost

sixty-five years, had made two attempts on different parts of the same; one of them was unsuccessful, the other, after going to the depth of one hundred feet, at great cost, procured a little water, but a very inadequate supply.

Besides, it was only in the summer time that a little cold water was needed for drinking purposes, there being then no ice put up, but the river water was universally preferred, as being more wholesome and palatable.

FUEL.

Stone coal, if even then discovered, was not made use of generally until long after the American days. There was no need of it, wood being abundant and cheap all over the country. Even as late as 1825, when the supply in the near vicinity began to grow short, it was brought on rafts from the upper rivers, and sold at from $1.25 to $1.50 per cord. The little fuel used by blacksmiths was charcoal burnt near the villages.

AGRICULTURE.

The agricultural operations in the early development of the settlement were on a very limited scale, confined at first mainly to corn for their bread; potatoes and turnips, pumpkins and melons in their common fields, and no more of these than were necessary for their own consumption, as there would

AGRICULTURE.

have been no market for any surplus, and each one his little garden patch contiguous to his residence, where he raised his little supply of kitchen truck.

In a few years, after the erection of Laclede's water mill, they added wheat to their bread stuffs. The cultivation of these products constituted the whole of their agricultural labors during these early years. They needed no meadows, the wild prairie grass abounding all over the country affording abundance of nutritious hay for their animals, upon which they thrived and kept in the best of condition throughout the year, grain seldom being given, except occasionally to a working animal, they had no need of oats. Their gardens furnished them peas, beans, cabbages, beets, carrots, etc., the woods and prairies plenty of wild game, the streams plenty of fish, and with their beef, poultry, eggs, milk and butter there was abundance in the land, because the consumers were but few.

The only article in the country on wheels for long years was a charrette, a primitive cart, constructed of two pieces of scantling some ten or twelve feet long framed together by two or more cross pieces, upon one end of which the body, of wicker-work, was placed, and the front ends rounded to serve as the shafts, and the whole set on the axletree of the wheels.

Almost the only use they had for it was to haul in

their corn and hay to their barns back of the village. It was sometimes used to take ladies and children out on a ride. All the males and most of the females made their riding on horse-back. Laclede brought up his family from Fort Chartres in 1764 in one of these carts, and the writer rode up in one from Ste. Genevieve in 1818 — rather rough.

Their agricultural implements were very limited in variety and of the most primitive construction, such as ploughs, hoes, spades and shovels, grubbing hoes, rakes, etc.; occasionally, a harrow, a joint-stock concern serving a neighborhood.

AMUSEMENTS.

For the men, the amusements were billiards, cards and pony races, for amusement only — rarely anything staked. For the females, fiddling and dancing and the usual amount of gossiping and small-talk. In 1767, the village hardly two years old, there were two billiard establishments, and a year or two later, a third. Their horses for many years being exclusively a small breed of Indian ponies peculiar to the country, mostly natural pacers, their races were seldom more than a few hundred yards in length, or at most, a quarter of a mile to the extent, usually in the prairie back of the village, there being then no race track.

After the Americans became possessed of the

country on the other side, larger horses were introduced here from Kentucky for work and draft only. And in 1818, when I came to the place, a horse of fifteen hands high was considered a large horse, and when the first Conestoga from Pennsylvania was seen here he created quite a sensation. They had no idea that there could be any such horses in existence.

Their dancing parties were sometimes on a Saturday evening, after the labors of the week were ended, and were always kept up until daylight the next morning. But more frequently on Sundays, afternoons and evenings, the Sabbath being considered over by most of the people at the conclusion of the High Mass at twelve o'clock noon, — the afternoons were devoted to amusement, a few only of the most devout, largely females, would attend the evening vespers.

Their judgment sales, by decree of the governor, always took place on Sundays at the church door, at the close of the Mass at twelve o'clock noon, that being the only idle day of the week when a small crowd could be gathered together for such a purpose, the most of the people being engaged during the other days in their various avocations, and with the majority of the people the religious duties of the day being discharged at that hour, and as all made it a special duty to attend the Mass, usually all the inhabitants of the place were there assembled.

Previous notice having been given of the sale, the property was cried out for three successive Sundays, and then awarded to the highest bidder on the third day ; as there were usually no other bidders than the two or three who might desire the house for a residence, the sale required but little time, the property was generally knocked off at the value of the improvements, the lot generally considered as part of the appurtenances of the improvements.

(No speculation in town-lots at that day.)

MARRIAGE CONTRACTS.

The laws and customs relating to marriages were those of Paris and Castile, designated " a community of interest,"— that is to say, unless otherwise specified in the civil contract, whatever property either party possessed before marriage made a common fund to be equally enjoyed by both. On the death of either party intestate ; the survivor was entitled to one-half of the estate, and the children of the marriage, if any, the other half ; if no children, then the legal heirs of the deceased party, — such as parents, brothers and sisters, etc., — hence it was customary upon the death of a married person to proceed at once to take an inventory of his or her effects. If so specified in the contract, the survivor could elect to " renounce " the community of interest, and withdraw whatever amount he or she may have put in. This did not prevent either party from leaving to the survivor the whole of the property where there were no children, which was the usual course, but in all cases where there were children they were to have one-half collectively. This was the civil marriage, the parties being afterwards united with the rites of the church by the parish priest.

Inventories being required in nearly all cases of death, where the deceased person possessed any property, it was the duty of the governor or commandant, on receiving notice of the death of any one, to repair to the residence of the deceased with his clerks and witnesses, and there take an inventory of the effects of said deceased, which being done, might remain in the custody of the survivor, or, if a single person, in charge of some responsible person appointed by the governor.

In the case of wills, where the party, from sickness or other disability, could not appear before him in his office, it was made his duty to repair to the bedside of the sick person and there have the will executed and attested in his presence.

All papers, to give them validity, had to be executed in presence of the governor.

The French word "*Livre*" signifies in English a *book*, a *pound weight*, and down to the date of the

French Republican Constitution of 1792, was the name of a *coin* of the value of 18½ cents of our currency, which for long centuries back under the ancient monarchy of France, was established as the unit of that nation in which all their money calculations were figured up and their account-books kept.

The French Revolutionists, in their zeal to do away with every thing that savored in the slightest of the "*ancien regime*," abolished the "*Livre*," and substituted therefor their new coin the "*franc*," which they made one mill or one-tenth of a cent heavier than the "*livre*," otherwise it would have been merely the "*same old thing*" with a new name; since which day the word "*livre*," as applied to a "money-coin," has become obsolete, and is known to but few of the present age. The par value of five livres by act of Congress was 92½ cents U. S. currency, and that of five francs 93 cents.

As this term "livre" occurs in every French document on record in our archives relating to money matters, the persons who were employed to translate these papers into English some years back, being doubtless ignorant that there ever had been a coin of that designation, have almost invariably translated it into "*pound*," thereby making the document translated meaningless in its most essential particular, the consideration.

Let it be understood that the above remarks in

relation to the "*livre*" apply solely to the mode of "*keeping*" their accounts, there being but little, if any, coin seen in the country, the circulating medium being furs and peltries at a fixed price per pound — 40 cents the finest, 30 for medium, and 20 cents inferior, whether established by law or custom does not appear; but unless otherwise stipulated by contract all transactions were understood to be in the above medium.* After the transfer to Spain, the coin of that kingdom began to appear, but in limited amounts, as we find a few transactions for "*hard dollars*," in contradistinction no doubt to the soft, or "*fur*" dollars. As to *paper* money, none had ever been seen in the country at that early day, and even had there been any, but few could have made out the denomination.

COMMONS AND COMMON-FIELDS.

Of those who were the first to come over to this from the other side, far the largest portion were tillers of the soil, who, by their labors in the field, produced their own subsistence and that of their stock. Some of them, in seasons when not engaged in their agricultural avocations, exercised the calling

---

* Even after the transfer to the United States, transactions were made in peltries, as we find that Judge Jno. B. C. Lucas made his first purchase of a house for his residence from Pierre Duchouquette and wife December 14, 1807, for $600 in peltries. (Book A, 525.)

of rough artisans, such as blacksmiths, carpenters, stone masons, hewers, etc., employed in building. Others, procuring small outfits of merchandise spent the winters trading with Indians and trapping, consequently it was a matter of prime necessity with them, so soon as they had erected their domicile in the village, to proceed at once to the production of their bread-stuffs. For this purpose the land immediately adjoining the village on the northwest, being the most suitable, was set aside for cultivation, and conceded in strips of one arpent in front by forty in depth, and each applicant allotted one or more, according to his ability to cultivate it. This was called the common-field lots, and the tract extended from a little below Market Street on the south, to opposite the big mound on the north, and from Broadway to Jefferson Avenue, east to west. The land lying southwest of the village being well watered with numerous springs and well covered with timber, was set aside for the village commons, in which the cattle and stock of the inhabitants were kept for safety and convenience.

These two tracts of land were at once enclosed by the people in 1764 and 1765, and their eastern fence formed the western boundary of the village for many years.*

---

* Col. Chouteau's testimony before the Board of Land Commissioners, 1806.

The idea that St. Louis was named in honor of the then king of France, Louis XV., first appears in print in Jno. A. Paxton's brief sketch of the place in his Directory of 1821, and has since been accepted by others in default of more reliable information on that head. This idea, to say the least, is preposterous, as can be clearly demonstrated.

At the time St. Louis received its appellation, its people had just been driven from the other side, where many of them were born, abandoning their little property, their homes, all the little comforts a lifelong laborious avocation had enabled them to acquire, by the act of this very man who was the cause of all their troubles and misfortunes, in transferring them and their country to a nation that they had always regarded as their natural enemies, compelling them either to live under a detested government or fly to another, and this latter alternative was their choice as the least of the two evils. Is it not more likely that, instead of honoring this man by naming their new location after him, they would unite in execrations on his head? A man who so far from being a saint was the very antipodes of one, leading a depraved and dissolute life, and who, had he lived at a later period in our history, would have doubtless perished on the scaffold, instead of his grandson and successor, the virtuous but unfortunate Louis XVI.

It received its name from King Louis IX., who, centuries back, had sacrificed his life in his zeal for the cause of religion and Christianity in the prosecution of the holy wars in the East, and was subsequently canonized by the head of the church. It always was and is yet, I believe, to some extent, the custom of devout Catholics in all places named after a saint to consider him or her the patron saint of the place so named, and for that reason the "Fete St. Louis," St. Louis' day, August 25th, was, in the early days of St. Louis, and for a number of years after my advent to the place, always observed with appropriate religious ceremonies and processions of the clergy and others through the cemetery and grounds of the church.

We conclude the first book of our annals, being its early French history, with a full catalogue of all the documents found in the archives, all written by, or in presence of, Joseph Labusciere, from April, 1766, to May 20, 1770, the day on which the French domination terminated in St. Louis, and that of Spain commenced, under the administration of Governor Pedro Piernas.

Copied from the original in the handwriting of Labusciere : —

Deeds for sales of lots and lands	61
Sales made under execution	11
Bonds and obligations	30
Bargains or trades	24

END OF THE FRENCH DOMINATION.

Marriage contracts	16
Exchanges of real estate	8
Engagements for services	11
Acquittances being receipts	5
Donations or gifts of property	5
Inventories of property of deceased persons	3
Do merchandise	4
Indentures	1
Copartnerships	2
Agreements	2
Emancipations of slaves	2
Affidavits	2
Ordinances or decrees	1
Powers of attorney	1
Wills	1
Leases	2
Miscellaneous	2
Documents in all	194

All the above enumerated papers were executed by Labusciere, as notary, and *ex-officio* secretary of the temporary government, in whose custody they were kept until handed over by him to Governor Piernas, May 20, 1770, on which day our infant village had grown to contain 100 wooden and 15 stone houses, a total of 115, with a population of about five hundred souls, in the six years since its commencement in the year 1764.

This house of upright posts, 35 feet front by 25 deep, built by Nicholas Beaugenou, Sr., at the southwest corner of Almond and Main streets, in the year 1765, was one of the first built in St. Louis, and in which the first marriage on record in the archives of St. Louis took place, on April 20, 1766, that of Beaugenou's eldest daughter, Maria Josepha, then in her eighteenth year, to Toussaint Hunaut, a young Canadian trader.

The house was occupied by the Beaugenou family for some years. Subsequently by others until 1815, when it was purchased by Gen. Wm. Clark. It was occupied by Major Mackey Wherry, our first Town Register, for a number of years from about that period, and was removed not many years back to give place to the present brick structure.

BEAUGENOU HOUSE, 1765.

[*Drawn by C. Heberer under direction of F. L. Billon.*]

ANNALS OF ST. LOUIS.

PART SECOND.

THE SPANISH DOMINATION.

1770–1804.

The Spanish domination in Upper Louisiana dates from May 20, 1770, on which day Capt. Pierre Joseph Piernas, appointed by O'Reilly, assumed authority as lieutenant-governor and military commandant of the upper portion of the province.

Piernas was a Spaniard by birth, and came to New Orleans, a captain in the Spanish service, with Count Ulloa in 1766. He was married in that city to Felicité Portneuf, a French lady of the place, and came to St. Louis with his family in the spring of 1770. On May 20 of that year Capt. St. Ange de Bellerive delivered over to him the possession of this Upper Louisiana, and from that date the Spanish rule on this side commenced.

The first official act of Gov. Piernas was the appointment of M. Milony Duralde to survey the lines of the village lots and out-lots that had been granted to individuals by his predecessors, the French authorities.

A small temporary log chapel was erected at the northeast corner of the church block — a tent having heretofore served the purpose.

In this chapel the Revd. Father Gibault, curate of Kaskaskia, who paid the new village an occasional visit, celebrated his first baptism in St. Louis on June 20, 1770, that of Felicité M., infant daughter of Lieut. Picoté de Belestre, and grand-daughter of Neyon de Villiers, the last French governor of Upper Illinois.

Under the laws and customs of Paris and Castile in force in the provinces of France and Spain, the governors exercised the powers and prerogatives of courts of justice for the trial of venial offenses. Several cases of this nature were heard by Gov. Piernas, — that of Michael Calas for slander, June 23; Amable Letourneau for seditious language, August 27; and one Jeannot for immoral conduct and disturbance, September 17, and each one found guilty and sentenced to ten years banishment from the province, under penalty of being publicly chastised should he dare to return.

AN AGREEMENT.

"Before us, Don Pedro Piernas, captain of infantry, lieutenant governor of the establishment of the Illinois, belonging to his Catholic majesty, personally appeared Mr. Louis Diard, merchant, usually at New Orleans, at present at the post of St. Louis, of one part, and Mr. John Datchurut, also a merchant, residing at the post of St. Genevieve, and at present also in this post of St. Louis. Said parties, of their free will and accord, to terminate the suit between them concerning a boat that Mr. Diard had loaned to Mr. Datchurut, which boat having descended to New Orleans for the benefit of Mr. Datchurut, had given an opportunity to Mr. Diart to cause Mr. Datchurut to appear before his lordship, Don Luis Unzaga, Governor-general of Louisiana, who, on the demand, principally of Mr. Diart, rendered a judgment against Mr. Datchurut on the 26th of January, 1770, which condemned him to keep on his own account all the goods that Mr. Diart would have taken down in his said boat. Said decree was signified to Mr. Datchurut at New Orleans, to Mr. Duralde, his agent, and was on the point of being executed, according to the order in the form of a decree, ordained by us the commandant, on the petition of Mr. Diart, the 28th of May last. But the said parties wishing to end and put a stop to a suit, which might be ruinous to both, and avoid all prosecutions, have by these presents agreed, and do agree before us, to refer to three expert arbitrators, knowing their business, to whom each will relate his reasons and argument, and make their award binding on them, and observe it, in all its particulars to its full extent, so that neither can appeal to any other tribunal in consequence of their decision. And to accomplish said agreement, said Mr. Diart names as his arbitrator Mr. Perrault, merchant, at present in this post of St. Louis; and Mr. Datchurut for his arbitrator, Mr. Laclede Liguest, also merchant in this place, and in case of disagreement between these two arbitrators just named, we name for the third, Mr. Lambert Lafleur, lieutenant of militia and merchant, to whom the two parties will submit their cases and documents, for their final award, to be carried out according to its tenor.

"The same to be submitted to us for confirmation.

"Thus it has been agreed and granted. Done and executed in the Government Hall at St. Louis, the year 1770, the 1st of June, in presence of Milony Duralde, merchant, and Joseph Labusciere, scrivener, who with the two parties and we, the commandant, have signed the same after being read.

"L. DIARD,   J. DACHURUT,
M. MILONY DURALDE,   LABUSCIERE,   PEDRO PIERNAS."

"Considering the foregoing agreement, we order that Messrs. Perrault, Laclede and Lambert heretofore named, will decide the matter between Messrs. Diart and Datchurut, and will make report to us of their award in the case, to be made known to whom it may concern.

"ST. LOUIS, June 1, 1770.

"PEDRO PIERNAS."

"Messrs. Diard and Datchurut having agreed in writing on the first day of the present month, before Don Pedro Piernas, Lieutenant-Governor, military and civil, to have appraised by us and Mr. Lambert (appointed umpire by Mr. Piernas, in case of disagreement between us), the damages and interests that have resulted to Mr. Diard, in the detention of the peltries and flour, deposited in the hands of Mr. Louis Chamard, at St. Genevieve, and for which there had been an award rendered at New Orleans, January 26, 1770, by Messrs. Breau and Rincon, and confirmed by a decree of Don Luis Unzaga, governor of the province of Louisiana, on same date at foot of said award, condemning the said Datchurat to pay the said Diard, at New Orleans, for the said peltries and flour, at their value there at the time said Diard arrived there, to commence his suit against said Datchurut.

"Considering all the circumstances of the case, upon mature reflection, deeming it unnecessary to call in Mr. Lafleur, the umpire, we have adjudged and decided that Mr. Diard should be indemnified for his losses by Mr. Datchurut at the same rate that his means lying at New Orleans, might have produced him in the Illinois country if he had gone up there to trade. In consequence of this abstraction, expenses of coming up, and expenses of boarding and storage incurred during a certain period; considering, also, that if he had had the funds in litigation, the risks he would run, as much in coming up from New Orleans to the Illinois country, as those he would incur in the sale of his effects, the proceeds of which are only realized after long waiting. We appraise the damages and interest that Mr. Datchurut has occasioned Mr. Diard at thirty-five per cent, which Datchurut will pay him on demand, on the amount accruing from the goods detained (a statement of which will be appended by us below), in conformity to the award made by Messrs. Breau and Rincon, confirmed by the governor at New Orleans. Mr. Diard not to claim anything more. And as to Messrs. St. Pierre Jussiam and Dupré, joint claimants with Diard as freighters, we have put off the decision of their claim, and adjudge that Mr. Datchurut will account to them for their capital at the same rate of 35 %, as soon as Messrs. Jussiam and Dupré may demand it. It is not to be taken from the bill of expenses, allowed by the judges to Mr. Diard in going to New Orleans, which is to be repaid him as the decision prescribes; and as to the legal expenses incurred by Mr. Diard, he will make a faithful account of them, which Mr. Datchurat will refund him.

"Executed in good faith, at St. Louis, June 9, 1770.

"Perrault,   Laclede Liguest,   Lambert,
 L. Diard,   Dupré,   Datchurut,
                  St. Pierre Jussaume."

EMANCIPATION BY LOUIS VILLARS.

" *To Don Pedro Piernas, Captain of Infantry of the Regiment of Louisiana, Lieut.-Governor of the Establishments of his Catholic Majesty at the Illinois:*

"Sir — Louis Villars, lieut. of infantry, in the battallion of Louisiana, humbly prays you, that he is the owner of a negress named Julie, about thirty years of age; that she has rendered him great services for a number of years, especially during two severe sicknesses your petitioner has undergone. The zeal and attachment she exhibited in his service having completely ruined her health, he desires to set her at liberty with a view to its restoration.

" For this purpose he respectfully supplicates your approbation, and, as in duty bound, will ever pray.

"St. Louis, June 2, 1770.

"Louis Villars.

" In view of the present petition and statement, to second the good dispositions of Mr. Villars, and knowing said negro woman to be of good conduct and behavior, we do, by these presents, grant her full and entire liberty, and declare her from this day free and enfranchised, to enjoy, she and the children of early age she may have, all the rights and privileges granted to the enfranchised, requesting all commandants and governors under whom the said Julia and children may find themselves, to cause them to enjoy said privileges, on the condition that said Julia bring by her good conduct, respect and honor on said Mr. Villars, on pain of being returned to her first condition of servitude.

" Done in the chamber of the government of Illinois at St. Louis, June 3, 1770, in presence of Messrs. Datchurut and Sarpy, merchants, witnesses, residing on the Spanish side, who have signed with us.

"Datchurut,
"Sarpy,
"Piernas."

PETITION OF MASSE AND LABASTILLE.

To Mr. Don Pedro Piernas, Captain of Infantry, and Lieutenant Governor of the Establishments of the Illinois and its dependencies, belonging to his Catholic Majesty:

"Your humble petitioners, Pierre Massé, *alias* Picart, and John Bap. Labastille, lead miners, living at the "*Mine Lamothe,*" respectfully represent that they took out lead and ore on a piece of land at that place, Mine Lamothe, that they always believed to be part of the Royal Domain. They were much surprised that, after they had done considerable work, and had taken out: the said Picart about eighteen thousand pounds of lead, and de la Bastille about two thousand pounds, they were interrupted by one Laroze, a miner, who forbid them to continue their labor, and at same time seized their lead and mineral, in the name of Mr. Datchurut, a creditor of said Laroze, from whom this last had acquired the said land. The petitioners always were, and still are, ignorant whether the land where they worked was acquired by the said Laroze, as he only had it surveyed long after your petitioners had taken out their ore, and that he never could shew them his lines. Considering this, sir, your petitioners have recourse on you, and think that as said Laroze did not have his land measured, and his lines established before the work done by your petitioners, that the replevy of their lead be granted them; and in case they are not on the six arpents square of said Laroze, acquired from said Datchurat, that they be protected in continuing their labor, and do justice, and will ever pray for your prosperity.

"ST. LOUIS, Nov. 30, 1770.

        "PIERRE MASSÉ Mark of
        " his x mark.   x
        "PICART.   LABASTILLE.

"Considering the petition, and the papers produced to us by Mr. Datchurut, relating to the ownership of the six arpents square of land, according to the grant made to Chatal and Gagnon, the deed of sale of Chatal and Gagnon to Mr. Bloin, the sale of Mr. Bloin to Mr. Datchurut, and the sale by Datchurut to Laroze:

we have ordered, and do order, that in default of Laroze having measured and marked his land, that the said Picart and Labastille may take away their lead and mineral which was seized by Datchurut and Laroze. We grant a replevin on the said seizure of lead, which was illegal against Picart and Labastille, directing them to withdraw from the six arpens square, if they are found to be on it, by an exact measurement, the centre of which shall be the hole which was made upon the first discovery of the lead. Releasing Mr. Datchurut from all demands, as security for said Laroze on the grant of the six arpents square of land sold by him to said Laroze, to whom and to his heirs we regrant it, based upon the title exhibited to us by Datchurut, and direct that the contract of sale between them shall have its full force.

Given in the government hall.

"ST. LOUIS, Dec. 1, 1770.

"P. PIERNAS, GOV."

BOND OF MR. KENNEDY.

"Before us, Don Pedro Piernas, captain of infantry, and lieutenant-governor of the establishments and dependencies of the Illinois, personally appeared Mr. Matthew Kennedy, merchant, residing ordinarily at Ste. Genevieve, now in St. Louis, who, by these presents, acknowledges to be indebted to Mr. Antoine Berard, also a merchant in this post of St. Louis, the amount of 2,100 livres in specie dollars, the balance of a sum of 3,400 livres 15 sols, which the said A. Berard loaned him at New Orleans, the 7th of Sept. of the past year, to complete the outfit and cargo of the last boat he dispatched to this upper country, on condition that, on his arrival at Ste. Genevieve, he would reimburse him, but not being able to fulfill his engagement to this day, and being about to ship a lot of flour arising from the sale of said cargo, said Kennedy, to secure to Mr. Berard the payment of the above amount of 2,100 livres still due him, mortgages for that purpose all the flour that he will send down from this country of Illinois, etc., especially the quantity of 12,000 lbs. which he is about to send at once to the post of Arkansas. Of this quantity Mr.

JNO. M. BUTAUD'S INVENTORY.

Kennedy agrees that Mr. Berard shall receive the payment in his stead to the extent of the amount of the balance due him, for which purpose Mr. Kennedy will deliver to Mr. Berard a draft for the amount due him on Mr. Orietta, commandant at said post of Arkansas; and if by any unforeseen circumstance the trip is prevented, or the payment suspended from any other cause, said Kennedy gives to Mr. Berard the same mortgage and security, as well on this last quantity of flour, if by any chance it should pass the post of Arkansas and go down to New Orleans, as on all he may send down by other occasions, until the balance due him is fully paid up.

"Done in the government chamber, in presence of Messrs. Laclede and Milony Duralde, requisite witnesses, who have signed with us this day, April 4, 1771, at St. Louis, of Illinois.

"A. BERARD, MATTHEW KENNEDY,
"M. MILONÉ DURALDE, LACLEDE LIGUEST,
"PIERNAS."

JNO. B. BUTAUD'S INVENTORY.

"On this day, May 17, 1771, at 10 o'clock a. m., we, Don Pedro Piernas, captain of infantry, lieutenant-governor of the establishments of the Illinois and its dependencies, belonging to his Catholic majesty, at the request of Jno. Bap. Sarpy, merchant, who informed us that Jno. Bapt. Butaud dit Brindamour had just died in his house of a natural sickness, and who requested us to repair there to take an inventory of the effects left by him, where we went, and in the presence of Jno. B. Hervieux, gunsmith, and Jno. Bap. Ortes, carpenter, Mr. Sarpy showed us the following articles: —

First, 6 white linen shirts, good and bad.
2 shirts, red cotton, checked.
2 shirts, blue, do.
3 pair large cotton breeches.

1 Beaufort bed sheet.
2 blanket capots, half worn.
1 blue jacket, 1 pr. blue wool stockings, half worn.
4 pairs old shoes.

6 cotton handkerchiefs, good and bad.
2 pair large breeches, cholet.
1 vest, 1 jacket of white cotton.
1 cottonade jacket.
1 old red cloth vest, an old trunk.
a feather bed with a skin cover.
a buffalo robe, a pillow, and an old couch.
an old gun, and hat, 7 pewter spoons, and a plate.
2 iron forks, pair scissors, pair brass buckles.

" Mr. Marie says the deceased told him ' that Laurent owed him a small amount, he does not know how much.'

" L'etang owes him something, he don't know how much."

" Mr. Sarpy declares that the deceased gave him a note of Mr. Hubert to take care of, which he handed to us, saying ' the deceased was awaiting the payment of the note to pay his own debts.' The note reads: —

" ' I will pay to the order of Brindamour, Senr., in the course of May next, the sum of five hundred livres in peltries, deer skins, or beaver, for his wages, and in full payment of all accounts with him to this day.

St. Louis, this 15th February, 1771.

' [Signed] HUBERT.'

" And after diligent search, and said Sarpy said there was nothing more to his knowledge, the said note copied above, with the other effects in this inventory, were placed in the hands of Mr. Alexis Marie, his brother-in-law, who relieves the said Sarpy, and who promises to produce all when so required by us, and as a depositary of fees of justice.

" W. S. SEGOND, ORTES, MARIE, SARPY."

BOND OF LUPIEN.

" Before me, Don Pedro Piernas, captain of infantry, lieutenant-governor of the establishments of the Illinois and dependencies belonging to his Catholic majesty,

" Was personally present Peter Lupien, called Baron, a joiner, and militia officer, residing at the post of St. Louis, who by these presents acknowledges to owe, and promises to pay to Mr. Eugene Pouré, called Beau Soliel (bright sun), militia officer, merchant at post St. Louis, present and agreeing, the sum of 498 livres and 2 sols, in beaver or deer skins as current in this place of St. Louis, subject to examination, and this for good and marketable merchandises which the said Beau Soliel has sold, advanced and delivered to Mr. Baron in his need, and at his request, which he thus acknowledges.

"Said sum of 498 livres and 2 sols, said P. Lupien, Baron, promises and pledges himself to pay and deliver to said Mr. Beau Soliel or the bearer of the present, in all the month of May of the following year, 1772, without fail, on pain of all costs, damages and interest. And as security for the said sum, the said Lupien, *alias* Baron, has by these presents, pledged and mortgaged a billiard table which he has set up in this place, St. Louis, comprising a building, billiard table, cloth, maces, queues and balls, and four feet of ground around said billiard room — which billiard the said Baron can neither sell or dispose of, until said Beau Soliel is fully paid, but must remain exclusively pledged to the payment of the amount due Beau Soliel.

"For thus it has been agreed, &c., &c., by the parties.

"Done in St. Louis, in the government chamber, in presence of Messrs. Joseph Labusciere and Benito Vasquez, witnesses, who, with us, the commandant, have signed these presents.

"July 9, 1771.

      "Baron,   Labusciere, Witness,
"Piernas,   Benito Basquez."

DETAILLY'S INVENTORY.

"October 25, one thousand seven hundred and seventy-one, at 8 o'clock a. m., before me, Don Pedro Piernas, captain of infantry, lieutenant-governor of the establishments of the Illinois and dependencies belonging to his Catholic majesty:

"According to the information we have just received that Denau Detailly had just died, who was interpreter at this poste, I repaired immediately to the house where he died, accompanied by don Antonio De Oro, officer of this garrison, Mr. Alvarez, sergeant, and Mr. Joseph Labusciere, and Mr. René Kiersereau, where we found an Indian woman, his wife legally married, whom we told to produce to us the effects which said Detailly left, and there being no place to which we could affix our seals, said widow Detailly presented them as follows: —

"An old feather bed covered with skin, another with ticking, four delf plates, an earthen pan, 7 pewter spoons, 4 iron forks, an axe, a saw, a tin pan, shovel, an oven, a table, four old chairs, two sheets, two pair old cotton breeches, ragged and holy, a shirt worn and torn, an old blanket coat, a straw hat, and mittens, a paper parcel, we did not examine, but took to the commander for that purpose. She declared there was due to her by one Mongrain thirty livres for a pirogue sold to him, which is all said widow declared she knew of, and not being able to write, made her mark to the same, day and year above.

"RENE KIERSEREAU, EUGENE ALVAREZ, N. CHABOT,
"LABUSCIERE, ANTONIO DE ORO."

1771, Nov. 16th. — The first auction sale on record in the Archives of St. Louis was of a box of packs of playing cards. It took but little time to get the people together at this sale, for besides fiddling and dancing, cards and billiards were about the only amusements in the village at that early day.

The bell ringer went through the village ringing his bell and crying out loudly the purpose of it, and a sale of playing cards drew at once the whole village, ladies and all, as we find amongst the purchasers the governor's lady, and another noted lady of the place, La Giroflée (Gilly flower), who, it appears, must have been fond of cards, as she was the first purchaser, and paid the highest price for three packs. They went off like hot cakes.

CONTENTS OF VIGE'S TRUNK.

" The year one thousand seven hundred and seventy-two, the 18th March, at 9 o'clock a. m., by order of Don Pedro Piernas, captain of infantry, lieutenant-governor of the establishments of the Illinois, we, Augustin Nicholas Vincent, sergeant of the garrison at this post, Benito Basquez and Pedro Baron, militia officer, we repaired to the house of Mr. John Gautier to open a trunk belonging to one named Vigé, a fugitive, in presence of witnesses we have inventoried it as follows, viz: —

	Livres.	Sous.	
A trunk without a key	10	...	
An iron stamp of two letters	1	10	
A scraper to shave skins	...	5	
A handle of a rudder	2	10	
An iron curling tongs, unserviceable	...	10	
A plane bit	...	15	
A lottery pointer	2	...	
10 packs cards	...	...	
3 old calines	1	...	
	18	10	$3.70

" Fourteen old billiard balls, 2 brushes, a billiard marker, all part of Vien's billiard table.

" VINCENT, BARON and BENITO BASQUEZ, witnesses.

" I received this amount in payment for 450 lbs. of flour which Vigé owes me, for that amount I paid for him to one of his hands.

" ST. LOUIS, March 18, 1772.

" VINCENT."

JEAN LOUIS LAMBERT,

a merchant and militia officer, came early to St. Louis, he died at Ste. Genevieve, December 26, 1771, his widow, Catherine Lepine, then at New Orleans, with her six children, Louis 15, Catherine 12, Martiniere 10, Marianna 8, Felicité 4, and Leonora 18 months, applied to the governor-general in that city, March 17, 1772, for authority to have an inventory taken of his property in St. Louis. The inventory was taken July 29, 1772, in presence of the Lieut.-Governor; Louis Dubreuil and Aug't Condé, appraisers; Pierre Chamard, attorney.

	Livres.	Sous.		Livres.	Sous.
1 Trunk	20		1 do.	30	
5 Handkerchiefs, 12	60		1 Umbrella	30	
4 do. 8	32		1 do.	20	
1 do. silk	10		Ribbon	12	02
8 do. 6	48		Silk	4	
3 do. 2	6		Thread	4	
1 do.	1		Pins	1	10
13 do. ½	6	10	2 Mattreses, 20	40	
2 pr. Stockings, silk, 5	10		1 Feather bed	20	
24 do. 3	72		1 Blanket	30	
1 do.	2		1 Coverlet	15	
2 do. 1	2		2 Sheets, 10	20	
22 Shirts, 8	176		1 Bed curtain	40	
4 Night caps, 10 sois	2		1 Pillow case	1	10
4 do. 10	2		Calico	2	
6 do. 15	4	10	3 Table cloths, 4.10	13	10
4 Drawers, 1.10	6		1 Gun & horn	50	
1 do.		5	3 Cravats, 3 sols		15
1 Sword belt	33		1 Gold watch	200	

LAMBERT'S INVENTORY.

	Livres.	Sous.		Livres.	Sous.
1 Gold button........	25		Hunting knife........	12	
1 Sil. snuff box.......	30		1 lb. Powder...........	1	5
3 Pair sil. buckles, 15.	45		Ox hair...............		10
3 do 7.10	22	10	2 Purses, 5.............	10	
1 Sil. cross...........	15		2 Looking glasses, 6....	12	
1 Sil. cap.............	20		Yard stick............	3	
1 Sil. spoon...........	25		Candle stick..........	2	10
1 do	15		Brush.................		10
1 Sil. forks, 15.......	30		Powder bag...........	1	5
2 do. rings, 2.10.....	5		Clock.................	26	
306½ Dollars...........	1,532	10	Muff..................	5	
1 Regimental coat.....	30		Capot.................	1	5
1 do. vests, 30.	60		Curling iron..........		15
1 Red velvet	30		Plates................	12	
1 Camlet do..........	20		Tureen................	4	
2 Summer do. 15......	30		Bottles...............	5	
9 do. 10	90		Basket................	2	10
1 do.	5		Bowl..................		10
1 do.	3		Pot...................	2	
1 do.	2	10	2 do. 2.10............	5	
5 do. 2.......	10		Copper kettle.........	5	
1 Pair breeches.......	12		Barrel................	1	10
4 do. 8......	32		Bird & cage..........	2	10
3 do. 6......	18		Deer skins...........	53	
1 do.	1	10	Dressed do...........	70	
1 Hat.................	20		Sundries.............	48	5
1 do.................	10				
Indian pipe...........	6			3,347	17

MEMORANDA OF NOTES, OBLIGATIONS, ETC., DUE HIM.

No.	Livres.	Sous.	No.	Livres.	Sous.
12 Francois Marc St.Gen	289		63 Claude Roussel.....	60	
13 Thomas Bernie......	72	12	64 Same...............	454	
14 Blouin at Kas..	116		65 Carriard...........	50	
15 Perrin..............	1,206		66 Pierre Oliver.......	360	
16 Bulchy..............	25		67 Pierre Abel.........	91	
17 Vaudry, St. Louis...	82		68 Decoigne....	120	
18 Condé, to collect....	20,327	7	69 Bazile Danoyer......	40	
19 Same, goods........	1,025	10	70 Tous Gaillard........	190	
22 Blouin, Kas,to collect	558	5	71 Francois............	30	
24 Sans Chagrin........	14		72 Tous Gaillard.......	35	

		Livres.	Sous.
25	Muslin Barbe	104	
26	Barré	11	5
27	Duchemin	49	2
28	Guille Paget	13	5
29	Chamard	200	
30	Anté Regis	903	10
31	Baudry	29	
32	Lamarguilliere (to collect)	2,815	16
33	Francois Franciscus	18	
36	Several orders	212	10
37	Jacques Renard	538	12
38	Juan De Large	862	12
39	Bois Doré	20	12
40	Joseph Blais	65	12
41	Joseph Lafleur	32	
42	Pierre Montardy	1,955	
43	Kennedy	100	
44	Pertuis, Senr	12	10
45	Cavalier Brothers	3,697	13.6
46	Joseph Cochon	123	19.6
50 to 55		1,272	5
57	Noel Gallien	70	
58	Antoine Couillard	133	
59	Anté Mallet, et als	200	
60	Bernard Moran	25	
61	Toussaint Gaillard	400	
62	Francois Jean Morrisot	150	

		Livres.	Sous.
73	Le Goffre, *alias* Le Bretan	64	
74	Martin the Spaniard	215	
75	Pelletier	67	10
76	St. Marc	75	
77	Joseph Oliver	24	
78	Denis Dufaulx	77	10
79	Lissot	844	
	Lefebvre Debruisseau	480	
	Datcherut (to collect)	17,539	9.8
	Legrain	61	
	St. Germain, bot. brandy	5	
	Grammon, do	5	
	Paul Segond	30	
	Dorioncourt	308	
	Sans Quartier (bot. Rhum)	5	
	Vincent Lesperance	265	
	Mat. Kenneday	79	
	Table	5	
	Bedstead	10	
	Desk	25	
	3 pieces iron, 15	45	
	House & lot	1,000	
		63,830	3.2

ITEMS OF NO. 36.

	Livres.	Sous.
Labonne, 2 bot. wine	10	
Mallet, 18 lbs. peltries	36	
Motard, 4 lbs. nails	8	
Do. 2 lbs. sugar	6	
Do. a blanket	30	
Labuscière, 3 lbs. nails	6	
Do. bottle Rhum	5	
Do. 5 yds. cord	1	10
Do. nails	15	
Do. bottle wine	5	

	Livres.	Sous.
Resar, 2 bottles wine	12	
Debruisseau, 4 bars soap	51	
Same, peltries	12	
Hervieux, 1½ lbs. nails	3	
Lapierre, bottle wine	5	
Laville, yard & ½ ribbon	4	10
Cottin, quart brandy	2	10
	212	10

JEAN DELAGE'S WILL.

ITEMS NO. 18 WITH CONDÉ.

	Livres.	Sous.		Livres.	Sous.
Nich's Royer............	474	17	Lefebvre & Carrose....	181	6.6
Jno. B. Papillon.......	423	17.6	Hervieux..............	57	10
Morissey & Co..........	3,422	10	Azean, *alias* Berthoud.	24	
L. & B. Desnoyers.....	163	10	Molard................	102	10
Ant. De Oro...........	145	8	Pierre Hubert.........	35	
Chas. Du Chemin......	47		Pirroquet.............	31	10
Sans Quartier.........	96		Berthoud & Piroquet...	8	10
Marechal..............	105	12	Francois Barbe........	165	
Labusciere............	129	12	Claude Tinon..........	31	
Barsalon..............	51	15	Gaudrain..............	30	
Feauché...............	682		Gramon, 7 bot. Rhum..	35	
Gramon................	65		Francois Pichard......	8	10
Blouin................	708	17	Lavigne, tailor........	44	
Case neuve............	75		Martigny..............	137	
Louis Blanchet........	1,438	4	Louis Vige............	100	
Sans Quartier.........	5		The Troops...........	490	
Julien Le Roy.........	83		Small bills...........	472	7
Francois Cadien.......	103	10			
Seraphim.............	126	15		10,300	11

(Signed)   Louis Dubreuil — Aug't Condé, Appraisers.
Pierre Chamard, Attorney.

P. Piernas.

JEAN DELAGE'S WILL, ETC.

"Substance of the will of Jean Delage, born in the parish of St. Pierre d'Olien, Angoumois, diocese of Perigueux, France.

"At St. Louis, July 16, 1772, at 10 o'clock a. m., before Lieut. Don Antonio de Oro, Governor Piernas being absent at St. Genevieve.

"First.—He commends his soul to God, to the glorious Virgin Mary, to Holy St. John the Baptist, his patron saint, and to all the Saints of Paradise, beseeching them with compunction and repentance to implore the Almighty to place his soul in the kingdom of the blessed.

"He leaves all he possesses to Alexander Langlois, as a testimony of acknowledgment for favors received from him.

" He thinks he is not under obligations to include his relatives among his heirs, because it has all been acquired by his own labor.

In presence of Silvester Labbadie, Louis Blondeau, Joseph Labrosse, Joseph Taillon and Jean Cambas, witnesses.

Approved, July 26, 1772.   "JNO. DELAGE."
PEDRO PIERNAS.

"The year one thousand seven hundred and seventy-two, August 4th. We, Pedro Piernas, captain of infantry, and lieutenant governor of the establishment and dependencies of the Illinois, on the application of Mr. Alexander Langlois, an inhabitant of this post of St. Louis, calling himself the general heir of the estate left by Jean Delage, who died at this post on August first of the above year, by the will which the said John Delage indited himself on the 16th of July of this present year, asking that it be done on removing the seals, which by our order were attached to the aforesaid effects of Jean Delage immediately after his death, and proceed to the inventory of them. We repaired to the house of said Alexander Langlois, where said testator died and left the above effects, where we summoned the said Alexander Langlois, to show and to declare to us all that he knows to belong to said deceased, and after he showed them to us, and recognized that our seals were whole and unbroken, we removed them and proceeded to the inventory, as hereafter declared, in presence of Mr. Nicholas Augustus Vincent, sergeant of his Majesty's troops, and Martin Duralde, assistant witnesses, and Messrs. Rene Kiersereau and Jno. B. Provenche, arbitrators named by said Alexander Langlois, and Mr. Francis Bissonet, third arbitrator officially named, to appraise and value each article, on their souls and consciences, according to the oath to that effect they took before us and the witnesses in the usual manner, all to be valued at prices in silver.

First opened a trunk and found as follows:

An ordinary coat and vest valued	25 liv.	5 cotton handker., red and blue.	12 liv.
A camlet coat.	10 "	3 pair cotton stockings.	12 "
A vest and breeches, brown Cadiz.	12 "	2 pair silk.	4 "
		Cotton band, ribbon, etc.	6 "
3 Breeches, 1 cloth, 2 Limbourg.	15 "	A worked towel and pillowcase.	2 "

JEAN DELAGE'S WILL. 115

2 do. 1 green cloth, 1 plush	10 liv.	2 spring knives, snuff-box, brushes.	1.10.
A cotton vest and large breeches.	20 "	A hat, gold band.	10 "
3 pair do. of cotton.	15 "	The trunk containing foregoing.	10 "
1 vest, white, and large breeches.	10 "	A cake of soap, French, 4 lbs. in a chest.	4 "
3 large breeches, 2 linen, 1 cotton.	5 "	9 pieces of soap do.	4 "
3 pr. gaiters, 2 calico, 1 Spanish	6 "	2 pr. old breeches, do.	1 "
		Small roll of tape.	1 "
2 pr. large linen breeches	3 "	Case of two razors, horn and ivory combs, etc.	3 "
A linen Birette, scull cap.	10 "	An old blanket capote.	3 "
A winding sheet.	8 "	A bunch of white thread.	5 "
3 pr. large linen breeches.	6 "	A mason's square and hammer.	6 "
2 linen shirts, fine trimmed.	12 "		
2 do. not so fine	10 "	2 basins, 4 plates, a pewter goblet.	10 "
2 do. fine.	12 "		
4 do. do.	20 "	5 empty bottles.	3 "
1 wool blanket, 2½ points.	5 "	An old pair stockings and hat.	1 "
2 red woolen caps.	2 "		
2 silk caps.	3 "	2 pr. mocksins.	1 "
3 cotton caps.	1	A poor small pistol.	1.05
A butcher knife, fish line, towel, &c.	2 "	A pen knife.	.05
		17 pewter vest buttons.	1 "
5 or 6 lbs. lead, shot & ball.	1.10.	A paper of pins, &c.	.10
A wooden box and key.	5 "	A gold hat band.	2.10
Another, partly broken.	3 "	A piece of linen galloon.	.10
A gun, horn and shot pouch.	15 "	A small English casket.	3 "
An iron pot and lid.	10 "	A power of attorney from Pierre Jourdan to Jno. Delage to collect from Pierre Becquet eight livres in silver.	8 "
7 carrots tobacco, about 10 lbs.	10 "		
2 pr. shoes and pr. brass buckles.	7 "		
A blanket capote	6 "		
A feather bed and ticking, a faucet, pillow and linen cover.	25 "	Amounting to	446 livres
A pr. large shoe buckles, pr. small do., pair sleeve buttons, all silver.	25 "		

A memorandum of those who Delage said were indebted to him.

"And after a careful investigation by us to see if there was nothing omitted belonging to the estate of said Jno. Delage, deceased, we finished the present inventory, amounting to the sum of four hundred and forty-six livres, and left with Mr. Langlois all the above mentioned articles, in presence of the same witnesses above mentioned, to be produced whenever it will be necessary to proceed to their sale. St. Louis, same day and year above.

" JEAN B. PROVENCHÉ, BISSONET'S x mark, VINCENT, M. DURALDE,
" RENÉ KIERSEREAU,   PIERNAS."

"In the year one thousand seven hundred and seventy-two, the fourth day of the month of August, before us, don Pedro Piernas, captain of infantry and lieutenant-governor of the establishments and dependencies of the Illinois, personally appeared Mr. Alexander Langlois, an inhabitant of this post of St. Louis, who, having been informed of the multiplicity of the creditors of the above named Jno. Delage, who died at his house the first of the said month, and considering the scantiness of the estate of the said deceased, who named him his heir general by his will of the 16th July, of the same year, has declared that he declines, and totally renounces the estate, and claims only what is due him by the deceased Delage for his board, lodging and other necessaries he furnished him during his sickness, placing himself on the same footing as the other creditors. In testimony of which, and that no one claiming from the estate can have any cause of action against him in consequence of having been made its heir, he executes this present under his mark in the presence of Nicholas Vincent, sergeant of this garrison, and Mr. M. Duralde, witnesses thereof, at St. Louis, the same day and year above.

" M. DURALDE, VINCENT, ALEXR. x LANGLOIS, PIERNAS."

"In the year one thousand seven hundred and seventy-two, the twenty-sixth of October, at 9½ a. m., I, don Pedro Piernas, captain of infantry and lieutenant-governor of the establishments and dependencies of the Illinois, on the application of Mr. Alexander Langlois, an inhabitant of this post of St. Louis, calling himself a creditor, and not the heir, of the deceased John De Lage, who died at Langlois' house on the first day of the month of August of this present year, in virtue of the relinquishment he made before us and the witnesses at the foot of the general inventory of the effects of the said deceased Jno. Delage, executed the fourth day of August of the same year; we repaired to the house of said Langlois, and after giving notice in all the public places of this post, and the public being assembled, it was announced that the purchasers would pay the price of their purchases in deer skins, beaver, or silver dollars, according to the valuation of this day, during the course of the month of May, 1773, and will be held to give good security resident in this post.

"(The sale then proceeded, and was concluded on the next day, the 27th, producing the sum of 836 livres, nearly double the amount of the appraisement, and just sufficient to liquidate the liabilities of the estate.)

"OCT. 27, 1772.

"MARTIN DURALDE,
"PEDRO PIERNAS.

"We, the undersigned creditors of Jean Delage, certify to having received altogether the proceeds of the auction sale of his effects, the sum of eight hundred and thirty-six livres in silver, to wit:—

"I, Alexander Langlois, boarding, &c........................ 530.10
Martin Duralde, legal fees, &c............................... 127.10
F. Valentin, Curate, church..................................... 67
R. Kiersereau, grave 8
Lachance, a debt 13
Conand, medical bill... 60
Aug. Condé, do 20
Louis Dubreuil, an acct... 10

836

"Settled by Govr. Piernas, Sept. 1, 1774.

BILL OF EXCHANGE.

"This day, September 16, 1772, appeared in the government chamber before us, Don Pedro Piernas, captain of infantry and lieutenant-governor of the establishments and dependencies of the Illinois, belonging to his Catholic Majesty, Mr. Louis Perrault, merchant, residing in this post of St. Louis, who asked us to grant him the registration of the following paper, to have recourse to it in case of necessity, said paper was then registered as follows: —

"For *8500* livres." "NEW ORLEANS, February 15, 1772.

"SIR: You will please pay by this first of exchange, if you have not paid my second or third, to the order of Mr. Louis Perrault, your brother, the sum of 8500 livres, in dollars at five livres, for value received of him in six negroes, including a negress, which he sold and delivered to me. Said amount you will pay from the first funds you have received, or are to receive from the effects arising from the estate of the deceased Miss Duplessis, for which you have our power of attorney to sell the same, and receive the proceeds without further advice.

"I am your very humble and obedient servant,
"[Signed.]" "OLIVIER DEVEZIN & DUPLESSIS OLIVIER."

"To Mr. James Perrault, Merchant, Quebec, Canada:—
Endorsed: "My brother James Perrault, pay to yourself the within amount, and place it to the credit of my account,
N. O., February 27, 1772.
LOUIS PERRAULT."

"This day, May 7, 1772, appeared before the undersigned notaries public in Quebec, Mr. James Perrault, citizen and merchant of this town, residing in the street of the Sailor's falls, on behalf and with the power of attorney of his brother, Louis Perrault, merchant at New Orleans, bearing the order from him of February 27, last, on the bill of exchange of 8500 livres, drawn by Mr. Olivier Devezin and Duplessis Olivier, his wife, residing in New Orleans, February 15, last, on said Mr. James Perrault, bearer of their power of attorney for the estate of Duplessis, laid before the undersigned notaries, who protested against the payment of said bill of exchange; that whereas, in the first place, he has at present no funds in hand belonging to said estate; secondly, that the draft being for 8500 livres, he is satisfied that the estate will not produce sufficient to meet it, adding besides such other protestations as in such cases are but just and proper, of which said Mr. Perrault, in said name, requested from the undersigned notaries a statement in writing for his benefit, which in justice was accorded him.

" Done at Quebec in the office of Mr. Saillant, place of the notaries, undersigned in duplicate, the day and year above, after being read, and was signed by the parties and notaries.

" SAILLANT, PANET, JACQUES PERRAULT."

" The original bill of exchange was immediately returned to said Louis Perrault, and these presents deposited in the government chamber for reference when needed, in presence of Messrs. Don Antonio de Oro, officer of this garrison and M. Duralde, witnesses, who with us, the governor and party have signed after being read.

" L. PERRAULTE, MN. DURALDE PEDRO PIERNAS."

BOND OF DE ORO.

" Before us don Pedro Piernas, captain of infantry and lieutenant-governor of the establishments and dependancies of the Illinois, belonging to his Catholic Majesty, was

personally present, Mr. don Antonio de Oro, an officer of the garrison of St. Louis, who by these presents acknowledges that he is indebted to and promises to pay Mr. William Lecompte, merchant, residing at present in this port, the sum of 1705 livres in money, for good merchandize that said Wm. Lecompte has this day sold and delivered to him, and with which he is satisfied — said amount of 1705 livres in money, said de Oro binds himself to pay in all the month of May of the year 1774, in two modes to wit: 1500 livres in coin dollars, and the 205 livres in peltries at the current valuation of this post, in default of which, all costs, damages, and interest; and in the event that said de Oro is compelled to leave this Illinois country by the King's order, to which he is liable, said de Oro promises to pay to said Lecompte, or holder of this obligation, the said amount of 1705 livres, one-half in coin dollars, and the other half in peltries, at the current valuation in this post, in the course of the month of May, 1773, the sale and delivery of the goods having been made here, the parties consent that the payment of the same be also made in this place, notwithstanding any absence or change of residence of said de Oro.

Executed in St. Louis, in the government chamber, in presence of Vincent, a sergeant of the garrison, and Martin Duralde, witnesses called in, who with us and the parties have signed the same with the exception of W. Lecompte, who declares he knows not how to sign, after being read.

St. Louis, Oct. 7, 1772.
M. Duralde, Vincent,
Antonio X. Joseph de Oro.
Piernas, Witnesses.

I certify that I have received the amount of this obligation, and release Mr. de Oro, annulling the same as of no value.

St. Louis, June 8, 1775.
Lecompte's,
x
mark.
M. Duralde.
witness.

MABILLE LETTER.

"Paris, July 28, 1772.

"*Mr. John B. Berard, Bordeaux*:

"Sir—On receipt of your letter of the 21st, I had the honor to see Mr. Bezodis, whose mother owes an annuity of 150 livres to Mr. Renout. He tells me had written to you on the 4th of this month, and said to you that having paid in December, 1765, all the arrearages of that annuity up to and including that year, 1765, nothing then remains due but from January 1, 1766. The payments he made up to that time are very regular, and for which he has receipts in presence of notaries. As to the arrearages due, since, they are assigned by the said Mr. Renout to Messrs. Dyvernay, priests and missionaries in the Illinois, who had advanced him a sum of about 1,000 livres, until it would repay them; besides that assignment, of which these gentlemen are holders, they made opposition in the hands of Mr. Bezodis for the security of their payments, so when they will be in readiness to receive they will take from it more than what may be due, including the entire year 1772, which can be paid but with a life certificate of 1773.

"You see that you can expect nothing from that annuity from now until the end of the next year, for those gentlemen will still receive it, and the payment that your son has made to his grantor for fourteen years of that annuity falls to the ground, and the transfer that said Renout may have made to your son is an illusion; in consequence you should forget that matter, and if Mr. Renout should yet live for some years, and you are able to prove that he receives his life annuity every year, and that he has not transferred it to any other person, you may in two years think of the affair.

"I would have been pleased to have given you more satisfactory information, but it appears to me that your son has had to do with men of but little conscience.

"I have the honor to be, sir, your very humble and obedient servant

"A. MABILLE."

This J. B. Berard was the father of Antoine Berard, a young merchant who died in St. Louis, 1776.

A BRIEF WILL.

"Before me, Don Pedro Piernas, captain of infantry and lieutenant-governor of this western part of the Illinois, in pressence of Pierre Laville and Pierre Montardy, witnesses, I, Foubert La Grammont, born at Grandville, diocese of Coutance, France, being about to leave for Detroit, and considering the danger of the journey, I name in case of death as my heir Mr. De Volsey, either in this country, France, or any other place. So that he may enjoy all I possess, in this or any other place. So that no other person can make any opposition thereto. This being my last will, which I have signed in the presence of the above witnesses, in St. Louis, September 17, 1872.

"LAVILLE, MONTARDY, Witnesses. FOUBERT.
"PIERNAS."

SALE OF AN ANNUITY.

"Before us, Louis St. Ange de Bellerive, late captain of infantry, formerly commanding the province of Illinois and dependancies belonging to his Catholic Majesty, appeared Lady Felicité Robineau de Portneuf, wife of Don Pierre Joseph de Piernas, captain in the battalion of Louisiana, lieutenant-governor of the establishments of the Illinois and dependancies of his Catholic Majesty. The said Lady Robineau de Portneuf, with the consent and authority of said Mr. de Piernas, her husband, as the sole heiress of the deceased, Mr. Louis Nicholas Robineau de Portneuf, and also as heiress of half the estate of the deceased Mad'e Marguerite Phillipe D'Aneau de Muid, widow of the deceased René Robineau, Esq'r, lord of Portneuf, according to her holograph will of May 8, 1770, deposited in the office of Mr. Panet, royal notary at Quebec — said Lady de Piernas as heiress aforesaid, and with authority of her said husband, does by these presents, cede, transfer and convey, and promises to guarantee from all trouble and hindrances of any nature whatever, except primitive acts, to Mr. Louis Dubreuil, merchant, at present of the Illinois, in the dependancy of his Catholic Majesty, now present and accepting purchaser for himself, his heirs and assigns, the sum of 81 livres, 12 sols 9 deniers of annuities to be taken from 261 livres 5 sols of annuities, created and registered at the City Hall in Paris, July 27, 1722, which were reduced from a capital of 418 livres of perpetual revenue, established on the excises and impost on salt, by agreement executed before Courtois, a notary of Paris, January 31, 1715, for the benefit of Peter Robineau, René Robineau, James Robineau and Louise Catherine Robineau, wife of Francis de Sourdy. And also 48 livres 19 sols 8 deniers of annuity to be taken from that above mentioned 261 livres and 5 sols, being one-half of the annuity of 97 livres 19 sols and 4 deniers, which belonged to said Lady D'aneau, widow Portneuf, on said excises and imposts of France on said contract of creation, which said half is now the property of the said Lady de Piernas, as co-heiress in the estate of the said Lady D'aneau de Portneuf, with demoiselle Catherine Robineau de Portneuf, the two ladies being the daughter and grand-daughter of the said deceased Lady de Portneuf, according to the intent of her before mentioned will, said two sums, forming together the sum of 131 livres 12 sols and 6 deniers, for said Mr. Dubreuil, his heirs and assigns, to enjoy and dispose of the said annuity of 81 livres, 19 sols and 9 deniers, and of that of 48 livres 19 sols and 8 deniers, now due to said Lady de Piernas, by the decease of said Lady D'Aneau, widow Portneuf, her grandmother, in full ownership and belonging to him, entitled to receive the arrearages from the day they became due — to that end the said Lady de Piernas making to said Mr. Dubreuil all transfers necessary concerning said two portions of the annuity belonging to her as sole heiress of one-half in the estate of said deceased Lady D'aneau, widow of Mr. René Robineau de Portneuf, her grandfather, to whom by decree of the court of the City Hall, in Paris, dated July 10, 1767, it was ordered that said annuities belonged as follows, to

	Livres.	Sols.	Den.
Mr. Nicholas Robineau de Portneuf..	81	12.	9
Dec'd Mad'e D'Aneau widow Portneuf	97	19.	4
Miss Catherine de Portneuf............	81	12.	9

———————261 livres 5 sols.

"This present transfer is made for the price and sum of 5,225 livres, for both the principal of said annuities, and the arrearages now due and to become due to the said Madame de Piernas in the estate of her deceased father, and half that in the estate of said Madame de Muit de Portneuf, her grandmother. Said amount of 5,225 livres said Lady de Piernas acknowledges having received from said Dubreuil, from which she releases him in full.

"Done in the government chamber at St. Louis of the Ilinois, in the presence of Messrs. A. Berard, Martin Duralde and Joseph Labusciere, of said place, witnesses, who have, with the parties and myself, former commandant, signed the same, after being read in accordance with the law.

St. Louis, Nov. 2, 1774.

"It is also expressly agreed that the sale made by the lady De Piernas to said Dubreuil, July 10, 1771, is null and void and of no effect, this last sale superseding it and being the only one in full force and value.

    PEDRO PIERNAS,   FELICITÉ ROBINEAU PORTNEUF PIERNAS.
    LOUIS DUBREUIL,   A. BERARD,
    MN. DURALDE,   LABUSCIERE,
                  ST. ANGE.

In the year 1774, there being no village prison,* Gov. Piernas had Laclede to have constructed a small one of ten by twenty feet, as an appendage against a gable end of Laclede's house, a part of which he then occupied as the government office, where it might, at all times, be under the personal supervision of the orderly sergeant and soldier or two who had charge of the government chamber, and were constantly in attendance on the governor.

A detailed account of its cost is among the papers in the archives, of which the following is a consolidation, in the handwriting of Auguste Chouteau, the governor furnishing the materials and the people assisting in the work: —

	Livres.	sols.	den.
Stone-work, by Antoine Roussel	267.	11.	8
Carpenters' and joiners' work, and roof by Francis Delin	405		
Iron and work on the fastenings, grating, nails, &c., Guion & Labbé	132		
18 barrels lime for mortar, by Deschenes	36		
	840.11.8—$165		

---

* NOTE.—There must have been something of a prison before this, as we find Trille in one in 1768.

Dec. 24. — The first church bell, named Pierre Joseph Felicité, after the governor and his lady, whose gift it was, was blessed by the first curate, Father Valentin, in the presence of the assembled inhabitants of the village. It was hung on a temporary scaffold outside the church. After the ceremony they resolved to erect a permanent church.

ST. ANGE'S WILL.

"The will of Louis St. Ange de Bellerive, first military commandant and acting governor of the post of St. Louis, upper Louisiana, Dec. 26, 1774:

"Before me, Pedro Piernas, lieutenant-governor of the establishment of Illinois and its appurtenances, belonging to his Catholic Majesty, at the request of Louis St. Ange de Bellerive, captain of infantry, in the service of his C. M., I repaired to the house of Mad'e Chouteau, at St. Louis, in which the said St. Ange de Bellerive lodges, attended by Joseph Labusciere and Benito Basquez, witnesses — being there we were introduced into the room where the said St. Ange is sick in bed, but nevertheless sound of mind, memory and understanding; considering that death is certain, and the time of its coming very uncertain, being dangerously ill, and desiring not to be overtaken by death, without having disposed of the few goods which God has given him, he has made and dictated the present testament to me, the lieutenant-governor, and in presence of the after-named and undersigned witnesses, in the following form and manner, viz. : —

"*First.* As a good Christian, Catholic, Apostolic and Roman, he has commended his soul to God, to the blessed Virgin, and the saints of the celestial court, beseeching them to intercede for him with the divine Majesty, that it may please the Lord to receive his soul into the Kingdom of the Blessed. The said testator wishes and ordains, that if he should die of his present sickness, his body be buried in the cemetery of this parish among the other faithful.

"He wishes and ordains principally, that all his debts be paid by his testamentary executor, and out of his goods.

"The said testator declares he owes Madame Chouteau his board from the first of August of the last year, one thousand, seven hundred and seventy-three, to this present day, according to the price agreed upon, and he commits to his testamentary executor, the settlement of this amount; declaring to have paid the sum of three hundred and ninety livres in money, which must be deducted therefrom.

"He declares that he owes to one Deschenne for twenty-five loads of wood.

"He declares that he owes to Laville, a tailor, for making a riding coat, a waist-coat, and two pairs of breeches, in payment of which said Laville has received forty livres in peltries, an old velvet waist-coat, and one pair of breeches, which the testator sold him.

"He declares that one named Francois de Lui owes him seventy livres, for money loaned him.

"He wishes and ordains that there be celebrated the day of his funeral, a solemn service, and as soon as possible twenty-five low-masses for the repose of his soul, and in case the goods should be more than sufficient to pay all his debts, the said testator gives and bequeaths, for the construction of the church of this parish, the sum of five hundred livres in money, which shall be paid out of his goods, by his testamentary executor.

"He gives and bequeaths to one named Antoine Breda (Anthony Barada) the sum of three hundred livres, for the good services he has received from him.

"He gives and bequeaths to Madame De Volsay, his niece, the sum of three hundred dollars.

"He declares that he has three slaves, named Angelique, an Indian woman, Charlotte, aged about nine years, and Antoine, aged about sixteen months, children of the said Angelique. He desires the said Angelique to belong to his niece, Madame Belestre, as a slave for life, and as regards the two children, they shall serve Mad'e Belestre and her heirs until they attain the age of twenty years, after this time shall have expired, he wishes and ordains that the said two children be free — beseeching the commander of this country to interfere by authority for the execution thereof.

"And as regards all the other goods he possesses now, and may possess in future, he gives and bequeaths them, after his debts are paid, to Madame Joachim Devilliers, wife of Belestre, and to Francois Devilliers, who is blind; the above-named nephew and niece, residing now at New Orleans, shall partake in equal portion of the remainder of his inheritance, as his general and universal heirs, and in case the said Francois Devilliers should be dead, the part accruing to him, shall revert to Louis Devilliers, god-son of said testator, such being his will and intention.

"And for his testamentary executor the said testator has named and appointed by these presents, Pierre Laclede Liguest, his friend, beseeching him to give him this last proof of his friendship, delivering into his hands all the goods belonging to him, to be employed according to the aforesaid will, declaring he has not contracted any marriage to this day. All the foregoing being the will and intention of the said St. Ange, he revokes and annuls all other testaments and codicils which he may have made before this present one, which will be executed according to its form and tenor.

"And the said will having been read and reread to the said testator, he says he understands it well and that it is his last will.

"Done and executed in the house of the said Madame Chouteau, in the room where the said St. Ange is in his bed, the year one thousand seven hundred and seventy-four, the twenty-sixth day of December, at 2 o'clock p. m., in the presence of the said Benito Basquez and Joseph Labusciere, attorney, witnesses, and of Antoine Berord, merchant, Joseph Labrosse and Jno. B. Martigny, captain in the militia, residing in the same place, who have signed these presents, with the said testator and me, the Lieut.-Governor, the day and year above said.

BENITO BASQUEZ,
LABUSCIERE,

ST. ANGE,
A. BERARD,
JOS. LABROSSE,
J. B. MARTIGNY.
PEDRO PIERNAS.

Capt. St. Ange died the same night, and was interred on the following day, December 27, 1774, by Father Valentin, the first parish curate;* his age is not stated.

After Gov. Piernas had assumed the government, Capt. St. Ange was admitted into the Spanish regiment of Louisiana, with the same rank as captain, on half pay.

April 19, 1775.— Easter festival the inhabitants assembled again, and having perfected their plans and specifications for a church of 30 feet front by 60 feet in depth, and 14 feet high, of hewn posts set in the ground, and made their award for the building of the same; the agreement was signed by the seventy-eight householders of the village, some thirty with their autograph signatures, and the others with his accustomed mark of a cross x.

The foregoing comprise about all the official acts of Gov. Piernas of any public interest, his others relating entirely to individual matters.

Gov. Piernas and lady, during their residence here, had the misfortune of losing their two young children, a son, Charles Rafael Victor, March 20, 1774, and a young daughter on January 9, 1775.

---

* As per record in the parish church register: —
"In the year 1774, the 27th of December, I, the undersigned, have interred in the cemetery of this parish the body of Mr. Louis St. Ange, captain attached to the Louisiana regiment, administered with the sacraments of the church. BRO VALENTIN, *Curate.*"

The death of Capt. St. Ange de Bellerive also occurred on Dec. 26, 1774.

The administration of Gov. Piernas continued just five years, terminating on May 20, 1775, on which day he relinquished the government to his successor, Gov. Francis Cruzat.

The exercise of authority by Gov. Piernas of this upper portion of the country was so much more mild and conciliatory than the French inhabitants here had any reason to expect, considering their long delay in placing the Spanish in possession, and the open resistance to the assumption of Spanish authority below at New Orleans, that at the close of his administration the principal inhabitants of the village held a meeting and united unanimously in expressing their satisfaction at the same in the following testimonial to that effect, as follows:—

" *To Pedro Piernas, at the close of his Administration, May 19, 1775:*

" We, the undersigned inhabitants, merchants, tradesmen, hunters and traders of the post of St. Louis, assembled in the government chamber, by direction of Governor Don Francisco Cruzat, of the Illinois, certify to all whom it may concern, that we have no subject of complaint to allege against the manner in which we were governed by his excellency, the late Governor Don Pedro Piernas, that he rendered us all the justice to which we were entitled. That neither himself, nor the company of soldiers he commanded in this post, ever committed any excesses or extortions, or were guilty of any wrong on any of the inhabitants, that said company occasioned no trouble, nor gave any scandal nor bad example; that no one received any violence or bad treatment without cause; that we are not aware that he had any pecuniary agreement or understanding with any one whomsoever, on this or the other side, in regard to business. It was never perceived by any one that he had injured the public in restricting trade; that he never exacted any thing either from traders or merchants for licenses or pass-ports necessary for their affairs, neither in setting out nor on their return. That he never excluded any one from the benefit of this trade, which he distributed alternately each year to the best of his judgment for the public interest, and the number of traders. That no one received any ill treatment from the Indian tribes for having been badly received by him at this post. That they never heard from said Indians any complaints of him, his behaviour, nor of the Spanish government, and that they are peaceable and contented, as well as we ourselves.

"In short, we can only speak well of him, and with respect and gratitude."

"ST. LOUIS, June 6, 1775."

Signed by 50 names, comprising the largest portion of the male adults of the post, in presence of Francisco Cruzat. Copy presented Piernas July 8, 1775.

LIEUT.-COL. FRANCIS CRUZAT

succeeded Capt. Piernas as lieutenant-governor of this upper part of Louisiana on May 20, 1775, appointed by Gov.-Gen. Unzaga.

He was of Spanish birth, as was also his lady, a man of middle age, having attained the rank of lieutenant-colonel of the regiment of Louisiana.

We find but few official acts of his during his first brief administration of three years which would seem to merit any particular notice; the principal occurrences were : —

1775, June. — The unaccountable disappearance of Father F. Valentin, the first curate of the parish, no where found of record either in the archives or parish register.

Sept. 15, the death of old Pierre Lapointe, over one hundred years of age.

Sept. 22, the death of Francis Xavier Cruzat, a young son of the governor.

Oct. 18, the death of Peter Lupien, *alias* Baron, the contractor then engaged in building the church.

PETITION OF ETIENNE BARRÉ.

" The undersigned has the honor to represent to you, that having received on board his boat at New Orleans, six barrels of rum and a quantity of dry goods from Mr. Boisdoré, according to receipt, at the rate of twenty-five dollars freight on each barrel, all to be delivered to Benito Basquez, in the Illinois on paying the freight according to agreement. The undersigned having delivered to Basquez, the 6th instant, the above articles by one Roy, of this place, said Basquez proposed to pay him his freight in peltries, which was not his agreement. He refused, demanding his freight in dollars as per agreement, he being obliged to pay his outfit and expenses in dollars. After repeated demands, he is compelled to have recourse to your justice to compel said Basquez to pay him as per agreement; and in default of the same to sell such portion of the goods as may be necessary to pay him the one hundred and fifty dollars.

St. Louis, May 10, 1775.

"Etienne Barrè.

" *To Lieut.-Gov.*
  " *Francisco Cruzat.*"

On the same day Cruzat notified Basquez to appear the next day, Thursday the 11th, and make answer to the above.

The distinction between a fur trader and a merchant was this: The trader was one who went among the Indians, usually for the winter, trading off his goods, and receiving in payment their furs and peltries; the merchant was one who resided permanently in a place, furnishing the outfits for the traders on credit, and receiving in payment the proceeds of his trade, usually the following spring.

The exclusive trade with the Indians of the Missouri, claimed by the house of Maxent, Laclede &

Co., under their license from Gov. Kerlerec in 1762, came to an end with the establishment of the Spanish authority in 1770, when the trade was opened to all who chose to embark in it. In the year 1776 there were some six or eight merchants in St. Louis then engaged in it. As much of the peltries brought to the place by the traders were more or less damaged through the neglect of their owners in properly caring for them, and as they were becoming almost the only circulating medium of the country, there being but very little coin in the country, and it in the hands of a fortunate few, the merchants united in a petition to Gov. Cruzat, for the purpose of creating some regulations on the subject which would conduce to the mutual interest of both parties, merchant and trader, in which they present their views as to the rules they deemed it expedient to adopt for the benefit of all concerned.

"*To the Lieutenant Governor of the Illinois:*

"SIR: We, the undersigned, merchants in this village, with due respect, have the honor to present to your consideration, that for some time back, the custom has grown up between the merchants, traders and hunters of settling the accounts between them with *furs and peltries*, at certain prices, which vary according to the kind, quality and condition, etc., etc.

"ST. LOUIS, March 4, 1776.

"Signed, MARTIN DURALDE, BENITO BASQUEZ, J. M. PAPIN, "SARPY, ANTE. BERARD, J. F. PERRAULT, JOS. MOTARD.

" After examination and considering the foregoing memorial of the merchants of St. Louis, and the forcible reasons with which it is supported, it is

"*Decreed*, that from this time in future, no skin shall be weighed before it is thoroughly examined and passed inspection as sound; but in order that no merchant can hold back from this reform, nor delay on frivolous pretexts the time of examination, and after the refuse is separated, the skins that are to be warranted shall be exposed to dry in the sun and air to be disposed of. And it is further *ordered* that it is the merchant's business to examine and discriminate his own skins, soon after the trader has delivered them to him, and shall have them weighed immediately, so that by this method no injury nor detriment will be done the trader.

"Done in the government hall, March 5, 1776.

"FRANCO. CRUZAT."

ANTOINE BERARD.

One of the names attached to the foregoing petition was that of Antoine Berard, who had left his native France a young man with bright prospects before him to come to Louisiana, the El Dorado of North America, in pursuit of fortune, and one of the many who soon fell victims in its pursuit to the deleterious effects of the climate, particularly upon Europeans at that early day of its settlement.

Antoine Berard, son of Jno. Bap. Berard, a merchant of Bordeaux, and Antoinette Vallé, was born in the parish of St. Pierre in that city in the year 1740. He came like numberless others in search of wealth to New Orleans, and about the year 1768, following the footsteps of Laclede, a friend and fellow-countryman, he arrived in St. Louis and embarked in business. Being well educated and of fine business capacity he soon acquired prominence, and during the few years of his life he was quite successful and acquired property, when his days were suddenly cut short.

In the year 1774 he became the purchaser of the quarter block at the northwest corner of Main and Locust, with a small house of posts divided into four small rooms, his store, bed room, kitchen and store room, nearly double the usual number of that day, where he had resided for a couple of years. He died on October 13, 1776, at the age of 36 years, at the house of Alexis P. Marie, at the southwest opposite corner, to which he had been removed for better nursing, and was interred in the cemetery grounds the following day.

His will, a brief one, was made on the 12th October, in the presence of the Governor Cruzat, his friends, Laclede, Sarpy and others. " He left his sister, Genevieve, then living with her parents at Bordeaux, his sole heiress, and names his friends above to execute his last will and testament. His house was purchased by another young merchant not long in the place, Dominick Bargas, who had barely occupied it a couple of years, when he, too, followed Berard to his last home, dying suddenly with appoplexy, on the night of July 18, 1779, at the age of

38 years, found dead in his bed the following morning. A somewhat singular coincidence regarding these two gentlemen, both merchants from Europe, unmarried about the same age, and owners and residents of the same house at death.

PIERRE MASSE AND FR^S. VALLE.

" 1875, February 23, Peter Massé, alias Picard, petitions Don Pedro Piernas, and complains as follows: In May, 1773, he entered into an engagement in writing with Peter Gadobert, of Ste. Genevieve, to work for six months at the lead mines of said Gadobert at Mine Lamothe, for one hundred francs per month, to be paid him in lead at five cents per pound, the current price at that time.

" When the time was out he applied to Mrs. Gadobert, who had charge of her husband's business in his absence, for his wages. She went with him to Mr. Vallé's, who had her lead in his possession. Lead had advanced in price, and Mr. Vallé proposed to pay him in money, as he had the other hands at the rate of eight cents the pound; declining this, an altercation ensued, and he was thrown violently on a trunk by Mr. Vallé, who threatened to have him imprisoned, and directed his clerk, Mr. LeClerc, to write on the back of his engagement paper an acceptance of his pay as proposed by Mr. Vallé, and a relinquishment of his claim on the lead, and this over his mark of the cross, which he had signed when he entered into the agreement to work with Mr. Dagobert, all this in the presence of Madame Dagobert, and Mr. Carpentier, the attorney of Mr. Dagobert at Ste. Genevieve. Your petitioner then applied to Mr. Carpentier, who told him he had no control over the lead, it being in the hands of Mr. Vallé as security. Your petitioner therefore applies to you for redress, and for proof of his statement refers to Mr. Carpentier, who was present and witnessed it.

PIERRE x MASSE DIT PICART.

March 10, 1775.—Gov. Piernas refers the petition and papers to Mr. Carpentier, to investigate and report the result. The papers were, first, a copy of agreement, May 2, 1773; second, Massé's receipt to Mr. Gadobert, relinquishing his claim to the mineral, November 9, 1773 — registered at Ste. Genevieve by Mr. Vallé, February 8, 1775; third, Madame Gadobert's statement that she had settled with Massé in full — taken by Louis Villars, lieutenant-commandant at Ste. Genevieve, November 29, 1774, and a copy sent to Gov. Cruzat, March 24, 1775.

March 30, 1775.—Testimony of Mr. Carpentier taken by L. Villars, by order of Piernas — Juan Purzada and Louis Chamard, witnesses.

31st.—Statement of Francis Vallé, and request to Gov. Piernas, with Madame Gadobert's account of lead.

1775, June 4. — Governor Cruzat's decision exonerates Vallé, and condemns Massé to a public retraction and an apology to Mr. Vallé, for the injurious imputations cast on him in his petition above, in the presence of three notable citizens, to be selected by Don Louis Villars, and eight days' imprisonment.

Nov. 7. — Massé asks permission to lay his case before the governor-general below at New Orleans.

Nov. 20. — Permission granted him by Gov. Cruzat.

The decision was confirmed, and the retraction and apology to be made in the Government hall in St. Louis.

1776, June. — Governor Cruzat's notice that he appoints Pierre Laclede, Henry Carpentier, and Martin Duralde to receive the apology, and Diego Blanco, sergeant, and Juan Olivier, soldier, witnesses, and will give due notice of the day.

Oct. 28. — The Lieut.-governor fixed a day early in November.

Nov. 2. — Mr. Vallé, being sick could not attend in person, and named Joseph Conand, merchant of St. Louis, to represent him.

On the day appointed Massé declined making the apology, saying "he had not given any offense to Mr. Vallé." Subsequently, however, it appears he changed his mind on reflection; and on

Nov. 12. — Informed the governor in writing that "he would comply with the decision in the case."

This must have ended the matter, as we find no further mention of it in the archives, his written acquiescence in the decision being accepted as apology sufficient, where it would appear that he considered himself the injured party, or it may have ended in smoke.

Massé died in St. Louis four years later, on July 24, 1780, at the house of Doct. Reynal, on the north side of Market Street, east of Third, between it and the alley, opposite the cemetery grounds, where he was interred.

The temporary chapel, built at the northeast corner of the church block in 1770, being now too small to accommodate the increased population, a meeting of the inhabitants took place December 25, 1774, at the priest's residence, at which they resolved to build a new church of 30 by 60 feet.

April 19, 1775.—They awarded the contract to Pierre Lupien, a carpenter, to be finished in the fall. October 18, Lupien, the contractor died, church unfinished.

January 28, 1776.—Another meeting was held. Jean Cambas agreed to finish it, which he did in the course of the summer, when it was consecrated.

FATHER BERNARD THE NEW CURATE.

May 19.—Arrival of Father Bernard de Limpach, the new parish curate, bearing his credentials, and

CHURCH AND PARISH RESIDENCE, 1776.

[*Drawn by C. Heberer under direction of F. L. Billon.*]

the transfer of the parish from the Diocese of Quebec to that of Cuba.

"Father Dagobert de Longwy, principal Capuchin Priest, and Vicar General of the Mission of Louisiana, in the diocese of Havana de Cuba, to our very dear Brother the Reverend Father Bernard, de dix Par, a professed Friar of that order, in the province of Liege, and apostolic missionary of this mission.

GREETING:

"Well and sufficiently knowing your good habits and capacity, desirous also to conform in all things to the commands of his very Christian Majesty, who, by his letters-patent, registered at the registry of the Superior Council of this colony, to grant in proper and due form, appointments, as curates, to our missionaries who merit it, to those parishes and posts of which the mission had formerly been deemed as entitled to, and to place them in legal possession — the patronage, emoluments, and all other arrangements being reserved to our position as the head — until his Catholic Majesty should otherwise direct. We have therefore given and conferred, and by these presents do give and confer on you, the curacy, or parish church, of St. Louis, of Illinois, Post of Pain-Court (a short loaf), with all its rights and appendages, upon condition of actual personal residence there, and not otherwise, until a change or revocation by us or our successors. Requiring, in consequence, the services of the deputy of the king's attorney, to see you placed in actual possession of said curacy of the parish of St. Louis of Illinois, in accordance with custom and the usual solemnities. Granted at our parsonage, under the seals of office, the eighteenth of February, in the year of grace one thousand seven hundred and seventy-six.

FRIAR DAGOBERT, Vicar General.

NEW ORLEANS.

I certify that this present document is an exact copy of the original appointment presented to us by the Reverend Father Bernard de Limpach, to be deposited for safe keeping in the archives of the Government Office in St. Louis of the Illinois.

FRAN'CO CRUZAT.

MAY 19, 1776.

In due time Father Bernard arrived in St. Louis, and presented his appointment to the Governor as above, and on the above day, Sunday, May 19, 1776, he was formally placed in possession of the parsonage in presence of the assembled inhabitants, by the gentlemen selected for that purpose, whose names are affixed to the document, and entered upon his clerical duties—Dubreuil, Perrault, Basquez, Hubert, Sarpy, Laclede, Berard, Barré, Chauvin, Condé, Conand, Labusciere, Fran'co Cruzat.

September 1, 1776.—At another meeting of the people, they resolved to build a new stone residence for the curate, in place of the old one of logs, now dilapidated. It was commenced in July, 1777, and completed in the spring, 1778.

November 29.—Death of Doctor A. A. Condé, the first and oldest physician of the place.

DRAINAGE OF THE BACK LOTS.

It would appear from the following, that everything, however trivial, advisable to be done for the public benefit in those primitive days of our little village, could only be accomplished through a town meeting of the people.

" On this day, March 15, 1778, at the close of the mass, the inhabitants of this post assembled in the government hall, in presence of Don Francisco Cruzat, lieutenant-governor, to consider as to the most convenient means of giving a proper drain-

CLOSE OF CRUZAT'S FIRST ADMINISTRATION. 141

age to the rain-water that settles in the back lots of the village along the back streets; and they agreed that a gutter or canal should be made at once down the street or road between the lots of Francois Bissonnet and Conand (now Chestnut street), to draw the water to the Mississippi, and to allow a constant drainage to the water from the gullies and sink-holes; and for this purpose, they named Lapierre, Taillon, Deschennes, Lachanse and Baccanet to devise a plan for the same, and have it done, etc., etc.

LACHANSE, his x mark.	DUBREUIL,	JOS. LABROSSE,
BACCANET, his x mark.	A. CHOUTEAU,	ORTES,
DESCHENNES, his x mark.	LABUSCIERE,	ROUBIEU,
TAILLON, his x mark.	BARADA,	BARGAS,
BISSONNET,	PERRAULT,	
CONAND,	BENITO,	FRAN'CO CRUZAT.

Whether Gov. Cruzat, was removed to make way for his successor or recalled at his own request, there is nothing in our archives to show, as all the public documents of a political character, or that related in any manner to the official doings of the governors, were carried below at the transfer to the United States.

He was a man of estimable qualities, and universally respected, as is shown by his re-appointment after the untimely death of De Leyba.

CAPTAIN FERDINAND DE LEYBA,

a native of Barcelona, Spain, appointed by Don * Bernardo de Galvez, succeeded Francis Cruzat as lieutenant-governor in St. Louis June 17, 1778. His brief administration of two short years was remarkable as the most eventful one recorded in our early annals.

1778. — He had been in office but three days when our yet infant village sustained an irreparable loss in the death of its early founder, Pierre Laclede Liguest, which sad event occurred at the mouth of the Arkansas on June 20th, while ascending the Mississippi River on his return to his home in St. Louis from a winter's sojourn in New Orleans.

This event was followed a few days later by the surprise and capture of Kaskaskia on July 4th by Col. Geo. R. Clark, and the subjugation of all the country on the east side of the Mississippi to the authority of the State of Virginia, an event which, although occurring in the territory of a neighboring power, was destined in but a few brief years to

---

* This gentleman, Bernardo de Galvez, had succeeded Unzaga as governor-general of the province January 1, 1777, as colonel of the Louisiana regiment, although but twenty-one years of age, yet of brilliant talents. His father was the highest Spanish grandee of America, Viceroy of Mexico, and his uncle Prime Minister of Spain.

influence the future greatness and prosperity of all the country in the great valley of the Mississippi.

LACLEDE'S SUPPOSED WEALTH.

Much has been said at various times in regard to the large estate it was thought by some that Laclede had left at his death. The idea was based upon the supposition, a very natural one, that as he was the original proprietor here, and had received several grants of lots and lands, and during his residence of fourteen years here had transacted a large and apparently prosperous business, he must have acquired a handsome property. But the reverse was the case, Laclede died comparatively poor, barely, if even solvent, for after his estate was closed there was little, if anything, left.

Laclede was not the manner of man to look far into futurity with an eye to the acquisition, while they could be obtained for the mere asking, of large grants of land for future wealth; he lived altogether in the then present, taking no more land than he had use for at the time. He first selected his block as the nucleus of his future village, and built thereon his store and warehouse, — this was the property of the firm of Maxent, Laclede & Co., of which he was only a junior partner, with but little if any capital of his own; next, he took a lot for his own dwelling-house, which as soon as completed he conveyed at once to Mrs. Chouteau and her children, and from that day never owned another lot in the place.

Next he purchased from Taillon in 1767 the mill T. had put up a couple of years previously on the little creek back of the village, not from an expectation of deriving profit from it, as he well knew that a mill that could barely run one-half the year from an insufficiency of water, could not prove a profitable investment, but for no other purpose than to furnish bread-stuffs for the people of his village.

Laclede expended on this mill during his ownership of ten years large sums of money in a new building, two pair of mill stones, raising the dam, etc., and received a concession of 8 by 40 arpents, on which it stood, as a small consideration for his large outlay, the only concession he ever received, so unselfish was the man in his aspirations.

Laclede had also a farm in the big prairie northwest of the village on land he had purchased from others, and had made the improvements by his own negroes to furnish the necessaries for his family.

The above was all the real estate Laclede ever possessed in his fourteen years' residence in St. Louis, and of which at the period of his death he possessed but his mill and farm.

In the fall of 1776 important business required the

presence of Laclede in New Orleans, where he spent that and the following winters, until the beginning of May, 1778, when he set out on his return voyage to St. Louis, engaged in looking after the interests of certain parties who had intrusted them to him; but mainly in his efforts to arrange the business of his firm, which had fallen largely in arrears, to his senior partner, Col. Maxent, and others; to secure whom he executed a deed of relinquishment December 13, 1777, to Col. Maxent of whatever interest he might possess in the square of land and buildings in St. Louis, which then became the exclusive property of the Colonel.

In the operations of the house during the fourteen years of its continuance a large amount of worthless and doubtful paper had been suffered by the leniency of Laclede to accumulate, forming no inconsiderable portion of the assets of the firm, and was the chief cause of its embarrassment on the unlooked for death of its active business head.

LACLEDE'S DEATH.

Laclede's death occurred on June 20, 1778, but three days after De Leyba had succeeded Cruzat in the governorship of this upper portion. He died at the mouth of the Arkansas on his way up from New Orleans.

As soon as the news of his death reached here, an inventory of his personal property was taken, and a public sale of the same made on July 19th. On the 21st Lieut.-Gov. De Leyba wrote to Gov.-Gen. De Galvez at New Orleans, apprising him of "Laclede's death and of the bad condition of the buildings" then occupied by De Leyba as quarters for himself and his company (the soldiers on the ground floor, and his [family above). On September 2nd De Galvez replies to De Leyba as follows:—

"In consequence of the notice you give me of the death of Mr. Laclede, and at the request of his creditors, I direct you to take charge of his estate and effects until further instructions; with the exception of the provisions, etc., which are perishable, and which you will sell to the best advantage.

"God have you in his keeping.
"NEW ORLEANS, September 2, 1778.
"BER'DO DE GALVEZ.
"To Mr. FERDINAND DE LEYBA."

Auguste Chouteau went down and spent the winter of 1778-79 in New Orleans in adjusting the affairs of the firm.

1779, January 15.—Gov. Galvez writes to De Leyba as follows:—

"As the estate of the deceased Laclede is largely in debt to Mr. Maxent, he has instructed Mr. Chouteau, the bearer of this, to take charge of the proceeds of what has been sold, as also of the effects remaining unsold. You will deliver them to

Chouteau, well understood free from the existing debts, which must be first satisfied, provided such creditors produce documentary proof of the clearness of their respective demands.

"God have you in his keeping,
"NEW ORLEANS, January 15, 1779.
"BENARDO DE GALVEZ.

"Endeavour to have the heirs of Laclede satisfied as far as possible in regard to what is due the deceased.
"To Mr. FERDINAND DE LEYBA."

When Chouteau returned from New Orleans appointed by De Galvez to settle Laclede's affairs, he petitioned De Leyba to authorize him to sell the mill, and farm to avoid their deterioration, which request was granted. The sale took place July 4, 1779. The mill, with the 6 by 40 arpents on which it stood, was purchased by Chouteau for 2,000 livres, four hundred dollars, and the farm in the big prairie, 6 by 80, with the improvements, a house of posts 80 feet long with several rooms, negro cabins, barn, orchard, garden, yard, etc., by his mother, Mrs. Chouteau, for 750 livres, one hundred and fifty dollars. The two pieces of property producing together the sum of 2,750 livres, five hundred and fifty dollars.

After Chouteau had spent over a year in closing up as far as possible the affairs of Laclede's estate, in the early summer of 1780, he descended again to New Orleans, to make report of his stewardship, of which we find the following memorandum:

"Notes, etc., of various parties irrecoverable 27,891 livres.
do   which may be collected...................   7,527
do   more solvent.............................   927.19
do   of Martigny..............................   845. 2
do   of Cardinal for 1 ½ arpents land...   140
do   of Fran's Bissonet for an arpent do....   80
do   for a mare.................................   120

Which amount to the sum of (37,531.1).. 38,523.13.7
And what he has delivered to Maxent............ 2,625. 2.1

                                                  41,148.15.8

From all which I release said Chouteau from any responsibility, he having executed his commission.

FERNANDO RODRIGUEZ, ⎫   GILBERTO ANTE. MAXENT,
PETER CONLEY,   ⎬ Witnesses.   AUGUSTE CHOUTEAU.
ADRIEN DE LA PLAZA, ⎭

                                LEONARDO MAZENGE, *Notary.*

Up to the period of the death of Laclede, Chouteau had been in the employ of Maxent & Co., as chief clerk of the house. After he had closed up the affairs of Laclede he continued in business for his own account.

For some unexplained reason Col. Maxent, now the owner of the square and buildings, made no disposition of the property for some ten years afterwards, it continuing to be occupied by the lieutenant-governor and soldiers as tenants, he being the colonel of the Louisiana regiment, was perhaps satisfied with the rent he received. In meantime for want of the necessary repairs the property was rapidly going to decay, until finally the owner concluded to sell it, as appears from the following documents —

"Col. Gilberto Antonio Maxent informs me that he will send by this opportunity his power of attorney to Mr. Gabriel Cerré to sell, as he may deem best, either at public or private sale, the house and lot he acquired from the estate of Mr. Laclede, deceased, of which I apprise you that you may facilitate said Cerré, permitting him to sell the same as he may deem best for the interested parties.

"If the purchaser of the property will put the necessary repairs on the house, now occupied as your company's quarters, which are indispensable to make it fit and comfortable for their occupancy, you may rent it, taking care to exchange contracts with said purchaser, and to observe the greatest possible economy for the royal interests.
"May God have you in his keeping.
"NEW ORLEANS, May 13, 1788.
"STEPHEN MIROT, Gov. Genl."
"To MR. DON MANUEL PEREZ,
"St. Louis."

Substance of the deed of sale: —
"A piece of ground 300 feet square, unenclosed, with a stone house 60 by 23 feet, falling to ruins, the roof rotten; another stone house, 50 by 30 feet, no floors, also in ruins, and another small house, the property of Col. Gil't A. Maxent, as principal creditor of the deceased Laclede, according to the relinquishment made by Laclede, Dec. 13, 1777, and the decree of Bernard de Galvez, of Jan. 15, 1779, for three thousand dollars cash, possession from this day. St. Louis, Jay. 6, 1789.
"AUGUST CHOUTEAU, CERRE.
"In presence of Louis Dubreuil, James Clamorgan and M. Papin.
"MANUEL PEREZ, Comd't."

"*Antoine Gilbert Maxent, Colonel and Indian Agent at New Orleans, to Gabriel Cerré, at St. Louis, May 10, 1788:*

"Power to sell a piece of ground in St. Louis three hundred feet square, with three houses, bounded north by ground of Tayon, and south Mr. Wm. Hebert, with full authority as to price and terms.*

"ANTOINE RODRIGUEZ, } Witnesses.   "GIL'T ANTE. DE MAXENT,
"FRANCO. CARCASSES, }   "AUGUSTE CHOUTEAU,
       "before the Notary,   "CERRE.
              "RAFAEL PERDEMO."

In September, 1764, when this house was completed, Laclede brought over from Cahokia Mrs. Chouteau's family. They were domiciled in it until 1768, when Laclede's own dwelling, at the corner of Main and Chestnut, being completed, they moved into that.

Afterwards it was occupied by the lieutenant-governors for a number of years, commencing with Piernas in 1770, their families in the upper part, and the soldiers quartered in part of the ground floor. Laclede had transacted his business in it from 1764 to 1778, 14 years. The ground was originally enclosed with a fence of stakes.

After Laclede's death it went rapidly to ruin, only the soldiers being quartered in it until purchased by Chouteau in 1789.

---

* The sale was approved and ratified by Col. Maxent, at New Orleans, June 9, 1789.

CHOUTEAU MANSION.
AFTER ITS RENOVATION, 1795.
[Drawn by C. Heberer under the direction of F. L. Billon.]

In the year 1775, August 28th, one Jno. B. Perrault, *alias* Duchene " being about to go among the Indians," and for fear of his death occurring while absent on his perilous "trip," made his will, in which he names his friend Lieut. Jos. Piernas as his universal heir to his little property, after the payment of his debts. It was no unusual thing in those early days of our settlements, for any one, particularly a devout Catholic, going on a voyage or journey, involving some personal risk, to leave a will disposing of his property, and directing prayers to be said for the salvation of his soul.

It seems he returned in safety from this first adventure, as going again on a similar voyage, August 18, 1778, he made another will, in which he substitutes for Piernas, who had left the country, the new Governor De Leyba as his heir and executor, saying he would find in his trunk at Mr. Labrosse's, notes for the money owed to him. Who he was does not appear, as his name is not again found in the archives but that he had faith in men of high position is clear from his making choice of a governor, and a brother of another for his heirs.

JOSEPH MARCHETAUD DENOYER AND CLAUDE TINON.

" 1. *To his Excellency the Governor:*

"Your petitioner has the honor to state to you that one Tinon, an inhabitant of Catalan (Carondelet), sold him, about three years since, a lot in this place, between Beaugenou and Coussot, for a yearling heifer, which I delivered him at once. This lot being afterwards found to be the property of one Lardoise (Vachard), by a concession from Don Pedro Piernas, our ex-lieutenant-governor, I demanded from Tinon the return of my heifer, which he refused, and which he yet retains. She has now become a mother cow, having had a calf this last spring.

"As all should in justice belong to me, I pray you condemn him to return the cow and calf, and pay the costs and damages.

St. Louis, Oct. 14, 1778."

"Joseph x Marchetaud."
Denoyer.

"Furnish a copy of this petition to Tinon for his reply within three days. — De Leyba."

Substance of Tinon's reply :—

"2. Claude Tinon respectfully states that under the government of St. Ange he received a concession of a lot and an half lot; he built and established himself on the lot, reserving the half lot for necessary outbuildings. He afterwards sold the lot and house to Francis Henrion, reserving the half lot, which he had inclosed and used as his garden. Subsequently deciding to remove to Catalan, he sold this half lot to Marchetaud Denoyer for a heifer and pair of cart-wheels, which heifer he received, but has not as yet received the wheels. Your petitioner has frequently offered to make him a deed, but D., being too stingy to pay the costs, has always deferred it and allowed the fence and ground to go to ruin, although Henrion, his neighbor, has several times summoned him before Gov. Piernas to keep up the division fence, which he was obliged to do, but afterwards tore them up and sold them to one Gascon, and removed to Catalan, where he has received no concession, proving his negligence. The indolence and laziness of the said Denoyer obliged Gov. Piernas to reunite the lot to the public domain and to re-grant it to Lardoise. Denoyers did not dare appear before Gov. Piernas, but waited until Gov. Cruzat succeeded him, before whom he presented himself with the hope of imposing on him, but this commandant, having learned all the facts of the case, cast him, and adjudged the heifer to your petitioner, who is still more astonished that at this day the said Denoyer ventures to present himself before your tribunal with a claim of the kind. He sees that by his own neglect he has lost his lot, and that by the care of your suppliant the heifer has become a cow and a mother, and this is why he seeks by unlawful means and subtlety to surprise justice, as he attempted through Mr. Cruzat to extort the cow of your petitioner.

"The original concession of the lot and half is entered in St. Ange's register of concessions in the archives; a copy of this was given to Henrion when he purchased the lot and house, consequently it could not go to Marchetaud with his half lot. Under these circumstances your petitioner has recourse to your authority that it may please you to cast a second time the said Denoyer, that you sentence him to leave your petitioner in peaceful possession of the cow, that he delivers over the pair of cart-wheels which he owes to your petitioner, and that he pay all the costs and expenses of this suit and the lost time and expenses he has entailed on your petitioner at this time of harvesting the corn crop. And your petitioner, as in duty bound, &c., &c.

St. Louis, Oct. 9, 1778.

"Claude Tinon."

Counter suit — Claude Tinon *vs.* Jos. Marcheteaud Denoyer.

"*To his Excellency the Governor:*

"Your petitioner respectfully represents that for nine years past Joseph Marc'd Denoyer owes him the squared timbers of a house he purchased from Mr. Dubreuil, as per the inclosed transfer, which he has repeatedly promised to deliver, but has never taken care to keep his word, and has put it off as long as possible, telling your petitioner to have patience, which through kindness he has always granted him. But as he now sees that Denoyer has no intention of ever keeping his word, he is compelled to have recourse to your authority, sir, that you please to order him to deliver without further delay the timbers he contracted to get out for Mr. Dubreuil, with the exception of fifty-three stakes, which he delivered to me. Besides to return him seventeen shingle blocks loaned him to shingle the house of the deceased

Lacroix, also the spokes for two wheels likewise loaned him, and further, two days' wages for a man to assist him in making wheels. Your petitioner hopes, from your justice, that you will order the said Denoyer to satisfy these claims, and he will ever pray, &c. St. Louis, Oct. 9, 1778. CLAUDE TINON."

"Having heard this day the parties in the above case at our audience, and the said Denoyer admitting the justness of the claim of Tinon, and begging a delay of three weeks to get out the timbers, we allowed him the same, without any further delay, under penalty of additional costs, and sentenced him to pay the costs, &c., &c. Oct. 16, 1778. DE LEYBA."

" Decision of the Governor — 'After mature consideration and full examination we decide that Denoyer, having forfeited his lot by his own failure to comply with the requisitions of the laws on the subject, furnishes him no pretext for withholding from Tinon the consideration for said lot. Consequently we decide the cow to be the property of Tinon, and direct Denoyer to deliver to him the pair of cart-wheels, and pay the costs of this suit.
" 'FERN'DO DE LEYBA.'
ST. LOUIS, Oct. 3, 1778.

PETIT *vs.* MENARD.

One John B. Menard, an inhabitant of the newly established village of Catalan's prairie (now Carondelet), at the house of Clement Delor, in that village, in presence of several ladies, in speaking of the wife of John B. Petit, of that village, accusing her of faithlessness to her marriage vows, applied to said lady very offensive and degrading terms. The facts being reported to the governor, Menard was brought before him and ordered to produce his proofs of what he had alleged against the honor and reputation of said lady, failing in which he should receive the punishment his offense justly merited, to which he replied as follows: —

"To Don Fernando de Leyba, Captain of Regiment of Louisiana, and Commander-in-Chief of the Western part of the Illinois, &c. :

"Sir, Jean Bap. Menard takes the liberty of informing you, that by virtue of your order at the foot of the petition presented you by Mrs. Petit, against him, by which he is required to prove what he stated against the honor and reputation of said Mad'e Petit, or to publicly retract, or to undergo the punishment it may please you to inflict on him, said petition and order being notified to him at the prison bars. Consequently, sir, as your kindness gives me choice of my punishment, I accept that of public reparation, and I declare that it was wickedly and wrongfully that I made to these ladies the statements I did; that it was while under the influence of liquor that I calumniated her honor and reputation, having always known her, as I now know her, for a virtuous woman, with nothing with which to reproach her integrity. I crave pardon from God, the king, and the said lady, begging her to forgive me, and promising to respect her on all occasions, beseeching you to ask her the kindness to accept the present declaration, which I am ready to make to the said lady, publicly, whenever you may deem proper, and I will ever pray for your prosperity.

"ST. LOUIS, 4 Decr., 1778.

his
" JNO. BAP. x MENARD.
mark.

"Considering the gravity of the offence, and that the written recantation is not adequate to the injury done the lady, we order that the said Menard be conducted, on the next Sunday, to the door of the parish church, at the close of the mass, where he will publicly make the necessary reparation, as stated in his written recantation. And will then undergo an imprisonment of 15 days, as an example to others. And is also condemned in the costs and expenses of the suit.

"St. Louis, Dec. 4, 1778.
"Fernando de Leyba.

"Sentence publicly executed, Sunday, Dec. 5, 1778, by John B. Lachapelle, constable."

"Trial of Louis Mahas, an Indian, Decr. 31, 1778: —
"*To Don Fernando de Leyba, Lieut.-Govr., &c. :* —

"Joseph Labusciere, Silvester Labbadie and Francois Beaurosier, citizens of this post of St. Louis, respectfully submit to you, that they have been appointed by the citizens of the place to make known to you that several years since there appeared in this place an Indian named as above, who had been a slave in Canada. For six or seven years this Indian has lived, at intervals, in this village and in the woods, committing a number of outrages, stealing, running off cattle, debauching slaves with liquor, insulting citizens, even trying to shoot some one, committing all sorts of atrocities, threatening to take the scalps of French and Spanish. As we all know him capable of committing any excess, and that he might take the life of some one of us, or of our slaves while at work in the fields, and that it would be dangerous to any one to punish him if left at large at this poste, as he would revenge himself at the first opportunity, on ourselves, our children or slaves, we apply to your authority to have said Mahas arrested and banished from this colony, as one dangerous to the peace and safety of our people, having already committed various acts that should have been punished, and that he be sent to the superior authority below to be there disposed of.

"Joseph Labusciere,
"Silvester Labbadie,
"Frans. Beaurosier.

"I direct an investigation of this matter.
"De Leyba.

"1st. I, Angelo Isaguiere, soldier of the garrison, testify that about two years ago, one evening after retreat, about 7 o'clock, I had occasion to go to the rear of the guard house, where I encountered this Mahas armed with his tomahawk. As soon as he perceived me he rushed at me, raising it to strike, which I succeeded in warding off with a large stick I fortunately carried, and after a fierce struggle succeeded in wrenching it from him, and gave him a severe blow with it on the left arm, the mark of which he will carry with him to his grave. He then cried out, 'you have cut me,' to which I replied, 'why did you attack me? You sought it.' He said, '*it's true*,' and then walked off without another word. "ANGELO ISAGUIERE, Soldier.
"JANY. 2, 1779.

"2nd. I, Noel Langlais, testify that Louis Mahas, the Indian, former slave, now claiming to be free, was at one time the slave of Mr. Darpentigny, captain of the Canadian troops, who sold him to an English trader, whom the said slave Mahas assassinated, and then made his escape among the Indian tribes of Canada, who drove him off, and he then came to St. Louis, where he has shewn himself a bad subject. "NOEL LANGLAIS."
"JANY. 2, 1779.

"I, Joseph Mainville Deschenes, testify, that some four years ago, during the governorship of Mr. Cruzat, Louis Mahas, the Indian, passing along in front of my house about eight o'clock in the morning, with his gun, without the least cause, but from pure wickedness only, fired his gun at my cow inside of my yard, which my negress was just on the point of milking, from which shot the cow fell dead, and which came near killing my woman.

"When asked the reason for this outrage, he replied, 'it was only for fun,' and he would pay me for the cow, and having made my complaint before Govr. Piernas, then about to leave the country, and also before Govr. Cruzat, his successor, he was ordered to give security for the payment, which he could never find, and to this day I am in for my cow.
JANUARY 2, 1779.

his
JOSEPH x MAINVILLE.
mark

ORTES, Witness.   JOS. M. PAPIN, Witness.

"I, Francis Villet, St. Cloux, certify, that on the first of this month of December, 1778, being hunting on the Illinois river, at Honorés camp, the said Louis Mahas being near by, took his gun, saying he would kill some Frenchman, and fired the shot with that intention, but I, St. Cloux, having escaped the shot, he grappled me around the body, and seeing that he would overpower me from his superior strength, and wicked design to take my life, I called on some river hunters who were near us for assistance, when we secured him by tying him with thongs. The next morning being untied, he came down with me in the boat to St. Louis. He boarded with me, and arriving home, he went up to the loft, and brought down his scalp-lock, saying he had dressed long enough as a Frenchman, he would now dress as an Indian warrior and go and take scalps. The same day the sergeant with the guard came and arrested him at my house. I know this Indian as going frequently with the neighboring Indian tribes, and capable of instigating them to the perpetration of great mischief to the people of our village. And that he should be driven from the country, for if he is let loose from the prison, he will doubtless revenge himself on some one by taking his life.

FRANCIS VIELLETTE.

JANUARY 2, 1779.   P. M. PAPIN, Witness.

" January 3 the Governor sentenced him to perpetual banishment from the country, to be sent below for the governor-general's disposition.

While in the prison here to be sent below, he made his escape on the night of the 27th, by filing off his shackles, and making a hole in the bottom of the wall, through which he passed out.

LOUIS RICHARD,

DIEGO BLANCO, Sergeant.   PHILLIPPE FIRAZANO, Soldiers.

Trial of Lorine, negro slave of Gaspard Roubieu, for an assault on Marianne, the mulatto slave of Govr. De Leyba, at 10 o'clock a. m., January 22, 1779.

Govr. De Leyba being the owner of the injured woman, placed the matter in charge of Capt. De Volsay, then post adjutant, for investigation, and report his decision.

Doctor Reynal's written report, as to the condition of the woman on the 22nd and 23rd, much hurt but not dangerously so.

First witness.—Fanchon, negress of the widow Dodier, sworn:

"Yesterday at 10 a. m., being on the ice at the mill creek, washing, Marianne was washing in a hole in the ice, and had some words with Louison (Duralde's slave), about the right to use the hole, and they gave each other some slaps. Afterwards, Lorine, who was washing at some little distance off, rose from her place and came and assaulted Marianne, who tried to defend herself, but Lorine being the strongest threw Marianne into the water, and would have drowned her but for this deponent, who ran to her assistance, and drew her out. Then Lorine attacked her again, giving her several blows, and knocking her into the fire, from which the deponent drew her, and did all she could to separate them."

Melanie, negro woman of Rev. Father Bernard, the curate, sworn and testified to about the same purport.

Joseph Cotté, aged 14 years, grandson of Mad'e Dodier, sworn and testified, in substance as before. Said that "after the few slaps between Louison and Marianne, Lorine, who was washing some distance from the first two, ran from her place without any apparent cause, and came and fell upon Marianne, throwing her down and giving her several blows on her head and body, and who was rescued again by Fanchon. Marianne then started for the village crying, with her clothes partially burnt."

Sentence by De Volsay:—

"To receive one hundred lashes, fifty to be inflicted this day at 4 o'clock, on the public place, and fifty to-morrow, the 24th, at the same hour and place, and that henceforth she refrain from any further violence towards said Marianne, as to all other persons, either by word or deed on pain of more severe chastisement.

"Ordered furthermore, that Mr. Roubieu and wife, owners of said slave Lorine, be held responsible for her appearance in case of the death of Marianne, and until her perfect recovery, and that they pay the surgeon's bill for attendance until her complete recovery, and all costs and charges of this prosecution.

"Diego Blanco, witness. "Labusciere, *Notary*.

"De Volsay."

LABBADIE *vs.* MARIE.

Block No. 9 is that between Chestnut and Pine, and Main Street and the Mississippi. The north half was granted by Laclede in 1765 to René Kiersereau, one who came over in the first boat with Chouteau. He built a good house on it the same year at his Pine Street corner, where he lived ten years and sold it in 1776 to P. Alexis Marie. The south half Laclede granted to one Beor, who also built a small house on it the same year, 1765, sold it to Pepin Lachance, a stone mason, in 1768, who built a stone house, which he sold in 1771 to Joseph Conand, surgeon. C. lived in it near seven years, and sold in to Silvestre Labbadie, merchant, March 1778. After Kiersereau and Beor had built each his house they enclosed their respective lots, putting the division fence as near on its proper line as they could then ascertain it at that early day of the village, with neither land-marks nor surveyors to guide them, and caring nothing for a few feet of ground more or less on either side. As soon as K. had enclosed his ground he improved it by making a garden, orchard, etc.; he set out a row of six apple trees along and just inside the south fence, for the fruit and shade, as also grape vines, etc., etc., which thrived well and soon produced fine fruit. Things went on thus very harmoniously and neighborly for some ten or twelve years, but shortly after Labbadie had become the owner of the south half block, he perceived that it was not quite as large in front as the north half, he had it surveyed, and found that the division fence ought to be removed some ten feet or so further north to give him the same quantity as the north half.

On representing the matter to Mr. Marie, who thought it a small business in Labbadie to claim what he had never owned, they each having bought their respective lots just as they found them, and just as they had existed from the very earliest days of the village, yet being an accommodating man, he made no objection to Labbadie's demand, removed his fruit trees and the fence, and relinquished to him the strip he claimed. But this liberality on the part of Marie did not satisfy Labbadie; he wanted the fruit trees, and insinuated that Marie in removing the trees took away that which was not his to take, and then petitions the governor for damages and costs.

"*1. To Mr. Don Fernando de Leyba, Captain of Infantry and Commander in Chief of the western part of the Illinois, and Lieut.-Governor of same:*

"Sir — Silvestre Labbadie takes the liberty to represent to you, that since the last year he perceived that Mr. Marie, his neighbor, had encroached on his lot fourteen feet at one end, and about six feet at the other, that the first owner of the lot of Mr. Marie planted six fruit trees and a grape vine on that said encroached piece which produced much fruit. Your petitioner finding himself much restricted by the deprivation of this piece of ground, requested Mr. Marie to move back his fence, which he did as requested; but from downright malice, cut down and rooted up said trees, after the division fence had been made, despite the remonstrances and prohibitions of your petitioner. These trees being an ornament to the ground, their removal is a manifest injury to your petitioner, causing him much pain and chagrin — and that such violent acts are not permitted, but prohibited, by the laws. The petitioner resorts to you, sir, that it may please you to order, with all the rigors of the law, and condemn him in the damages done to your petitioner, and also to the expenses.

"St. Louis, March 6, 1779.
"Silvestre Labbadie."

"2. Alexis Marie takes the liberty to reply before you to the petition of Mr. Labadie, by shewing you how pained and hurt in his feelings he finds himself, in being compelled to defend himself from the charges, altogether without foundation, that Mr. Labbadie has taken so indirectly to annoy him by bringing this suit before you.

"The points presented by Mr. Labbadie have no connection with those which existed and which still exist. The forestalling of the ground of which Mr. Labbadie complains, your petitioner had no hand in, as the lot was sold to him as it is at present. He had the right to remove the trees, which are the cause of the suit, as they were part of the lot acquired by your petitioner; and Mr. Lachance, prior owner of the lot of Mr. Labbadie, never understood that he sold to Mr. Conand, the second owner, but the lot as then enclosed, and that said Conand never sought any difficulty with your petitioner about it, who himself made no objection to restore to Mr. Labbadie the ground he claimed had been fore-occupied; and the said Labbadie himself said to your petitioner, when requiring the fence to be set back, that if I (Marie) did not remove the trees, that he would cut them down himself; that they were old and good for nothing. Again, your petitioner removed back the trees while removing back the fence, and not after the fence was made, as improperly stated by Mr. Labbadie. Said Labbadie said I had torn up a grapevine, when it was himself that cut it off, and when the fence was changed nothing was left of it but the stump, besides it was barren and never produced any fruit.

"Mr. Labbadie falsely states that he forbid me to remove his trees; he forgets that it is only the orders of the lieutenant-governor that are to be respected at this post; as to the interdict of Mr. Labbadie, your petitioner gives them no consideration.

"Mr. Labbadie should not forget the proposition, unjust and indiscreet, that he made me, that if I would give him an apple tree, that he would send me six, or even twelve, that he could take them from Mr. Laclede's orchard, and that he would send them to me, and which I refused, which evinces the little delicacy of Mr. Labbadie; besides he cut down himself one of the trees which was in the line of the fence with Mr. Marie.

"Mr. Labbadie said several times to your petitioner that if he did not remove his trees he would cut them down, on account of the shade they gave his garden, which injured his vegetables, proving that your petitioner was never actuated by spite, as Mr. Labbadie declares in his petition.

"Your petitioner thinks he had the right to remove his trees, as both Lachance and Conand, two prior owners of Labbadie's lot, never considered them as theirs, and that they never had the slightest difference about them, which Mr. Lachance is ready to certify whenever required. Besides, Mr. Chancellier, of this place, was present when Mr. Labbadie said to your petitioner that he would not give 20 cents for those trees, and that he might remove them, which Mr. C. likewise offers to affirm.

"All this, which your petitioner takes the liberty of submitting to you, sir, proves sufficiently the obstinacy, the disturbing mind and the litigious disposition of Mr. Labbadie.

"In these circumstances your petitioner hopes that it may please you to decide said trees his property, which he had a right to remove as part of his purchase, as any other movable included in the sale, and that Mr. Labbadie be condemned to all the costs.

ALEXIS MARIE.

ST. LOUIS, March 8, 1779.

Testimony of the following witnesses taken before the governor in the case, all being duly sworn on the holy cross as Roman Catholics: —

First. "Jean M. Pepin dit Lachanse: Am about 40 years; was one of the first owners of the lot now Mr. Labbadie's; that he never considered these trees as his; they were planted by Kiersereau, who sold his lot to Mr. Marie, and always thought they belonged to him. I never had any pretensions to them. When I sold my lot to Mr. Conand, I always thought I had my quantity of ground, and I never would have sought any trouble on that head, and by the sale to Conand he was not including the trees, knowing they did not belong to him, but did legitimately belong to Kiersereau, who afterwards sold his lot to Mr. Marie. That it was himself, Lachanse, that planted the stakes that separated the lower parts of their lots, and he thought at the time he was putting them up on the true line.

"MARCH 8, 1779.

"JNO. M. PEPIN x dit LACHANCE."
his mark.

Second. "Louis Chancellier, farmer of this place, aged 37 years: Passing along the street lately with Mr. Marie, in front of Mr. Labbadie's house, they there met him, to whom Mr. Marie remarked: 'I come from Mr. the commander, to speak with him about these trees. He tells me that the tax on trees is 50 sols (cents); that I could arrange it with you, if you wished them, as I was the owner.' To this Mr. Labbadie replied that 'he wouldn't give 5 cents for all the trees; they are good for nothing, and you can keep them, and do as you like with them.'

"MARCH 8, 1779.

"LOUIS CHANCELLIER."

Third. "Nicholas Francis Guion, blacksmith, about 39 years of age: Assisted in removing the trees from where they originally stood to where Mr. Marie transplanted them, at which time the old fence had been removed, but the new one not yet put up.

"MARCH 8, 1779.

"NICHS. F. x GUION."
his mark.

Fourth. "Louis Lirette, boatman, aged 37 years: Assisted in transplanting the trees; the old fence was gone, but the new one was not then put up.

"MARCH 9, 1779.

"LOUIS x LIRETTE.
his mark.

"In presence of LOUIS RICHARD, soldier, and JOS. LABUSCIERE.

"Between Sil'e Labbadie, merchant, and Alex's

Marie, resident. The governor recites the evidence and gives his decision, viz. : —

"All this examined and maturely considered, we find that there was no occasion for a suit between these parties. That by the testimony of Mr. Lachanse and the three other witnesses, there were no grounds for the action of Mr. Labbadie against Mr. Marie; that it proceeds from a spirit of chicanery and obstinacy subversive of the harmony that should exist between neighbors.

"Finding, besides, neither motive nor reasons for condemning Mr. Marie, it being proven by Messrs. Guion and Lirette that Mr. Labbadie was lacking in truth, in falsely alleging in his petition that Mr. Marie tore up and cut the trees, after the new division fence had been put up, the contrary being proven by said deponents. Therefore,

"In view of the facts, and to render justice in the case, we throw out of court Mr. Labbadie's demand and pretensions, as they have no foundation in reason, condemning said Labbadie in the costs of this suit, which will be executed.

"Given at St. Louis, in the government chamber by us the governor.

"MARCH 10, 1779.

"FERNANDO DE LEYBA.

"I executed the above decree this 13th of March, 1779, by delivering to Mr. Labbadie in person, at his own residence, a copy of the sentence with a notification to conform thereto, so that he may not pretend ignorance.

"DEMERS, Constable."

FIRST INQUEST.

Domingo de Bargas, a young Spanish merchant, who came to the place about the year 1777, died suddenly in the night of July 18, 1779.

Father Bernard, the parish curate, being uncertain as to the cause of his death, and the propriety of interring his body in consecrated ground, for fear he had died from intoxication, or some other unnatural cause, Governor de Leyba directed Doc. Bernard Gilkins to hold a *post mortem* examination of the body, and report as to the cause of his death. Repairing to the house of the deceased, he examined the following witnesses: —

"1. Joseph Mainville testified, that M. De Bargas came across the street to his house yesterday afternoon, and remained there until about 5½ p. m., in conversation, apparently in good health and not having been drinking. From my house he recrossed the street to his own."

(Mainville lived at the southeast corner of Main and Locust, and De Bargas diagonally across, at the northwest corner of the same.)

"2nd. Ignace Laroche and wife testify: Said De Bargas came to their house last evening, at about nine o'clock, to invite them to supper with him, but Laroche being already in bed declined the invitation. De Bargas then cut a piece from a cake he had with him, and gave it to them and retired instantly; did not appear to have been drinking, and seemed apparently well."

(Laroche's were neighbors at the n. e. corner of Locust and Second.)

"3rd. Francis Larche, another near neighbor at the s.e. corner of Locust and Second, reported to Governor de Leyba at 5½ a. m. that he found De Bargas' dead body on his bed, whereupon the governor, attended by Sergeant Blanco and Labusciere, repaired at once to the house and placed his seal upon the property of De Bargas, he being single and living alone.

Doct. Gilkins made his report: —

"That De Bargas had died from apoplexy superinduced by the excessive heat."

De Bargas was 38 years of age, and was interred on the 20th.

THE BOAT CASE OF VASQUEZ AND MOTARD.

Early in the summer of 1779 a party of five men descended the Ohio River to Louisville, on their way to join Clark at Kaskaskia. At Louisville they found a boat in charge of one Slater and one Callender with a family on board bound, as they stated to the party, for Kaskaskia. On this boat the party of five — Andrew McDonald, Aaron Barrett, Paterick Shone, Andrew Coil and Tarrence Mooney — took passage for Kaskaskia. Entering the Mississippi, the boat continued its course down the river as far as the River St. Francois, where, meeting a batteau with two Spanish gentlemen, Messrs. Motard and Benito, bound for Ste. Genevieve, they were undeceived, and learnt that they were 150 leagues below the mouth of the Ohio; whereupon they took possession of the boat in the name of the States, made prisoners of Slater and his hand, and commenced their return up the river, accompanied by the two Spanish gentlemen in the batteau, who took passage with them. When they reached the mouth of the Kaskaskia River, being entirely ignorant as to their locality, they passed it and reached the landing at Ste. Genevieve, where these Spanish gentlemen hoisted the Spanish flag, and gave protection to the two prisoners, threatening the Americans with violence if they made any opposition. On the following day, June 11th, the party having crossed to Kaskaskia, made affidavit of the facts before Col. John Todd, judge and civil commandant of the county of Illinois, who addressed the following note: —

"*To Col. Geo. R. Clark:*

"SIR — Included herewith you have the depositions of several persons, which indicates a conduct but little generous on the part of some gentlemen of the other side, which is perfectly known to Monsieur Cartabona; a remonstrance from you I think would not be illy received by him. If the Boat and prisoners are restored to Justice, as by the depositions they should be, the Spanish honor will remain untarnished.

"The crew being of your command, en route to join you, should consequently be under your jurisdiction.

"I am with respect, Sir,

"Your very humble servant,

"JOHN TODD, *Judge.*"

"Declaration of several witnesses concerning a certain Boat and Passengers landed at Ste. Genevieve — taken before me, John Todd, Judge at Kaskaskia, June 11, 1779, to wit: —

"Andrew McDonald, Aaron Barrett, Patrick Shone, Andrew Coil and Tarrence Mooney, being all passengers in a boat, coming from the falls of the Ohio River to the Illinois, have together and with one accord made the following narration, viz.: 'Relying on a certain Slater, who commanded or steered their Boat, and who had a description of the Ohio river; the said Slater brought them as far as the River St. Francis, the declarants believing all the time that they were in the Ohio; and declare that they are very certain that the said Slater and one named Callender were perfectly knowing of the place where they were, but that their design was to take them to Natchez, or so near it that it would be impracticable to return. Meeting a Spanish Batteau, they were undeceived, and learnt that they were one hundred and fifty leagues below the Ohio. Upon which the said affiants seized, in the name of the States, the said Boat and the persons who thus deceived them, and who by that proved traitors to their country, in trying to escape to the English and taking with them your affiants.

"Having possession of said Boat they rowed her up stream, without any assistance from the cowardly runaways, to try to reach Kaskaskia.

"The affiants having taken as passengers Messrs. Benito and Motard, Spanish subjects, who profited by the ignorance of the affiants of the places on the Mississippi, and brought them to Ste. Genevieve, telling them they were going to Kaskaskia; notwithstanding all the enquiries they made to learn the entrance into the Kaskaskia River, these parties kept constantly telling them that they had not yet arrived there, and thus deceived them until they arrived at the landing in sight of Ste. Genevieve, where these Spanish gentlemen hoisted their Spanish flag on the Boat of the States, and gave Spanish protection to the two aforesaid prisoners, on the same Boat that had been seized in the name of the States by the affiants, and threatening them with violence if they made any opposition.

"In conclusion they affirm that they seized the above Boat and equipments in the name of the States for having violated their fidelity, and that they compelled them to return, with the intention of taking them to Kaskaskia to prosecute them for their offense, and were able and would have accomplished it, and delivered them to justice, had the Boat and prisoners not been taken under the protection of the Spanish flag by the deceitful and treacherous artifice of those Spanish Passengers.

"ANDREW MCDONALD,
"AARON BARRETT,
"TARRANCE MOONEY,
"ANDREW COIL,
"PATRICK SHONE.

"The above affiants were solemnly sworn as to the truth of the foregoing deposition before me this 11th June, 1779.

"JOHN TODD, *Judge.*"

The facts of this case having been forwarded to Gov. De Leyba, by his lieutenant and commandant at Ste. Genevieve, Don Francisco De Carta Bona; he summoned these two parties, Benito and Motard, to appear before him and answer to the charge.

Their defense was that "when they got on board the boat, they arranged for their passages with the man Slater, who claimed to own the boat, to take them to Ste. Genevieve, and as those who had assumed control of the boat to bring her up to Kaskaskia, their destination, did not deny his ownership, and although they were aware of the intention of the captors to take the boat to Kaskaskia, finding they knew nothing of where Kaskaskia was, and desiring to land at Ste. Genevieve, they allowed them to pass the mouth of the Kaskaskia, and come up on to Ste. Genevieve."

Having heard the statement made by these parties in their defense, after maturely considering the case, he sentenced them to pay the value of the boat to the proper parties, whoever they might be, residing on the American side.

VALUATION OF THE BOAT AND CARGO.

In the year one thousand seven hundred and seventy-nine, the 30th of June, at 10 o'clock a. m., by order of Don Fernando de Leyba, Captain of Infantry, and Commandant and Lieutenant-Governor of the Western part of the Illinois, of the 22nd inst., before me, Don Francisco Vallé, Captain of Militia, and

Civil Judge of St. Genevieve, were present: Daniel Murray and Thomas Tyler, appraisers named by Col. George Rogers Clark, Colonel of the United States Troops on the east side of the river, and Francis Lalumandiere and Louis Bolduc, residents of this place, and also appraisers, proceeded to appraise, on their souls and conscience, the said American barge and cargo, to wit:—

The barge of nine oars, chains and seats................	400 livres.
A lage wooden chest of old clothes and linen..............	100 "
Another do do	100 "
A middle size box, filled with flax for spinning.	100 "
A do do do do	100 "
A small box of do do do	75 "
3 small do do do	100 "
10 iron pots, 1 large brass kettle, and several kitchen utensils	450 "
A lot of pewter and other household utensils...............	100 "
3 feather beds, 6 sheets, 3 bolsters, 3 blankets, all old..	200 "
2 small spinning wheels....................................	60 "
4 old rifles...	400 "
	2185 "

And the aforesaid effects were left in the keeping of the patroon of the boat and his family.

  Thomas Tyler, Daniel Murray,
           his
  Lalumandiere, Louis x Bolduc.
           mark

In presence of Juan Purzada and —— Dupré.
            Francois Vallè.

1779.—This year witnessed another declaration of war on the part of Spain against England, the effects of which, although but little felt in this remote region, yet tended in a large measure to further complicate the then existing state of affairs between the four nations, the young republic of the United States being involved therein.

A SLANDER SUIT.

In the year 1779, there lived in the vicinity of Main and Elm Streets, a coterie of middle aged married ladies, who found it pleasant to spend some of their surplus time in scrutinizing into the affairs of their neighbors, and in disseminating among themselves the result of their observations. One was Mrs. Deschamps, at the northwest corner, a lady of a certain age, which gave her precedence. Another, Mrs. Louis Desnoyer, at the southwest corner, a star performer of great brilliancy on an instrument called "the unruly member," and a third, Mrs. Louis Ride at the northeast corner, younger than the others and not long in the neighborhood, figured more as a good listener than a participant in their slanderous tales.

A Mrs. Montardy, wife of a somewhat prominent man in the place, happened to incur the ill-will of this Mrs. Desnoyer, who, in giving loose reign to her tongue, related to the others certain matters in the conduct of Mrs. Montardy that she had witnessed, with innuendoes as to her character, etc., and that "she thought her no better than she should be." Whereupon Mrs. M., feeling herself aggrieved, petitioned the governor for redress, and that Mrs. Desnoyer be punished for defamation, etc. The governor, having had all the parties before him, examined on their affidavits, rendered the following decision.

He recites the several papers in the case, sums up the evidence, is particularly severe on the wife of Descamps, as the principal instrument in fomenting discord and dissensions between the parties, and concludes his decision as follows: —

"All attentively considered and examined, it appears that there are no grounds for a suit in this case, it being at most but the idle scandal of babbling women, which took place long since and now revived by dissensions and broils among themselves. I throw the matter out of court as too trivial. Impose silence in future on the subject on all complicated therein, strictly forbidding any reflections on each other that might tend to the injury of their reputations, under the utmost rigor of the law, to be imposed upon the first transgressor; and condemn the two parties in the case, each to one-half the costs and expenses of the suit.

"FERNANDO DE LEYBA.

"Done in the government hall, St. Louis, October 7, 1779.

COMPLAINT OF JOSEPH ROBIDOU.

"*To his Excellency, Govr. de Leyba:*

"Your petitioner respectfully represents to you that he finds himself shamefully injured in name and reputation by the wicked calumnies invented against him by individuals always ready to injure their neighbors, and blacken the purest reputations.

"Having, for some time past, visited the daughter of Mr. Bequet, the blacksmith, with a view to marriage, and having obtained the consent of the young lady, asked her hand from her father, who appeared pleased with the proposal, and asked for three days to consider it, your petitioner was very much surprised at the expiration of the time, that Mr. Bequet should say to him that he would not give his consent to the marriage because he had learnt that there were some in your petitioner's family who had surrendered their souls to the devil, and as there were no wicked ones in the Bequet family, *he* would not introduce any; that Pierre Bequet, uncle of the young lady, had told Mad'e Laroche, her sister, that he had learnt that your petitioner had an uncle who had killed his wife, and that having made his escape, he had killed a citizen for whom he worked, and that after these murders he had retired to Cahokia, on the American side, and that he stole and carried off the wife of one Agon, and took her to Post Vincennes.

"Your petitioner having found an opportunity of speaking to Miss Bequet, she told him of her father's prohibition, and what had been said against him, which compelled him to demand from Mr. Bequet from what source he derived these foul aspersions, which he B. refused to give him. This compelled your petitioner to obtain from old inhabitants and travelers from Canada, who knew his family, to ascertain if there was any blemish or stain on it. These persons have given him certificates, here accompanying, which prove that there never was any stain of dishonor on his family's good name, and that it never was tarnished by the law, and that all that has been said against him is false and calumnious.

"Your petitioner not being able to obtain from Mr. Bequet the names of dis informants, determined to obtain himself light on the subject, and applied to old Mr. Tabeau, a Canadian resident of this place for many years, who knew your petitioner's family connections.

"'Of what are you accused?' asked he. 'There is nothing to repeat about your family. I know them, and it is through mischief only that these things are said.' Your petitioner replied that Pierre Bequet told the mother of Miss Bequet that one Demer, an uncle of your petitioner, had killed his wife and employer, and carried off the latter's wife. That Tabeau said it was true that T. Bequet had inquired from him, but he answered him that it was false, and that he knew of no stain on the family of your petitioner.

"Having demanded of Pierre Bequet who told him all this, replied that he could not inform him on that point. For this reason your petitioner prays you to compel Bequet to disclose his informant in your presence. Your petitioner not being deterred by the avowal of Madame Bequet, mother of the girl, that it was Mr. Marly, blacksmith, and Mr. Robert, Sr., both of this post, who put these injurious reports into circulation, and that it was from them that Mr. Bequet had forbidden his daughter to speak with your petitioner.

"As he finds himself injured in the most sensible point to an honest man, and that his reputation is seriously injured in the public estimation, by the malicious reports of Marly and Robert, he relies on your justice, that it may please you to order these two men to prove what they so wickedly advanced against the honor of your petitioner's family, and that they be held to repair authentically and publicly the gross wrong done his character and reputation.

"The petitioner re-assures himself of your uprightness, and hopes from your justice that the said Marly and Robert will be restrained in their calumnies and slanders against him, and he will continue his vows for your prosperity.

"St. Louis, Jany. 28, 1780.

his
"Joseph x Robidou."
mark.

To this petition are appended certificates testifying to the respectability of his family, from Louis Lambert, Raymond Quenel, Hubert Lacroix, L'ange Nicholas, Louis Vachard, Grigue and Tabeau.

"The respondents, Louis Robert, Senr., and Jno. B. Marly, both respectable citizens of St. Louis, deny the truth of Robidou's allegations, that they ever said anything about him whatever, as they knew nothing at all of this particular Robidou.

Governor De Leyba, in his decision of the matter, refers to the evidence pro and con as pretty evenly balanced, throws the case out of court, enjoining upon all parties to curb their tongues in future, and particularly recommends it to Robidou to procure the requisite documents from Canada in support of the respectability of his branch of the Robidou's, and gives a year to establish it in court. Whether Robidoux took in good part the kindly advice of Gov. De Leyba, and profited by it, or it was the result of chance, he became a successful business man of our place, and was prominent as a merchant, dying in easy circumstances, and leaving a half dozen sons, one of whom in time became the founder of the city of St. Joseph, Mo.

GRATIOT AND SANGUINET SUIT.

During the winter of 1779-80, the people of Cahokia were very much exercised by the continued fear of an attack on their village by the British and their Indian allies with a view to its recapture. However, as the winter wore along without bringing with it the expected attack, apprehensions in a great measure subsided, and with the approach of spring, matters resumed their usual routine.

In the month of March, 1780, Charles Gratiot, then doing business in Cahokia, of which place he had been a resident something over a couple of years, to replenish his stock of merchandise, came over to St. Louis and made a purchase of an invoice of goods from Charles Sanguinet, for which he gave his note, payable in July following, and took them over to his store in Cahokia. Some little time after this purchase, and apprehensions of an attack were revived, in the month of April Mr. Gratiot, at the urgent request of the people of that village, went at great personal risk in search of Col. Clark, then engaged in building Fort Jefferson, at the iron mines on the Mississippi, a short distance below the mouth of the Ohio, to urge him for assistance to repel the anticipated attack.

Mr. Gratiot, fearing that in his temporary absence on this mission the expected attack might occur, and knowing well that the Indian allies of the British were only tempted by the expectation of pillage and plunder, took the precaution to send his goods and valuables across the river to St. Louis, where he knew they would be perfectly safe. He sent them over by his clerk, Ducheneau, who left them in the care of Mr. Charles Sanguinet, the only person he knew in St. Louis, who gave him a receipt for the same.

After Mr. Gratiot's return to Cahokia from his unsuccessful mission in search of Clark, who had gone up to Louisville through orders from the governor of Virginia, and apprehensions of an immediate attack had subsided, desirous of having his goods for sale, he sent the same clerk over to St. Louis for them, but Mr. Sanguinet declined returning them unless Gratiot gave him another indorser on the note he had given for the goods in March, alleging that the first indorser was an insolvent. Hence the suit commenced by Gratiot May 8, 1780, and terminated by Gov. De Leyba's decision in his favor May 26, 1780, day of the "grand coup."

" *To Don Fernando De Leyba, Captain and Lieutenant-Governor of the Western Part of the Illinois, and its Dependencies, &c., &c.:*

SIR — The petitioner has the honor to inform you that he purchased from Mr. Sanguinet this last spring, merchandise for about sixty bales (peltries), for which amount he gave his obligation, which is not due until July next; that at the earnest request of the inhabitants of Cahokia, having gone to solicit from Col. Clark, prompt assistance against the incursion of the Indians, with which they were menaced; that he caused to be sent over to said Mr. Sanguinet, with his approval, and to guarantee his payment in case of misfortune to which all men are liable, the said merchandise, with the intention of retaking them on his return from his journey, to sell them and meet his obligation. That Mr. Sanguinet, on his request for the same, absolutely refused to return not only them, but also those that belonged to Mr. Gratiot, and which had also been deposited with him.

"The petitioner, sir, is also the more surprised at such a refusal, as they belong to *him*, the time of payment for them not having as yet arrived. That Mr. Sanguinet sunders, by this ill-advised step, all obligations, formal and reciprocal, having already received on account of the above-mentioned obligation, fourteen bales. That he withholds, moreover, goods that in no wise belong to him; that he acts contrary to all established laws of commerce and against the fidelity of the depositor.

"In view of the above, may it please you, sir, to order Mr. Sanguinet to restore me without delay the above mentioned merchandise, and the other effects placed with him on deposit.

"In so doing you will be rendering justice.
"St. Louis, May 8, 1780.
"Charles Gratiot.

"Ordered, that a copy of this be furnished to Mr. Sanguinet, for his reply within three days from this date.
"May 8, 1780.
"Fernando de Leyba.

"To Mr. don Fernando De Leyba, Commander-in-Chief and Lieut.-Governor of the Western Part of the Illinois:

"Sir — Charles Sanguinet takes the liberty of respresenting to you, in reply to Mr. Gratiot of the 8th, that it is true that Mr. Gratiot delivered up to him a quantity of merchandise as security for 54 bales of peltries that he owes to Mr. Sanguinet, according to his note due in July next.

"Mr. Gratiot, before his departure to seek Col. Clark, sent him word by his clerk to receive these goods at his warehouse as security for what he owed him, for fear of accident, which your petitioner willingly accepted, owing to the critical state of affairs.

"The receipt given for them by your petitioner proves, sir, that he received them but as security for what Mr. Gratiot owes him, and which Mr. Gratiot says himself in his petition. The petitioner has never refused to deliver the goods and other effects to Mr. Gratiot, but thinks he is justified in delivering them, to require from Mr. Gratiot a security to pay him, in case of his default at the maturity of the note, as Mr. Gratiot might at that time be absent on business or accidentally.

"At the time Mr. Gratiot purchased from the petitioner he gave his note jointly with one Cardinal, who is at this time insolvent, and the business even of Mr. Gratiot may be much deranged.

"It is absurd for him to say that he has paid on account to your suppliant fourteen bales, as he has paid him only 5½ bales, and that he has at Mr. Dubreuil's about 8 bales, without a receipt and to whom he owes a considerable number of bales. He must admit that he delivered to your suppliant these goods only as security for what he owes him, since he says so in his petition, and that the receipt of the undersigned conforms to it. Besides, he has never refused to deliver these goods, but he thinks himself, as already said before, justified in asking an endorser resident at this post. If Mr. Gratiot knows himself above board in his business matters, he can certainly find an endorser. It is all that your petitioner asks for his safety. It is unjust to now omit a guarantee that Mr. Gratiot had agreed to, and which he now withholds from his creditor, giving grounds for a suspicion to the disadvantage of Mr. Gratiot in refusing to furnish the aforesaid indorser, inasmuch as he resides on a foreign shore, and in present circumstances his business might be embarrassed in the event of a war which threatens them.

"The petitioner has the honor to inform you, sir, that yesterday, the 9th inst., in presence of Duchesne, perceiving that Mr. Gratiot had not asked him for a casket which contains documents (as was told him by Mr. Gratiot's clerk when leaving it in his care), he offered it yesterday to his above named clerk, under the supposition that Mr. Gratiot might have occasion for the papers it contained, and that he might, perhaps, use it as a pretext for an injurious suspicion of your suppliant in having retained it in his custody. He again, sir, offers to return it to Mr. Gratiot in the same condition as he received it.

"In view of these circumstances, he prays you, sir, to enjoin on Mr. Gratiot to give him a good and sufficient endorser of this place, and to accept his goods in the same condition that it had been received by him, and in which he had already offered to return it, both goods and peltries, and condemn Mr. Gratiot in all costs and expenses.

"Your suppliant continues his wishes for your prosperity.
"St. Louis, May 10, 1780.
"Charles Sanguinet.

"Ordered, that a copy be passed to Mr. Gratiot, to be replied to in writing within three days from date of this decree.

"St. Louis, May 11, 1780.

"Ferd'o De Leyba.

"Copy of Charles Gratiot & Jno. B. Cardinal's note: —

"In the course of the month of July next, we promise to pay to the order of Mr. Charles Sanguinet, the sum of five thousand, nine hundred and seventy-one livres, in beaver and deer skins, for value received from said Sanguinet, and we will pay in the course of the next month as much as comes to five hundred livres on account of the above.

"St. Louis, March 13, 1780.

"Charles Gratiot.
his
"Jno. Bap. x Cardinal.
mark.

"St. Louis of Illinois, May 11, 1780.

"We, Don Fernando De Leyba, Commander-in-Chief and Lieutenant-Governor of the Western part of the Illinois:

"Having been informed by Francis Duchenau, clerk of Mr. Gratiot, of the instructions he had received from Mr. Gratiot to bring over to this side his goods, &c., being duly sworn to tell the truth, Declares that Mr. Gratiot instructed him to seek a house in St. Louis, to store his goods, some peltries and other things. Knowing no one in St. Louis, he applied to Mr. Sanguinet, who said to him, 'if you will put your goods in my house, they will there be safe, and you can retake them when you choose;' that the affiant agreed to it, and delivered them to said Mr. Sanguinet, who gave him a receipt worded contrary to the understanding and intention of your affiant — not knowing how to read, and having had it read to him subsequently, he discovered that Mr. Sanguinet had given him a receipt in different terms from Mr. Gratiot's instructions, and stating in the receipt that they 'were received as security for what Mr. Gratiot owed him,' when, on the contrary, he had only deposited them for safe keeping in the fear that they might be plundered by the Indians if left in Cahokia during the absence of Mr. Gratiot. That he then ran back to

Mr. Sanguinet to get from him a different receipt, which he refused to give, saying, ' don't be uneasy; I know very well that you leave Mr. Gratiot's goods with me only for safe keeping, and that you can take them when you choose.'

" Question: ' Was any one present when you ran back to Mr. Sanguinet for a new receipt? '

" Answer: ' No, there was no one present,' and he again repeated that Mr. Sanguinet said to him he knew very well the goods were only left with him for safe keeping, and not for security, and that he could have them whenever he chose to come for them; that seeing the frankness in which Mr. Sanguinet spoke to him, he left all to the good faith of that gentlemen,' ' which is all he had to say; ' it being read to him, he said it contained the whole truth, ' to the best of his knowledge,' and not knowing how to write, he made his mark in presence of Antoine Stefanelly and Mr. Joseph Labusciere, witnesses, who with us, the governor, have signed these presents.

" LABUSCIERE,
" ANTOINE STEFANELLY,

his
FRANCIS x DUCHENAU.
mark.

" FERN'DO DE LEYBA.

" We order Mr. Sanguinet to deliver to Mr. Duchenau a small casket of papers, which he has in his possession, belonging to Mr. Gratiot, and which is not included in the receipt for goods he gave to M. Duchenau.

" ST. LOUIS, May 11, 1780.

" DE LEYBA.

" *To Don Fernando De Leiba, Commandant-in-Chief and Lieut.- Governor of the Western part of the Illinois:*

" SIR — In reply to the petition presented you by Mr. Chas. Sanguinet, of the 10th inst., your petitioner has the honor to express to you his surprise at the small amount of truth that his adversary alleges in his defense, in stating that the goods of your petitioner that were taken to the house of the defendant, were deposited with him as security for a sum of money which is not due him until July next, a statement of which it is easy to prove the falsity, by the affidavit of the clerk of the plaintiff, who proves on oath that they were deposited only for their safety in the absence of your petitioner, in his mission to Col. Clark for assistance to repel the attack of the Indians, with which we were threatened on our side of the river, and the petitioner had no other view than to retake his property on his return, to sell them and fulfill his obligations to the defendant.

"As to the receipt which Mr. Sanguinet gave your petitioner's clerk, it proves his lack of sincerity, by the reiterated assurances made to him that he could carry away the goods whenever it suited him, saying to him that your petitioner owed him nothing, but when the said clerk had returned to this village, and that he had had read to him the said receipt, not being able himself to read nor write, he was very much surprised to see that the tenor of the receipt differed from the assurances that the said Sanguinet had given him, upon which he immediately returned to said Sanguinet to shew him that the receipt did not in any wise conform to their agreement, and formally refusing such conditions.

"To which in reply, Mr. Sanguinet said to him 'that he might if he wished, take his goods at that very moment, or that he would take care of them until he or your petitioner should think fit to take them away; that if he had, as was true, put at the foot of this receipt that he had received them as security for money not yet due him until in the course of July next, it was merely that in case of death, or other grievous occurrence at that critical period, and that he sought to render a service, and be useful to your petitioner as much as lay in his power.'

"It is by these means, sir, he imposed on the good faith and credulity of the clerk of your petitioner, who, believing that after such promise Mr. Sanguinet would not be so dishonest as to disown or retract what he had said, and refuse to restore to the plaintiff his goods on his demand for the same, made in the presence of Mr. Dubreuil, alleging in reply that he was sustained by the tenor of his receipt. Facts which he now denies by his statements made to you, that he requires but an indorser residing on this side as the one he had exacted at first at the time he sold the goods, is, as he now pretends, insolvent, and that the business of the plaintiff might be found embarrassed.

"Your suppliant is very much surprised to see that Mr. Sanguinet assumes to see so clearly into the business transactions of your petitioner, and would be pleased that he would point out to him in what, and towards whom he has failed to fulfill any engagement he has entered into. It would seem by his statement as if he was seeking to injure your petitioner's credit, with the view of sustaining his own cause, but he deceives himself; he is dealing with a tribunal too upright, a judge too wise and enlightened not to discern the just and reasonable demand of your petitioner, presenting him nothing without the proofs to sustain his position.

"As respects the peltries which the petitioner states he sent to Mr. Sanguinet, his receipts can convince you that it was to him and not to Mr. Dubreuil, that they were sent, and in regard to the merchandises, they were never deposited as security with him, as your petitioner has already previously explained, seeing that he owes him nothing at this time. That if he had them sent over to him, it was to endeavor to insure them from the possible events they were daily expecting to occur on this side; that he even sent all his private valuable papers, and he believes that neither Mr. Sanguinet, nor any other one whomsoever, can controvert the propriety of the act.

"It would seem as if Mr. Sanguinet was endeavoring, in acting contrary to all the laws of commerce, in abusing the good faith and confidence of the trustee, in even seeking to affect his credit, alleging in his statement only acts, the falsity of which are so well proven, shows that he is sensible of the weakness of his cause in straying so far from the truth.

"Perceiving all this, will it please you, sir, to order, in the event of his refusal to return at once the goods which belong to your petitioner, that he keep them for his own account, and for which he will pay according to the bill which will be presented to him by the plaintiff; and that he be required to pay all the costs, expenses and damages arising therefrom — and your petitioner will not cease to address his vows to heaven for your prosperity and just decision in the case.

"CAHOKIA, May 12, 1780.

"CHARLES GRATIOT.

"Considering the present petition, we summoned Mr. Chas. Sanguinet to appear before us, to declare if he consented to keep the goods which he has in his hands belonging to Mr. Charles Gratiot, for himself, according to the prices Mr. Gratiot fixes on them. Who replied that ' he agreed to keep them if the prices set on them by Mr. Gratiot is reasonable, and in case he values them too high, that we please to name four arbitrators in this post to fix a price that will be neither to the disadvantage of Mr. Gratiot nor to himself; that he had no knowledge of the quality and amount of the goods that are contained in the bales that had been placed in his hands, requiring that before taking them for his own account, the eight bales that are at Mr. Dubreuil's be sent him on account, according to the receipt which shall be made for them by the arbitrators.'

"Which he signed in the presence of Mr. Jos. Labusciere and Louis Richard, soldier, witnesses, St. Louis, May 13, 1780.

"LABUSCIERE, LOUIS RICHARD.   CHARLES SANGUINET.

"A copy of which reply we direct to be furnished to Mr. Gratiot, with the present order, so that said Mr. Gratiot may send us the invoice of the said goods within three days of the present order, with the prices he intends to fix on said merchandise.

"FERD'O DE LEYBA.

"Given at St. Louis, May 13, 1780.

"*To Don Fernando de Leyba, Capt. of the Regiment of Infantry of Louisiana, Commandant-in-Chief and Lieut.-Governor of the Western part of the Illinois:*

"SIR — According to the order at the foot of the petition which your suppliant had the honor of addressing to you from this place, and the reply that Mr. Sanguinet made thereto, by which he accepts and consents to keep for his own account the merchandise, provided the plaintiff puts them at a reasonable price; if not, he prays you to name four arbitrators to fix their value. To which your petitioner has the honor to represent to you that, although Mr. Sanguinet has unjustly and without any legitimate grounds, kept his goods, and refused to return them when demanded, and that the plaintiff has left them with him since for his own account, seeing that he was bent on keeping them; that he does not intend to fix any higher price on them than he is accustomed to sell them at here; and that he does not think that Mr. Sanguinet possesses the least right to have assessed the goods that do not belong to him, and which your petitioner decidedly opposes and rejects. Seeing they are articles subject to fluctuations in their prices, according to their abundance or scarcity in the country, and which your petitioner himself purchased at exorbitant prices.

" Consequently, may it please you, sir, to order him to keep the goods at the prices which your petitioner sends you in the memorandum herewith enclosed, being the prices at which he sells daily the majority of the articles mentioned. And that it please you to appoint two persons, or allow each party to appoint one, to make an inventory of said goods, in the presence of the clerk of your petitioner, and append the prices as given in the memorandum, which the plaintiff has the honor to send you, to make out the invoice and foot up the amount, of which Mr. Sanguinet will render him a statement.

" In regard to the peltries which your petitioner has in the cellar of Mr. Dubreuil, as per receipt of the defendant, and which your petitioner thinks are coming to him from Mr. Sanguinet, he does not consider himself under obligations to send them to him, seeing that he expects to receive some from him, as he owes him nothing. But, nevertheless, if the balance is in favor of the defendant, the plaintiff agrees with pleasure to remit that amount, and even a larger amount if necessary.

" In view of the losses of the sale of my goods since the time I demanded them from him up to to-day, may it please you to condemn him in all costs, expenses and damages, should he refuse to keep the goods at the prices named in the schedule, and do justice, &c.

" CAHOKIA, May 16, 1780.

" CHARLES GRATIOT.

" Ordered, that a copy of the present petition and the memorandum of prices of the merchandise attached be furnished to Mr. Sanguinet, to reply within three days from this date.

" ST. LOUIS, May 18, 1780.

" FERNANDO DE LEYBA.

"No. 8 is the memorandum of the prices of the goods belonging to Charles Gratiot, and left for the account of Mr. Charles Sanguinet, merchant of St. Louis, unnecessary to copy.

"*To Mr. Don Fernando de Leyba, Commandant-in-Chief and Lieut.-Governor of the Western part of the Illinois, &c.:*

"Sir — Charles Sanguinet has the honor to represent to you that in reply to the petition of Mr. Charles Gratiot, which was notified to him the 18th inst., with the memorandum in which he fixes himself the prices of the goods which he placed in the hands of the petitioner, and which he finds excessively exorbitant, and pushed to the utmost limits. Mr. Gratiot does not reflect that such a proposition cannot be entertained, and that the prices are higher even than retail prices. Your petitioner, sir, will willingly accept the goods, but not at a price which would entail the ruin of himself and family, especially as Mr. Gratiot should recollect that the petitioner sold to him at 150 % less than the prices he fixes on them to-day, and for that reason he should not resort to such cunning devices to pay off one who so generously profited him, and who would not have withheld the goods if Mr. Gratiot had informed him at the time he purchased of his resources for paying for them, but which in the position in which the country is now found, fortune changes from day to day, and your petitioner's only reason for requiring an endorser was to be certain of receiving the payment of his goods at the time when it became due. But since he offers his goods your petitioner accepts them, but not at Mr. Gratiot's prices, who, in a litigious transaction of this nature, should not expect to be the sole arbiter, and fix the prices so utterly beyond all reason as those he sets down in his memorandum, since the retail prices at this time are much lower, and in a sale of this nature it is not to be expected to establish them at retail prices, and your petitioner in selling them asks only to be refunded the amount at which they will be charged to him in the valuation, &c. This is why he persists, in conclusion, that it may please you, sir, to appoint arbitrators to value the said goods, the said arbitrators to be sworn by you, sir, to conscientiously value the same according to the present value of the articles, or permit each of the parties to name one each, who may appoint a third one, and condemn Mr. Gratiot in the costs and expenses.

"ST. LOUIS, May 20, 1780."
"CHARLES SANGUINET.

" In view of the present petition, together with those heretofore presented by Messrs. Gratiot and Sanguinet, we order both parties to appoint each one arbitrator, who will meet at 8 o'clock a. m. on Monday next, at Mr. Cerré's house in the post of St. Louis, whom we officially appoint in conjunction with the two named by the respective parties, to assess the value of the goods in question and report their action in the case.

"ST. LOUIS, May 20, 1780." "FER'DO DE LEYBA."

" Appointed by Don Fernando de Leyba, captain of the regiment of Louisiana, commandant-in-chief and lieutenant-governor of the western part of Louisiana. We met by his order to arbitrate and estimate the merchandise belonging to Mr. Charles Gratiot, and deposited with Mr. Charles Sanguinet. When about to commence Messrs. Gratiot and Sanguinet presented themselves — the one declaring to us that no one in the world but himself, had the right to value his goods, and the other having challenged the arbitrator appointed by the adverse party, we unanimously renounced the arbitration, and returned back all proceedings therein between these parties to the judicious enlightenment and decision of Mr. de Leyba. "CERRÉ.

"ST. LOUIS, May 21, 1780."

" Between Charles Gratiot, merchant of the village of Cahokia, plaintiff, versus Charles Sanguinet, merchant of this post of St. Louis, defendant.

" *Decision.*—All the evidence in this case having been attentively examined and duly considered, we decide that Mr. Sanguinet is not sustained in his defense, that he wrongfully retained the goods of Mr. Gratiot, that had merely been entrusted to his care for safe keeping, as is proven by all the evidence in the case.

"In consequence we condemn the said Mr. Sanguinet in all the costs, expenses and damages of this suit, and direct him to restore to Mr. Gratiot all the merchandise, etc., deposited with him by said Gratiot for safe keeping, under the penalty of imprisonment, etc.

"Given at St. Louis in the government room by we, Don Fernando de Leyba, commander-in-chief and lieutenant-governor of the western part of Louisiana.

"FER'DO DE LEYBA.

"ST. LOUIS, May 26, 1780."

No better proof can be adduced of the impartiality and uprightness of De Leyba as a judge than his decision in this case of Gratiot and Sanguinet.

Sanguinet, a Canadian, was identified with St. Louis, where he had resided for some years engaged in business, had married a daughter of Dr. Condé, a former surgeon in the French service, with an extensive and lucrative practice, who had come over to this side with Laclede, with numerous family connections and influential friends in the place, who could not but feel interested in his success.

Whereas Gratiot was almost a stranger in the place, but little over two years in the country on the other or American side of the river, without a single relative or connection in the country, and his business heretofore confined exclusively to Illinois. Yet with all these advantages in favor of Sanguinet, of which Gratiot was well aware when he declined arbitration, we find De Leyba, regardless of the sympathies of the friends of Sanguinet, deciding the case according to his conscience in favor of Gratiot, regardless of the effect it might produce on his own personal popularity.

The causes which led to the affair of May 26, 1780: Four years previously (1776) the British colonies on the Atlantic coast had renounced their allegiance to the mother country and asserted their independence.

Two years later (1778) the Virginians under Clark had surprised and taken possession of the English or Illinois side of the Mississippi.

In the winter of 1778-79 the British from Detroit under Hamilton had retaken Vincennes from the Virginians, and expected to be soon able to retake the whole country and again establish the authority of Great Britain.

This Illinois side had been British for fourteen years, a number of its principal inhabitants were either Canadians or Englishmen, and had thriven and acquired property under British rule, consequently were Tories in sentiment and interest, with a firm belief on their part, as with many on the Atlantic border, that the *rebellion* of the American people of the colonies would soon be put down, and the rule of the legitimate sovereign restored.

The Illinois Indians were at that period all under the influence of the Canadian traders and their emissaries, hence the troubled and unsettled condition of the Illinois side, more particularly at Cahokia, where the next attempt of the British to recover possession was more especially apprehended. But not so the Spanish portion on the west side, where the people were mostly all French; they had lived in peace and harmony with the Indians since the first settlement of the country, and there was no cause whatever for apprehension, nor did they feel the least, as the sudden inroad on to their side was so totally unexpected and astounding as to create as much surprise as consternation.

In proof of the condition of affairs on the American side of the river at that period, and the constant apprehensions of the people over there of another attempt of the British to recapture Cahokia from the Americans. I append an extract from the correspondence of Charles Gratiot, then a resident over there.

CAHOKIA, December 16, 1779.
"*Col. Montgomery,* Kaskaskia*:

"I write you in haste by Mr. Girardin to apprise you of the calamitous occurrences with which we are threatened at every moment.

"This night at about midnight I was awakened and told that

---

* American officer then in command at Kaskaskia.

INROAD OF MAY 26, 1780.

the cantine (soldiers' dramshop), near the place of Mr. Labbé, was taken by the Indians. I got up immediately to go to Mr. Lacroix's to know the truth of the report; reaching there I found a Peoria Indian, a hand at the said cantine, who told me 'that he had started yesterday with Charley, an Indian interpreter, and son of the Wolf chief of the Kickapoos, to go to the mammelles, on the hills about a league distance from the said cantine, that on arriving there they found a large Indian lodge with a number of Indians in it, who immediately seized Charley and tied him; for himself, a woman warned him that if he did not escape at once he would be killed with the others.' He also said the son of the Wolf was complicated with the other Indians of the party. From what I see and learn they are *Wabash Indians*, and may number about 50 or 60 men, having eight lodges united as one. Whereupon, to be prepared against so pressing a danger, I immediately caused to be assembed all the people at my house, to deliberate on what we should do, where we determined to at once despatch twenty of the bravest and most resolute of our young men, well mounted and armed, with a written order to Mr. Saucier as their commandant, 'to demand from these Indians the reason why they made a prisoner of Charley, and to bring him to the village,' and if the Indians opposed it to charge on them like brave soldiers; and if the Indians wanted to enter into a parley, to have nothing to say to them, more than 'that they send with them two or three of their chief men to confer with the old inhabitants of the village.' I have just this moment despatched the said horsemen well armed with a white flag to offer them peace or war.

CHARLES GRATIOT.

In another letter later in December, in reply to one from Col. Montgomery, Mr. Gratiot says:—

"All has been very quiet since that time, and we have heard no further rumors of the approach of any enemies."

"P. S.—As soon as I received your last, I sent it to Cardinal, who lives on the Mississippi a few leagues above Cahokia, translated into French, with instructions to caution all those of the other side, who had any intention of going up the Illinois river, not to expose themselves to the risk seeing the danger they would incur in so doing.

" CHARLES GRATIOT."

This day, Friday, May 26, 1780, had been set by the governor for his final judgment in the Gratiot-Sanguinet suit, at which were assembled in the government hall the principal business men of the place, all greatly interested in the decision of so important a matter. While so engaged, and doubtless at the very hour itself, this marauding party of savages, for it was nothing more, were also engaged, at a safe distance from the village, in their hellish work of shooting down in cold blood those innocent and unsuspecting inhabitants whose lives were so ruthlessly sacrificed on that eventful day.

All the circumstances connected with this massacre, all the facts and occurrences previously, prove conclusively that no combined attack was ever made, if ever meditated, on St. Louis, with whom the Indians were and always had been on a friendly footing, but that it was the design of the British to make one more attempt to re-establish their authority in Illinois by the surprise of Cahokia, the easiest assailable point on that side, if it could be accomplished with but little or no loss to themselves, but which attempt, if ever conceived, subsequent events admonished them to abandon as hopeless; and that some few of their Indian allies, disappointed in their chief inducement for aiding in it — pillage and plunder — crossed the river to seek revenge for their disappointment by shooting down any straggler they might come across in the fields, taking good care to keep at a safe distance from the village, as the nearest body found, that of Amable Guion, was on his land more than a mile from the village, and the others from one to four miles distant; and as there was no Indian found dead, it is conclusive that there was neither battle nor attack on the village, but simply a one-sided affair, in which the lives of seven peaceable persons, theretofore their friends, were barbarously sacrificed in the gratification of malice and revenge.

And here let me add that when, long since, I first read all that had been alleged against De Leyba by the few early writers on St. Louis, I imbibed to a great extent the prejudices unjustly entertained by them against him; but after I had become familiar with his decisions on cases brought before him, and read his impartial and apparently just decisions in most of these cases, I became convinced that he had been a much villified and abused man and grossly misrepresented, and when we consider the troubles and perplexities of his brief administration of the government, coupled with the irreparable loss of his young wife, leaving two motherless little girls to the care of strangers in a strange land, it should not excite surprise that he should become somewhat intemperate in his latter days, as is alleged against him by some of those early writers, although without proof.

Gov. De Leyba's decision in the Gratiot and Sanguinet case seems to have been about his last official act as governor, as we find nothing further from him in that capacity in our archives.

He took to his bed with his last illness very shortly after the sad affair of May 26th, sending to Ste. Genevieve for his lieutenant, Don Silvio de Cartabona, to be at hand to administer the government, in the event of his death, which it appears he anticipated.

On the arrival of Cartabona, he executed his last will on June 10, 1780, in the presence of this latter and others, and expired on the 28th, a brief month after the sad affair of May 26th, his death doubtless hastened by the occurrences of that day, and his remains were interred in the body of the church.

Brief sketches of those who were killed on May 26, 1780: —

1. *Amable Guion, Sr.*, came from the vicinity of Fort Chartres with his wife and infant son Amable, among the first to come here in 1765. He

built a stone house on his lot, the north half of block No. 5 (the s. e. corner of Main and Elm), where he lived until his death on the above day, at the age of about thirty-eight years.

His widow married Wm. Hebert Leconte, a trader, a native of Quebec, on November 3, 1780, about five months after the death of her first husband, Guion. She died in 1835, leaving a numerous progeny of grand and great-grandchildren, all descended from her only child, the Amable Guion No. 2 above mentioned.

Guion had a forty arpent concession extending from Broadway to Jefferson Avenue about a mile north of the village where Cass Avenue is now located, a part then in cultivation on which he was killed. The writer of this sketch occupied a part of this old stone house in 1818–19.

2. *Charles Bissette* was born in Montreal, Canada, in the year 1747, and was amongst the first that came over from Fort Chartres in 1765, with an older brother, Wm. Bissette, a thriving business man, who died unmarried in 1772, and several married sisters.

Charles B. married January 29, 1774, at the age of twenty-seven, a Miss Marie Christine Pepin, aged twenty-eight years, likewise a native of Canada, daughter of Jno. M. Pepin, dit Lachanse, a stone mason, who built several of the early stone houses of the village.

About the time of Charles Bissette's marriage, he built a stone house of 40 by 20 feet, a large one for the day, on his lot, the south half of block No. 54, at the northwest corner of Poplar and Second, where he was living at the time of his death, May 26, 1780, at the age of thirty-three, leaving his widow and two small boys, Paul and Antoine, and Marie, an infant daughter, who when grown became the wife of Louis Boissy.

After the death of Chas. Bissette, his widow, Marie Christine, married a second husband on September 1, 1781, one Jno. Baptist Provencher, a wheelwright, who died in 1813 at the northeast corner of Pine and Second, where now stands the *Boatman's Bank*, of which lot he was the original owner in 1765, and where his widow died a few years after him. The Bissette stone house on block No. 54 became in time the property of old Pierre Didier, a watch-maker from Paris, about the year 1795, who, after the transfer of the country to the United States, was for a time the treasurer of the territory, and several of our early Fourth of July celebrations came off in " *Old Didier's Apple Orchard.*"

Charles Bissette owned a tract of $2\frac{1}{2}$ by 40, 100 arpents, in the Grand Prairie, between the concessions of Mme. Hebert and Mme. Dodier, of which he had a few arpents in cultivation. He was killed on this land, or between it and the village.

3. *Joseph Calvé*, whose son, a young lad, was also one of the victims, was an early settler of the place, having received from St. Ange the second recorded concession of a lot in the village, April 30, 1766, being the east half of the present block No. 61, on the west side of Second Street, from Chestnut to Pine, running back to the alley, upon which he built a small log house, where he lived a couple of years. He bore an indifferent character for honesty, and being suspected of robbery, absconded in the night time in 1768. We find, however, his family living at the southeast corner of our Vine and Second Streets in January, 1770, and until 1786. This Calvé was a trader, and spent most of his time with the Indians. The age of his son killed is not stated nor where found.

4. *Joseph Chancellier's* negro. — Nothing is found respecting this person, his name, age, nor any other particular except the bare fact that he was interred, with the others named, by the priest, Father Bernard, on the same day, May 26, 1780.

These comprise the four whose bodies were brought into the village and interred on the same evening.

5. *John Marie Cardinal* and wife Marianne, came over from the little village of St. Phillippe, a few miles above Fort Chartres, near the southwest corner of the present Monroe County, his family being one

of the fifteen then constituting the little village, all of whom abandoned the place and came over to this side in 1765, except the commandant of the post, whom they left there "*alone in his glory.*" He lived on the southeast quarter of block No. 26, being the northwest corner of our present Main and Green Streets. Cardinal when killed was a man somewhat advanced in years, having a family of several children, his eldest daughter, Genevieve, wife of Jno. B. Vifvarenne, being about twenty-three years of age, with a couple of children.

He was killed on a piece of land he owned in the Grand Prairie, about three miles northwest of our present court-house, east of the Fair-grounds, now Lindell Park, and was buried where his body was found.

6. *Francis Hebert.* — There were two Hebert families here from the start. One, the Heberts proper, from Fort Chartres, and the others, the Heberts Leconte, from Canada.

Previous to the establishment of St. Louis, Ignace Hebert, the father of this Francis, died on the other side, at Fort Chartres, as his widow, Helene Danis, was here and possessed a house and lot, the south half of block No. 38, prior to the concessions.

Francis Hebert (called Belhomme), their son, was born at Fort Chartres about 1750. He married in

St. Louis on February 4, 1774, at the age of twenty-four, the daughter of Julien Le Roy, aged about fifteen. He lived at the time of his death in a house built by his uncle, Joseph Hebert, on the southeast quarter of block No. 39, the northwest corner of Main and Poplar, which he had purchased from this uncle.

He was killed on a piece of land of eighty arpents he held in the Grand Prairie about four miles west of the court-house, survey No. 1287, now a part of Forest Park near the n. e. corner. He was just thirty years of age, and, like Cardinal, was buried where found on his land.

Francis Hebert's widow, Madeleine Roy, was married to her second husband, Jno. B. Truteau, on May 1, 1781, one year after Hebert's death. Truteau (a corruption, properly Trudeau) was the only village schoolmaster of the Spanish days, and continued to teach his little French school for almost half a century until near his death in 1827, more than twenty years after the transfer to the United States. His widow survived him for some years. They lived for a long time on the south side of Pine, a little east of Second, where old Batiste Trudeau's name is found in our first St. Louis Directory of 1821. They had several married sons and daughters. The compiler knew them well.

7. *Pierre Gladu*, a Canadian, was the seventh victim.

In a recent thorough examination of the old "parish church records of interments," I made the following discovery, viz. : —

"1792, March 21. — Pierre Gladu, a good and honest man from Canada, was killed by the Indians on May 26, 1780, in the Little Prairie and buried there; his remains were taken up and re-interred in the cemetery.

"By FATHER LEDRU, *Curate.*"

This Gladu's name is no where found in the annals but in this one instance, and was not identified with the village. This completes the list of victims of the fatal day.

The will of Don Fernando De Leyba :—

"Before me, Don Francisco de Cartabona, Lieutenant of Infantry in the Battalion of Louisiana, garrisoned in the post of St. Louis, in default of a notary therein, at the request of Don Ferdinand De Leyba, captain of the Regiment of Infantry of Louisiana, Commander-in-chief and Lieutenant-Governor of the western part of Illinois, I repaired to the Government Room in order to receive the last Will of the said Don Fernando De Leyba, where I found him in bed dangerously ill, but sound in mind, in memory and judgment, as appeared to me and to the undersigned witnesses.

The said De Leyba, knowing the certainty of his death, and desiring not to be overtaken by it without having disposed of his goods, and to put his business in good order, has requested me to receive the present testament, which he has dictated in the following manner, to wit:—

First.—As a good Catholic, apostolic and Roman Christian, he commends his soul to God, beseeching the Blessed Virgin Mary, and all the Saints of the celestial court to intercede for him, so that the Almighty may receive him among the Blessed.

" The testator wishes and ordains that his body be buried in the church of this parish by the side of his deceased wife, and a solemn service be celebrated the day of his funeral; moreover, fifty low masses and one Solemn Service at the end of the year for the repose of his soul, and that of his wife.

" The said Testator having two daughters born of his marriage, the one named Pepita, and the other named Rita, he acknowledges them as being his legitimate daughters.

" He wishes and ordains that there shall be remitted out of his goods to Madame Joseph Viscageaux, his mother, at Barcelona, the sum of one thousand hard dollars, which sum she shall receive without any charge or cost, and if there be any, it shall be on account of the heirs of the said testator, and as regards all the other goods which he possesses in this colony, he leaves them to the care of M. de Galvez, governor-general of Louisiana, to be invested, and the annual interest thereof to be employed in educating his two daughters, either in the convent or any other boarding school.

" The said Testator has appointed for his Testamentary Executor, Francis Vigo, merchant, residing in this post, and for his substitute, Benito Vasquez, Lieutenant of Militia, requesting them to take this charge, and placing in their hands all his goods.

" The said Testator declares that all the furniture existing in the Government House is his personal property, so that no person can claim anything thereof, excepting, nevertheless, the goods which Mr. Vigo has brought upon his last voyage, and which belong to the presents for the Indians.

" The testator wishes and ordains that all his personal goods and effects, whatever their nature, be lawfully valued, and those which may be sold here to advantage to be sold; as regards those which may be more advantageously sold at New Orleans, Mr.

Vigo will send them to that City with his deceased wife's clothes, and the silver plate shall be divided between his two daughters.

"The said Testator, not having regulated his business with the said Vigo, he has given him two bills of exchange, one for the sum of two thousand four hundred and twenty dollars, and the other for fourteen hundred and fifty-two dollars; by means of these sums all accounts between the testator and the said Vigo are liquidated and settled; and if after the death of the testator, there should be found notes or bills due by each to the other, they shall be null of full right.

"The testator wishes and ordains that Mr. Sarpy, who has transacted business with him, and all others in the same case, should render their accounts to the said Vigo, his testamentary executor.

"All the above said has been dictated to me, Don Francis de Cartabona and the undersigned witnesses by the said Don Fernando de Leyba, and this present deed having been read to him, he has declared to have understood it well, and wishes the same to be executed according to its form and tenor as being his last will and intention. Revoking and annulling all other testaments, codicils or other testamentary dispositions which he may have made before this present one, to which he adheres, and wishes the same to be executed in everything as contained therein.

"Made and executed in the Government Hall, St. Louis, where Don Fernando de Leyba is in his bed, the year one thousand seven hundred and eighty, the tenth day of June, in the presence of Joseph Labusciere, residing at this post, Diego Blanco, a sergeant of this garrison, Jean Pursada, sergeant, and Louis Richard, soldier, attending witnesses, who have signed with the said Testator, and with me, Don Francisco de Cartabona, the same day and year above.

"Fernando de Leyba.

"Diego Blanco, Juan Purzada, Labusciere, Louis Richard, Benito, Vigo,
Silvio Francisco de Cartabona.

"First copy delivered to Bernardo de Galvez, governor-general; second copy to Francisco Vigo."

INTERMENT OF DE LEYBA AND HIS WIFE.

Governor de Leyba died, and was interred on June 28, 1780, in the body of the village church, alongside his wife, who had preceded him some nine months, as per the following records in the church register:—

"In the year one thousand seven hundred and seventy-nine, the sixth of September, I, Capuchin Priest, apostolic missionary, Curate of St. Louis, have inhumed in this church, in front of the right hand balustrade, the body of Madame Marie, of the Conception and Zezar, consort of Don Fernando de Leyba, commandant of this post, captain of infantry, invested with all the sacraments of penitence and extreme unction.

"In testimony whereof I have signed this, the day and year as above.
"FATHER BERNARD, *Missionary.*"

"In the year one thousand seven hundred and eighty, the twenty-eighth of June, I, Capuchin Priest, apostolic missionary, Curate of St. Louis, of Illinois, province of Louisiana, diocese of Cuba, have inhumed in this church, in front of the balustrade on the right, the body of Don Ferdinand de Leyba, captain of infantry of the battalion of Louisiana, commandant of this post, with all the Sacraments of our holy mother church administered to him.

"In faith whereof I have signed the present the day and year above stated.
"FATHER BERNARD, *Missionary.*"

DON SILVIO FRANCISCO DE CARTABONA

came up to St. Louis with Capt. Ferdinand de Leyba in 1778 as the lieutenant of de Leyba's company of the Louisiana regiment of infantry, and was left by him at Ste. Genevieve as military commandant at that post, Francois Vallé being the civil commandant.

When de Leyba found himself very ill, with but little hope of his recovery, he sent for Cartabona to come up to St. Louis, to be near him in the event of his death, to take charge of the government *ad interim* as the next officer in rank. He reached St. Louis about June 9th, as on that day his signature first appears in the archives for de Leyba, then too ill to write. His official acts commence on June 10, 1780, with de Leyba's will, and conclude on September 22d — a period of three months, when Cruzat appeared to re-assume the command.

Cartabona then returned to Ste. Genevieve, where he remained until the place was swept away by the high waters of 1784, after which we lose sight of him altogether.

FRANCIS CRUZAT'S SECOND TERM.

After the death of De Leyba, the governor-general, de Galvez, re-appointed Col. Francis Cruzat, who had made himself very popular with the people of St. Louis in his first administration, lieutenant-governor of Upper Louisiana. In meantime Cartabona officiated until the return of Cruzat and his resumption of authority on September 24, 1780.

Previous to this inroad, none of the few villages in the upper part of the Illinois country were in any manner fortified or protected from the Indians. There had been no necessity for any such protection, all being heretofore peaceable. But on the return of Cruzat, to guard against any such mishap in future, he deemed it best to erect some protection against any future attempt of the kind; thereupon he directed Auguste Chouteau,* who had made the original plat of the village for Laclede in 1764, to

---

* Chouteau, who was no military man, albeit a good pensman, and had never seen any other fortified town than his native place, New Orleans, copied from that as his model, and gave to St. Louis quite a formidable appearance on paper, with its bastions, towers, demilunes, palisades, sally-ports, scarps and counter-scarps, etc., all laid down *secundem artem*, and the people set to work with a will in their immediate erection; the palisades were soon planted, and two or three of the towers and the northwest bastion commenced, but the alarm having measurably passed over, they progressed very slowly, and were soon abandoned in an unfinished state.

mark out on the same a line, to include within its limits all the houses then in the village, upon which to put up a stockade of posts and erect a few stone towers at suitable points on the line, and this was the origin of the so-called fortifications of St. Louis.

DUBREIUL'S AUCTION SALE.

Louis Dubreiul, having gone down to New Orleans to remain during the winter of 1780–81, concluded to sell a portion of his household effects he had left in St. Louis. For this purpose he appointed his friend and connection, Charles Sanguinet, and sent him authority to do so.

"The year one thousand seven hundred and eighty, the 23rd day of the month of December, we Don Francisco Cruzat, Lieut. Colonel of the Louisiana Regiment, Commandant-in-Chief and Lieut.-Governor of the western part of the Illinois, at the request of Charles Sanguinet, merchant of this place, in the name of, and authorized by Louis Dubreiul, absent at New Orleans, which requested our attendance at his house, to proceed to a sale by auction, of the cast off effects of Mr. Louis Dubreiul, where the public being assembled, it was proclaimed to them that the purchasers will pay the price sold at, in deer skins or beaver, at the current rate at this post, or in money, in the course of the month of May next, in giving good security resident in this place, and then proceeded as follows: —

	Livres.	Sols.	Purchaser.				
					404	10	
A cradle, 2 pans	5		Horttiz.	Several books of history	12	10	Reynal.
Ropes, knives, &c., &c	16	10	Taillon.	Pitcher, pots, box, corks	15		Horttiz.
A turreen, 8 pans	5		Demers.	12 table knives	25		Same.
A do. 8 small pans	8		Coussot.	Castors, 9 flagons	30		Blanco.
5 spoons, 3 plates, 2 pans		2	Sanguinet.				

LAFLEUR ET ALS. *VS.* CHAS. GRATIOT.

Item			Item		
Pots, rods, 4 lbs. balls	10	Horttiz.	About 100 empty bottles.	39	Sangui't.
2 earthen pots	5 10	Sanguin't.	12 china plates	36 10	Same.
Pitcher of grease and vinegar	20	Blanco.	12 do.	30	Blanco.
A large iron oven	55	Tardif.	20 carots tobacco	40	Belkemier.
A small do	25	Horttiz.	20 do.	30	Blanco.
A churn, 7 sickles, 2 scythes..	20	Chevall'r.	20 do.	41	Chancel'r.
Hammer, pincers, draw knife	15	Sanguin't.	26 do.	43	Horttiz.
2 picks, iron & bolt	6 10	Blanco.	12 plates	26 10	Reynal.
1 pick, hoe, boat-hook	2 10	Same.	5 dishes	27	Horttiz.
20 carots of tobacco	37	Same.	6 goblets, a coffee cup	14	Blanco.
1 demijohn, 1 pitcher grease	19 10	Cheval'r.	A funnel, piercer, corks, &c	10	Sangui't.
6 small shirts, traders	39	Sang't.	A scarlet cloak	40	Reynal.
3 boxes	12 10	Chartran.	A pot of shooting powder	51	Renaud.
1 box old iron	15 10	Guion.	Locks and old iron	12	Demers.
2 gridirons, fork, tripod, &c	15	Sanguin't.	1 pair of oxen	399 10	Guyon.
1 mattock, 8 lbs	40	Taillon.	1 tumbrel	40	Horttiz.
1 do. 4 lbs	30	Chevallier.	Livres	1360 10	
Up	404 10				

"And after tramping around until 6 o'clock p. m., finding nothing more to sell, we closed the auction, amounting to 1360 livres and 10 sols in skins or money, to be paid at the time above mentioned into the hands of Mr. Sanguinet, and signed the same the day and year above.

Diego Blanco,
Chas. Sanguinet, } Witnesses.

Demers, *Constable.*
Labusciere, *Notary.*

LAFLEUR ET ALS. *vs.* CHAS. GRATIOT.

About the beginning of the month of March, 1780, Mr. Chas. Gratiot, then a resident of Cahokia, sent up a barge with provisions and stores to Prairie du Chien, with a license from the American authorities, Cols. John Todd and George R. Clark, and also from Govr. De Leyba, of the Spanish side, to be disposed of to the people of that place. The boat was in charge of Jno. B. Cardinal as master and pilot, with a crew of five hands.

When arrived at Turkey River, ten leagues below the Prairie, then still held by the British authorities, they were surprised by a party of British and Indians, who captured the boat and cargo, and took their prisoners to Mackinaw, from which place Cardinal after a time, for his defiant language, was sent in irons to Montreal for trial.

After having made their escape from Mackinac, after an imprisonment of a year, and their return to St. Louis, three of these hands, Peter Lafleur, John Marie Durand, and Francis Chevallier, presented a petition to Governor Cruzat, July 9, 1781, in which they allege that " they applied to Mr. Gratiot for the wages due them, as hands on his boat 130 livres,— $26 each, — which he declined to pay them, saying ' he had not expected to pay them after the loss of his boat and cargo, until he was himself recompensed for his heavy loss;' " they therefore petition the governor to compel Mr. Gratiot to pay them the wages they claim, plainly insinuating collusion between Mr. Gratiot's partners and the captors of the boat.

Petition filed July 9, 1781, and copy furnished to

Mr. Gratiot, who in his reply to the same, July 12, says :—

"1st. True, as stated by his accusers, that being detained by pressing matters in Illinois he sent under the charge of his employé and pilot, Jno. B. Cardinal, his Boat loaded with stores and provisions to be disposed of either on the voyage or at the Prairie, only to traders or Indians with whom they were engaged in trade, as proven by the licenses granted by De Leyba to him and others so engaged.

"2nd. Indignantly denies the insinuations of his accusers of collusion with their English enemies, being then absolutely ignorant of the declaration of war between Spain and England.

"3rd. Cites the affirmations of James Matthews and Louis Lamarche, two others of the hands of his Boat who were also carried prisoners to Mackinac, in direct conflict with the statements of his three accusers, whom he denounces as base slanderers, and demands that they be compelled to appear before the governor and prove their accusations or incur the penalty thereof — and concluded his reply in testifying to the integrity of Jno. B. Cardinal in the following words: —

"If Cardinal, who exposed himself to the most rigorous punishment from our enemies for his attempt to divert the Indians from coming to war on us, if he had any orders from me to assist the designs of our enemies, would he have exhibited as much constancy and firmness in his rigorous confinement? has he not in every particular comported himself as a brave and faithful subject of his Catholic Majesty? could such a man be capable of betraying his country? would he have abandoned his wife and child on this side to become a party in so infamous an accusation? No, sir. CHARLES GRATIOT."

"I certify that I engaged myself to Mr. Charles Gratiot, in the month of March of the year 1780, and left the village of Cahokia on a barge loaded with merchandise for Prairie du Chien, with a license from Col. Montgomery, then in command at Kaskaskia — came to St. Louis where we remained two days, and where we took on board a part of the goods belonging to said barge, with the permission of Mr. De Leyba, commandant of said post — from there started on our voyage under the charge of Jno. Bapt. Cardinal, manager and pilot of said barge, and completed our trip without accident as far as Turkey River, ten leagues distant from Prairie du Chien; but as soon as we arrived at that place, we were surrounded by an army of English and Indians, who plundered us of the Boat and cargo, and unexpectedly took us prisoners. From this point we were taken to Prairie du Chien, where we were separated from each other. Shortly after our arrival at this Post, not being allowed to see or speak to Mr. Cardinal, our principal, I learnt that he had been very badly maltreated and put in irons for having spoken to the Indians and advising them not to undertake the war against the Illinois country, telling them that the Spaniards, the French and the Americans, were but as one, and that they would be in a pitiable condition if they drew upon themselves the wrath of those three powers."

"That the said Mr. Cardinal was sent with us to Mackinac, and on his arrival there, and during the time he was detained, he remained in irons up to the time of his departure for Montreal, where he was sent.

"I further certify that I have no knowledge whether Mr. McCrae, the former partner of Mr. Gratiot, received the payment for the merchandise of the barge, believing that he would not have risked applying for payment, for fear of being suspected of holding secret correspondence with the Spanish and Americans, as we found a number of charitable individuals who would have endeavored to mitigate the rigors of our captivity, but were deterred by the fear of exciting the suspicions of the British Government to their injury. I certify to the truth of the present certificate. "JAS. A. MATTHEWS."

"ST. LOUIS, 30th July, 1781.

Another certificate of Louis Lamarche, also one of the crew of the barge, verbatim with the above, concludes as follows: —

"I have given my certificate under oath, and not knowing how to write, I have put my ordinary mark to the same in presence of witnesses. LOUIS LAMARCHE.
"His x mark."

"CAHOKIA, Aug. 1, 1781.
Affirmed on oath before me. JNO. BABT. LA CROIX, *Justice*.

"Before me, Don Francis Cruzat, Lieut.-Governor of the western part of the Illinois, and Mr. Linctot, officer in the service of the United States of America, and the undersigned witnesses, appeared in person, Peter Lafleur, Jno. M. Durand, and Francis Chevallier, residents of Cahokia, who solicited me to allow the withdrawal of a petition dated June 8, 1781, which they had presented to me against Mr. Charles Gratiot — protesting that they never had any intention whatever of assailing the honor of said Mr. Gratiot in anything that might have appeared in their petition, it being simply as they supposed for their wages only; and that everything therein that tended to asperse the reputation of the said gentleman did not emanate from them, but from the person whom they employed to prepare the said paper, who imposed upon them, inasmuch as neither of them can read, and they would be very much perplexed to produce any proof of anything asserted in that paper. In testimony of which, not being able to write, each has made his ordinary mark, in presence of the undersigned witnesses and of Mr. Linctot.

"St. Louis, 4th Sept., 1781.

"CERRÉ,
"FRANS. CAILHOL,

his   his   his
"PETER x LAFLEUR,   JNO. M. x DURAND, FRANCIS x CHEVALLIER,
mark   mark   mark
"PERRAULT,   DUBREUIL,   S. DE CARTABONA,
"GODFREY LINCTOT,   FRANCO. CRUZAT."

"The undersigned arbitrators, I, Gabriel Cerré, for Chas. Gratiot, and I, Francis Cailhol, for the hands Lafleur, Durand and Chevallier, for the purpose of settling the matter of the wages they claim to be due them for a voyage they made up the Mississippi with a loaded barge for Mr. Gratiot, and which was captured last year by the Indians who came and attacked * *

(*2 or 3 lines here illegible*)

"our decision is that said engagés should not lay claim to any wages — that if hereafter Mr. Gratiot should be reimbursed for the loss of said cargo he will be under obligations to pay them.

"In testimony whereof we give the present, at St. Louis the 4th of September, 1781.

"CERRÉ — CAILHOL.

"In view of the above decision of the arbitrators, the parties will abide by said decision.

"St. Louis of Illinois, this 5th Sept., 1781.

"CRUZAT."

CHARLES GRATIOT

was a resident of Cahokia from December, 1777, until the summer of 1781 — three and one-half years — during which period he was one of the firm of David McCrae & Co. of Cahokia, McCrae being of Montreal.

During this period, Gratiot being one of the few educated business men of the place and familiar with both the French and English languages, on the surprise of the country by Clark in 1778, he soon became on intimate terms with him and all the American officials, had extensive business transactions with them, rendered them many important services, and although not filling any official position he was so prominently identified with the public events of the period, and his influence in Cahokia so very great, that his views were usually consulted on public matters of the day.

In the summer of 1781 Mr. Gratiot removed from Cahokia to St Louis, married his wife, and identified himself with the place, in which he continued to live for thirty-six years, until his death in 1817. One of the principal reasons which induced Mr. Gratiot to change his residence from Cahokia to St. Louis, was to enable him to participate in the trade of the Missouri Indians, from which he was excluded by the Spanish laws of the country as they then existed.

In September, 1781, Mr.. Gratiot, in closing up the business of McCrae & Co. at Cahokia and Kaskaskia, having in his possession a large amount of claims against the State of Virginia for supplies, etc., furnished by them and others to Clark and his successors, placed these claims, amounting to some eight or nine thousand dollars, in the hands of one Philip Dejean, to collect, if possible. A list of the same was filed by him in the archives of St. Louis September 27, 1781, viz: —

"A note of Capt. James Harrod, Nov. 13, 1778 $ 114
An obligation of Major John Williams, Nov. 9, 1778   1.440
                                                     —————
       With an interest % upon the above — total   1.862
A note of Capt. Dodge, Sept. 28, 1780   90 $2/5$
Another of same, approved by Col. Montgomery,
       Sept., 1778,   146
A bill of exchange on Treasury of Virginia by Col.
       Montgomery, Oct. 18, 1780   5.102 $1/6$
Another on the same by the same, Sept. 28, 1780   321 $4/5$
Bill of exchange by Col. Clark on Oliver Pollock, at
       New Orleans, Nov. 23, 1778   800
                                                     —————
                                 Total $8,322 $2/6$

This Dejean, not succeeding in collecting the foregoing, returned them to Mr. Gratiot.

VILLAGE LAWS.

In the year 1782, the village having been enclosed by the palisades erected after the attack of May 26, 1780, it was deemed expedient to adopt a more perfect code of laws for the government of the inhabitants of the village.

" DECREE.

"The undersigned, sindics nominated by the assembly of the inhabitants, which was held in the government hall on the 22nd September of this year, 1782, by Mr. Don Francisco Cruzat, lieutenant-colonel by brevet of infanterie, commandant-in-chief, and lieutenant-governor of the western part and district of Illinois, for the purpose of establishing fixed and unalterable rules for the construction and repair of streets, bridges and drains of this village, and vested with the authority of the public who elected us to that effect, have in the said government hall, and in the presence of the aforesaid Don Francis Cruzat, on this day, the 29th of the same month, agreed upon what follows, and to which every one shall regularly conform in future: —

"1. — On the first day in every year an assembly of all the inhabitants of this post shall be held in the government hall, and in the presence of the lieutenant-governor, in which there shall be nominated by the plurality of their votes, two sindics, to watch together the repairs to streets, bridges and drains of this village, whose duty it shall be to cause the following regulations to be observed exactly : —

"2. — The first duty of the sindics, as soon after their election, must be to examine by themselves the interior of the village, and to cause to repair, without delay, the streets, drains and bridges by the persons that are bound thereto, and whom we shall indicate hereafter; and should any body refuse to do the same, they shall have recourse to justice to compel them to fulfill a duty so indispensable for the public convenience.

"3. — All the inhabitants whose lots face a street through which passes a rivulet shall be obliged, to give a current to that water to the Mississippi river, to make the necessary drains and bridges; to repair the same, and put at all times the street practicable for the circulation of public vehicles.

"4. — Besides the cases explained in the foregoing articles, the streets in general shall be repaired and kept in a proper condition by the owners of the lots fronting on them, it being well understood that their neighbors opposite shall co-operate therein by equal portion should the case require it.

"5. — Lastly, the bridge on the little river, as well as all roads which are without the village, shall be made and kept in repairs by the public.

"Done and passed in the government hall, and in the presence of the lieutenant-governor who has signed with us the same day and year as above.

"PERRAULT, BRAZEAU, CERRÉ, RENE KIERCEREAU.
 his   his
JOSEPH x MAINVILLE,   JOSEPH x TAILLON,
 mark   mark
"AUG'T CHOUTEAU, CHAUVIN, FRAN'CO CRUZAT.

"We the undersigned, the sindics appointed by the assembly of the inhabitants which was held in the government hall on the 22nd of the month of September of this year, 1782, by Mr. Francisco Cruzat, lieutenant-colonel by brevet of infantry, commander-in-chief and lieutenant-governor of the western part and district of Illinois, for the purpose of establishing fixed and unalterable rules for the construction and keeping of the fences of the common of this village, being vested with the authority of the public who elected us to that effect, have in the said government hall, and in presence of the aforesaid Don Francisco Cruzat, on this 29th of the same month, agreed upon what follows, and to which every one shall regularly conform hereafter: —

"1st. — On the first day of every year there shall be publicly appointed in the government hall, in the presence of the lieutenant-governor, one sindic, and immediately after eight umpires, who shall make the first inspection of the fences of the common.

"2d. — The fences of the said common shall every year be made and perfected by the 15th day of April at farthest, and received the first Sunday after this date, by the eight umpires appointed as aforesaid.

"3rd. — The aforesaid umpires shall not receive the fences unless they are constructed in such a way that cattle shall not be able to get out of the common and go into the townfield of the inhabitants to injure them.

"4th. — It shall be the duty of the said eight umpires to render an account of their inspection of the enclosure to the sindic, who shall immediately name eight other umpires for the purpose of verifying the exactness or the negligence of the first ones, and should fences be found not to be in the condition requisite for their reception, and the first umpires had not reported them as such to the said sindic, each of them shall be condemned to pay a fine of ten livres.

"5th. — When it shall come to the knowledge of the sindic that any fence is not in the condition described in the third article of these regulations, it shall be his duty to inform thereof the owner of it, in order that without delay, he may make suitable repairs thereto; and should this latter, through caprice or otherwise neglect this just duty, the sindic shall cause it to be repaired at his expense.

"6th. — If the last one that shall have made the inspection of the fences, had not informed the sindic of the state in which he found them, and that within the interval of his inspection and that which is to follow, it was found that animals had got out and made some damage, he shall be bound to pay therefor; and should it happen that the sindic having been informed of the bad condition of the fences, had neglected to advise the owners thereof, then he shall be held accountable for the damage, and obliged to pay for it himself; likewise in the case the owners have been warned by the sindic to go and repair them, and they had not done it immediately, they shall be subjected to the same penalty.

"7th. — If during the time that animals had got out and done damage many fences were defective; in order to remedy the bad consequences that commonly result from such facts, it is enacted, that said damage shall be made good by those whose fences shall be defective; however, should it happen in the time between two inspections, the fences having (in the first inspection) been found in good order by the sindic or the persons appointed for those purposes, that animals had passed through some opening made by unknown malefactors, or through some unexpected event, then the damage shall remain to him who has sustained it.

" 8th. — If animals let loose are found in the fields without their owners having aided their egress from the commons, they shall not be obliged to pay for their arrest, nor held responsible for the damage, in case any has been done.

" 9th. — When it shall be proven that the keeper of the fence-gate, has by his neglect or otherwise, let pass through it animals of any kind, whatever, he shall be obliged to pay for the damage thus done.

" 10th. — So soon as the fences are received, it shall not be allowed to any one to cross over them, under penalty of a fine of ten livres for the first time, and of twenty-four for the second, with twenty-four hours imprisonment in the jail.

" 11th. — Malefactors caught in the act of making breaches in the fences, either to pass through themselves, or to cause animals to cross them, whatever may be their motive, shall be condemned, besides the damage done thereby, to pay a fine of fifty livres, and be imprisoned 15 days in the jail.

" 12th. — It is ordered to all who shall find any person committing the offense specified in the preceding article, to give most prompt information thereof to the lieutenant-governor, and to lead himself the offender to jail, if able to arrest him. But if any one through a mistaken indulgence or particular interest should not fulfill this duty, and it were proven that he told other persons of his having surprised somebody in this offense, he shall be reputed an abettor of the crime, condemned to pay the same fine and damage, and be subjected to the same penalty above mentioned.

" 13th. — The owners of fences shall be required to stamp them with their names in full, under the penalty of a fine of 15 livres.

" 14th. — The person who shall take a horse tied in the prairie to use it without the consent of the owner, shall be fined 25 livres, and imprisoned 24 hours; and should any accident befall the horse, he shall pay therefor according to the appraisement which shall be made.

" 15th. — If horses or animals tied in the prairie, breaking their ropes, should be taken in the fields, those who take them up shall require five 5 livres for each head, and the owner of the land upon which they are arrested, shall require the payment of the damages to be valued by umpires.

" 16th. — When it shall be proven that any person has taken away the rope of an animal tied in the prairie, he shall pay ten livres for it, besides the damages caused thereby according to the appraisement thereof by umpires.

" 17th. — It is forbidden to any person to tie horses or other animals upon the land of another person, without his special consent; should it be otherwise, the owner of the land may seize the animals and require from those to whom they belong five livres per head, and it shall be lawful for him to claim the damage in case any had been done.

" 18th. — When slaves shall be found to transgress any of the foregoing articles, their masters shall pay the fines, arrests and damages prescribed, and the above said slaves shall be punished by whipping, according to the gravity of the case.

" 19th. — All the fines shall be deposited with the sindic appointed by the lieutenant-governor from the two that are to be nominated yearly for the police and keeping of the village, and they shall revert to the public works of the community.

" Done and passed in the government hall in the presence of the aforesaid lieutenant-governor, who has signed with us the same day and year as above.

" PERRAULT, CERRÉ, RENÉ KIERCEREAUX, BRAZEAU,
   mark of   mark of
MR. JOSEPH x TAYON.   MR. JOSEPH x MAINVILLE.
CHAUVIN,   AUG'TE CHOUTEAU,   FRAN'CO CRUZAT.

CHARLES GRATIOT.

During the progress of the American revolution, the country, as all well know, had become flooded with continental scrip which had so depreciated as to be almost worthless, and of which Mr. Gratiot possessed a large amount, which as an enthusiastic American he had cheerfully accepted from the American officers in Illinois, having unbounded confidence in its ultimate redemption. After some unsuccessful endeavors to collect a portion of his claims through the agency of others, Mr. Gratiot, in the the spring of 1783, hostilities between the United States and Great Britain having ceased, and negotiations for peace then pending, thinking he might realize at least a portion of his claims on Virginia if he presented them in person, set out on horseback, the only mode of locomotion at that day in the wild west, and after a journey of 1,500 miles through the almost trackless wilds of Illinois, Kentucky and West Virginia, arrived in safety at Richmond, the then new capital of Virginia, being the first actual resident of St. Louis that ever up to that time had made the journey.

After an absence of over a year, in which he made the personal acquaintance of Patrick Henry, Thos. Jefferson and other Revolutionary worthies of the day, he got home to St. Louis late in June, 1784, unsuccessful, however, in the object for which he undertook his long and hazardous journey, the exchequers of the United States and Virginia being then exhausted.

I append here the action of the Virginia authorities on two or three of his claims, found among his papers, as curious documents, exhibiting the spirit of the times :—

"FORT PATRICK HENRY, IN THE ILLINOIS, 11th Aug., 1779.
"Exchange 405 2/3 Dolls., No. 151.

"On sight of this my first of exchange (the second of the same tenor and date not paid), please pay Mr. Joseph Anderson, or order, the sum of four hundred and five dollars and two-thirds, it being his pay for going express from Kaskaskias to Kentucky, and for sundry articles lost, provisions furnished for himself and comrade as per account to me rendered, with or without advice from, sir,
"Your most obedient humble servant,
"*To the Treasurer of Virginia.* WM. SHANNON,
Comdr.-General, etc.

INDORSED.

AUGUST 12th, 1779.
"Received of Capt. Helm, the amount of the within bills in cash on behalf of the State.
"JOSEPH ANDERSON."

"I do assign the within to Mr. Josh. Andrews; it being for value received.
"LEONARD HELM."

"I do assign the within to Pierre Mallet, June 10, 1780.
"JOSEPH ANDRÉ."

"I do assign the within to Charles Gratiot, June 10, 1780.
"PIERRE MALLET."

"On this day, being the tenth day of July, in the year of our Lord one thousand seven hundred and eighty-three, I John Beckley, mayor of the city of Richmond, in the Commonwealth of Virginia (there being no notary public in said Commonwealth), at the request of Charles Gratiot aforesaid, did exhibit the original of which the above bill of exchange is a true copy, to the treasurer aforesaid, on whom the same is drawn, and demanded payment thereof; whereunto the said treasurer gave for answer that he would only pay twenty pounds * for the same, which was refused by the said Charles Gratiot.

"Therefore, I the said Mayor, do hereby at the request of Charles Gratiot aforesaid, solemnly protest against the drawer of said bill, and against all other persons concerned, for all change, exchange, reexchange, costs, interest and damages suffered and to be suffered for want of payment of the said bill. This done and protested in the said city of Richmond on the day, month and year aforesaid. In testimony whereof I have caused the seal of said city of Richmond to be hereunto affixed.

"JOHN BECKLEY, *Mayor.*"

"Received of Joseph André twelve bottles taffia, at different times, for the use of friendly Indians, two bushels of corn, one hog. Fort Patrick Henry, May 20, 1780.

"VAL'E THOS. DALTON, *Dep. Indian Agent.*"

THE STATE OF VIRGINIA.

"12 bottles taffia .... 20 dollars, 240
2 bushels corn............................ 10
1 hog.. 30   280 dollars."

INDORSATIONS.

"I assign the within to Pierre Mallet, June 10th, 1780.
"JOSEPH ANDRE."

"I assign the within to Charles Gratiot, June 10, 1780.
"PIERRE MALLET."

---

* 20 pounds Virginia currency $66.67.

"On this day, being the tenth day of July, in the year of our Lord, one thousand seven hundred and eighty-three, I, John Beckley, Mayor of the City of Richmond, in the Commonwealth of Virginia (there being no notary public in said Commonwealth of Virginia), at the request of Charles Gratiot, aforesaid, did exhibit the original of which the above certificate is a true copy, to the auditors of public accounts of the Commonwealth of Virginia, who by the laws of the said Commonwealth are authorized to liquidate and pay all claims and demands whatsoever against the said Commonwealth, and demanded payment of the same, whereunto the said auditors gave for answer that they would only pay seventeen pounds ten shillings for the same, which was refused by the said Charles Gratiot. Therefore, I, the said Mayor, do hereby, at the request aforesaid, solemnly protest against the drawer of the said certificate and against all other persons concerned, for all change, exchange, re-exchange, cost, interest and damages suffered and to be suffered for want payment of the said certificate.

"This done and protested in the City of Richmond the day, month and year aforesaid. In testimony whereof I have caused the seal of the said City of Richmond to be hereunto affixed.

(SEAL)
       "JOHN BECKLEY, *Mayor*."

"The State of Virginia, Dr. to Joseph André. Provisions found four Delaware chiefs four days, two dollars each, thirty-two dollars, being in council at St. Vincents, April 5, 1780.

I do certify the above to be true.
      "VAL'E THOS. DALTON, *Dep. I. A.*

"Indorsations : —
"I assign the within to Pierre Mallet, June 10, 1780.
      "JOSEPH ANDRÉ.
"I assign the within to Charles Gratiot, June 10, 1780.
      "PIERRE MALLET."

"On this day, being the tenth day of July, in the year of our Lord, one thousand seven hundred and eighty-three, I, John Beckley, Mayor of the City of Richmond, in the Commonwealth of Virginia (there being no notary public in said Commonwealth), at the request of Charles Gratiot, aforesaid, did exhibit the original, of which the above certificate is a true copy, to the auditors of public accounts of the Commonwealth of Virginia, who, by the laws of the said Commonwealth, are authorized to liquidate and pay all claims and demands whatsoever against the said Commonwealth, and demanded payment of the same, whereunto the said auditors gave for answer that they would only pay three pounds for the same, which was refused by the said Charles Gratiot. Therefore, I, the said Mayor, do hereby, at the request of the aforesaid, solemnly protest against the drawer of the said certificate and against all other persons concerned, for all change, exchange, re-exchange, costs, interests and damages suffered and to be suffered for want of payment of the said certificate. Thus done and protested in the said City of Richmond, the day, month and year aforesaid. In testimony whereof I have caused the seal of the said City of Richmond to be thereunto affixed.

"JOHN BECKLEY, *Mayor.*"

[SEAL]

During his stay at Richmond Mr. Gratiot effected an arrangement with the Virginia authorities respecting aportion of his claims, for which they agreed to give him lands in Kentucky so soon as land offices were established and lands surveyed, but I believe he never realized anything from them.

1784. — The annual floods of the Mississippi and Missouri Rivers usually occur at different periods in the spring of the year, that from the Missouri the earliest. In the early summer of 1784 they occurred at the same time. The combined waters of the two rivers caused a destructive inundation at all points below their junction. As this was the first occurrence of this nature noticed in the experience of our earliest settlers, it became a noted epoch in its annals, and the year 1784 was always from that period designated by the French inhabitants "l'année des grands eaux," the year of the great waters.

The original village of Ste. Genevieve on the flat near the river, a couple of miles below the present one, was swept away entirely, the present town of Ste. Genevieve dating from the year 1785. By marks kept at Ste. Genevieve and Kaskaskia the flood of 1844 rose some four feet above that of 1785.

Nicholas Francis Guion, a blacksmith, had his shop on the north half of block No. 14 in 1769, and kept it there for a number of years, the farthest house at the north end of the village. He died up the Mississippi River in 1784. The inventory of his estate was taken by Governor Cruzat on December 4, 1784, at the house of his friend and neighbor, Jno. Bap. Ortes, the carpenter, viz: —

Personal effects	459 livres.
Magdalena, 31 years, an Indian Slave	600 "
Alexis, 10 " do.	400 "
Joseph, 4 or 5 " do.	150 "
Amable, 2 " do.	80 "
A trunk with a plated cross,	5 "
A receipt of Joseph Viez for	100 "
	Total livres 1794.

Emilien Yosti,
Joseph Mainville, } *Appraisers.*
Luke Marly,   Francisco Cruzat.

He had disposed of his house, which is not on record.

SUIT AGAINST ISABEL BISSETTE VACHARD.

"Marie Cardinal, the widow of Jean M. Cardinal, murdered by the British Indians, May 26th, 1780, having a family of seven children, petitions your Excellency for an inventory of the property of her deceased husband's estate, to enable her to dispose of the same, &c.," viz. : —

Valuation personal effects	510 livres.
A pair of oxen	500 "
A cow	200 "
A horse	150 "
A mare and colt	300 "
	Total 1660.

By Louis Potier & Nicholas Hebert, } *Appraisers.*

Aug. 2, 1784.

Approved,
Fran'co Cruzat.

1784. — Action against Isabel Bissette Vachard, wife of Louis Vachard *dit* Lardoise, of St. Louis, on the complaint of Datchurut, Jno. B. Valle and Louis Bolduc of St. Genevieve, made Dec'r 11, 1783 to Don Silvio Francisco de Cartabona Lieut. and acting judge at St. Genevieve, for a violation of the laws, in this, in bringing in her boat from St. Louis to the salt works of Datchurut & Vallé, near St. Genevieve, articles of clothing and dry goods, which she traded off to slaves and others, for salt, corn, meal, grain, &c., to the manifest injury of these parties, in causing the slaves to steal from their owners, and in some instances to run off to avoid punishment.

Dec. 11, 1783. Affidavit of Jno. B. Racine, taken before Cartabona in St. Genevieve.

" 12. do. of Alexis Griffard, the boss at the Salt Works, do., establishing the facts set out in the declaration of the plaintiffs.

" 18 & 19. Affidavits of parties in St. Louis, confirming the above. Her boat and cargo were seized and confiscated, and sold at public sale at St. Louis, and the proceeds held by the governor, awaiting the issue of the suit, as to the claims of parties in St. Louis (ladies), who owned a part of the goods.

"1784, March 24. The prosecutors at St. Genevieve above named, considering her ignorance of the laws, the standing of herself, relatives and connections in St. Louis, relinquished their claims on her for indemnity for their losses, requiring her to pay all costs of the suit, and refund the amounts some of them had expended in the prosecution.

"Gov. Cruzat presented his general account of costs, &c. :
March 23. Amount realized from the sale   1095 reals of 12½c. 136.87½

	"	Paid Demers, constable, services at sale	21 reals.	2.62¼	
April 4.		" costs at St. Genevieve papers, &c., &c.	85 "	10.62½	
" 19.		" to Charles Vallé exps. to & from St. Louis	272 "	34.	
May 3.		" affidavits, papers, &c. &c. at St. Louis	185 "	23.12½	
			563	70.37½	
" 3.		Balance returned to Isabella Bissette	532	66.50	

1785. — A Joseph Verdon, a cabinet maker and turner, had married Victoire Richelit, widow of a Jean Soyé, at Point Coupée, Louisiana, about the year 1773. They came up to St. Louis, and both being industrious and frugal they prospered in the world, and in 1783 bought a lot with a small house on the east side Main, below our present Myrtle Street; but notwithstanding their thrift, it appears that their tempers not being congenial they kept matters pretty lively at home with continual bickerings and quarrels for a period of twelve years, during which they became the parents of five children, when they held a council of war and decided that "for the salvation of their souls" they had better live apart the balance of their days; and as divorces were not countenanced in the Catholic church, they repaired to the governor's office and there entered into the following agreement: —

Copied *verbatim* from the English translation in the archives: —

"In the year one thousand seven hundred and eighty-five, the seventh of the month of March, before noon, before me, Francis Cruzat, commander and lieutenant-governor of the western part of Illinois, personally appeared Joseph Verdon, an inhabitant of this post, and Marianne Richelet his wife, who declare that after twelve years of marriage, not being able to sympathize together, and wishing to put an end to their disagreements, have *unanimously resolved* of their own free will to contract by these presents an act of separation, hoping by this means to ensure the safety of their souls which each appears to desire, not being able to do so on account of their continual quarrels in their conjugal state; for these reasons they have consented, covenanted and agreed between themselves that Marianne Richelet, wife of the said Joseph Verdon, her heirs or legal representatives, shall remain in peaceable possession and hold all the goods, real and personal, which they this day own, and which they jointly acquired during their marriage; the said Verdon being bound not to trouble her nor make any demand for a division, withdrawing only the following articles, viz.: his gun, bed, clothes, two axes, and all implements of turner and cabinet maker, these being indispensably necessary to him. And the said Marianne Richelet binds herself from this day to pay all the debts they may have contracted while living together, and should there be any hereafter unknown to her, they will be on account of the said Verdon individually. Each renouncing all the rights and goods which may accrue to them individually, they cannot compel each the other to furnish any pecuniary assistance for the future, and as the said Richelet by these presents finds herself in possession of all the property, the said Verdon will be entirely released, and without being held to any examination, from the dower which he acknowledged in the marriage by and before Don Balthazar de Villiers, commander at the time at Pointe Coupée.

"As regards the children, the issue of said marriage, they being four in number, two male and two female, the parties have agreed that they shall remain under the care and charge of the said Richelet, their mother, who binds herself to take charge of them, and raise them in honor and in the fear of God.

"Thus it has been covenanted and agreed in the government hall in St. Louis, in Illinois, the same day and year as above, in presence of Mariano Izaguire and Josef Bermeo, attending witnesses, the parties declaring they knew not how to write.

her   his
"Marianne x Richelet,   Joseph x Verdon, Josef Bermeo,
mark.   mark.
"Mariano Izaguire.   Francisco Cruzat."

After the abdication of old Joe Verdon, and he had retired to the privacy of his turner and cabinet shop, his better half, who had always bossed the concern, although uneducated, yet was a strong-minded and self-willed woman, learnt to scratch her name in regal style, "La Verdun," and made an occasional trading voyage by boat to Ste. Genevieve and Kaskaskia with merchandise, and bringing back in return salt and other products, by which she acquired a snug little sum. She died in 1796, having named in her will Auguste Chouteau for her executor, who settled her estate in 1797, dividing it between her sons and daughters. Her second daughter, Victoire, was married to Joseph Charleville, from whom there are many descendants now living. Old Joseph V. died in 1813, his age said to be ninety-five years.

1786. — This year brought to St. Louis the first Episcopalian family that settled in the place, that of the Rev. Ichabod Camp. He was a clergyman, born in Connecticut in 1726, went to England expressly to be ordained, which could only be done by a bishop, and there was none at that early day in America. He was made a priest in March, 1752, at the age of twenty-six, by the Bishop of Lincoln at Westminster, London, and on his return home to America officiated for nine years in his native State.

In 1761 he removed with his family to Lunenberg County, Virginia, and the next year, 1762, to Amherst County, where he had a very extensive parish and where he lived for eighteen years. In 1779 he left Virginia with several other families coming out west, and settled in Kaskaskia May 1st of that year. In this place his third daughter, Catherine, was married to Jno. B. Guion, a Canadian Frenchman, in 1785.

This Guion, a passionate man and inclined to drink, treated her so unkindly that she left his house and sought shelter at her father's. This incensed Guion, and one night while somewhat in liquor he went there to force her away, and while the old gentleman stood at the door remonstrating with his son-in-law, Guion drew his pistol, while crazy with passion, and shot him. He died immediately, April 20, 1786, and was buried in Kaskaskia.

A short time before this sad affair Stella Camp, the second daughter, had married Antoine Reilhe, an European French gentleman of St. Louis, and with them Mrs. Camp and her three other daughters removed over to this place, arriving here May 15, 1786.

Guion does not appear to have been prosecuted for this murder, but died soon after this occurrence.

Gov. Cruzat met with several severe family afflictions during his residence in St. Louis in the loss of his wife and three children.

First, a son, Francis Xavier, on Sept. 22, 1775.

Second, a daughter, Josette, Oct. 12, 1784, aged four years.

Third, another daughter, young, Feb. 1, 1786.

Fourth, and greatest, his wife, April 15, 1786.

The record of her interment is found in the parish church register as follows: —

"April 15, 1786, under the first bench of the main aisle, against the balustrade along side of the sacristie, I have interred the body of Madame Nicanora Ramos, consort of Don Francisco Cruzat, lieutenant-colonel, captain of grenadiers, and commandant of the Illinois, with the sacraments of our holy mother Church.

"FATHER BERNARD, *Curate.*"

Accidental killing of Mrs. Chouteau's negro man, Batiste, on the evening of Dec. 27, 1785.

Doctor Reynal's inquest on the body:—

"I, Antoine Reynal, surgeon, residing in this post of St. Louis, in obedience to the orders of Governor Cruzat, went on the 27th December, 1785, after eight o'clock in the evening, to the Barn lot of Mrs. Chouteau, on the hill in rear of this village. There we found a negro lying dead on his back, on the ground in front of the door of the barn, head to the east, feet west. He had been killed by a ball from a gun, which had gone through his body and lungs, from one side to the other, which must have caused his immediate death.

"DEC. 28, 1785.
"REYNAL, *Surgeon.*"

"To *Governor Francisco Cruzat, Sir:*

Marie Therese, widow Chouteau, takes the liberty of informing you, sir, that on the evening of the 27th, at about 8 o'clock in the evening, her negro man Baptiste discovered the runaway Indian slaves, who had fled from the village some time ago, on the hill of Barns in rear of the village. He spoke to them, and by some pretext kept them there until he came and apprised Mr. Papin, whose slave was one of them, and that no time was to be lost, if he desired to catch him, and told him where they were. Mr. Papin, without giving him time to run and get permission from his mistress, gave him a bottle of rum, and sent him back to the place he left, and by giving them drink to try to detain them until he, Papin, could get the assistance necessary to come and arrest them. He got together a few without loss of time, and arrived on the ground but a very short time after the negro Batiste. I do not know if the slaves made any movement to escape, but in a moment several gun shots were fired by Mr. Papin's party, which unfortunately killed the negro of your petitioner.

"As Mr. Papin acted so very hastily and inconsiderately in in this matter, not appearing to reflect on the danger to which he exposed my negro man between his party and the runaways, and was the occasion of his death, in sending him on his dangerous expedition without my knowledge or permission, I ask your authority that I be paid for his loss. His services were invaluable to me, sir; his good qualities, ability, his attachment to the family, the care he continually took of my interests, not only in his own work, but overlooking the others, so that I could safely trust him with the management of all my slaves, in the flower of his age, no money can remunerate me for his loss. And as my demand is based on the laws, which forbid the employment of a slave unless with the knowledge and consent of the owner, you will compel the said Papin to pay me the sum of *$1,000* dollars, which, considering his great value to me, will be but small remuneration for my loss.

"DEC. 29, 1785.

"VEUVE CHOUTEAU."

Joseph M. Papin, in his reply to the foregoing, addressed to the governor, January 5, 1786, gives a long history of the affair, filling six pages of large fools-cap closely written. I give a condensation. He says:—

"'*His mother-in-law's negro man*,' was killed in a contest sanctioned by the authorities, and supported with zeal by the soldiers and militia, occasioned by the unexpected appearance of two runaway slaves, and then claims from *him* remuneration as being the author of the affair," and then goes on to give his version as follows: "Eight free Indians, former slaves, deserted from this post after robbing their former masters of horses, guns, blankets and ammunition, taking with them several negro slaves, and from appearances setting on fire two or three places, with a view of destroying the village. After a month's absence, pillaging an American and his wife on the waters of the Meramec, and others, subjects of the King, and murdering another in that section, four of them left the others in their place of concealment, and came near our village to try and persuade some female slaves to abscond with them. Two of these went to the village of the "*little hills*" (St. Charles), where the people having received some intimation of their visit, one was captured, the other, however escaped. The prisoner, brought here and questioned by the governor stated that they were to slip into the village, favored by the darkness, and come to my lot. Being present at this avowal, I received orders to go to my house and take the necessary steps and precautions to capture these assassins by the assistance of such of my circumjacent neighbors as I might select, and place them under my command at such points on my lot as to ensure their capture. Hardly had I executed this order when my mother-in-law's negro arrived in hot haste, to apprise me 'that two of the runaway slaves were at his mistress' barn, that he had come for a bottle of rum to keep them there while I took the measures necessary to cut off their retreat and capture them.' Not relying solely on my own judgment in the matter, and always ready to be guided by superior knowledge, I availed myself of the brief interval to send word to the governor of what had transpired. I sent my brother-in-law Labbadie, who seconded me in these operations, to inform our lieutenant-governor of the steps I had taken, and for reinforcements, to run less risks, and by our numbers compel them to surrender. This he did, he immediately sent from his company two detachments, one around the fort by a passage through which the slaves might have escaped, the other near to me, to act in concert with me. As time pressed I lost not a moment. After instructing all not to fire unless in defense of his own person, I divided my band of soldiers and militia into two equal parts, each to take a separate road so as to surround easily the spot where the criminals were. Reaching the place of the combat, after repeating the injunction not to fire, I sprung into the quarry with a brave militiaman who would follow me, when we were immediately assaulted, not only by our enemies in front, but by a general discharge of gun shots on both sides by our own people.

"Preserved, both of us, by a Providence who watched over our days, it was only the unfortunate negro who received his death by a chance ball, without the satisfaction of witnessing the glorious end of the action.

"After having exposed myself to the greatest danger for a matter of public concern, acting only by express orders, would it be just that the whole burden should fall on me, and that I should be compelled to pay for the negro who volunteered himself, and when I had a right to command, etc., etc., etc.

"JOS. M. PAPIN."

Inquiry — In this village of St. Louis of Illinois, this ninth day of January, 1786, in view of the petition presented by Dona Maria Teresa, widow of Mr. Chouteau, demanding payment from J. Marie Papin for a negro named Baptista who was killed at the time of the apprehension of the Indian criminals now imprisoned in the common jail of this village, and the answer in reply and declaration of Mr. J. M. Papin in his defense to the petition of said Mad'e Chouteau, and for a clear understanding of the matter, we have taken the necessary depositions of the parties to, and witnesses of the affair, in manner and form as follows, in the presence of Sergeant Fernando Lisoro and Corporal Mariano Izaguire, assistant witnesses, for the purpose, who with myself the governor have signed the same.

"FERNANDO LISORE, MARIANO IZAGUIRE, FRANC'O CRUZAT.

"On the day, month and year as above, personally appeared before me, the Lieut.-Governor, 1st. Pedro Torrico, a soldier of this garrison, who being duly sworn, by making the sign of the cross with his upraised right hand, in response to questions propounded to him, deposed as follows, viz. :

"Was born in Belme, Jaen, Spain — a Roman Catholic — and a soldier of the Stationary Regiment of Infantry of Louisiana, and 34 years of age. On the day named, Decr. 27, 1785, was in the Commandant's house, when Mr. Silvestre Labbadie came to ask for aid necessary to apprehend two fugitive Indians, discovered lurking at the barn or stable of Madame Chouteau — in consequence

KILLING OF BATISTE.

the Lieut.-Governor directed the deponent to go to the soldiers' quarters, and take five men and a corporal and hasten with them to a deep trench or hollow near the said barn to prevent the escape of said Indians and apprehend them if possible. Knows but little of what occurred during the capture of the said Indians, being stationed in the hollow, only on hearing a tumult of voices and gunshots he and his men flew immediately towards the spot where they encountered them, bound and secured them, and marched them to the public jail of the village, and soon afterwards your deponent heard it said, that a negro man had been killed in the tumult. Does not know who took the Indians — in the darkness of the night, objects could hardly be distinguished, but it was understood by Mr. J. M. Papin, Mr. Silvestre Labbadie, Mr. Charles Tayon, and the soldiers Juan Antonio Dias and Francisco Bonda.

"Pedro x Torrico.
his mark.

" 2nd. Juan Antonio Dias, soldier, sworn in like manner, deposed :

" Was born in the town of Lugo, Gallicia, Spain, Roman Catholic, age 24 years. On the day cited, at seven o'clock at night, was named by first Sergeant Fernando Lisore to aid in apprehending two Indians discovered furtively secreted in the barn or stable of Mad'e Chouteau by the orders of Don Silvestre Labbadie. Issuing from our quarters with said Don Silvestre Labbadie, he conducted us to the house of Don J. M. Papin, where the deponent with Francisco Bende, Don J. M. Papin, Don Silvestre Labbadie, Don Carlos Tayon, a servant and the negro Baptiste, were detached by the direct street to said barn or stable of Mad'e Chouteau, and the soldiers Joachin de Roxas and Phe. Menzedes with two militia men not known to your deponent, by another route, so that all being near the said barn, one party on the one side, and the other party on the other side to prevent their escape, and reached the place in this order: Baptiste entered the barn, followed immediately by Don Carlos Tayon with his gun levelled and fired, but no one issued at the shot, and immediately there jumped into the barn Don Silves. Labbadie, J. M. Papin, and the other Frenchman, discharging their firelocks at same time, and at the same instant one of the Indians darted out to escape, and the soldier Menzedes discharged his gun at him, and the deponent and his companion took him prisoner. The deponent close to the others in the operation understood it said in Charles Tayon's stable, that the shot was fired by Mr. Papin involuntarily. The deponent heard a shot, not knowing who fired it, as the said Tayon crept towards the Indian with the intention of seizing him by the hair. The deponent with Francis Bende bound him securely. Soon afterwards a soldier came who stated that the negro had just expired from the shot received at the encounter at the stable. The affair terminated by conducting the prisoners to the public jail of the village where they were incarcerated, and have nothing further to add.

his
JUAN ANTOINE x DIAS.
mark.

"3rd. Francis Bende, soldier, sworn in like manner deposes:
"Was born in the village of Ginamar, Grand Canary Isle, aged 28 years; his testimony in substance same as Dias, but more brief; assisted in capturing the two Indians and in conducting them to prison and only learnt of the death of the negro on his return to quarters.

"*4th. Phe. Menzedes*, soldier, sworn as the others, was born at Abulo, Isle of Gomana, Canaries, a Catholic, and thirty years of age: —

"On the day designated, was ordered by Sergeant Lisoro at 7 o'clock, p. m., with three other soldiers to assist in apprehending the runaway Indians. Marched from their quarters, conducted by Mr. Labbadie to the house of Mr. Papin. Word being given in a loud voice, heard by all, that the time had arrived, we sallied out from Mr. Papin's, divided by our corporal into two parties, one party to go direct to the barn, and the other, myself and comrade, Rosas, with two militia men, whose names I did not know, to take the road that led to the back part to prevent their escape that way, and be there at the same moment. Having just made that disposition, he heard a discharge of fire-arms from the opposite party without knowing the cause, immediately after the discharge, one of the Indians, endeavoring to escape close by us, we seized him, put him in the barn and then, having captured the other, bound them and conducted them to the village jail. Is ignorant of Mr. Papin's instructions to the negro when he gave him the brandy, and knows nothing of the killing of the negro by some of the other party, only learnt after their return to quarters that the negro had been killed.

his
" PHE. x MENZEDES.
mark.

" 5th. *Joachim de Rosas*, soldier, sworn in like manner, born at Tagonana, Isle of Teneriffe, Roman Catholic, thirty years of age. Testified in substance as the preceding, but a little more at length, and only learnt of the negro's death after their return to quarters.

his
" JOACHIM x DE ROSAS.
mark.

" 6th. Mr. Silvester Labbadie, duly sworn, testified: —

" Am a native of Vigonia, in France, a Roman Catholic, married, and a merchant. On the aforesaid day solicited aid from the Lieut.-Governor to more surely apprehend the runaway Indians. A corporal and ten men were detailed for the purpose, instructed to proceed at once to the duty. Having started with four of the soldiers went direct to the house of Jos. M. Papin, where the negro, Baptiste, of Mrs. Chouteau came and notified us that it was now time. The deponent set out at once from the house with his company divided into two portions, one through the lane leading direct to said barn, the other for the back part so that none might escape. Being prepared, Mr. Papin and Mr. Tayon advanced together with the deponent and a servant man of said Papin and entered the barn. The Indians, perceiving this, sprang up, and one not able to gain his gun, tried to defend himself by blows, in the interval the deponent, by the light of a flash from the priming of a gun, was able to see, without knowing by whom the shot was fired, in a moment after a discharge of fire-arms took place, ignorant by whom they were fired, the deponent had no other weapon with which to defend himself than a sword. In this discharge the negro, Baptiste, was shot dead and one of the Indians wounded. They were immediately bound and conducted and deposited in the prison of the village. Saw the negro lying dead at the door of the barn. Does not know who killed him, nor who first discovered him.

SILVESTER LABBADIE.

"7th. Charles Tayon, duly sworn, testified:—

"Born at Fort Chartres, eastern part of the Illinois, is 26 years of age, married, a farmer, and Second Lieut. of the militia of the Post.

"On the day named Mr. J. M. Papin came to my house, with the commandant's orders and auxilliaries, to apprehend an Indian fugitive who had appeared at the Barn of Madame Chouteau. Mr. Papin's negro man having notified us that the time had arrived, we at once set out on the march in two parties, to be on opposite sides at the ground, so that neither could escape. The deponent anticipating formidable and violent resistance, offered to Mr. Papin to go with his servant man and a soldier stealthily in the darkness, and suddenly spring upon them in the Barn before they could prepare to resist. Thus accompanied he entered the Barn suddenly, and found himself a lone between the two Indians, one of whom sprang out of the door; in a moment's time two shots were fired from in front of the Barn door to stop him, which killed the negro.

"The deponent cannot say with truth who is at fault, nor who fired the two shots that opportunely prevented their escape. He came solely to assist in apprehending the Indian slave of Mr. Papin, with no power but to aid Mr. Papin, whose life would have been in danger from these Barbarians, who violently pushing aside the deponent, got out of the door of the Barn, where being met by Mr. Labbadie one was thrown down and held by him while calling for help for fear he would be assassinated, when in a moment's time your deponent and one of the soldiers jumped upon him, bound him, and together brought him to the public prison of the village.

"CHARLES TAYON."

"*Appraisement.* — In the village of St. Louis, July 13, 1786, before me, the lieutenant-governor, the undersigned selected to carefully consider and correctly appraise the qualities, intelligence and value of Mrs. Chouteau's negro man, Baptiste, who was killed in the affair of the capture of the Indian slaves discovered in the barn of said Mrs. Chouteau, unanimously appraise him at the value of six hundred silver dollars, as a full compensation for his loss.

" CERRÉ, DUBREUIL, CHAS. SANGUINET.

"*Decision.* — In virtue of the action had in this suit, I pass it over to the Superior Tribunal at the capital for examination and final decision.

" Awaiting this the constable of the village will notify the parties.

" ST. LOUIS, Jany. 14, 1786.

" FRANCISCO CRUZAT.

"*Final Decree.* — Considering the payment to be made by the owners named in the suit of the Indian runaways belonging to several inhabitants of the district of St. Louis, of Illinois, to Madame Chouteau, for the negro man named Baptiste belonging to her, who was killed in the expedition to capture said Indian runaways, the same is approved.

" NEW ORLEANS, July 31, 1786.

" ESTEVAN MIRO, Govr.-Genl.

" Before me, Fernando Rodriques.

"*Assessment.* — In this village of St. Louis, of Illinois, the fourth day of May, 1787, I, Francisco Cruzat, commandant and lieutenant-governor of this western part of the district of Illinois, in default of a notary, personally appeared before me in the hall of this government, Senors J. Marie Papin, Silvestre Labbadie, Alexis Marie, Antoine Vincent, Charles Vallé, Genevieve Rouquier, widow of Louis Bissonet, dec'd, and Marie Therese Bourgeois, widow of Auguste Chouteau, deceased, all owners of the Indians mentioned in the suit against them. And the judgment against them by Senor Don Estevan Miro, colonel of the regiment of Louisiana, and governor and inspector-general of this province of Louisiana, with the opinion of his legal counsellor being read to them, to the end that being informed of its contents, they may not plead ignorance, but conform strictly thereto, which they have acquiesced in, and with me, the governor, have signed the same, except those who could not write, who have signed with their accustomed cross, the day and year above.

"J. M. PAPIN, SIL LABBADIE, ALEXIS MARIE, ANTOINE VINCENT,
      her   his
"GENEVIEVE x ROUQUIER, CARLOS x VALLÉ,
     mark   mark
"MARIE THERESE CHOUTEAU.   FRANCISCO CRUZAT.

"*Finale* — I, Marie Therese Bourgeois, resident of this village, and widow of the deceased Auguste Chouteau, formerly of New Orleans, have received of Senor Don Francisco Cruzat, commandant and lieutenant-governor of this western part of the district of the Illinois, the sum of six hundred dollars of silver, value of my negro named Baptiste, who was killed in the expedition against the runaway Indians who belonged to differennt inhabitants of this village, being the amounts paid by the several owners of these runaway Indians, in conformity to the mandate of Senor Don Estevan Miro, colonel and governor-general of this province of Louisiana, in his decree issued July 31, 1786, in accordance with the opinion of his legal counsellor. St. Louis, May 15, 1787.
        MARIE THERESE, VEUVE CHOUTEAU.
"JOSEPH BERMEO,
"MARIANO IZAGUIRE, Witnesses."

This affair was one of absorbing interest to the inhabitants of our little community, furnishing the gossips of the day a fruitful topic to engage their attention for the whole period of 16 months that the affair was before the public, from the date of the killing of the negro, Dec. 27, 1785, to its grand *Finale* May 15, 1787. Not so much from the death of the negro itself, for that was a circumstance of minor importance at that day, as from the high social position that all concerned in it occupied in the community, being of the "*elite*" of the village, the three most conspicuous parties being "*son-in-law, brother-in-law and mother-in-law,*" a fact which Mr. Papin in his elaborate defense took especial care to allude to in a somewhat sarcastic manner.

In its military aspect it was a complete burlesque on military stratagem; the three commanders, after first holding a council of war, and deciding upon the safest plan of capturing the enemy — two runaway Indian slaves — in his stronghold, Mrs. Chouteau's barn, backed by ten regular soldiers and some militiamen, divided into three detachments to surround him and prevent his escape, rushed upon and captured him with the loss of but one life, the poor negro messenger, who died, in the expressive language of Mr. P., "without the satisfaction of witnessing the glorious end of the action."

SALE OF A HOUSE IN MARSEILLES.

"In this town of St. Louis in Illinois, the thirtieth of the month of July, in the year one thousand seven hundred and eighty-seven, in default of a Notary public, before me, Don Francisco Cruzat, commander and Lieutenant-Governor of this western part and district of Illinois, province of Louisiana, and in presence of the undersigned witnesses, hereinafter named, personally appeared John Baptist Ferret, a trader with the Indians, residing in this post of St. Louis, who has sold, ceded, relinquished and transferred, now and forever, and in perpetuity under title of a simple and irrevocable sale to Jno. Joseph Motard, merchant of the town, here present and accepting, a four-story house, such as it stands, situated in the City of Marseilles, in the quarter of St. John on the harbour, being at the corner of the street, Notre Dame de la Nativité (our lady of the nativity), bounded east by the Port, south by the house of Francis Ronstant, north by "Notre Dame" Street, and to the west by "la place St. Jean" (St. John's Square), the said house being at present occupied by John Baptist Ferret and his wife, father and mother of the vendor, the said property having been given to him by the will of Rose, widow of Antoine Dominique, his maternal grandmother; this house thus sold, is released and free of all rights, seignories and other incumbrances whatever.

"The said sale is made for the consideration of the sum of twenty thousand livres, which the vendor acknowledges to have received from the purchaser in current money of this place, for which he is released and discharged; and in virtue thereof the said Ferre- has abandoned the said house in favour of the said Motard, transferring to him all his rights of property and possession, maintaining it to him against all persons; and as guarantie for the said sale, the said Ferret binds all his goods actual and future, as the parties have agreed. Done and executed in my government, in presence of Don Antoine Bonnemain, merchant, and Jean Pierre Pourcelly, master baker, in the said place, who with the parties and myself the Lieut.-Governor above named have signed.

"JNO. B. FERRET, J. MOTARD, BONNEMAIN, JEAN P. POURCELLY,
FRANC'O CRUZAT.

A fatality appears to have attended the families of our three first Spanish governors while in the place: —

Gov. Piernas, the first, lost two children in his five years.

Gov. Cruzat, second, three children and wife.

GOVERNMENT HOUSE, 1765.
[*Drawn by C. Heberer under direction of F. L. Billon.*]

THE GOVERNMENT HOUSE.   245

Gov. De Leyba, third, his wife and himself.

In the year 1783 the old Laclede mansion, the upper part of which had been occupied by the successive governors as their private residence and government hall, from its ruinous condition being no longer tenantable, Governor Cruzat purchased from Jno. B. Martigny his stone house diagonally opposite, at the southeast corner of Main and Walnut, for his residence and government business. It was a large, well-built house for the times, 40 feet front on Main Street by 25 deep, and divided into four rooms.

This house he occupied for the last four years of his residence here, disposing of it to Auguste Chouteau when about to leave the country at the close of his administration, November 27, 1787. After which it continued to be occupied as the Government Mansion during the remaining portion of the Spanish Domination.

CAPT. EMANUEL PEREZ

Succeeded Francisco Cruzat as lieutenant-governor of this upper part of the province on November 27, 1787, appointed by Governor-General Miro. Of his personal history we find nothing more in our archives than that he was a captain in the stationary regiment of Louisiana when appointed, and after his return to New Orleans at the close of his governorship in 1792, he was promoted to the rank of Lieut.-Col.-Major of New Orleans for his Majesty. His administration of four years and eight months was an uneventful one in our annals, furnishing us but little, if anything, of sufficient general interest to require any especial notice.

LIEUT. DE ORO.

In 1774, Lieut. Antonio de Oro was ordered from St. Louis to Ste. Genevieve, where and around about he was stationed for some twelve or thirteen years, until he had risen to the rank of captain. He died in August, 1787. An inventory of his effects was taken by order of the lieutenant-governor, Perez, by Henry Peyroux de la Coudrenaire, commandant at Ste. Genevieve, viz.: —

A uniform coat	$25	½ barrel clay pipes	3
Another do	15	94 lbs. coffee	46

THE WILL OF MADAME PEYROUX.

Another do. (old)	4	
2 Satin breeches	16	
2 Cloth do	10	
2 Cottonade do	6	
2 Breeches & vests	6	
17 Shirts	40	
2 Breeches, vest & draws	7	
2 Breeches & buckles	3	
2 Blanket overcoats	2	
Old coats, vest & breeches	12	
4 Old cloaks & vest	4	
24 yds. calimanco	12	
6 ells of linen	3	
5 ells red cloth	10	
20 ells of satteen	16	
A blue cloth cap	2	
36 Blankets	36	
1 piece gingham	4	
A pair of pistols	25	
A sword	8	
pair sil. epaulets	4	
2 sil. spoons, 3 forks	11	
Walnut wardrobe	35	
A trunk	6	
An old gun	2	
31 Razors, 10 knives, 16 pewter spoons, 32 iron forks, 24 wooden combs, 1 lb. thread.	11	
140 lbs. powder at 60c		
100 lbs. do 25c		
9 muskets, bad order	18	
1,000 flints	2	
2 bars lead	16	
60 lbs sugar		
50 lbs. Beaver		
43 deer skins		
7 Cat, 2 Fox skins		
A yoke of oxen and cart	60	
A chaise and horse	50	
A copper clock	2	
Negro woman, Theresa, 20 years	400	
do, Polagie, 25 years	400	
House of posts, 20x25, with lot, usual size	100	
A book of account, No. 1		
Bundle of paper " 2		
Another do " 3		
Packet of letters " 4		
2 certifs. of Baptism		
5 coms. from the King " 5		
A note of some one. " 7	175	
Do of John Dodge " 8	100	
Do of Lachance " 9	6	
Do of ―― " 20	50	
Another for $50		
On which paid 21 25		
Balance $28 75		
Due by same 11	39 75	
A deed for negro woman No. 10		
A receipt of Jno. B. Valle, with four notes for bread, for the troops, paid No. 12		
	$1796 75	

EUGENIO ALVAREZ & MARIANO IZAGUIRE witnesses.
PRATTE, FRIAR LEWIS GINGES, Curate. DOROTHY DE ORO, FRANCIS LECLERC, HENRY PEYROUX DE LA COUDRENAIRE.

WILL OF MAD'E PEYROUX, OF STE. GENEVIEVE.

In the town of St. Louis, May 26, 1788, before me, Manuel Perez, Captain and Lieutenant Governor of the establishments and dependencies of the Illinois, personally appeared Dona Margareta Susanne Jouolt, widow of Charles Peyroux, who about leaving for Ste. Genevieve dictates her will, as follows: —

First. She has been married, and is now the widow of Charles Peyroux deceased, and before she departed from France, all the property she possessed was given to Henry M. Peyroux and Maria Juanna Gravila and Margarete Susanne, her son and daughters, at the request of her eldest son, Pierre Charles Peyroux, as a proof of his fraternal affection towards his brother and sisters. Besides that, Pierre Charles Peyroux, paid out himself, all the expenses of the voyage from France to this country, and for the support of said Margaret Suzanne with all the care of a good son. Now she desires and instructs that all she possesses at the present time is to be the property of said Charles Peyroux, so that neither his brother nor sisters can claim any part thereof, requesting her said son, if she should die to celebrate a service and thirty masses for the repose of her soul, and to take charge of her funeral.

She annuls any former wills she may have made. Done at St. Louis the day and year above mentioned in presence of
JOSEF HORTIZ, JEAN PIERRE, PEDRO DE SANTOS, BARRERE, ROBIDOUX, BONA COLLELL,
Witnesses,
M. S. JOUALT PEYROUX.

MANUEL PEREZ.

KEER AND FAMILY KILLED BY INDIANS.

An Englishman named Keer, with his family, who had removed over from the Illinois side, was living on a new place about $6\frac{1}{2}$ miles north of St. Louis on the Bellefontaine road, improving the place for James Clamorgan. In the afternoon of June 21, 1788, this man Keer, his wife, a son and two daughters, five in all, were murdered by roving Indians. A son of 15 or 16 and a daughter of two years escaped.

KEER AND FAMILY KILLED BY INDIANS. 249

The brief account of it is found in the archives.

TRANSLATION.

"In the town of St. Louis of Illinois, on the twenty third day of the month of June, one thousand seven hundred and eighty-eight, I, Don Manuel Perez, commander and Lieut. Governor of the western portion of Illinois, In consequence of the misfortune that occurred on the twenty first in the afternoon of the present month, on the farm of Don Santiago Clamorgan, and on the person of Mr. Keer, an Englishman, who, himself, his wife, one son and two daughters, were killed by Indians, and who were residing on said farm, having the management thereof: one son fifteen or sixteen years old, and one daughter two years old, having escaped. I repaired at about 4 o'clock P. M. to the dwelling of the said Santiago Clamorgan, a resident of this Town, where all the movables and other effects belonging to the said deceased were conveyed, to take an appraised and general Inventory of the whole, for which purpose I officially appointed Benito Basquez, Bentura Collell and Santiago Chauvin, appraisers, all residents of this Town, and having duly administered the oath to them, they proceeded to discharge their duties truly and faithfully as such; valuing each article presented them, in current money of the country, and the Inventory was commenced in the presence of the attending witnesses, Mariano Izaguire and Joseph Hortiz in the following manner —

	Livres		
			1,218
1 Horse	100	6 Tin measures	3
2 Cows and Calf	300	1 Tin Coffee pot	15
1 Large hog	100	1 Tin Tea Pot &c	15
2 Sows	150	2 Iron Candle sticks	2
9 Womens' dresses	150	1 Side Saddle	30
2 Gowns	50	4 Iron Ovens	150
8 Jackets	20	1 Frying pan	2
1 Pellerine	30	7 Wooden buckets	7.10
5 yards black Silk	75	1 Pump	15
7 Handkerchiefs	35	1 lot of Keys	10
5 Caps	1	1 Water bucket	10
5 Chemises	40	3 Spades	15
1 piece of Cloth	10.10	2 Axes	15
2 pairs Stockings	7		

1 Apron	7.10	1 Feather Bed	40
2 Pillow cases	3	3 Blankets	22.10
1 looking glass	5	2 Smoothing Irons	10
4 leather gloves	5	1 Trunk	10
2 pair Silver Buckles	35	4 Chairs	25
3 Snuff-boxes	5	1 Beaver Hat	10
1 Old File	1.10	1 Bedstead frame	5
2 pair Shoes	15	1 Plough	40
a box of pewter Spoons	3	1 Spinning Wheel	50
a pewter dish, etc	20	1 Gun	20
6 pewter Plates	10	1 Cock, 6 Hens, 13 Chicks	33
11 cups and Saucers, ware	30		
5 plates, ware	7.10	Total	1773
forward	1218		

SEPARATION OF BARRERE AND WIFE.

In the year 1775, there came up to St. Louis from New Orleans a Francis Barrere, a native of a place in France called Mundé Marchant; a baker by trade, with his wife, whom he had just married at New Orleans, whose maiden name had been Maria Genevieve Catoise, and at the date of her marriage to Barrere, was the widow of one William Paille with an infant child. She and her first husband had commenced the world with nothing, and at his death they had accumulated the sum of four hundred and fifty-one dollars, one-half of which, two hundred and twenty-five $\frac{50}{100}$ dollars, was according to the French marriage law of community of interest, the daughter's share of the estate. The widow's half, $225.50, she invested in her second marriage with the above Barrere, who brought to the partnership his whole capital of one hundred and sixty dollars, so the new firm set out with a joint capital of three hundred and eighty-five dollars and one-half. They were industrious and frugal and they prospered.

They were married in New Orleans, May 1, 1775, their contract signed in the presence of their friends, Arnold Magnan, Nicholas Tarde and Henry Roche, was certified to by Andres Almonester y Rosas, notary. They came to St. Louis immediately after their marriage.

On January 14, 1776, they purchased the house and lot at the southwest corner of Third and Elm, a quarter block, 120 by 150 feet, house of posts 40 by 20, then a large house, for two hundred and fifty pounds of deer skins ($100).

On October 23, 1785, they also purchased the house and lot, northwest corner of Main and Elm, 55 front by 150, with a house of posts 26 by 21, barn, etc., for $600.

Notwithstanding their worldly prosperity, it seems they were not happy, for in less than four years after this we find them entering into the following mutual agreement to live apart:—

"In the year one thousand seven hundred and eighty nine, the thirty first of the month of July, a. m., before me, Don Manuel Perez, Captain of the Regiment of Louisiana, Lieut. Governor and commander-in-chief of the western part of Illinois and its districts (in default of a notary), personally appeared Frances Barrère, a resident of the post, and Genevieve Catoise, his wife, who by these presents and of mutual accord, and of their own free will, and in virtue of the proceedings commenced on the 9th of the present month, have voluntary consented, and do consent to a separation to the end of their lives, and to remain separated, one from the other, being absolutely unable to reside together, nor remain united on account of the difference of their dispositions, and reciprocally desirous of avoiding daily quarrels, and to spend the remainder of their days in peace, and to procure the salvation of their souls, which they can not do peaceably, living together, in consequence of their continual disputes, and no longer being able to bear them ; and in consequence of the deed of partition, dated the 30th Inst, not wishing to have any recourse on each other's property, now being individual as well actual as future ; regarding each other as strangers, as if no alliance had ever taken place. The said Madame Genevieve Catoise acknowledging and confessing that she has received by the aforesaid act her dower, and the property belonging to her daughter, as also half the goods of the community with the said Francis Barrère, which community the parties declare broken and dissolved. Therefore the said Genevieve grants a full and entire release and discharge to the said Barrère without any expectation of return.

" Done and executed at the office of the Government, in presence of Bonaventura Collell and Manuel Moro, attending witnesses, and of Messrs. Joseph Hortiz, Joseph Robidou and Gaspard Roubieu, who attended in the capacity of arbitrators, as well at the Inventory as at the deed of the partition, who have signed with the contracting parties, and Lieutenant Governor at St. Louis in Illinois, the same day and year aforesaid.

"FRANCOIS BARRERE, GENEVIEVE CATOISE,
JOS. HORTIZ,   GASPARD ROUBIEU,   MANUEL MORO,
ROBIDOU,   BONAVENTURA COLLELL,   MANUEL PEREZ."

An inventory of their property and a partition of the same was made by the three gentlemen above named. The house and lot on Third was assigned to Barrere, and the one on Main Street to Mrs. B., all the proceedings and documents in the matter are recorded in the archives.

Barrere, who was a man well thought of, continued his bakery business in the same house until his death in 1803, leaving his property to his wife's daughter by her first husband, whom he had adopted as his own, and educated until she was fifteen, when she married. Of the few residents on Third Street at that early period of our history, Barrere being the most prominent one, the Street was frequently called "Rue Barrere," Barrere's Street.

ABSCONDING OF LAPIERRE AND WIFE.

On the night of September 10, 1789, one Jno. Bapt. Lapierre, a blacksmith, absconded from the village, and with his wife, their clothing, bedding, etc., crossed in the night to the other or American side of the river. This Lapierre was a great scamp and bore a very indifferent reputation for veracity and integrity, as evidenced by his various acts.

At the time of his flight he lived in a small house of posts at the southeast corner of Main and Olive. This lot of 25 feet at the corner, a part of Alexis Picard's half block, which he had located in 1765 under Laclede, and upon which he was then living, had been *swapped off* by Picard to Francis Guion, a blacksmith, in 1773, for a cow, and Guion to fence it in, and had come into the possession of this Lapierre, how, it does not appear, as there is no record from Guion to Lapierre, however, he was living and had his shop on this lot at the time of his flight.

To illustrate, I append the official proceedings of Governor Perez in the matter:—

"This day the twefth of the month of September A. M. one thousand seven hundred and eighty nine at the post of St. Louis in Illinois: Before me Don Manuel Perez, Captain of the Regiment of Infantry of Louisiana, Lieutenant Governor and commander in chief of the western part and District of Illinois Personally appeared at the Government hall, and in the presence of Don Benito Vasquez and Bonaventura Collell, the person named Amable Flamant, a mason, who declaring that while residing at the house of John Bapt. Lapierre, a blacksmith, a resident of the said Post, he was much surprised and astonished on waking at day break to find all the doors open, the greater portion of the furniture and beds carried away, and could not find either the said Lapierre nor his wife Marguerite Dupuis in the house, declaring also that on the previous evening nor at any other period before this, there was not the least appearance of the removal of the said Lapierre and wife, swearing also that he had not the least notice, nor heard anything of their intended departure, nor of the removal of their effects, he being buried in the most profound sleep at the time thereof.

"In consequence whereof I repaired, accompanied by the above attending witnesses, and said Flamant to the residence of said Jno. B. Lapierre and wife, to take cognizance of the affair and to make a general and appraised Inventory of all the effects movable and immovable abandoned and left by the said Lapierre and his wife, and I appointed for this purpose Joseph Motard and Joseph Robidou, appraisers, who voluntarily accepted the commission and promised under oath to value truly and conscienciously the whole, and I commenced as follows:[1]

A large walnut wardrobe, without a lock	100	livres
An old bureau, one drawer missing, without lock	30	"
An old walnut bed stead, straw bed and teaster	10	"
Eight old chairs	7	10
An old earthern pot	2	10
An old kneading trough	6	
A small walnut table with drawer	10	
An old walnut do	4	
A small cupboard without key	5	
About two minots of peas in a barrel	15	190
A lot of ground 72 1-2 feet by 150 with a house of posts in the ground 35 by 18 feet, on the main street of the village, opposite Charles Simoneau, north a cross street, south Antoine Vincent, rear the Mississippi.		1250

JOSEPH MOTARD } Appraisers. Total............ 1440 livres.
JOSEPH ROBIDOU }

MANUEL PEREZ.

1792, June 29. — Perez preparing to leave St. Louis, sold his furniture at auction.

July 23. — Archives mention a sale of slaves by Aug't Chouteau to Manuel Perez, the account was filed but not recorded.

Perez and Chouteau had large transactions together; Chouteau gave Perez a bond to secure P. in

---

[1] This Jno. B. Lapierre and wife being indebted to Charles Sanguinet in the sum of 1750 livres, had given Sanguinet a mortgage on the property to secure him, on Sept. 10, 1789, only two days previous to their flight from the place. Sanguinet sold it to Louis Brazeau.

the sum of $2,625, dollars, dated July 23, 1792, payable in five years. Chouteau being in New Orleans in the winter of 1795-'96, anticipated the payment some 18 months, as per

"Receipt January 10, 1796, at New Orleans of Manual Perez Lieutenant Colonel Major of New Orleans, for his majesty, to Aug'st Chouteau of St. Louis."

Capt. Perez had been promoted.

CAPT. DON ZENON TRUDEAU,

appointed by governor-general, the Baron de Carondelet, entered upon his administration July 21, 1792. He was a Canadian by birth and a well educated man with a family of several sons. The two last of the Spanish governors of this Upper Louisiana, Trudeau and Delassus, although in the Spanish service, were Frenchmen by birth and their appointment was due to some extent to this fact, as will be made evident.

After the peace of 1783, the American settlements in Kentucky gradually extended west of the falls of the Ohio into the Green River country, until they had almost reached the Mississippi at the close of the century. The Kentucky trade down the Mississippi to New Orleans had likewise materially increased. In 1787 Col. Morgan, of Pennsylvania, had commenced the establishment of New Madrid. The first record of Americans becoming Spanish subjects in St. Louis, we find in the archives of 1782, after which they increased in number for a few years, from Illinois and Kentucky, until towards the close of the century, when they amounted to a goodly number, mostly farmers settled on the waters of the Meramec, Joachim and Plattin, in the district between St. Louis and Ste. Genevieve. The increase of the Americans in the country added to the complications between the Spanish custom house officials at New Orleans and our western people, growing out of the violations of the treaty between the two nations for the reciprocal navigation of the Mississippi, by the exaction of illegal fees from our people by the Spanish officers, and the threats of our people to retaliate, caused apprehensions on the part of the Spanish that a rupture of peaceful relations might soon occur, and as a matter of precaution they commenced the erection of some new works of defense at St. Louis, and the completion of the unfinished towers.

These were completed in 1794 under the supervision of a Col. Howard, who had come up from New Orleans some time previously with a few additional troops, which with those previously here, were quartered in their new barracks in the Fort on the hill.

FENCES OF STE. GENEVIEVE.

"We, Don Zenon Trudeau, Captain in the Regiment of Louisiana, and commandant in chief of the western part of the Illinois, in conformity to the orders of Monsieur the Baron of Carondelet, Governor General of this province, to establish a beneficial stability and assure to the inhabitants of Ste. Genevieve and surroundings the crop of corn during the time that the fences of the fields should be strong and open. We certify that we repaired to said

FORT ON THE HILL, 1794.

AS SEEN FROM FOOT OF WALNUT STREET.

[Drawn by C. Heberer under direction of F. L. Billon.]

village the seventh day of the present month, where, on our arrival, we convoked a meeting of all the inhabitants and citizens of the parish and its dependencies to consider the most convenient method for the advantage of all to establish the fences of the Fields and preserve the crops from the depredations of animals.

"All the inhabitants having expressed their views, it was decided by the majority that it was important to the safety of the crops that the lands should be all enclosed, conformably to the regulations of the present year, of which a copy is in the archives of said village of Ste. Genevieve, to remain so the whole year, excepting a certain interval of time, when it is allowed to turn in cattle, after the crops are gathered in, to give them pasture, and that only to the time when the Trustee will be required to order the execution, or shall himself so order, which must be executed without opposition on the part of the owners of animals, to restore the said fields for ploughing and sewing anew, under the guarantee of their same fences. This we have (conformably to the orders of the Governor General) agreed to, and ratified, to remain permanent, in accordance with the wishes and intentions of the large majority of the people of said village. Wherefore, we order all others to conform to this regulation in its full sense, which each year's sindic will see duly enforced, under the penalty of offenders being treated as refractory to good order and government.

"Done and agreed to at the village of Ste. Genevieve, before Messrs. Francois & Batiste Vallé, the requisite witnesses, who with us the commandant in chief, have signed the seventh day of the month of September, one thousand seven hundred and ninety-three.

"Francois Vallé,
"J. Bte. Vallé,   Zenon Trudeau."

SALE OF THE CREPEAU HOUSE.

"*To the Lieutenant Governor:*

"Eugenio Alvarez, an inhabitant and resident of this town of St. Louis in Illinois, with due respect appears before you, and says, that one Louis Crepeau is the owner of an old and dilapidated house on a piece of ground in the town, bounded one side by the widow of Jacques Labbé, on another by the widow of Lardoise, on another side by the second principal street, and on the other by a cross street, and the said Louis Crepeau being absent for six or seven years, having contracted some debts, and particularly a sum of considerable amount to the petitioner, and desirous that the said house should not be entirely ruined, no one living in it, to the prejudice of its owner and of his creditors, humbly requests you to order a valuation to be made of said ground and house,[1] by sworn arbiters, so that the person named Alexander Grimeau, the brother in law of the said Crepeau, may take possession thereof before it falls entirely to ruin, the said Grimeau remaining responsible for re-imbursing to said Crepeau, or to his creditors, the full amount of the valuation. A favor he expects to receive from your well known justice.

"EUGENIO ALVAREZ."

"ST. LOUIS IN ILLINOIS March 20, 1794."

"Petition granted, for which purpose I appoint Don Joseph Robidou, Don Bentura Collell and Don Gregorio Sarpy to make the valuation of the house to-morrow the 21st before me, and the said Grimeau may remain therein, for the price of the appraisement, for which he will be responsible to the said Crepeau, or to his creditors. TRUDEAU."

SYLVESTER LABBADIE.

Silvester Labbadie Sr., son of Dominick Labadie and Anne Beclac was born in Tarbes, Bearne, France — his name is first found in the Archives of St. Louis in the year 1769, and in 1773 associated in

---

[1] This lot, at the corner of Second and Poplar, was cut up by a deep gully through it, had no enclosure, and a very old house of posts, 20 by 16 feet, was valued at sixty dollars.

business with Jos. M. Papin. He was married July 27, 1776, to Pelagie the second daughter of Mrs. Marie Therese Bourgeois Chouteau. After a successful business of some 20 years, in which he acquired a handsome competency, he died on June 19, 1794 — his age is not stated.

HIS WILL.

" In the town of St. Louis of Illinois, the eighteenth day of the month of June, in the year one thousand seven hundred and ninety four, Don Silvestre Labbadie, merchant in the said town, has declared that he had made his will, in the presence of Pedro Pedesclaux, notary public in the City of New Orleans, on the twenty eighth day of May, one thousand seven hundred and ninety one; and that for the satisfaction of his conscience and that of his heirs, he will add as a codicil, what follows, to wit: That his Majesty having allowed to Fathers of Families the right of appointing such intelligent persons as they wish, for dividing their estate and regulating their interests, the said Silvestre Labbadie, using this privilege has named Bernard Pratte, his nephew (son in law) and Auguste Chouteau his cousin (brother in law) to make the Inventory and the division of all his property, according to the form prescribed in the said will, and he wishes and ordains that Pelagie Chouteau, executrix, appointed in the same will for the same purpose, shall execute it in what is not contrary to this present codicil, which shall remain in force and vigor.

" Made and executed in the presence of Antoine Reilhe, Manuel Gonzales Moro, Benito Vasquez, Mathurin Bouvet, before me Zenon Trudeau, captain of the Regiment of Infantry stationed in Louisiana, Lieutenant Governor, and commandant of the western bank of the Illinois, in default of a Notary in this jurisdiction.

Don Silvestre Labbadie.

" M. Bouvet, Benito Vasquez, Manuel Gonzales Moro, Ant'e Reilhe.   " Zenon Trudeau.

Silvestre Labbadie died on the next day, the 19th June.

When the estate was finally closed in November, 1795, there were five children living, all minors, Silvestre, Emily, Pelagie, Sophie and Marie Antionette. Emily, the oldest, had been married to Bernard Pratte a month before her father's death.

LOUIS CHAUVET DUBREUIL,

was born at Rochelle, Aunis, in France, in the year 1736, son of René Chauvet Dubreuil, attorney for the king, and Marie Dagnau. He came to St. Louis in 1765, at the age of twenty-nine, and married there on September 19, 1772, Miss Susanne Saintous, aged seventeen, daughter of John Saintous, deceased, and Subada Tuyaret.

Louis Dubreuil's will is dated July 15, 1794; he died four days afterwards, on the 19th, leaving to his widow and nine children, two sons and seven daughters, all minors at his death, a handsome property he had acquired in his business. They all lived to become married men and women.

It is somewhat singular in the lives of these two men, Labbadie and Dubreuil, that they both came from the western part of France, were friends and near neighbors for over 25 years, and died within a month of each other, each leaving a large family of children, all minors, and all living to become married.

MANUMISSION.

"This day the 21st day of April 1796 before me Don Louis Charles Blanc, Captain in the Army of the King, civil and military commandant of the Post of Natchitoches and dependencies. In default of a Notary in this place, was personally present Mr. John Baptist Grappe, inhabitant of this district, who declares and affirms by these presents, that he voluntarily gives freedom to his mulatto woman named Catiche, aged about twenty six years, whom he purchased from Mr. Louis Fontenau of this said place, recorded in this office the first of this present month of April. This is granted her so that she may enjoy it without any hindrance, with all the privileges granted to the enfranchised for this is the pleasure of the donor, who forever renounces all claims of service upon said liberated slave.

"Done at said place of Natchitoches in presence of Mr. Joseph Tauzin and André Rambin witnesses who with said Jno. B. Grappe and myself the above commandant have signed the same.

JOSEPH TAUZIN, ANDRÉ RAMBIN, LOUIS DEBLANC.
JNO. BAPT. GRAPPE.
DON LOUIS CHARLES DE BLANC, *Captain of Infantry.*

ORIGIN OF NEW MADRID AND FIRST CENSUS.

"NEW MADRID, Dec. 31, 1796.

" *To Mr. Charles Dehault Delassus, Lieut. Colonel admitted into the Stationary Regiment of Louisiana, and Military and Civil Commandant of the Posts and Districts of New Madrid:* —

" SIR, THE COMMANDANT,

"Before handing you the first census of New Madrid under your commandment, I have ventured upon a sketch upon the origin of the settlement of this Post, and the causes which have retarded its growth and chiefly its cultivation. If former defects have kept it until this time in a species of stupefaction, your sagacious views and the zeal you exhibit to second the good will of Mr. the Governor General of this Province towards this settlement, can in a little while efface the trouble it experienced in its birth.

"I was present Mr. Commandant when you pronounced with effusion these words, which I wish that all the inhabitants might have heard; words which depicted so frankly your kind intentions, and the interest which Mr. the Governor takes in us.

"'The Governor,' said you, 'is surprised at the languor exhibited by this settlement and its little advance, he desires its prosperity. I will reflect 'upon its failure,' added you, 'and will endeavor to remedy it, I ask your assistance. If the inhabitants need encouragement, if they stand in need of help, let them inform me of their wants, and I will convey them to the Governor General.' This offer was appreciated by those near you, little accustomed to hear the like they wondered at you, admired you, and appeared to rest content.

"Nevertheless, different statements were spread amongst those who heard you; Why so long a silence since your generous offer? Is it distrust on their part? Is it mistrust of their own misunderstanding? Is it profound reflection to better further your views? or may it not be self-interest that induces some to remain silent? I am ignorant of their motives, and limit myself to the hope that they will eventually break their silence and make known to you their salutary reflections.

"If my knowledge equalled my desires, I would hasten with all my power, sir, the commandant, to tender you the homage of my services, but they fall too far short to allow me to hope that they could be of any utility to you. I will confine myself solely to communicate to you such knowledge as I have acquired, and my reflections thereon since I have been at this Post, and may a series of these reflections assist in your benevolent heart some happy idea that may tend to the advantage and prosperity of this colony.

"Some traders in pursuit of gain, came to *l'anse a la graisse*, (*cove of fat or grease*,) a rendezvous or gathering place of several Indian nations, and where, as we are told by tradition, they found abundance of game, and especially bears and buffaloes, hence the name of l'anse a la graisse. A first year of success induced them to try a second, and to this others. Some of them determined to establish their homes where they found a sure trade and unlimited advantages, divided there among themselves the lands. The bayou, named since St. John, was the rallying point, and the land the nearest to this then became settled, therefore we find that Messrs. Francis and Joseph Lesieuer, Ambrose Dumay, Chatoillier, and others, divided among themselves this neighborhood ; property which Mr. Fouché, the first commandant considered as sacred, and which he did not disturb. The profits of the trade of *l'anse a la graisse* having been heard of as far as the Post Vincennes, the St. Maries, the Hunots, the Racines, the Barsaalou's, &c., of that place accomplished for some years, very advantageous trips, they congratulated themselves moreover that the Indians of *l'anse a la graisse* (you might call the fat of the land) traded with them amicably, whilst those of the United States were treacherous towards them, and made them averse to inhabit a Post where their lives were in constant danger.

" Nevertheless an unfortunate anarchy, a singular disorder, prevailed at *l'anse a la graisse;* all were masters, and would obey none those of who set themselves up as heads or commandants of this new colony. A murder was committed by an inhabitant on another — then their eyes were opened, they began to feel the necessity of laws, and some one at their head to compel their observance, they bound the culprit and sent him to New Orleans ; everything tends to the belief that the commandants of the Posts of Ste. Genevieve and of St. Louis had during these transactions apprised the Governor General of what was occurring at *l'anse a la graisse;* but a new scene was in preparation.

" One Morgan having descended the Ohio, the first year that traders settled at *l'anse a la graisse,* he examined in passing, the land, and found it suitable to fix here a settlement. Returning to America (U. S.) he removed and succeeded in bringing down to this Post several families, he selected for the village the elevated ground where are at present the habitations of Jackson and of Waters near the Mississippi ; they built some houses on the land ; and full of his enterprise and the success he expected from it, Morgan descended to New Orleans to obtain, not encouragement simply in his plans, but proprietory and honorary concessions beyond measure, he was baffled in his pretensions, and did not again set his foot in the Colony.

" These various occurrences determined the Governor general to send a commandant to this Post, and M. Fouché was selected. Men are not Gods, they all possess in some respects the weaknesses of human nature, the predominant one of the first commandant was self interest, and who in his place would not have been so? Sent to a desert in the midst of savages, to bring the laws of a regulated government to new settlers as barbarous as the Indians themselves; what recompense would he have received for neglecting his personal interests? What obligation would the new colony have been under to him? None.

" Mr. Foucher was the man that was wanted for the creation of this colony; busying himself at the same time with his own interests as of those of the inhabitants, with his own amusements as well as theirs, but always after having attended first to his business, and by a singular address if he sometimes plucked the fowl, he not only did it without making it squall, but set it dancing and laughing. M. Fouché remained but a very short time at this Post, and done a great deal; in eighteen months he divided out the country, regulated the land necessary for the village, and that of the Inhabitants; he built an imposing fort, promulgated the laws of the King, and made them respected, he was the father and friend of all, lamented, regretted, and demanded again from the Governor General down, by the unanimous voice of all the inhabitants.

" In all his labors was Mr. Fouché assisted by any one? Had he overseers at the head of the works he prescribed? Not at all; he alone directed every thing; he laid out the work, penetrated the Cypress Swamps to select the useful trees, he walked with the compass in hand to align the streets and limit the lots, he demonstrated by his example to the perplexed workmen how much men with but little main strength, but with intelligence and dexterity, can multiply the extent of the same and surmount obstacles. His administration was too brief to ascertain the good he might have done, had it continued the ordinary period, what is certain is that during the 18 months that he was in command, there came to New Madrid the largest portion of families that are still there, and it was he that attracted them there.

" M. Portell successor of M. Foucher, commanded this post during five years, the population did not increase under his administration and the growth of agricultural labour was but slightly perceptible. M. Portell[1] did not value the inhabitants sufficiently to do them a substantial favour, nor did he use the proper means to improve the condition of the colony, he was not a man of the people, and when by chance his interest required him to assume the character, he was extremely awkward in it, they peceived that he could not play his part, and that a residence at court would have infinitely better suited him than one in a new settlement mostly ill-composed. M. Portell had a good heart, he was by nature noble and generous, but his mind was somewhat mistrustful and suspicious, and his age placed him in a position to be influenced by his surroundings. I am convinced that if M. Portell had come alone to this colony, he would have exhibited much less weakness, and that his time would have been much more taken up for the public good, than it had been. The little progress made by the Colony, must not however be attributed to the apparent indifference which seemed to form the base of M. Portell's character, physical and moral causes retarded its advancement.

"At the period when M. Portell assumed his command, he found the inhabitants at this post made up of traders, hunters and boatmen, trade was still pretty fair for the first two years of his residence here, so that nearly every one, high or low, would meddle with the trade, and not a soul cultivate the soil. It was so convenient with a little powder and lead, some cloth, and a few blankets, which they obtained on credit from the stores, to procure themselves the meat, grease and suet necessary for their sustenance and pay off a part of their indebtedness with some peltries. Some of them, but a very few, seeded, equally well as badly, about an acre of corn, and they all found time to smoke their pipes, and give balls and entertainments. How often have I heard them regretting those happy days, when they swam in grease, and when abundance of every description, was the cause of waste and ex-

---

[1] M. Portell, a man of distinguished merit, equally in the military as in the cabinet, was superior to his position, and if he failed, it was because he did not place himself on a level wtih the sort of people he had to govern.— P. A. L.

travagance, and the stores of fish from their drag-nets gave them whiskey at 4 or 5 reaux (bit of 12 ½) a gallon, and flour at 4 or 5 dollars a barrel maintained and kept up these festivals and pleasures, which only came to an end when the purses were exhausted.

"Mr. Foucher, a young man, who during his command of the Post, never neglected his work or business for amusements, yet, found time to be at them all, and often was the first to start them, but M. Portell was not so sociable in this respect, he found fault with this giddiness and folly, and judged that a colony peopled by such indviduals could not attain a very brilliant success.

"At last game in these parts becoming scarcer, the Indians removed themselves further off and were seldom here, the traders knew very well where to find them, but the inhabitants waited for them in vain, then grease, suet, meat and peltries being no longer brought by the Indians it was only a few resident hunters and the traders themselves that provisioned the village, the unfortunate habit of not working had gained the day, it was too difficult to overcome it, so, great distress was often seen in the country before they could snatch a few ears of green corn from a badly cultivated field, three or four Americans at most, as far back as 1793, had risqued the settlement of farms on large tracts of land, the creoles under valued them, did not eat their fill of dry corn bread, and smoked their pipes quietly, they were however surprised to see that with several cows, they often had not a drop of milk, while these three or four Americans gorged themselves with it, and sold them butter, cheese, eggs and chickens &c.

"By dint of looking into the matter, and waiting in vain for the Indians to supply them with provisions, it struck them that the most prudent thing they could do, would be to become farmers. It became then a species of epidemic, and the malady spreading from one to the other, there was not a single one of them but who, without energy, spirit, animals or ploughs, and furnished only with his pipe and steel, must needs possess a farm.

"It was towards the close of the year 1793, that this disease spread itself, and towards the spring of 1794 all the lands in the vicinity of New Madrid were to be broken up and torn into rags, to be seeded and watered by the sweat of these new farmers. Who can tell how far this newly awakened enthusiasm might have been carried? It might have produced a salutary crisis, and self love and necessity combined, we should be supplied with farmers at all hazards, and whose apprenticeship might perpaps have resulted in some success.

"An unlooked for occurrence calmed this effervescence, all were enrolled into a militia to be paid from January 1, 1794, and they found it much pleasanter to eat the King's bread, receive his pay, and smoke his pipes, than to laboriously grub some patches of land to make it produce some corn and potatoes. These militia men were disbanded about the middle of 1794, their pay was already wasted, they found it a great hardship to be no longer furnished with bread by the King, the largest portion of them had neglected their planting, they found themselves at the year's end in want, and clamored as thieves against the King, saying, 'it was all his fault.' M. Portell knew well his people and disregarded these outcries.

"In the meantime five gallies had come up in the course of this year, and had passed all the summer at New Madrid, and they had caused a great consumption of food; M. Portell found nothing in the village for their subsistence and drew his supplies for them in part from Illinois and from Kentucky. He did not let pass the opportunity of making it felt by those of the inhabitants of long residence, that should have been in a condition to have furnished a part of these supplies, but the blows he struck came too late and made but little impression — the hot fever which had occasioned the delirium, where every one saw himself a farmer, had now subsided; no one thought any more of it, some of them who had made a trial of their experience at Lake St. Isidor, had so poorly succeeded, that the laugh was not on their side, and it needed but little for hunting, rowing and smoking the pipe to resume their ancient authority over nearly all the colony.

"In 1795 a new fit of the fever struck the inhabitants, the settlement of Fort St. Fernando occasioned a hasty cleaning out of the little corn there was in the colony. Kentucky furnished a little, and Ste. Genevieve supplied a great deal, even to New Madrid that fell short after having consumed her own supply. This example struck the inhabitants, they saw that if they had harvested extensively, they could have well disposed of their surplus — new desires to go on farms to raise stock and to make crops.

"During these occurrences several American families came to New Madrid, some of them placed themselves at once on farms, and like children, our creoles from a state of jealousy, clamored against the Americans whom they thought too wonderful, jealousy stimulated them and they would also place themselves on farms.

"It is in reality then only since the year 1796, that we may regard the inhabitants of this post as having engaged in cultivation, and that it is but yet absolutely in its infancy; a new scarcity they have just experienced before the last crop, has convinced them of the importance of raising them, not only to provide against such inflictions, to enable them also, with the surplus above their own consumption, they may procure their other indispensable necessaries.

"The population of the years 1794, 1795 and 1796, is nearly about the same, but the crops have increased from year to year, and all tends to the belief that this increase will be infinitely more perceptible in future years.

"In the year 1794 the corn crop was 6,000 bushels.
"   "   1795   "   "   10,000   "
"   "   1796   "   "   17,000   "

"It was in this condition of things that M. Portell left his command.

"It was perhaps impossible, from the foregoing facts, that the settlement at New Madrid could have made greater progress than it has up to this time. It was not husbandmen who came and laid the foundation, it was tradesmen, cooks and others, who would live there with but little expense and labor, who being once fixed there, having their lands and their cattle, the Indians having removed themselves to a distance, and trade no longer within the reach of all the world, necessity taught them that to procure the means necessary to live they must resort to tilling the soil. The first attempts were difficult, but the inducement of disposing with ease of their crops determined them to labor.

"The first steps have been taken, nothing remains for a wise

Commandant but to manage everything with prudence, according to the views of the Government, to firmly repel idleness and laziness, to welcome and encourage activity, and exhibit to the industrious man that he is distinguished above others, and has earned the protection of the government; in giving him tangible proof, either by preference in purchasing from him, or some other manner of recompense. The honest man, the active and industrious man is sensible of the slightest proceeding on the part of his Superior, and it is to him a great expansion to reflect that his labors and fatigues have not been ignored, and that they have given him a claim on the good will and benevolence of the heads of a Province.

"What a vast field is open to a Commandant who would reap advantage by these means, and gain the benedictions of all the worthy inhabitants of a Colony.

"I stop here, Mr. Commandant, what I might say further would add but little to the good purposes you design for the progress and success of this place. I have made a concise narrative of the origin of the post of New Madrid, and the reasons of its slow growth in agriculture. The census which follows will give you a correct view of its present position. It will prove to you that courage and emulation need but a slight support to emerge from the giddiness where they have so long remained. But for certain the creoles will never make this a flourishing settlement, it will be the Americans, Germans and other active people who will reap the glory of it.

"Observe if it please you, sir, that amongst the habitations granted long since, those given in by Francis Racine, by Hunot, Sr., the Hunot sons, Paquin, Laderoute, dec'd, Gamelin, Lalotte, &c., have not yet had a single tree cut on them; that those of the three brothers Saint Marie, Meloche and other creoles are barely commenced. You will see, on the contrary, that the Americans who obtain grants of land have nothing more at heart but to settle on them at once and improve them to the extent of their ability, and from this it is easy to draw conclusions.

"Another observation which will surely not escape you, sir, is that the total of heads of families amount, according to the census I exhibit to you, to 159, and that in this number there are 53 who have no property. This, I think, is an evil, to which it would be easy for you to apply a remedy. In a country destined to agricultural pursuits and to the breeding of domestic animals, it is too much that one-third of its inhabitants should stand isolated from the general interest, and that the other two-thirds should be exposed to be the victims of a set of idle and lazy people, always at hand in their slightest necessities to satiate their hunger by preying on the industrious.

"I think Mr. Commandant that several habitations left by persons who have absented themselves from this post for a long time should be re-united to the Domain.

"The following are of this class: —

"One Enie Bolduc, absent for over 2 years, had a place at Lake St. Francis No. 2.

"John Easton, absent over three years, had a place at Lake St. Eulalie; it is now abandoned. Mr. Waters says he has claims on it. What are they?

"Tournay had a place at Lake St. Isidor; he associated with to cultivate it, one Gamard. Tournay returned to France, and Gamard has worked for two years at Fort Saint Fernandez.

"M. Desrocher, why has he not worked his place in the Mill prairie, which he holds for over four years — has he not enough with the one he holds at St. Isidor?

"M. Chisholm holds three places; he lives on one he has just commenced to clear; a second is in litigation, and for over four years he has done nothing on a third near the village — has he not enough with two? Why hold land uselessly, and above all near the village?

"The examination you will give the census and the information concerning the property of each head of a family will lead you probably to other reflections. I append to the whole a new map of the village and its environs, as taken after the last abrasion of lands by the Mississippi; this work claims your indulgence, it is not that of an artist, but of one of the most zealous subjects of his majesty; and the only merit it may possess is to demonstrate to you with correctness the number of places that have been conceded in the village, the houses that are built thereon, and the names of the proprietors on the general list, which correspond with the same numbers as those placed on each conceded place.

"I pray you to believe me with profound respect,
"Sir, the commandant,
"Your very affectionate & devoted
"Servant,
"PETER ANTHONY LAFORGE.

"NEW MADRID,
Decr. 31, 1796."

FENCES OF FLORISANT.

"*To Captain Zenon Trudeau, commandant in chief of the western part of Illinois —*

"SIR, being clothed with full authority, and having charge of the public affairs of the village of Florisant, in regard to the young men who refuse to connect with the public enclosure owning stock, who are Antoine Riviere, Sr., and Antoine Riviere, Jr., Joseph Riviere, Jr., and Francis Riviere, Jr., and little Blanc, and Bonaventura Marion, and we have Americans who made the said connexion without any difficulty.

"Sir, we remind you that you granted us the commons verbally, and it began by costing the village one day's time of Mr. Beaurosier and twelve men with him to mark it out, and secondly it cost the village to survey it and mark its bounds, thirty-four minots of wheat, also 12 men's labor, without the above named being at any cost. Sir, it is Mr. Antoine Riviere, Jun'r, who acts for all the above named, and tried to hinder the Americans from making their share, but they did not listen to him, as it is for their interest as well as ours, first for fire wood, next, for hay and thirdly for the live stock.

"Done at St. Ferdinand this April 17, 1797, the foregoing statement approved by Mr. Francis Dunegant, with the signatures of all the former sindics, and of Mr. Amable Gagné, the present sindic for this service chosen by the people.

"Joseph x̶ Rapieu, Antoine x̶ Marechal, Francis x̶ Maurau, (his mark.)

Francis M. x̶ Challe, Pierre x̶ Devos, Francis x̶ DeLaurier, (his mark.)

Amable x̶ Gagné, (his mark.)   Francis Dunegant."

" St. Louis, Aug't 21, 1797."

" All Citizens without land united to that which it is desirable to enclose, are not liable for the Commons enclosure, which protects them from animals; but said citizens should contribute in all that is of public benefit, as roads, bridges, commons for stock, and other matters that they make use of, consequently should assist in paying the survey of the commons, the men's hire, &c.

" Zenon Trudeau."

LECLERCQ AND FATHER DIDIER.

" *To Mr. Zenon Trudeau Lieut. Colonel of the Stationary Regiment of Louisiana, and Lieutenant Governor of the Western part of the Illinois,*

" Sir, Augustus LeClercq, a resident of this town informs you that after the presentation that has been made at several times, to your knowledge, to Mr. Joseph Didier, curate of this town, of a note for two thousand and fifty livres, drawn by him in my favor, the one half payable on January first next, and the other half on January 1st of the succeeding year, for value received by him in the proceeds of the goods which your said petitioner had left to his children, on his departure for France in the month of June, 1792. Said demand simply requesting the said Mr. Didier to convert said note into two others jointly for the same amount, each for one half at same dates, to your said

petitioner, and after re-iterated replies which said Didier made, that 'he did not owe the amount of said note to said petitioner, that he would neither change nor pay it when it became due,' your petitioner, who is about to depart for New Orleans, has reason to believe that the above mentioned Mr. Didier will make the same answer when the note becomes due. To obviate trouble and to know on what to depend before he leaves the town, he has recourse to you to interpose, for a settlement between Mr. Didier and himself according to what you might be pleased to direct, and you will render justice.
" LeClercq.

" St. Louis, October 11, 1797."

" Mr. Pierre Joseph Didier, Benedictine friar, curate of St. Louis, replies to the above petition read to him, that he consents to assign the reasons he has for refusing to pay the amount of the note which Mr. LeClercq reclaims, before arbitrators chosen by the two parties, by means of which, if his refusal is not a just one, he consents to pay it.
" Pierre Joseph Didier.

" St. Louis Oct. 11, 1797."

" In view of the above demand and reply, the parties will each choose his arbitrators, who being sworn will meet where it may suit them, to terminate with another one officially appointed, the controversy in question.
" Zenon Trudeau.

" St. Louis Oct. 11, 1797."

Mr. Leclercq selected Charles Sanguinet and James Clamorgan, and Father Didier selected Charles Gratiot and Antoine Reilhe.

REGULATIONS FOR THE GOVERNMENT OF NEW ORLEANS.

" Don Manuel Gayoso de Lemos,
" Brigadier of the armies of the King, Governor General, Vice Royal Patron of the Provinces of Louisiana and West Florida, Inspector of the Regular Troops and Militia of the same, &c.

Desirous of maintaining good order and the public tranquility, upon which depends the safety of the inhabitants, we have deemed it proper, following the established custom, to publish the following order or regulations, for the execution of the same we will employ all the authority and power which his Majesty has deigned to confide to us in giving us charge of this Government.

"I. All persons, of whatsoever class it may be, who, under any pretext whatever, will have the audacity to blaspheme the name of God our Lord, the Virgin Mary our Lady, or sacred things, or make use of threatening oaths, will incur the penalties established by the laws of these kingdoms. All workmen or artisans, without exception, of whatever class or profession it may be, who will be convicted of having worked on Sunday or a holy day, during which one can only attend to work in cases of necessity by especial permission, will be sentenced to a fine of ten dollars, or if he is insolvent, to six days' imprisonment; and his employer will pay double the amount.

"It is prohibited, under penalty of 24 hours' imprisonment to run carts on holy days and Sundays.

"II. No person of whatever state, sex, quality or condition he may be, can keep, neither in his or other persons houses, nor in the suburbs or vicinity of this city, any game of cards or dice, or other forbidden games, and notably those known under the names of Lansquenet, Monté, Albures, Primera, Rolette, Crabs and others, which are, unfortunately, but too much in use causing the unhappiness and destruction of the young. Whoever may infringe this prohibition, will be punished rigorously to the extent of the law, by a fine of fifty dollars on the one who plays, and of one hundred on the keeper of the house. And for the second offense the fine will be double, and for the third the fine will be again doubled, and they will be sentenced to banishment. And in the case of the insolvency of the parties, the players will receive six days' imprisonment, and the proprietors twenty days for the first offense, and a proportionate increase for repetitions. If slaves, they will be chastised with twenty-five blows of the whip.

"III. All those who carry arms that are prohibited by law, either fire arms or especially poignards, sheath-knives, butcher-knives, flemish knives, bayonets, or all other descriptions of penetrating instruments, that are prohibited which the wickedness of mankind has, or may invent for the destruction of his fellow man, will be punished with the utmost rigor of the law, without any exception and without regard to privileges.

"IV. All vagabonds and vagrants without homes, and of vicious life, who follow no trade or known employment in this city, by which they may prove the employment of their time, must leave this jurisdiction within three days, after which term, they will be arrested and made to work in such manner as may be judged suitable, giving notice that no one shall secrete or harbor them in his own or the houses of others, under a penalty of twenty-five dollars, or ten days' imprisonment for those who may be insolvent.

"V. To compel the observance of these regulations and others, which have for their object the maintainance of good order and tranquility in this city, they will uphold in all its strength and vitality the proclamation proclaimed by my predecessor the Baron of Carondelet, the 26th January, 1792, on the division of the city into four parts, and the appointment of their magistrates or trustees, reviving in its full force the 3rd Article of the said Proclamation, in which it is provided that so that the Government may have a perfect knowledge of all the individuals who compose these divisions, and of those who come to and leave the City, whoever lets out a house or a room, or furnishes lodging to any stranger, must make it known during the day, or the day following at the latest, to the magistrate or commissioner of his division, under a penalty of two dollars for the first offense, and four dollars for the second; and for insolvents eight days' imprisonment for the first, and fifteen days the second offense; those who neglect it the third time, will be condemned to a much longer imprisonment, or to such other punishment as the government may deem proper to inflict.

"VI. Taverns and Billiard-rooms must be positively shut up at the hour of the tattoo, at all seasons, under a penalty of eight dollars fine for the first offense, and sixteen for the second, besides that, the proprietors of said places will forfeit the privilege of keeping them. The said Billiard-rooms must not be opened on

Holy days until after the High Mass; and on working days, mechanics and workmen will not be permitted to frequent them during working hours; as to minors and slaves they are forbidden to be found there at any time, under the penalties expressed above.

"It is permitted, however, to have in the doors of Taverns a wicket of a foot square, through which to deliver those articles of great necessity that sick persons may require at unseasonable hours; well understood, however, that the door is not to be opened for any purpose whatever after retreat (tattoo) until the dawn.

"VII. To escape as far as possible the harm caused by fires, it is again recommended to follow the fifth article of the above cited Proclamation, which prescribes that there shall be at the house of the Magistrate of each division, a place of deposit for buckets, axes, and ladders, which will be distributed by him to all those who may come and offer themselves to work; with the understanding that the government will take the most effective measures to locate the Engines in various quarters, so that the Magistrates of the quarters having knowledge of the same may make use of them promptly whenever requisite. With the same view, it is ordained to all proprietors to open within fifteen days, on his lot, one well at least, of a sufficient diameter, and to all tenants to have it done at the expense of the owner, otherwise it will be done at their expense by the galley slaves. The Magistrates of the quarters will appoint each month from the citizens of their respective districts, fifteen men used to handle the axe, and fifteen bucket carriers, to whom he will distribute axes and buckets, so that so soon as they find that a fire has broken out in their quarter, they will immediately repair to the place with their axes and buckets, where they will obey no orders but from an experienced citizen of the quarter, who will be appointed each month for that purpose by the commissioner. In cases where the fire may make rapid progress, the Magistrate of the Quarter may ask assistance, without for that reason that other citizens, carpenters and masons, can consider themselves exempted from assisting as much as they possibly can, as it is their duty to do on occasions of the kind.

"VIII. The Register of the month, whose turn it may be to perform the functions of clerk of the market will post up in the City every Saturday the price of meat, of beef or pork, and bread for the succeeding week, and he who sells at a higher price, or does not give the full weight or measure, will pay a fine of four dollars for the first offense, and eight for the second.

"IX. No retailer of game, fish or other eatables whatever, coal, wood, lime, etc., will be allowed to go outside the gates of St. Charles, St. Louis, St. John and St. Ferdinand to find those who sell, or inhabitants who come from the vicinity and different directions to sell their provisions, for the purpose of purchasing and bringing them into the city as belonging to them, and within the enclosure of the City they can only purchase them after eight o'clock A. M. during the summer, and after ten o'clock in winter, and after they had been exposed for sale for over two hours, so that the people may promptly provide for themselves; no one either can sell the provisions he may bring in the night time, before he has exposed them the day following up to the hour indicated as above for the summer and winter, under a penalty of four dollars fine for the first offence.

"As a general rule, it is forbidden to all retailers to purchase within the distance of five leagues from the City, without giving notice to the Government or Register for the month. No negress or mulatress slave will be permitted to sell in the streets, or on the levee without a written permission from the government, and a list of her articles for sale signed by her master.

"Free negresses and mulattresses, that it would be more suitable to see employed in some more useful manner, will also not be allowed to sell in the streets without a like written permission, and a list for their articles signed by the commissioner of the Quarter.

"X. No person, without exception, can sell to slaves, without a written permission from their masters, guns, balls, or powder, nor any fire arms whatsoever, under a penalty of fifty dollars fine, or one month of imprisonment for those who are insolvent.

"XI. No person is allowed to sell on credit, traffic, nor purchase from the soldiers, without permission in writing from their officers, nor to children without that of their parents, nor to slaves without that of their masters, under penalty of twenty dollars fine for the first time, and forty for the second, and in case of other relapses, justice will inflict on the delinquents imprisonment or banishment and the loss of the articles bought or traded for, and which if found to have been stolen, the said delinquent will be tried as an accomplice and receiver of stolen goods.

" 'This article is applicable to the Indians also, from whom it is only allowed to purchase wild meat obtained from hunting and peltries.

"XII. Whoever sells to Indians, or to slaves without permission from their master, liquors, wine or brandy, will be sentenced to four or six dollars penalty for the first offence, and to double the amount for the second; and should it be a dram shop keeper, his license will be forfeited, nor can he in the future obtain another.

"XIII. No one can keep a Tavern, without a written permission from the Government and the Intendant, under penalty of ten dollars fine, or one month's imprisonment if insolvent, for the first offence, and of double for the second.

"XIV. Every citizen will be required to keep the sidewalk along the whole front of his lot, in a good and clean condition, and to have the same swept and sprinkled, at least once a day in summer, and to have the mud cleaned off every time it may be practicable in the winter, under a penalty of two dollars' fine for the first neglect, and four for the second, and if the delinquent has not wherewith to pay, he will be punished by four days' imprisonment the first time, and eight the second; and in all cases, where the first notification has not been complied with, the owners of the lot will be required to pay whatever has been expended to have it put in good condition.

"XV. Every citizen is expressly required under the same penalties to keep the chimnies of his house in good repair, and to have them cleaned out at least once a month in winter, and once in two months in summer.

"XVI. Under no pretext, nor for any reason whatever, either in building or repairing houses, will it be permitted to put the enclosure outside the curbstone, nor to deposit on the sidewalk at any time, lime, earth or other materials which would obstruct the passage.

"XVII. No one will be allowed to throw into the streets, rags, scraps of leather or cloth, &c., nor garden stuffs, house litter, oyster shells, broken glass or china, &c., &c., nor leave in the streets, carriages, carts, &c., day nor night unless in use at the time.

"It is expressly required that all vacant lots shall be enclosed within the period of one month, and in case of neglect it will be done at the cost of the owners of the same.

"XVIII. No vehicles, Coaches, Caleches nor horses will be allowed on the Levee, under a penalty of six dollars fine. Hereafter no one will be permitted to erect on the Levee any house cabin, &c., and those that are at present there, cannot be repaired under the penalty of forfeiting them, excepting therefrom those that are used for the support of the orphans, and still less will it be permitted to excavate cellars or vaults thereon.

"It is positively prohibited to stow away and saw drift-wood, and put away fire-wood either on or outside the Levee, from the gate of St. John to beyond the last cabins of the careening place.

"The goods that are unloaded on the Levee can remain there no longer than is necessary for the Custom-house examination, under a penalty of four dollars fine.

"It will not be allowed under any pretext whatever, to deposit such materials as lime, bricks, wood or timber on or outside the Levee from the gate of St. Louis as far as the careening place, and whatever is landed there must be removed within twenty-four hours.

"Fire-wood and lumber for Carpenters and fences, must be exposed at public sale, outside the gate of St. Louis, in a place to be fixed upon by the commissioner of this quarter, taking care to always leave clear the landing place.

"It will not be allowed under any pretext to wash clothes below the careening place, under penalty of two dollars fine for whites and free colored persons, and ten lashes of the whip for slaves.

"Water carriers are required to take their water from the river, outside the gate of St. Louis, under penalty of four dollars fine, and twenty lashes of the whip for slaves.

"Dirt must be thrown in the river in front of the quarter, under penalty of four dollars fine, and twenty whip lashes for slaves.

"It is positively prohibited to empty foul water into the gutters that run into the streets.

"Dead animals must be put under ground, under penalty of four dollars fine.

"No one can raise or keep swine within the enclosures of the town; but it will be permitted to kill and scald them there, on the express condition that no fire for the purpose must be made of shavings, chips or straws, which is positively prohibited in view of the grievous consequences which may result therefrom.

"If any one desires to singe his hogs, he will be held to do it outside the city, where the public slaughter-house will also be established.

"The manufacturers of hair powder must have their work-shops outside the city, owing to the infectious odor exhaled by putrified flour.

"XIX. No slave can be permitted to keep a room or a lodging house apart from that of his master, under the pretext of working by the day, unless it be a slave married in presence of the Church to a free woman; and the masters of such slaves are required to recall them to their homes, under penalty of four dollars fine for the first offence, and eight dollars for the second; and in case of other recurrences, such punishment will be inflicted on them as may be deemed suitable.

"XX. No person whatever will be permitted to keep in his store more than 25 pounds of gunpowder at a time, under penalty of confiscation for the benefit of the poor, besides fifty dollars fine, or one month's imprisonment for those who are insolvent for the first offence, and of double for the second; and whoso ever carries powder in or outside the City without keeping it well covered and wrapped in tarpaulins, will pay a fine of ten dollars.

"XXI. All slaves found in the commons without a written permit from his master to go and cut wood, will be considered a runaway, and chastised with 25 lashes of the whip.

"XXII. Every Sailor or Boat-hand who has engaged himself for a voyage on a barge, a pirogue or boat, for either of the posts of the province, and who, after having completed the engagement, or received some money on account, should desert, will be condemned to two months hard labor to correct the intolerable abuse which has introduced itself in these cases.

"XXIII. After the period of three days precisely, all the dogs, curs, mastiffs and others of the species, that are found in the streets will be killed; all citizens who desire to preserve them for pleasure or use, being obliged to keep them confined.

"NEW ORLEANS, January 1, 1798."

PETITION OF THE MISSOURI TRADING COMPANY.

"*To Don Emanuel Gayoso de Lemos, Brigadier of the armies of his Catholic Majesty, Governor General of the Province of Louisiana*:

"MY LORD, Your humble petitioner, Joseph Robidou, Merchant, Lieut. of Militia, has the honor to lay before you, that he was calmly and advantageously pursuing his trade with the Indian tribes in the neighborhood of St. Louis, his residence, when on May 12, 1794, Mr. Zenon Trudeau, Lieut. Governor of this western part of the Illinois, desirous of extending the knowledge of the places under his jurisdiction, promote commerce, and wrest from the English nation a portion of the gains they fraudulently acquired from the dominions of his Catholic majesty, having assembled all the traders of St. Louis, proposed to them to unite in co-partnership, consolidate their respective capitals, and control the trade in peltries, then carried on in the Upper Missouri. Mr. Zenon Trudeau in suggesting this enterprise, explained to them, that his purpose was, at the same time, to enlighten the age, in regard to that portion of the Globe, as yet so little known.

"To this effect he required that in pursuing this trade, those engaged in it, would pay attention to unite to the employees they might send to the country, enlightened persons, who would use every exertion to penetrate to the sources of the Missouri, and beyond if posible to the Southern Ocean — take observations and heights of localities, and notices of the tribes who inhabit them, their habits and customs, the trade that might be established with them — note them as suitable marts for trade, or Forts for the protection of commerce, in a word to acquire a correct knowledge of a country until this period solely inhabited by Indian tribes, and almost entirely unknown.

"Your petitioner was one of the first to eagerly embrace a project so wisely conceived, and which was at an early day to cause the Colony to flourish, enrich all the members, and add to the glory of the Crown. It is unnecessary to enumerate to your Excellency, the names and the number of traders, who co-operated with your petitioner, and who perceived as himself, the good fortune and wealth to be derived from the enterprise, they are known to your Excellency. There were but two of them who, after having agreed, withdrew and renounced the partnership; more enlightened than your petitioner, they perceived in the undertaking their future ruin, which he has since found out, but too late, and which would not have occurred, had it been managed by an honest man. In fact sir, the act had but just been resolved upon, when, by a blindness your petitioner and his associates are amazed at, selected to place at the head of the enterprise, a man who was the least proper to its success. It was Mr. Clamorgan, whose private business affairs were in the greatest disorder and confusion, whose probity was suspected by several, intriguing, a fluent tongue, pliant, and even servile when it was politic to deceive to exalt himself, or to injure others. Such was the man that your petitioner and his associates chose, believing him the most competent to conduct great operations, which he said he had done all his life.

"The associates of Mr. Clamorgan, as I have just depicted him to your Excellency, fearing he might not act justly toward them, and trick them, to prevent which they associated Mr. Reilhe with him in the management, a man of established probity, that they thought was the proper one to watch over their suspected head, but this honest man became the dupe, he deceived and ruined him as he did the others.

"Your Excellency will feel surprised that an association placed at its head, one in whom they had no confidence — your Excellency will recover from this surprise when he will know that the co-partners not believing any of themselves sufficiently competent to conduct so extensive an enterprise, fearing that in assuming it they jeopardized their little fortunes and that of the association —

they flattered themselves, that in honoring Mr. Clamorgan, as head of the concern, the man would bear in mind the true principles of integrity, and that he would manage its affairs more honorably than he had up to that day managed his own, and that ambitious to merit the good opinion of his co-citizens, or to regain it if forfeited unjustly, he would strive to bring to his aid, all the light and knowledge he possessed to conduct with noble disinterestedness and expanded views an enterprise, which if well managed should work his fortune and those of his co-partners, the general advantage of the Colony, and add to the glory and renown of the Monarchy. Their hopes were deceived, and far from having opened to them the road to fortune, he led them, to the abyss of misfortune. Notwithstanding all the trust that his associates reposed in the ability of Mr. Clamorgan, however little they had in his probity, they thought it essential to their safety to adopt a code of regulations for the association, consequently under the auspices, and aided by the intelligence of Mr. Zenon Trudeau, the act of co-partnership, which is in your Excellency's custody, was revised and corrected, and sent to the Government for approval. That act was but little respected by Mr. C. he transgressed it whenever he thought it to his interest so to do.

"Mr. Clamorgan having been chosen and placed at the head, began his work. He was then entirely unprovided with merchandise, as were also several of the co-partners. Your petitioner not to delay the operations of the Company opened his store and loaned to Mr. Clamorgan, and to some of the co-partners, the articles they severally needed. We supposed that Mr. C., would select from amongst the traders, men of known integrity, skilled in the trade, and speaking various Indian dialects. We were surprised and chagrined that he selected but those who were known tr be the most worthless and corrupt, and that for the sole reason that they had long been in his debt; true, he selected a few honest ones among the number, but so ignorant and of such little experience in the business, that it is not surprising he did not succeed. He needed men, who, with their eyes open to the business, did not extort, and with whose aid he might without fearing imputations, have made judicious changes in the portions of the general outfit made by the several co-partners. From that moment it was feared that he was not going right, but it was only suspicion.

"If Mr. Clamorgan had really at heart the success of the Company, he would have selected intelligent, prudent, economical men, to manage an undertaking which required wisdom, system and economy to accomplish success for the benefit of the association and the Government. A course so lacking in honesty on the part of Mr. C. caused the loss of the first outfit, men poorly selected, goods in bad condition, damaged, necessarily drew on the loss.

"A second and third outfit, were not more successful, because nothing was properly done, several of the co-partners backed out after the first loss, not that they had changed their view of the adventure in itself, but rather that they perceived the faithlessness of the principal agent, that would occasion the loss of all other outfits they might make. At the last one your petitioner was the only remaining partner.

"Mr. Clamorgan in contempt of the articles of association, had acquired the shares of two of the partners, so that he was in himself Agent and Company, and your petition having but one share could neither oversee nor control in the least the outfits he C. thought proper to make, so that it resulted in the almost ruin of your petitioner who lost in the three adventures, ten thousand dollars. The petitioner would not have complained of his loss, had he no fault to find with Mr. Clamorgan's course, and had he acted like an honest man, but the petitioner cannot forgive, not only his mis-management, but of abusing the credit he had obtained with the Government through the mis-placed confidence reposed in him by his co-partners, and which it is but proper to expose to your Excellency the cunning and craftiness of Mr. Clamorgan.

"Mr. C. perceiving that the Missouri association would fall through for lack of means, since he had succeeded in nearly ruining the members—finding no longer the means of making new dupes, unwilling also to forfeit the reputation he flattered himself he had acquired by the crafty letters he had written to the Government, as by the notices he had caused to be inserted in your papers, "that he was the soul of an enterprise that would immortalize its projector." He forestalled a rich English Merchant of Canada, intent upon extending his trade as all the English are, he exhibited to him the great means he had in hand, to promptly realize a great fortune; he succeeded in gaining his confidence to such an extent that he put in his hands a large capital, solicited for him the exclusive trade of the Mississippi, hoping by this means to re-unite some future day, the same privilege for that of the Missouri, and so engross all the trade of the Illinois country — he was upon the point of succeeding, when death carried off at New Orleans this Merchant, who would have been a dupe as your petitioner was — the heirs will soon learn to what a man their Parent had surrendered himself.

"Your Excellency must perceive in this brief exposé that Mr. Clamorgan's aim was after exhausting the resources of a portion of the traders, to monopolize all the trade of the country, and to carry it on alone, on the ruins of those whose means he had the address to appropriate to himself.

"Your Excellency may perhaps imagine that the object of your petitioner is to demand from Mr. Clamorgan damages and interest on the losses he sustained, he is not so fond of litigation as to attempt such an enterprise, it would necessitate the lifting of the curtain which hides all the fraudulent tricks of Mr. C., probe an almost impenetrable abyss, and your petitioner's life would not be long enough to sweep over the ground, that such a pursuit would impair the tranquillity of soul of your petitioner. He does not intend to call Mr. C. to account for his depredations. He ventures only to pray you to withdraw from Mr. Clamorgan the exclusive privilege of the trade of the Missouri, which he monopolizes under the name of Todd & Co. — a privilege which, in changing the trade of the Illionis, brings no advantage to New Orleans, the center of all the trade of this country, inasmuch as all the peltries from this river go to Canada, and never are seen at the place which should be their proper destination, such as it was agreed on when the privilege was granted.

"Allow your petitioner to continue in the Missonri association, which he does not regard as a chimera although he lost largely.

"In praying you also that said society be reformed, that Mr. Clamorgan, who by his manipulations has made himself the perpetual head, be, not only excluded from all intermeddling but also to relinquish his stock and all those he bought or traded for, to the end that said company, remoddled and re-created under the auspices of your Excellency, and under the direction of Mr. Zenon Trudeau, the most sagacious, prudent, and zealous of Commandants, who has made his appearance in the Colony. If your Excellency deigns to entertain the request of your petitioner, he might recover his losses, and try again the enterprise risquing the remainder of his means, to attain the object which the society and the government had proposed to themselves. He hopes to obtain that boon from your kindness and your justice.

He has the honor to sign himself, My Lord,
Your most humble and Obed't Servant
JOSEPH ROBIDOU.

ST. LOUIS March 7, 1798.

SCHEME OF THE KING OF SPAIN TO REPLENISH HIS TREASURY 1798.

Translation.

"I send to your Lordship, by the King's order, four printed copies of the Royal decree directed to me by his Majesty.

"You will there see the urgent necessity that exists to provide for the defence and preservation of the Monarchy by the means there represented, and the greatness and magnanimity of the determination to prefer above all imposts the voluntary offerings of loyalty and patriotism. In truth his Majesty has seen with the liveliest satisfaction how much this course has animated the hearts of his subjects in his States, for hardly had the news been spread than considerable and repeated gifts have flowed, and continue to flow in, every day, each one contributing in proportion to his ability and even making admirable efforts.

"His Majesty being persuaded that he would find no less attachment on the part of his subjects who reside in his possessions in America, has resolved to have circulated there the said Royal order, to the end that following the example of those of this Kingdom, every one of them would strive to contribute to so laudable an object as that of providing for its conservation, hoping that they will give him this new proof of their loyalty, especially those who possess fortunes, and the persons who have the honor of serving in his Tribunals, they having greater reason to know the present necessities of the State and the easy manner taken by the King to supply them, they being also better able to appreciate the efforts of his Royal benevolence. I apprise you of this arrangement by his order, to the end that you make them known at the Capital and other dependencies of your government, and also that as those contributions are made, either by voluntary contribution or loan, you give me notice in naming those who contribute them, and particularly each one of them, so that I can place it all under the eye of his Majesty.

God have your Lordship in his holy keeping.
Aranjuez, June 20th, 1798.
Signed   SAAVEDRA.

To Mons. the Governor
of Louisiana.
Copy conforming to the original.
New Orleans, Feb. 28, 1799.
ANDRES LOPEZ.

Translation.

" The shackles and obstacles that the industry and commerce of my Spanish Provinces are made to suffer as the inevitable consequences of war, added to the stagnation in the funds and the precious productions of my Amerian possessions, are the causes why the products of my Royal revenues at this day are found much reduced, while on the other hand the extraordinary expenditures that are found necessary for the defence, the honor and the prosperity of the Monarchy accumulate and augment progressively; so that after having exhausted the resources to which in preceding times we had recourse, there remains a very considerable void, which it is urgently and indispensibly necessary to fill by some means equally extraordinary.

To impose new contributions is justifiable by the example of other belligerent nations, and by the concurrence of present circumstances, where the ties of interest and public duty compels every individual for the good and the preservation of the State to make sacrifices proportionate to their respective means; but as it is repugnant to the sensibility of my paternal heart to resort to this last remedy, before I have proved the insufficiency of the others, I have preferred to follow the impulse of a perfect reliance I entertain, that my dear and faithful subjects guided by the inclinations of their own honor, their loyalty and their patriotism, will make a generous effort to complete the sum necessary for present necessities. In consequence I have come to the conclusion to open, in Spain and in America two subscriptions: one for those voluntary gifts that persons of all classes and conditions may offer of their own free will, of such sums of money, or articles of gold or silver, that their zeal for the public cause may suggest to them, the other for a patriotic loan, without interest, which will be re-imbursable in the precise term of ten years, to commence running two years after the day of the announcement of Peace. So that in this manner each one may participate in the honor and satisfaction of having contributed to a purpose so essential to the State, without depriving himself of the use of the means he may need for ulterior purposes, or to further the progress of his industry.

" And for the best and most prompt accomplishment of all that is above written I desire that the following arrangements and conditions be observed and fulfilled.

" I. In Madrid and its jurisdiction, both Subscriptions will be received by the President of my council, or by one or more persons of consideration and worthy in every respect of the confidence of the people, to whom he may specially delegate his powers.

" II. In the principal large Cities in Spain, where my chancellorships and Royal courts are established, the said subscription will be made equally into the hands of the Presidents or principal officers respectively, who may delegate their authority to persons of distinction and of solid fortune, in the other cities, towns and villages of their districts; paying attention that none of my subjects have to go out of the place where they reside, nor to employ intermediate agents for that important service.

" III. The same course will be observed in America, by my Viceroys of New Spain, Peru, Santa Fé, and the Provinces of the Rio de la Plata, and by the Captains-General, Governors of Havanna, Porto-Rico, Caracas, Guatamala, Chili and the Phillippine Islands, who will take the greatest care that the honorable commission to receive these subscriptions be intrusted in each place to persons who unite external distinction to a well-established reputation for disinterestedness, integrity and patriotism.

"IV. There will be sent to all those who will be intrusted with this commission, printed forms of both subscriptions, so that it will only be necessary for them to fill the blank spaces, and that they uniformly follow one and the same method.

"V. The subscribers to the voluntary gift, will contract by the act of affixing their signatures, the distinct and formal obligation to send to our Royal Mints the articles of gold and silver of which they will designate the weight, or to remit to the order of my acting Treasurer-general the said articles, or the amount of specie money for which each one may have subscribed, and to effect said remittance, without deviating from the conditions established by themselves at the time of the subscription.

"VI. Accordingly as these subscriptions are gathered in, either by the Governor of my council, or the Presidents and heads of my chancellorships and Royal courts of Spain, or through their individual representatives, who will pass them over with the least possible delay, they will be sent to my Treasurer General to enable him to provide for gathering in the specie in the convenient time, and to receive the other precious articles by the most prompt and economical means, well understood that for the sake of good order and compatibility they will observe in these operations the usual formalities.

"VII. In America the Vice-Roys and Captains General will take the necessary steps to gather into the treasuries of my Royal exchequer, with punctuality, the sum total of these subscriptions, where they will be kept separately until the first opportunity to send them to Spain, or until I give them some other destination, in sending me notice by all opportunities of their actual condition.

"VIII. The patriotic loan will be composed of an indefinite number of shares of one thousand reals each, of which a certain number will be divided into four portions, so that even persons of very little means may, in depriving themselves for a time of the use of two hundred and fifty reals, procure for themselves the honour of perpetuating the memory of their zeal for the interest of the State.

"IX. The officers and persons appointed in Articles I., II. and III. to receive the subscriptions in the whole Kingdom, will also receive and send those for this loan to my Treasurer General, who will take suitable steps to pass them into my principal Treasury, or in those of the army or the nearest Provinces without any expense to the lenders, the amount of their shares, or portions of shares, for which they had subscribed, by giving or sending them letters of credit, issued in their favour, to the end that they may serve as legitimate titles for their loans.

"X. My Vice-Roys and Captains-general of the Americas and Phillippine Islands, will also see that there are given to Subscribers in the treasuries of my Royal exchequer, provisional acknowledgements of the amounts they have contributed, and so that in the three days preceding the departure of each messenger, the Treasurers remit them a single statement of receipts, which will include the said amounts as received for the account of my Treasurer General and to be sent to Spain, on which will be specified the names and residences of those interested; and by virtue of these papers, which the said Vice-Roys and Captains-general will send me by the conveyance reserved for the public treasure, my principal Treasury will despatch the certificates relative thereto, which will be sent to the same Principals, to be sent by them to the parties to whom they properly belong.

"XI. These certificates will be printed with a plate engraved expressly therefor; they will be invested with the signatures of my Grand Treasurer and Comptroller of my principal Treasury; there will be a blank space left to insert the name of the contributor, and in numbering them they will, pursue the ordinary usual mode, without leaving any one void.

"XII. The subscription will date in Spain, the 31st of December of the present year, 1798, and in America the 30th of June of the next year, 1799, the loan to be counted by the number of shares filled at that date.

"XIII. At the close of each of the ten years which will follow the two first years of peace, counting from the day it will be proclaimed, the one-tenth part of these certificates will be cancelled;

for this purpose they will draw lots for the numbers of those to be cancelled, and the full re-payment of their value will be made at the same place where the amount was delivered, or where the lender may find convenient.

"XIV. Seeing that this patriotic loan is for the defence and the common safety of the State, I declare, in my character of supreme administrator, that in all time it will be considered as a national debt, and in my own proper name, as in the names of my successors, I pledge all the revenues of my Crown to its punctual repayment in the manner before prescribed.

"XV. I desire also that the subscription to the voluntary gift, to the patriotic loan, or to both, be regarded as a positive act; and so that in all future time it may be distinguished as an act of honor and great merit in the persons of the subscribers and their descendants, there will be printed and published full lists of all their names, specifying the amount subscribed and the date of payment; and certified copies of these lists will be deposited in the offices of my Secretaries of State, in those of the Chambers of Castile and the Americas, and in all the other Tribunals, Royal Bureaus and public Archives of the nation in both domains, so that the memory of these services may be perpetuated, and that particulars may be drawn from it whenever it might become a question of dignity, employment and honor.

" Of this you will consider yourself apprised, and will issue the orders and instructions necessary for its execution.

" Signed by the Royal hand of the King, at Aranjuez, May 27, 1798.

"To Don Fran'co Saavedra."

" A copy conforming to the original Decree that the King has deigned to address to me. Aranjuez, May 28, 1798.
" Signed, SAAVEDRA.

" Copy conforming to the original.
" New Orleans, this 28th February, seventeen hundred and ninety nine.
" ANDRES LOPEZ, Signature.

The latter years of Trudeau's administration adds but little of general interest to our annals. Don Manuel Gayoso de Lemos had succeeded Baron de Carondelet as governor-general below in 1797. He died in New Orleans, July 18, 1799, and the Marquis de Casa Calvo, came over from Havana to act *ad interim*.

Trudeau's administration up here ended on August 29, 1799.

COL. CHARLES DEHAULT DELASSUS,

who had been commandant at New Madrid for the previous three years, and whose appointment as lieutenant-governor was made by express orders from Spain, succeeded Gov. Trudeau on the same day, August 29, 1799.

GIFT OF ZENON TRUDEAU TO THE SONS OF JNO B. TRUDEAU.

" Be it known by this indenture that I, Don Zenon Trudeau, Lieut. Colonel and Captain of grenadiers of the Regiment of Louisiana, declare that I am under grateful acknowledgements to to Don Juan Bap'a Trudeau, schoolmaster of this town, he having for some years educated my numerous family with particular care, and having received many favors at his hands, and being my relative, and my eldest son, Don Renato, being god-father to his eldest son, René Louis, with my free consent, without any inducement nor persuasion, in the best form of law, and well knowing my rights in such cases, I acknowledge and declare that I make a pure and perfect gift, which the law calls 'intervivos,' and irrevocable, to the male children born, and to be born, with the exclusion of the females, of the said Juan Bap'a Trudeau, of four hundred dollars which he owes me, which I advanced for the purchase of his house, and now henceforward and forever I relinquish and abandon all right, title, actions and recourse to the said four hundred dollars, and cede, relinquish and transfer them to the said male children of the said Juan Baptiste Trudeau, that he may administer the same during their minority, and that the interest thereof be applied to their suppport and education, without touching the capital, which must be delivered to them entire on their reaching the age of twenty-five years, or when their father may think them capable of managing their property. And I grant the said Trudeau full power in the name of his children, to hold possession of the said four hundred dollars. And I renounce the laws of large and general donations of all the property, because I have a sufficiency in my remaining property, and the sum donated does not exceed the five hundred 'sueldos' of gold allowed by law, and should it exceed this I empower the said Juan Bap. Trudeau, and any other person he may appoint to urge the same before the competent judge, making him approve thereof, and interpose his authority and judicial decree, and from this moment I consider the same acted upon and executed with the necessary solemnity, and request that any deficiency of clause requisite, or circumstance for the validity thereof be supplied.

"And I swear by the lord our God and by the sign of the cross, that I will not revoke by deed, will, or any other form whatever, neither tacitly nor expressedly, nor in any other way, although allowed to me by law, and should I do so (besides not being heard in law), it may be seen that I approve the same and invalidate it; adding strength to strength and contract to contract, for the due performance I bind my person and goods (estate), actual and future, and authorize his Majesty's justices, and especially those of this province, to whose jurisdiction I submit myself and goods, and I renounce my domicil and any other privilege conceded to me, and all laws and privileges in my favor and the general law that I be compelled thereto as if sentence had been given in the case, and with my consent.

"And I, the said Jno. Bap. Trudeau, here present, acknowledge to owe the said Don Zenon Trudeau, the aforesaid, four hundred dollars, and in the name of my male children, born and to be born, I accept the donation to be used as above stated, and highly esteem the kindness conferred on me, and to secure to my children the sum to them donated by this deed, I expressly mortgage a dwelling house to me belonging, situated in this town, bounded south by ground of Don Bernard Pratte, east (west) by Main street, north by another street which separates it from the widow Labbadie, and east by the river Mississippi, which is my own property, and was paid for with the four hundred dollars mentioned in this deed, and free from any other incumbrance whatever, and I now bind and incumber the same so that I can not sell or alienate it until the payment of the said four hundred dollars, and anything done contrary thereto will be null, and execution can be issued on said house, and I empower his Majesty's justices, and especially those of this jurisdiction to whom I submit myself and goods, and I renounce my domicil (legal residence), and any other privilege in my favour, together with all laws and ordinances in my favour, and the general laws in due form, that they may proceed against me as if sentence had been given, and with my consent. And I, Don Carlos Dehault DeLassus, Lieut. Colonel of the royal army, and Lieut. Governor of the western part of Illinois, bear testimony that the contracting parties are known to me, that they executed this deed before me, in default of a notary in this jurisdiction, in presence of the attending witnesses, Don Eugenio Alvarez and Joseph Hortiz, and they signed with me in St. Louis in Illinois the eighteenth day of the month of October, one thousand seven hundred and ninety-nine.

Zeno Trudeau,   Jno. Bap. Trudeau,   Joseph Hortiz,
Carlos Dehault Delassus.

The above is copied verbatim from the record in the archives. The translation from the Spanish is wretchedly absurd and ridiculous, rendering the English version almost incomprehensible.

Under the French and Spanish laws of the olden time, a man even free from debt, could not gratuitously give away his property beyond a certain amount, the one-half being in law the property of his wife and children, but when in debt his whole property was held to be mortgaged for his debts, even if not so expressed in writing, and he could make no legal disposition of it until his debts were paid.

A male was a minor until the age of 25 years, a female until 20 years.

MURDER OF ADAM HOUSE

on the waters of the Maramec, by Indians in 1800: —

I. Pierre Treget, commandant at Carondelet, pursuant to orders from Don Carlos Dehault Delassus, commandant at St. Louis, repaired to the Renault Forks, with the few militia men I could assemble, in pursuit of the Indians; on reaching the place, I found an old man dead, head cut off, and laid at his side, scalp taken and body full of wounds from musket shots, and a few paces off, a boy 8 or 9 years old, head cut off and lying near him, face smeared with blood, with a small piece of maple sugar in his mouth, no wound on his body from either musket or knife. A dead cow, one horn carried off, dead calf, head cut off, beds in the house cut to pieces, utensils broken and strewed about the house.

"Ascertained the murder had been committed by the Osages; buried the bodies, not known at the time.

"CARONDELET, March 19, 1800.
"PIERRE DE TREGET.

"RENAULT'S FORKS, March 25.

"I, Pascal Leon Cerré, Ensign of Militia, repaired to the above place by order of the Governor, where I ascertained that the persons killed were Adam House and Jacob House, his son — from his son John, 14 years of age, who escaped wounded by a musket shot, and finding no will in the house to ascertain his disposition of his property, I appointed as witnesses to the inventory of his effects, John Cummins and Joshua Donald. I appointed as guardian of the minors, Betsy, John and Peggy House, Mr. Robert Owen, of Marais des Liards (Owens Station).

"MATTHEW LORD, JAMES CRAIG,   PASCAL L. CERRE,
"ANDREW PARK, JOHN JOHNSTON,   ROBERT OWEN, *Guardian.*
"JAMES GRAY, ADAM STROUD,   JOHN BROWN, *Security.*
"JUDATHAN KENDALL, THOS. WILLIAMS, JNO. CUMMINS &
"JOS'HA MCDONALD,   Witnesses.
"BART HARRINGTON, LEVI THIEL & JOHN JACK, *Appraisers.*

The negro fork of the Meramec, is our present Big River, which is a large branch coming into the Meramec on the south side in Jefferson County. Fourche a Renault is Renault's fork, or mineral fork of Big river in Washington County, 8 or 10 miles north-west of Mine á Burton, now Potosi.

This is the Renault found in Gayarré and others, who came over from France about 1722 with a large force to work the mines, and brought the bricks necessary for the furnaces from Paris, with his name on them. Cozens unearthed one of them in surveying in that locality in 18—.

EDWARDS *versus* KISHLER.

"John Bishop sworn, saith that said Edwards embarked in said Kishler's pirogue at the forks of Licking, from whence said Edwards was only a passenger to Cincinnati, at which place he engaged himself to said Kishler to come as far as the falls of Ohio, which said Edwards performed and said Kishler paid him the full hire, which said Edwards confessed to said Bishop.

"That said Kishler engaged said Edwards again at the falls to come in his Pirogue to the Illinois, but that he, said Bishop, was not present at the bargain, but that he heard said Kishler say in presence of said Edwards that he, said Kishler, was to give to said Edwards one dollar per day for the time he should be coming down the Ohio, and one and a half dollars for every day he should be ascending the Mississippi; that the said Edwards took the charge of said Pirogue with said Kishler's family, the Deponent with his family being also of the Company, that they all left the falls in said Pirogue; said Kishler left the falls the day before by land, and they left the falls about the eighteenth day of September and arrived at Misere (St. Genevieve) the twelfth of October, of which time they were eleven days coming from Massac to Misere; that the said Pirogue was split and leaky when she left Licking & that they were obliged to repair her three times by the way; that said Edwards left said Pirogue at Massac because two of the hands out of the 5 hands he had were detained three days in prison, during which interval said Edwards made a bargain with a boat that was coming to the Illinois for a passage for himself and followers, and that said Edwards could not sell the Pirogue for more than one dollar, for which reason he made a hole in her and sunk her.

"Mrs. Bishop sworn and confirms the above.

"Miss Polly Jones sworn, and saith she knoweth nothing relating to the before mentioned affair.

"Nathaniel Porter sworn, and saith that he was sometimes in company with said Edwards, and that he could not perceive that said Edwards lost any time by neglect, that the Pirogue appeared to go as well as that of the deponent, and that he left said Edwards above Massac.

"Mrs. Graves sworn, and saith that said Edwards told her at Creve Cœur that he had no bargain with said Kishler, but that he intended to charge him only eighteen dollars, besides six dollars that he laid out on account of Kishler's family.

"Sworn and examined before me this 18th day of March, one thousand eight hundred.

"SANTIAGO MACKAY, Capt. Comd't.

"We the arbitrators find for Plaintiff, sixty two dollars, our judgment divided in respect of the Pirogue.

JAMES GREEN and SAM'L CULBERTSON.

Mr. Nathaniel Porter being chosen as a third to assist the two other arbitrators Mr. James Green and Mr. Samuel Culbertson, they have determined that the plaintiff shall pay to the said Kishler, the sum of twenty dollars for the said Pirogue out of the sixty-two dollars which is given in favor of the said Edwards consequently the said Kishler is now and hereby indebted to the said Edwards in the sum of forty two dollars.

"St. Andrew, March 18, 1800.   "James Green,
"Approved, Santiago Mackay.   Sam'l Culbertson,
                                                Nathan'l Porter."

ACTION AGAINST MOSES MOODEY,

of St. Ferdinand, for breach of the peace, and his imprisonment for the same.

Francois Dunegant dit Beaurosier was the first commandant at the village from about 1780 until the transfer.

His complaint against Moodey:

"St. Ferdinand, March 9, 1800.

"Sir: Mr. Griffin came to my house in the night, between Sunday and Monday the 9th inst., to complain against Moses Moodey, who had been living with him about fifteen days. Mr. Moodey came home between 11 and 12 o'clock at night, and asked Mr. Griffin's son 'if his father and sisters were in bed, because he wanted his things,' to which Mr. Griffin's son replied 'yes, they had gone to bed,' notwithstanding he entered Mr. Griffin's room and demanded of the girls his clothes, and one of the Miss Griffins replied that his things were ready except a shirt not yet washed; then he said to Mr. Griffin that he wanted to settle for the time he had been boarding there. Mr. G. then said to him that it was not the proper time to settle, and that he would see him again — but Mr. Moodey determined to know how much he owed to Mr. Griffin, reiterated his demand, to which Mr. Griffin replied, 'I made a trip for you to Meramec which took me about three days, about fifteen days' board for yourself and horse, the making up of several articles for you, and your washing, is altogether well worth twenty dollars.' Mr. Moodey flew into a violent passion, saying, 'you want to ruin me,' and drawing two pistols from his belt, presented one to Mr. Griffin's breast and the other to his wife. Griffin seeing his life and that of his wife menaced, sprang upon Moodey, who eluded his grasp and escaped, and Griffin says Doct. Wallis witnessed it all.

"I at once ordered six militia men to arrest Mr. Moodey, who brought him to me, and not having here a sure place to keep him, I send him to you in the custody of two of the militia, that you may exercise your discretion in the matter.

"I have the honor to be, sir,

"Your very humble and obedient servant,

"F. DUNEGANT.

"To Mr. CHARLES DEHAULT DELASSUS."

"Moodey was put in prison, and Governor Delassus being at the time otherwise engaged, he commissioned his adjutant Capt. Soulard to act in his stead, who repaired to the place, and in the presence of Dunegant and other witnesses, took the depositions of William Griffin and wife Barbara, and daughters Susie and Margaret and Doct. Geo. Wallis, James Richardson, Interpreter, and Robert Owen, Syndic of Marais des Liards, witnesses.

"After a month's imprisonment Moodey addressed a petition to Gov. De Lassus, April 7, 1800, 'acknowledging his offence which he much regretted it being his first, under the influence of liquor, proposing to pay all the costs, and asking to be liberated, promising to so conduct himself in future as to give no cause of complaint.

"Signed MOSES MOODEY.

"Under the circumstances, and with the acquiescence of Griffin, who joined in the petition, he was pardoned by the Governor and released.

"Copy of the costs of Justice:

				Dollar.	
Gov.'s fees — his decree and signature to Adjt. Soulard	8 reals	1 00			
Same. his sentence and signature	8 "	1 00			
Same. Sitting occupied in reading affidavits	22 "	2 75			
Tax on the costs of 12 pages, a real for 4 pages	3 "	37½			
Signature to the bill of costs	4	45	50	5.62½	
For Adjt. Soulard — A day's journey out of the town (4 ducats)		44		5 50	
Horse and feed each 8 reals		16		2 00	
2 Sittings taking affidavits — 2 ducats each		44		5 50	
8½ pages manuscript writing, 2 reals page		17		2 12½	
8 signatures — 4 reals each		32	153. 4	19.12½	
			198 reals.	$24.75	

JOHN COLGIN *VS.* RICHARD LYONS, AT ST. ANDRE.

Mr. Nathaniel Porter Deposeth that he heard John Colgin say that he could whip Lyons if he would come out, and that Lyons went out and he saw them enclosed, and heard Colgin say that Lyons was biting him, that he ran to part them, and that Lyons had let Colgin go, and that both of them were in liquor.

"David Cole Deposeth that he heard Colgin and Lyons quarrelling and that they were stripped to fight, and then he thought they had made it up, that he saw Lyons strike Colgin once, and then they quarreled again and he heard Colgin say if Lyons would fight him a fair fight, he would fight him, that they then went in the house and wanted Lyons to make friends, and he would not, that he heard Lyons say he would complain against Colgin to government, and then they quarrel again, and he heard Colgin say he could whip Lyons the best day he ever saw, and then he said Lyons struck Colgin twice, and then they enclosed again, and he heard Colgin say, Lyons you have bit me.

"Bery Jones Deposeth that he heard them quarreling, and that he saw Lyons catch Colgin by the face, and then they stripped to fight, and he heard Colgin say he could whip Lyons the best day he ever saw if he would fight him fair, and then they went in the house, and that I then started home, and after Colgin said he could whip Lyons that Lyons said you must do it now and that he saw Lyons strike colgin twice and then they enclosed, and he saw Colgin fall and said Lyons had bit him and that Pusley asked Lyons if he gouged him and said no and then he ast him if he bit him and Lyons said it was another man's business and that they I believe they ware both in liquor and that colgin wanted to drink friends and that Lyons said he would complain to the Government.

"George Pusley Deposeth that he was in company with colgin and lyons and others and that they ware all drinking and he saw lyons and colgin enclos'd and fighting and that he helped to part them they both went out of the house and striped to fight and neither of them would strike and then they went into the house and then we all started to go home and in the yard I heard colgin say lyons I can whip you the day you ever saw and that I saw lyons draw his fist and strike at colgin twice and colgin caught Lyons by the breast and they pusht one another about and Colgin fell and we ran to part them and Lyons got of Colgin and I askt lyons if he gouged him he said no. I then asked him if he bit him he said that was another man's matter and that I believe they were both in liquor.

"Wm. Tardy Deposeth that he heard Lyons and Colgin quarreling and he saw lyons strike colgin and was then parted and then they both stript and went out to fight and I heard colgin say he could whip lyons and they started to go home I saw them both a fighting, and believe they were both in liquor.

"As it appears to us J. Mackay command't of this District that the said Lyons is guilty of a breach of the Peace in a striking manner we have ordered him to pay to said John Colgin the sum of Eighteen Dollars Peltries, besides Two Dollars and half dollar silver Costs to Mr. Richard Caulk and Two Dollars to Mr. Carpenter, Sergeant of the Gard after which he is discharged.

"J. MACKAY.

"ST. ANDRÉ, Jan'y 29th, 1801."

"Whereas, I Richard Caulk Assistant to Santiago Macky and by his instruction have attended at St. André to hear a complaint of John Colgin against Daniel Lyons and he said Lyons has absconded himself from tryal and the substance of the evidence appears to be against him I do by these presents in the name of his Majesty the King of Spain seize all the property of the said Daniel Lyon in behalf of the complainant and his creditors until further tryal consisting of — one yoke of oxen pied, and one cow, five chisels, and one gouce, four files, and two rasps, four plains, two stocks of plains, and one plain bit, one gimlet, one pair of compasses and one saw set, and two gages, one kettle of 17 gallons at ace Musick, and one cappo that Gibson left there and one wood all one handsaw one smoothing plain two lots one formerly the property of George Pursley and the other the property David Cole one pair saddle bags which property I deliver into the hands and care of Christopher Carpenter as Sargent of the guard of this District in behalf of goverment.

" Received by order of Richard Caulk in behalf of government the above mentioned articles by me.

"CHRISTOPHER CARPENTER.

"ASA MUSICK,
"MICHAEL UDOM.

WM. BELL *vs.* JOHN COLGIN.

" Before us J. Mackay command't of the District of St. André, appeared William Bell, inhabitant of this said District who has brought the following charges against John Colgin also an inhabitant of this District, to wit: The said Wm. Bell (Plaintiff) saith that the said John Colgin (defendant) in the beginning of January last at the House of Mrs. Henry abused him with much bad language that he called him a damned lyar and that he could prove it — and that he had his Hogs & cast him, and he shook his tomihawk over his head. To support the said charges the Plaintiff brought the following evidences, John Ridenhour who hath sworn on the holy Evangelist that about the beginning of Jan'y last that he was at the house of Mrs. Henry in company with the Plaintiff and Defendant and Mordicai Bell and others and that on a dispute between the Defendant John Colgin and Mordecai, the plaintiff William Bell interfered by talking in favor of said Mordecai Bell on which said defendant called the Plaintiff a lyar and that he would call him a lyar when he pleased and that he cast him and that he had his hogs and that the Defendant shook his tomihawk over his head, on which the Plaintiff called witness and said that his hogs should come home, and further he saith not. John Murphy who hath sworn on the Holy Evangelist that on a quarrel between John Colgin and Mordecai Bell, the said Wm. Bell said that Mordecai was not fit to fight with Colgin because that he was lame and that said Colgin said to the Plaintiff Wm. Bell that he was a lyar.

"Mrs. Colvin sworn saith that some time after the trial in the winter before last John Colgin and John Bell quarreled at her house and that on John Bells making some reflections on the defendant the said defendant answered. I suppose you want to make me out a hog thief because I took 2 of your father's pigs to which said Jno. Bell son to the plaintiff replyed that he did not call him a hog thief, but he thought it was the next thing to it.

"Dan Richison sworn saith that on the same night, as specified in John Ridenhours affidavit, he was at Mrs. Henry's house where he heard the Defendant John Coligen say to the Defendant he was a lyar and recorded such that he could prove it and that he had his hogs.

"John Carpenter sworn saith that he was at Mrs. Henry's house when the said Bell and Coligen quarreled and that Coligen called Bell a lyar and he could prove it, that he was a damned hog and might go and stay with his hogs.

"Nathaniel Porter sworn saith that he heard John Colgin say to Wm. Bell, to hell with the lying Bells.

"Seeing by the testimony taken and examined, as before mentioned, that said Colgin was in the wrong. We have condemned the defendant John Coligen to pay said Wm. Bell, ten dollars in Peltries and twelve dollars in peltries for the costs.

"ST. ANDRÉ, the 19th Feb'y, 1801.

"J. MACKAY."

AGREEMENT TO MARRY.

"Upper Louisiana the year one thousand eight hundred and one, the first day of April. Before me Don James Mackay, commandant of St. André of Missouri, were present William Tardy and Madame Joanah Henry, inhabitants of this district of St. Andrew, who hereby declare that being on the point of being married together, their marriage contract has been agreed on, made and concluded on the following conditions viz: the said Madame Henry declares by this, that neither the said Mr. Tardy, nor his creditors, nor any person whatever on their part, never had any right, nor power to sell, or dispose of in any manner, none of the effects, or property belonging to said Madame Henry, which consists of four cows, two young steers, one heifer, three calves, sixty hogs, a furnished bed, two iron pots, an oven, six crockery plates, two pewter dishes, two sad-irons, a spinning wheel, the above articles with all the produce in future, being by right Mrs. Henry's property, are confirmed to her and her sucessors by this contract forever. And it is declared hereby, that neither their marriage, nor any other pretext, gives any right to said Tardy, or any other person, over the articles above mentioned, and that said Madame Henry alone has any right to dispose of as she thinks fit, any of the above articles. And said Mr. Tardy declares that he accepts all the above conditions.

In testimony whereof the contracting parties have signed with their marks, in presence of witnesses and I the commandant.

Hugh Graham	his William x Tardy. mark
Samuel Graham.	her Joanah x Henry. mark
James Mackay.	

In the year 1801, the northeast portion of this county, north of the present village of Baden, was under the charge of one Edmund Hodges, an uneducated but efficient man, as supervisor for Gov. Delassus of that portion of this district. The Spanish Pond, 12 miles due north of St. Louis, then the residence of Jacques De St. Vrain, a brother of Gov. Delassus, was the central point in the surrounding settlements.

A young man named Samuel Fallis, whose parents lived across the Missouri in St. Charles county, spent much of his time in this district. For some time back a number of horses had been missing from the pastures of some of the inhabitants, which at first were supposed to be stolen by roving Indians from both sides of the Mississippi, but from certain circumstances that subsequently transpired, Fallis was strongly suspected of being a party to their disappearance; thereupon he was apprehended by Hodges assisted by others and brought to St. Louis, where, after an examination by Gov. Delassus, he was committed to prison August 20th, 1801, to await his trial, pending which the following petition was prepared and presented to the governor: —

"*To Don Chas. Dehault Delassus, Lieutenant Governor of Upper Louisiana:*

"SIR.—Isaac Fallis and Susan Fallis petitioners, have the honor to represent to you, with all the respect which is your due, that the detention of their son Samuel, causes them great injury, seeing that he is the one of their children who is their greatest help in their old age.

SAMUEL FALLIS.

"Your petitioners are far from excusing their child, he is no doubt guilty since the law has punished him severely; but Sir, will you not allow yourself to be softened by the tears of a whole virtuous family, afflicted by the misdeed of one of its members, who all his life had been brought up in correct principles, with which they are themselves penetrated. Cannot the rigors of the law be softened on behalf of a son who was always correct up to the moment when, perhaps misled and encouraged by evil advice, he wandered from the straight path of duty, and brought grief to the bosom of his family, your heart is compassionate Sir, allow mercy to act in behalf of a father and mother, be pleased as judge to ameliorate the law which condemns our son, deign to grant pardon to Samuel Fallis, not alone to his parents but also to the honest inhabitants who join with us to obtain it from your clemency; Samuel Fallis raised in the principles of an honest man, will easily recover from the correction you inflicted on him, the punishment from which he will escape but by an especial favour is almost a certain guarantie that he will in the future conduct himself as he should, his parents may venture to be responsible to you on that score, and cheerfully pledge themselves to pay all the costs, which their son may have occasioned by his misconduct.

St. Louis Sept. 20th, 1801.

ISAAC FALLIS,	ALEXANDER CLARK,	JOSEPH TODD,
SUSANNA FALLIS,	ROBERT OWEN,	JAMES DE ST. VRAIN,
WM. PATTERSON,	JAMES MITCHELS,	SAMUEL DUNCAN,
JOHN BROWN,	HEZEKIAH CROSBY,	LOUIS LABEAUME,

"This may certify that I know no harm of him or any of the family before this. SAMUEL GRIFFETH.

M. JAMES DU B. BROWN.

"I John Lar do Her sartify that I Never Heard Anything of thay family Till this Time &c. AMOS RICHARDSON.

"This may Certify that I Never New any harm of him before this. VINCENT CARRICO.

"Mr. Samuel falas Dr. to Edmund Hodges, August the 4d 1801
By sining one pirtision for Mr. piper to fetch Mr. falas Before us to answer to Mr. piper's complaint   D. S.
                                                                    0. 4. 0

for one Days tendance on a troial
for one tachment to take Mr. falas hom
By going 2 Leags to Serve the tachment
for going one Day me and hors after Mr. falas to take him
19 of august, 1801
By one order to take mr. falas to St. Lewey
By going Down with Mr. falas 2 days to St. Lewey 7 Leags
By going with old Mr. falas to St. Lewey 2 days 7 Leags
the above is a verbatim copy of Mr. Hodges bill of costs —
" Samuel Dunken and William Heart and Larance Huf and Ira Nash you are Comanded to gow and take Amos Dunken and Conway to Sant Luis and ameadatly, fale not, given under my hand this 14 day of March 1801.
"EDMUND HODGES, *Comander.*

Translation.
" Regiment of Infantry of Louisiana, District of Illinois.
" Statement shewing the time the Englishman named Folis was fed by the company of this Post in this Fort of St. Louis, having entered it August 20th and left on Sept. 22nd 1801 — 33 days at two reals a day — amount in dollars $8.25.
"ST. LOUIS, July 3, 1802.
"JUAN ROBAYNA, *Serg't.*

The confidence of his parents in the future good conduct of their son was verified, as we find him a few years later purchasing from Adam Brown a farm of 140 acres near Owen's Station at $4 per acre, $560. A brother, Geo. Fallis had a large farm in the St. Ferdinand prairie.

SARPY *vs.* SAFFRAY.

" *To all who shall see these present letters, greeting:*
" Be it known that before us Don Thomas Portell, Captain of Infantry in the Stationary Regiment of Louisiana, and civil and

military commandant of the District of New Madrid, residing at Fort Celeste, undersigned, was present Mr. Saffray, an inhabitant of this district, who acknowleges that he is indebted to Mr. Joseph O'Neille residing usually at St. Louis, of the Illinois, at present in this town, in the sum of three thousand, six hundred and thirteen livres, eighteen sols, for goods advanced him in this Post up till the twelfth of May, one thousand seven hundred and ninety-four, which said sum of three thousand, six hundred and thirteen livres, eighteen sols tournois, said Peter Saffray promises and binds himself to pay to said Mr. O'Neille, or holder of this present bond, in one year from this day in current money of this place of New Madrid, under penalty of all losses, costs, damages and interests.

"And to further secure said Joseph O'Neille the payment due him by said Saffray, he by these presents has bound and hypothecated for security of said sum, — first, a farm on which he now resides, situated at the place called Lake St. Isidor, with all buildings and appurtenances now on it or which may be in future. Secondly, a town house on a lot of forty foot front on the public place in New Madrid, by the usual depth of one hundred and eighty, also three pairs of oxen, two cows and twelve hogs which said Saffray now owns, and also all the other effects which he may acquire up to the date of the payment of this bond, and all the animals he may acquire in any way from now to the same time, said Saffray consenting to make no sale of said effects nor animals until the said sum of three thousand six hundred and thirteen livres, eighteen sols tournois, which he owes to said Mr. O'Neille, are fully paid to him, or to the holder of the present obligation. However, said Joseph O'Neille hereby consents, that if said Mr. Pierre Saffray finds opportunity to sell the house in town above designated, he may do it, provided that the proceeds of the same be converted into live stock for the advantage of the farm of said Saffray, said live stock representing said house will remain bound for the payment of said sum due to Mr. O'Neille.

"Executed at Fort Celeste of New Madrid, April second, one thousand seven hundred and ninety four, Peter Anthony Laforge, commissary of police of that town, and John Barna y ferru Sola, at present in this town of New Madrid, being witnesses, who have with said O'Neille and Saffray, signed these presents, thus signed at the moment.

"P. SAFFRAY, JOHN BARNA Y FERRU SOLA, JH O'NEILLE,
"PETER A. LAFORGE.

"Before me, the commandant,   THOMAS PORTELL.
"I certify that the present is a copy of the original in the archives of this command of Fort Celeste of New Madrid, April 4, 1795.

"THOMAS PORTELL.

"The year eighteen hundred and two, the thirteenth of January, I, Peter A. Laforge, discharging the functions of notary at this poste of New Madrid, have informed and notified Mr. Gabriel Cerré of the decision rendered by M. the commandant of New Madrid, this day, at the bottom of the petition presented to him. And I have also informed, notified and given a copy to Mr. Peter Saffray at his known residence in this village, at the house occupied by Mr. Francis Pasquin, verbally to said Pasquin in person, of the petition of Mr. Cerré against him dated the twelfth of this month, and the order given in consequence by the commandant of this poste the next day, the thirteenth, so that all said gentlemen may be informed, and conform to it.

"In testimony of which I have signed said copy and this one.
"PETER ANTHONY LAFORGE."

INQUEST ON THE BODY OF JOSEPH BATES, DROWNED.

"In the town of St. Louis of Illinois, the 7th day of the month of July, of the year one thousand eight hundred and two.
"I, Don Joseph Horttiz, performing the functions of notary public in the place, being informed from Senor Don Carlos Dehault Delassus, Lieutenant Governor of this upper Louisiana, that at the lower end of the town on the bank of the Mississippi river, a body had been washed ashore. By order of said Governor, being in the Royal Service, I repaired to the place indicated, accompanied by Mr. Francois Valois and Joseph Robidoux, Jr.,

INQUEST OF PARISIEN.

to examine and identify the body which we found on the river bank opposite the residence of Pierre Gueret Dumont, and proceeded to the examination, which consumed much time to find any one who could identify it, when Calvin Adams, of this town, declared that it was the body of an American named John or Joseph Bates, who worked for his living in the settlement of St. Andre, on the Missouri, in this district, who had a brother in said settlement, and was a Roman Catholic, and about five or six weeks ago, a pirogue was destroyed and washed ashore at Cahokia.

"Thereupon said Adams went to the Governor with the permission of Father Pedro Janin, curate of this parish, to procure a coffin for said body, which was taken to the cemetery and there interred the same day.

"In testimony whereof, and by direction of the Governor, this certificate, signed and attested by the witnesses and myself, was made to serve if needed.

"Jos. C. ROBIDOUX, FRAN'S VALOIS, JOSEPH HORTTIZ,
DELASSUS.

INQUEST ON PARISIEN.

"In the town of St. Louis of Illinois, this 13th day of July, eighteen hundred and two: I, Joseph Horttiz, notary of this town, by order of Don Carlos Dehault Delassus, Lieut. Colonel, exercising the functions of Lieut. Governor of this Upper Louisiana, having received information that a dead body was discovered floating in the Mississippi river, between the plantations of Mr. Joseph Brazeau and James Coburn, about three-fourths of a league south of the village, I repaired to the place, accompanied by Francis Valois and Auguste Chereau, witnesses, to identify the body, which proved to be that of an Indian named Pierre Parisien, who lived at the establishment of St. Charles of the Missouri, and who, as we had heard from Don Carlos Tayon, had gone fishing on the 9th of the previous month, June, and had never been heard from. With the assistance of four men the body was drawn from the river, which being in too putrified a condition to be taken to the village, a grave was dug on the spot to the depth of five feet, and the corpse buried therein, and a cross placed at the head of the grave; all this in my presence. There being neither wounds nor bruises found on his body, it was declared to be a case of accidental death.

"AUGUSTE CHEREAU, FRANCIS VALOIS,

"Approved same day. JOSEPH HORTTIZ, *Not'y*.
"DE LASSUS.

MOTARD & LOISEL.

"In the town of St. Louis, of the Illinois, this 29th day of the month of October, of the year eighteen hundred and two: We, Joseph Motard and Regis Loisel, citizens of this town, have agreed with the present knowledge and consent of Mr. Charles Debault Delassus, Lieutenant Governor of Upper Louisiana, to come to submit ourselves to an arbitration in regard to the boarding of Joseph Motard at Regis Loisel's, as also some other matter of interest that there is to settle, and for this purpose they have appointed for arbitrators, Charles Sanguinet and Manuel Moro, the first for me, Joseph Motard, and the other for Regis Loisel, to whose judgment and decision we will conform in all, and if the said arbitrators disagree, and come not to one mind, it will then be passed over to the Lieut. Governor, to the end that he be pleased to decide it by a third arbitrator. In testimony whereof, we have signed these presents, the day and year above.

JOSEPH MOTARD. REGIS LOISEL.

"We, Charles Sanguinet and Manuel Moro, arbitrators chosen by Joseph Motard and Regis Loisel, after having heard the two parties in a strict examination of their arguments and understandings, have resolved and determined as follows, in regard to their difference, to wit

"As one of the two said parties asks a little too much for his boarding from the other, and that this other will not agree and give a fair price, and in view of the many verbal complications branching out from the main point, which would require further enlightenment, and having found both parties much soured against each other, and consequently difficult to lead to an agreement, we send it back to the Lieutenant Governor, so that it may please him to make such a decision as he may find suitable, or terminate their differences by such a decision as seems to him best.

"St. Louis of Illinois, November 17, 1802.
"Manuel Gonzales Moro.   Charles Sanguinet."

"In view of the statement of Messrs Charles Sanguinet and Manuel Moro, arbitrators appointed by Joseph Motard and Regis Loisel, in regard to their difficulty about the payment of the boarding. As it is a difficulty impossible for us to terminate, as there is no written agreement, nor other evidence than that of the interested parties themselves, and that can only be decided by a fair estimate made by impartial parties, we will appoint Mr. Hebert Lecompte, who with Messrs. Sanguinet and Moro, may be able to end the matter according to their souls and consciences.

"Chas. Dehault De Lassus.
"St. Louis, November 22, 1802."

"We the undersigned, with one accord, on our souls and consciences, have decided and decreed that Mr. Motard will pay Mr. Loisel the sum of one hundred and thirty-four dollars and five bits ($134\frac{62\frac{1}{2}}{100}$), that we have made up from their respective statements, in money current in this country. In testimony of which we have signed this present, at St. Louis of Illinois, December 1, 1802.

"Charles Sanguinet.   Man'l Gonzales Moro.
"Wm. Hebert Lecompte."

"The parties to the above judgment will be notified to conform to the same.

"Delassus.
"St. Louis, December 1, 1802."

---

[1] Old Motard died on the 29th December, at the age of 80 years, just four weeks after this feeding contest, so that Loisel just "*saved his bacon.*"

316 ANNALS OF ST. LOUIS.

OFFICIAL NOTES TO GOVR. DELASSUS, PRECEDING HIS EXPEDITION TO NEW MADRID.

"In compliance with your official orders of yesterday, Mr. James Boyer of the Saint Genevieve Company, and Mr. ——— of the Platin Company, bearers of the same, have orders to report themselves to you prepared to march.

"God have you in his holy keeping,
"FRAN'CO VALLÉ.

"ST. GENEVIEVE, Nov. 10, 1802.

"No. 74. I received by your messenger your official note No. 71 of the 19th Inst. I immediately dispatched the messengers, as you instructed me, to apprise the Chiefs of the Mascou or Taliposa Indians, who may be found in the vicinity of this district, that I learnt from one of the said tribe now at this post, they were in the direction of the Marameque; and I charged the said Messenger, that if he encountered old Canaloué, the Shawnee Mascou, to report with him at New Madrid the 15th Decr, proximo—to be present at the council there to be held in compliance with the instructions of the Governor General of New Orleans, in regard to the disposition of the Mascou prisoners now held there.

"God have you in his holy keeping,

"ST. GENEVIEVE, Nov. 22, 1802.
"FRAN'CO VALLÉ.

"To Gov'R CHARLES DE LASSUS.

"In reply to your official note No 72, I send you herewith a list of those persons at this post able to bear arms, and who possess arms and horses. St. Genevieve, Nov. 24, 1802.

"God have you in his holy keeping.
"FRAN'CO VALLÉ.

"To Gov'r CHARLES DE LASSUS.

"No. 76. In conformity to orders received in your official note No. 73, I have this day organized for active service the Detachment under my command, and they are ready for the march. I would have sent you the muster-roll, but that I was constantly expecting your arrival, as you had written me.

"God have you in his holy keeping.

"St. Genevieve, Dec'r 4, 1802.
"Fran'co Vallé.

"Don C. Dehault De Lassus,
"Lieut. Gov'r.

"No. 77. I received by your mounted orderly the orders of the 8th and 9th Insts., sent me by Don Camille De Lassus, Lieut. and Aid-de-Camp, and at once made them known to the commanding officers of the militia of Saint Genevieve and Platin, so that they may carry them into execution without delay.

God have you in his holy keeping.
St. Gevevieve, Dec'r 10, 1802.
Fran'co Vallé.

Don Chas. Dehault Delassus,
Commanding Officer.

78. Hereto appended is the roll of the New Bourbon Company, examined by myself. In execution of the orders of last evening, I ordered the St. Genevieve and Platin companies to re-assemble at 2 o'clock p. m., to have read to them the order of march.

God have you in his holy keeping,
St. Genevieve, Dec'r 12, 1802.
Fran'co Vallé.

Don Chas. D. Delassus,
Lieut. Gover'r.

"No. 1. Conformably to your official notice No. 23, I caused inquiry to be made in all the adjacent parts of this district, if there were any Indians of the Mascoux or Talipoux tribe thereabouts. I am assured that there are none of that nation hereabouts.

God have you in his holy keeping,
New Bourbon, Nov. 23, 1802.
Camille De Lassus.

"No. 2. Included is the list of those inhabitants of this post and district who possess horses and arms, and whom I have directed to hold themselves ready to repair to New Madrid, early in the month of December next, or when it may be requisite in the course of that month. Consequently apprise me in time to give them due notice, some of them living at a long distance from this Post. Apprise me also if these men are to carry with them their provisions for the journey, the length of time they may remain at New Madrid, and for their return to their homes.

"This is in reply to your official note, No. 24.

God have you in his holy keeping.
NEW BOURBON, Nov. 23, 1802
CAMILLE DE LASSUS.

"No. 49. Don Charles Dehault De Lassus.

"In conformity to your official note No. 64, which I received the 22nd inst., I repaired the next day and the succeeding one, to the village of the Loups and Chaouanons Indians and made known to them your orders.

"As they are nearly all absent on their hunt, I think there will be but few of them at the Council; however, the principal chief of the Loups will be present with some others.

God have you, Sir, in his holy keeping.
CAPE GIRARDEAU, Nov'r 29, 1802.
L. LORIMIER.

"No. 50. Don Charles Dehault De Lassus.

"Subjoined is the list of the Inhabitants of this Post able to bear arms, as you required of me by your No. 65.

God have you, Sir, in his holy keeping.
CAPE GIRARDEAU, Nov'r 29, 1802.
L. LORIMIER.

MILITARY ORDERS OF GOVERNOR DELASSUS,

in his expedition to New Madrid, Dec'r. and Jan'y. 1802–1803.

ORDERS OF THE 8TH TO 9TH DECEMBER, 1802.

The assembled inhabitants will recognize Capt. Don Francois Vallé, as Second in command of the expedition.

Lieut. Don Joseph Pratte as commandant of the St. Genevieve Company.

Second Lieut. Don Francois Vallé, Jr., as commandant of the Platin company.

Second Lieut. Don Camille Delassus as commandant of the New-Bourbon company, and aid-de-camp and Adjutant.

They will be obeyed in all their orders, verbal or written, for the King's Service.

This order will be read to-morrow on assembling the companies. After which the commandants will appoint the Sergeants and corporals of their respective companies.

DELASSUS.

ORDER OF THE 9TH DECR.

"Commencing this day, each company will appoint a mounted and armed Orderly, who will remain near the Lieut. Governor, and will be successively relieved every twenty-four hours; the Sergeants of each company will report every day at Sunset at the house of Mr. Eaugé to receive the orders of the Adjutant Don Camille De Lassus to the commandants of companies, for the observance of their respective commands. Should the Sergeants be engaged in other duties, which would prevent their being there at the time designated, he will be replaced by the first corporal, and so on successively.

DELASSUS.

ORDER OF THE 11TH DECR.

"Messrs. the commandants of companies will hold themselves in readiness to form on to-morrow at the hour which will be given them by the 2nd in command, Don Franc's Vallé, to hear read the order of March.

CHAS. DEHAULT DELASSUS.

ORDERS FOR THE MARCH OF THE EXPEDITION.

"1st. Seven men will be taken from each company to form the advance guard, which will be commanded by each Sergeant alternately.

"2nd. This guard will have twelve axes, and will start every morning, two hours before the main body of the militia — when towards noon they will have reached a suitable place for the noon-day halt, they will stop there and kindle two fires, at the distance of an arpent apart.

"3d. On the arrival of the main body at the halting place, the van guard will remount and proceed on to select the company ground for the night, where they will kindle five fires, at a distance of half an arpent apart, taking care to select the said camping ground, early enough to enable the main body to reach it a half hour before sun set.

"4th. The Van-guard will be relieved every morning, and will then form the rear guard for the day.

"5th. The Sergeant commanding the Van-guard will proceed on a slow trot in good roads, and at a walk in bad places.

"6th. Should there be met in the route which will be indicated to him, any serious impediments, such a srivers, creeks, bad crossings, &c., he will await the arrival of the main body of the militia.

"7th. Should he meet with any gathering of Indians, or other armed men he will at once communicate the same to the chief commandant, by a mounted messenger.

"8th. In such bad places as may not require his waiting for the main body, as per Article 6th, he will expedite the passage of the said body as much as possible, by cutting the ice if not strong enough to bear the horses, or bridging it with branches of trees, or saplings, to make the crossing practicable.

"9th. The main body of the detachment will start two hours after the van-guard, going on a trot in good places, and at a walk in bad, and will maintain as far as possible the order of march which will be given them at starting.

"10th. In all cases where Messrs. the Officers may command silence, or other orders, we doubt not that all who compose our Detachment will be eager to obey.

"11th. Immediately on arriving at a camping ground, a guard will be formed of seven men from each company, commanded by an officer, a Sergeant and a corporal, who will place the sentinels that the location may require to guard against surprises, and prevent the escape of any of the horses. The officer commanding the guard will report every morning, and his Sergeant will immediately take the command of the advance guard.

"12th. The officers will carefully watch over their respective companies, and have the roll called every morning, they will see that no arms are loaded without orders, and make their report on each day before resuming the march.

"13th. If while marching, the officer or Sergeant at the rear perceives that they go too fast, he will immediately notify the commandant at the front by passing the word to halt.

"14th. All the horses, packed or loose, with their drivers, will be placed between the Detachment and the rear-guard, allowing none to pass to the front by the flanks, nor remain in rear of the said guard.

"15th. The rear-guard will keep at about two arpents in rear of the Detachment, and will take care to pick up anything that may have been dropped. Should any one from sickness, or fault of his horse be compelled to drop behind, the guard will at once notify the commander by a messenger.

"16th. They will see that no horse driver remain behind, their place on the march being between the Detachment and the guard; should anything fall or become disarranged, they will call a halt and lend assistance to remedy it, and then resume their march at the proper distance from the Detachment.

This order will be read to each company under arms, by its respective commanding officer at the hour to be named by the Second in command, DON FRANCIS VALLÉ.

"NEW BOURBON, Dec. 11, 1802. CHARLES DEHAULT DELASSUS,

"CAMILLE DELASSUS."

ORDER OF THE 12TH TO 13TH DECEMBER.

"To-morrow, Dec. 13th at eight o'clock A. M., weather permitting, the advance guard, under the command of the Senior Sergeant Mr. Levrard, will set out, pursuant to the order of the 11th, to open the March; for this purpose the officers will appoint from their respective companies the number of men specified, taking their respective numbers in rotation so that the duty may be equally performed.

"The militia men of the advance guard of the two companies

now at Ste. Genevieve, will be joined in passing through New Bourbon, by the guard of that company, which the commanding officer of the same will take care to have in readiness to join the first to complete the said Van-guard. They will take the most convenient road, passing by the rapids of Salt river, and will then pursue the route, conforming to the order of March.

"The main body of the militia will form to set out three hours after the advance guard, the two companies will start from Ste. Genevieve, and the New Bourbon company will take its position in the line in passing through that Post. The Van guard having twelve axe men, five of the remaining six will march in front of the main body, at an arpen distance, formed by two's and one in front, and the sixth will keep between the detachment and the rear guard, with the pack trains.

" There being no van-guard for the first day's march, there will be detailed a corporal and three men from each company, who will march in rear of the Detachment after the baggage, and who will conform to what is prescribed for the rear-guard in the order of March.

"CAMILLE DELASSUS.   CHAS. DEHAULT DELASSUS."

ORDER OF THE 17TH DECEMBER AT CAPE GIRARDEAU.

" Don Louis Lorimier, commandant of Cape Girardeau, will be recognized as Captain of the militia of said Post, and Don William Lorimier as Lieut. of said militia, and they will be obeyed in all their orders, either verbal or written, in this expedition for the service of his Catholic Majesty.

"Afterwards Don Louis Lorimier, at the head of his militia will designate the sergeants and corporals of his company.

" From to-day an officer, a sergeant, and a corporal of the company of the Cape with twenty of her men will set out as an advance guard one hour before the Detachment; on arriving at the camping place they will kindle ten fires, at the distance of half an arpent from each other, they will clear the snow from around the fires so that the militia men may encamp there comfortably. The colours of the Cape Girardeau company will remain attached to its company, but it will be placed in the centre of the Detachment, with a guard of two men from each company who will surround it in the order in which we post them.

"On arriving at each camping place or settlement, the officer, Don Camille Delassus, will repair to the fire of the vanguard of the Detachment, and if in a settlement to the quarters of the commander in chief where the guard will repair.

"The eight axe men of the company of the Cape, will always march at the head of the main body of the Detachment, a half arpent in advance, and when in line, they will repair to the centre of the Detachment, where they will form themselves in the manner there indicated.

"The companies will be formed as follows: the St. Genevieve Company on the right, next in line that of New Bourbon, then that of Cape Girardeau, and then the Platin Company, all according to the seniority of the settlements.

GENERAL ORDERS, NEW MADRID, DEC'R 20, 1802.

"*1st.* The officers of the Detachment of the Posts of St. Genevieve, New Bourbon, Cape Girardeau, and Platin, in addition to the zeal and readiness they have displayed from the moment of our departure, will watch over with diligent care to see that all the respectable and worthy inhabitants of our Detachment be made as comfortable as possible in their quarters, and that the provisions for themselves, and forage for the horses be fairly distributed, requiring also that the sergeants and corporals have an eye to the same; they will inform me of the least innovation, so that if contrary to the orders I have given, that nothing be omitted necessary to their comfort during their sojourn in this place, I may remedy the matter by additional orders.

"*2nd.* Every day the guard of the Machekouy Indian prisoners, will be formed by the militia of New Madrid, that is to say, by the company on foot.

"*3rd.* The cavalry company of this Post will hold themselves ready at all times to mount their horses with those of the Detachment of the upper Posts, as before mentioned, and will perform the duty with them alternately.

"*4th.* Every day at eleven o'clock A. M. Mr. Henry Peyroux, commandant of this Post of New Madrid, Mr. Francis Vallé the second in command of the Detachment, Mr. Camille Delassus, my aid de Camp, and Mr. Pierre Antoine Laforge, adjutant of the militia of New Madrid, will come to receive the order that I will give them, to communicate the same to a sergeant of each company of all the militia in general; said sergeants will report themselves at noon at the garrison at the fort, where the senior officers and adjutant above will dictate it and the sergeants take it down in writing. To this end each sergeant will have an order book, commencing from to-morrow the 21st Inst.

"*5th.* The said commandant Peyroux, commandant of the detachment from above, Aid de Camp and Adjutant will receive the watch-word each day, which they will give in writing to each commandant of the guard of their companies, for which purpose the said officers will send an armed corporal at five o'clock P. M. to the said principal who will carry it sealed to his officer.

"*6th.* The watch-word is to receive the rounds, which will be made after this, according to seniority of the officers — these will give on arriving at a post the countersign, and being recognized, the sergeant will receive the sign and countersign. If it is senior rounds, that is made by myself M. Peyroux, M. the 2nd in command, or the aid de camp or adjutant, the corporal or sergeant of the guard will approach and receive from him the countersign, and being recognized, the commandant of the guard will give the watchword, that is sign and countersign, it being understood that all persons who wish to pass after retreat (tattoo) will be required to give the countersign, without which they will be arrested. The orders for the guard of the Indian prisoners will, until new orders are issued, remain in force as they are at this day.

"Every day at sunset the officers will be with their respective companies to have the roll called, they will make their report by a sergeant or corporal to Major Camille Delassus, who will apprise me of the least change; for this purpose each one will select a suitable place for assembling his company near the center of their quarters, and they will give notice to the men of their respective commands to arm and repair to the place where the Detachment brought by me to this Post is to form at a signal of alarm, by

EXPEDITION TO NEW MADRID. 325

the drum, a red flag and a blue light at the fort, assured by three cannon shots in the day time, and by five cannon shots in the night and the drum beating.

"In a case as above each commandant of a company will conduct his own, full, to the said place, as also the Cavalry Company of this Post, and the foot companies will await my orders to assemble as I deem it necessary.

"The guards and mounted orderlies will be relieved each day at 5 o'clock, for this purpose they will assemble at the Fort, from which the adjutant Don Camille de Lassus will despatch them to their respective posts, and the duties, until new orders, will be as follows: The guard by the foot militia of New Madrid for the prisoners of the Machecous Nation, will remain as at present. The color guard will consist of an officer, a sergeant, a corporal and four men of the militia who came here. Each of the companies here united will send each day a mounted orderly to the quarters of said Major Don Camille De Lassus — the sergeants and corporals of the companies who came here, will alternately every two days take their men to the fort, to be present at distribution of the rations which will be made them, for themselves and their horses. The commandants of companies will take care to read every day at the roll-call, the present order, and all those that I may give in future.

"It will be made known to the militia of this post of New Madrid, the officers of the arriving detachment, as follows: —

Don Francis Valle, Capt. Com'g. St. Genevieve Company, 2nd in Command.

"Don Louis Lorimier. " Cape Girardeau "
"Don Joseph Pratte, Lieut. " St. Genevieve "
"Don Francis Vallé, Sub. Lieut. Platin "
"Don Camille De Lassus, " New Bourbon, *Aid. de Camp.*
"Don William Lorimier, " Cape Girardeau
"Don William Strader, Standard Bearer.

"CHARLES DEHAULT DE LASSUS."

ORDER OF THE 22ND, DECEMBER, 1802.

" It is absolutely necessary to observe the greatest order for the public tranquillity, the officers will see to it this evening at the roll-call of their respective companies, that all the fire-arms are discharged, and that firing in the village is prohibited without orders, under any pretext whatever.

ORDER OF THE 23RD DECEMBER, 1802.

" The militia of this post having guarded the Machecous prisoners since the thirtieth of July last to this day, to enable them to take some rest, and organize themselves more easily, to be ready at the first order to commence from this day, the companies that came here and the cavalry company of this place, will furnish the prisoners' guard, that will be composed of an officer, a sergeant, two corporals and thirty men, who will mount guard on foot; the guard of St. Genevieve will furnish daily six militia men; that of Cape Girardeau will furnish ten, that of Platin, three, and that of New Bourbon will furnish seven.

" The color guard will consist but of one corporal and one militia man from each company and the orderlies of the Senior officer will be furnished as heretofore.

" Those persons at whose houses the recently arrived militia are quartered, will take good care of the horses of those on duty, with the forage which will be distributed to them for the purpose, whilst these last are on guard.

" The officers of the companies on foot of this Post, will give all their care, with the greatest possible expedition, to organize their respective companies, so that they may be ready and in a condition to join the others, at the signal to be given in case of necessity.   CHARLES DEHAULT DE LASSUS.

DECEMBER 25, 1802.

" Commencing to-morrow 26th, the roll-call and parade will be at nine o'clock A. M., to facilitate the distribution of the provisions and rations, as soon as the guard is relieved.

ORDER OE THE 27TH DECEMBER, 1802.

" For the signs of alarm, instead of the red flag and blue light, proclaimed by the order of the 20th inst., it will be a red light and the royal flag.

CHARLES DEHAULT DELASSUS.

ORDER OF THE 31ST DECEMBER, 1802.

" All the officers assembled at this Post, who will not be on duty, will meet on to-morrow Jan. 1, 1803, after the parade, at the house I occupy, and to be present at the council to be held there with the Machecou and other Indians.

CHARLES DEHAULT DELASSUS.

ORDER FROM 2ND TO 3RD JANUARY, 1803.

" The officers of the companies of Cavalry, will assemble their respective companies to-morrow at nine o'clock A. M. near their quarters; they will order arms to be loaded, and to take the the necessary precaution to strictly charge every man to exercise the greatest possible care that his piece is not discharged involuntarily without orders, and as soon as the companies are formed, each will advise me of it by an orderly he will despatch to me.

" Each commandant of said companies will await the cannon shot which will be fired from the Fort as the signal of assembling, and will march his company, according to orders previously given him to form the line, and the officers, sergeants and corporals will take their positions as previously ordered.

" The Adjutant Don Camille Delassus will detail a guard of a sergeant, a corporal, and one man from each company, to go for the standard, with drums beating, which having brought they will place it opposite the cavalry in the centre.

" When he will be commanded to carry the order to the officer of the prisoners' guard, to deliver up the criminal Tewanayé to the commandant of the Detachment of the Louisiana Regiment, he will repair there and cause his shackles to be taken off by the blacksmith he will find there for the purpose; and will give the order to the officer of the guard, to immediately place the four other prisoners on the gallery to enable them to witness the execution of Tewanayé.

"He will place himself at the head of the regiment of Louisiana, which he will march opposite the Standard where the sentence of Tewanayé will be read by Don Pierre Antoine Laforge, adjutant of the militia of this post, public writer, and appointed in that capacity for the instruction of the said prisoners, which sentence will be interpreted to them by the interpreter.

"Immediately following, the criminal will be conducted in the same manner to the place appointed, and there shot to death by the detail from the garrison for the purpose. The corpse will be placed in the coffin, and carried by the soldiers in the garrison to the place of interment, the detachment of cavalry will then form by fours on the right, at the command of the Adjutant, and will then pass opposite the grave, drums beating, and form as in the first position. The Standard will then be returned in the manner it was brought, to its place of keeping. The senior officer having brought back the detachment, will give an order for each company to return to its place of meeting near its quarters, where they may dismount for a brief period, leaving their horses saddled ready to remount at the first order, under the command of the sergeants and corporals of the respective companies, the officers having to assemble at my quarters to be present and witness the release of the other four prisoners, to which end the senior officer will carry the order to the officer of the guard to take off their shackles and send them with one-half of his guard to my quarters, to be restored to the Chief Agypousetchy of the Mashkou Nation.

"The guard and the orderlies will be relieved after the close of the council, according to orders which circumstances may suggest. "CHARLES DEHAULT DELASSUS."

ORDER JANUARY 3RD 1803.

"The guard, heretofore the prisoners, will remain until further orders, composed of an officer, a sergeant, two corporals, and the same number of militia men as formerly, as principal guard, and from this date will report themselves with arms and horses; the said guard will furnish two sentinels in the day time, one on foot, placed opposite the guard house, the other mounted, around about the powder magazine; in the night time she will furnish three, mounted, one in front of the guard house, and one in the rear, the third about the powder magazine. Commencing after night-fall, the officer of the guard will cause hourly patrolling to be made in all the streets of the village, and the patrol will consist of a sergeant who will alternate with the corporal and four men, all mounted. The patrol will arrest all suspected persons, and those who make noises in the streets, the rounds will be recieved as before, and this order will be passed from the officer of the guard being relieved to the one coming in.

"CHARLES DEHAULT DELASSUS."

ORDER JANUARY 4, 1803.

"The main guard armed, counting from to-day, will consist of an officer, a sergeant, two corporals, and fifteen militia men on horses, they will post a sentinel before the guard house, and another on the square of the powder magazine, they will be on foot during the day, and on horse at night for the rest observe my previous orders.

"C. DELASSUS."

ORDER JANUARY 6, 1803.

The militia of the upper Posts here assembled, will present themselves at three o'clock P. M. to receive their rations to Cape Girardeau. To-morrow at 10 o'clock A. M. they will assemble in the street opposite the Colours, and as soon as formed we will start for our first Camp at the hole — an officer, a sergeant, a corporal and seven men a company, will start at nine o'clock A. M. to prepare the encampment in the same manner as in coming.

The officers will be careful to have gathered up the axes brought with us, and to have them delivered to the van guard.

The main guard for this day will be detailed from the company of mounted men of this post, and will comprise a corporal and four men, who need not patrol the village, but only an armed sentinel on duty day and night.

CHARLES DEHAULT DELASSUS.

"ORDERS FOR THE MILITIA OF THE POST OF NEW MADRID.

" which the commandant of the said post will cause to be observed ; and of which each Captain will have a copy for his own observance, and that of the officers and men composing his company.

" Notwithstanding that the Mashkou Tewanayé has been executed in presence of one of his chiefs, and one of consideration of their nation, who have approved of his sentence, and who have promised us to live in the most perfect friendship with us, it may occur that some scoundrel of that nation or another may seek to revenge the death of their comrade — and to frustrate the accomplishment of such evil intention, it is absolutely necessary that the militia of this post, which to my great surprise, I found without the slightest order or organization whatever, for lack of disposition, although the same zeal that I found in the subaltern officers on my arrival here, should be put in better shape.

Commencing on the next Sunday, Mr. Henry Peyroux, commandant of this Post, will assemble all the militia men, including therein all persons able to bear arms, from the age of 14 years up to 50 and not above, as I perceived on my arrival here children of not more than 8 or 9 years, who were on guard of the Mashkous prisoners ; and each Captain, or commandant of each company, will organize his own in the best manner possible, and he will make them understand that no matter at what hour it may be, at the signal of assembling, which will be the same promulgated in our order of the ———— they will immediately report themselves at the place indicated for that purpose.

" Mr. H. Peyroux will immediately issue his orders to the military storekeeper, that he will always keep all the arms in the King's Storehouse in good order ready for service, and a sufficient number of cartridges ready for distribution in an urgent case to those persons who may not possess arms nor powder, and of lead for those who have arms.

" Should there be found some militia men living at distant habitations, and who are without arms, Mr. Peyroux will distribute to them a number of the guns from the King's Store, and some ammunition, to enable them to defend themselves, while awaiting such measures as the commandant may take to hasten to their assistance with the first who may repair to the place of meeting indicated ; the said militia men will give a receipt for the arms and ammunition that may be entrusted to them, and for which they will be responsible.

" Innovation or not the militia will assemble every fifteen days on Sundays, commencing on the Sunday next, and each commandant will exercise his in marching by file, or in sections of four and eight, according to the number of their men, to teach them the manual of loading and firing, to enable them to execute it promptly and with regularity.

"All enrolled militia men who exhibit an indisposition to comply with the order, by not appearing at the place of assembling when required, thus giving an unequivocal proof of his little love of country, will for the first offense be reprimanded by eight days imprisonment, and eight dollars fine — the second time double the length of imprisonment and fine, and for the third time, it will be signified to him to settle up his affairs within a reasonable period and leave the country. Understood that in the oath of allegiance administered to all new comers to the country, before a concession of land is granted him ; he must obligate himself to take arms against the enemies of the State, and all malefactors whenever it will be required of him. As there may be found some of the inhabitants who have not yet had the oath, the commandant will administer the same to all those he may find on each Sunday of assembling.

" In the event of an alarm, ascertained to be from Indians, or other malefactors who have committed any excesses, or who may be preparing to commit them, the Cavalry company will at once begin and contiue patrolling, for which purpose having purposely chosen persons of position and mounted, they should always be ready the first, and if the danger appears to be of some duration, the commandant will order a daily guard and patrol by all the militia according to the exigency of the case. It being ascertained that it is a premeditated attack, and that the enemy are in great numbers, the commandant of this Post will dispatch an express to the commandant at Cape Girardeau, Don Louis Lorimier, either to come and reinforce the militia of this place, or to keep himself on the lookout to which purpose we will give him the necessary instructions. This course should only be taken in a case well ascertained to be as explained above, and not from vague rumors emanating from cowardly persons, so that no useless alarm may be spread through the country, nor the inhabitants interrupted in their daily labors without an urgent necessity.

"As the position of the cannons, and the manner in which they are pointed in the square which encloses the flag, and the powder magazine, is contrary to all the general rules of tactics, considering also that there are no regular troops at this post, the commanding officer will avail himself of the militia men on the next Sunday, to place them in battery on the river, leaving the first that are mounted on pivots, to be enabled to fire in case of necessity on the four fronts.

"This order will be read to the assembled militia on every Sunday of meeting, as also those the commandant may deem necessary to issue.

"Orders will be issued to Mr. Francis Lesieur, Lieut. of the militia living at the little Prairie at the distance of ten leagues from this village, to strictly observe and report all he may learn of news and rumors of the Indians, and that he keep himself on the alert and send notice to this post of all he may learn of consequence, making him responsible for all inconsiderate and improbable reports that might cause alarm."

Governor Delassus appointed the following officers, viz. : —
Rich'd F. Waters Capt., Geo. K. Reagan Lieut., Jno. B. Barsalou Ensign, of the company of Cavalry.
John Lavallée Capt., Pierre A. Laforge Lieut., John Charpentier Ensign, of the first company of Infantry.
Robert McCoy Capt., Joseph Hunot Lieut., Jno. Hart Ensign of the second company of Infantry.
The Captains of companies to appoint Sergeants and corporals.

ORDERS CONCERNING TAVERNS AND DRAM-SHOPS.

GENERAL ORDER TO ALL TAVERN KEEPERS, TRADERS AND DRAMSHOP KEEPERS AT ALL THE POSTS OF THE UPPER LOUISIANA.

Mr. Charles Dehault Delassus, Lieut. Col. of the Regiment of Louisiana and Lieutenant Governor of Upper Louisiana and dependencies:

" In virtue of strict orders conveyed to us from his lordship, the Governor-General of this Province, to entirely eradicate the prime cause of all the disorders occasioned by liquors sold by tavern keeps, dramshop keepers, traders and other inhabitants to the Indians, in spite of the reiterated prohibitions of our predecessors and ourselves, and without the fines which have been paid by the delinquents serving as an example to prevent it, being generally proven that the said Indians commit no excesses but when drunk; this is proven by the assassination of Mr. Trotier by the Indians to whom he had traded liquor; all this compels us to use the most rigorous measures for the public tranquility.

" *1st.* At each post there shall be but a certain number of tavern and dramshop keepers that we will appoint, and who shall be persons of good conduct and devoted to the government; these, under no pretext can either sell or give liquor to Indians or to Slaves.

" They will give immediate notice of the least disturbance at their house which may lead to disorder, to the commandant or nearest Syndic of its occurrence, so that he may apply the most prompt remedy. And all other persons than those who shall be authorized to keep tavern, or dramshop, who shall be found to have sold liquor, will undergo for the first offence, three days' imprisonment and two dollars' fine, the second offence 50 dollars' fine and 15 days' imprisonment, and for a third relapse, they shall be sent to New Orleans under safe conduct at their own cost and expense.

" *2nd.* Every person whomsoever, either keeper of Tavern or dramshop, or any other who shall be found to have given or sold liquor to Indians will be at once arrested, put in irons, and sent under escort of a detachment of militia at his cost and expense to New Orleans, and his effects will be seized and sequestered, until the decision of his lordship, the Governor General.

"*3rd.* All commanders of every Post will be held responsible to the government for the least neglect of the articles above, and of the least negligence, in listening to the complaints which may be made him on the subject, and to make the strictest inquiry, and investigation to ascertain the truth.

"*4th.* For this post of New Madrid, one single tavern being sufficient, Mr. John B. Olive will be the only one who will have the privilege of selling and putting off liquors in conformity to present regulations, and for the convenience of travellers on the road to Illinois, in this district, Mr. Edward Roberson will have the right to sell and put off liquor, in conforming strictly to present regulations, and at the little prairie, Mr. Charles Guilbault, &c., &c.

"*5th.* The two tavern keepers above named will pay per annum such sum as a tax that the Governor General may deem just to be applied to the construction of a prison at this Post.

"This order will be translated into English by the Interpreter of the King, Mr. J. Charpentier, published and posted up in the public places of this post, and at the doors of the tavern keepers above named, and a copy will be sent to each district dependant on this post.[1]

CHOUTEAU *vs.* LISA.

In the year 1802, four merchants of St. Louis, engaged in the Indian trade up the Missouri River, viz., Manuel Lisa, Francis M. Benoit, Gregory Sarpy and Charles Sanguinet, entered into an association under the style of "Manuel Lisa, Benoit & Company," with a view to extend their trade with the tribes of the Little Osage nation.

In some transaction, Mr. Aug't Chouteau became

---

[1] The causes which led to the foregoing military demonstration will be found in Delassus' letter to Capt. Stoddard of March 30, 1804 on page.—

the possessor of an obligation of the company, which became due April 30, 1803, and which he presented for payment to Mr. Lisa, who declined paying it, and Mr. Chouteau had it protested and put in suit, whereupon Messrs. Benoit, Sarpy and Sanguinet wrote at once to Mr. Chouteau, proposing to pay each his respective one-fourth or three hundred and seventy-five dollars each.

" To Mr. *Charles Dehault de Lassus, Lieutenant-Colonel of the Armies and Lieutenant Governor of Upper Louisiana*:

" SIR: Auguste Chouteau humbly begs and has the honor to represent to you, that he is the owner of an obligation dated August 7th last, of the amount of fifteen hundred dollars, due this day, agreed to by the partners of the 'Trade of the Osage Nation,' under the name of 'Manuel Lisa, Benoit and Company,' from which associates your petitioner demanded payment of the said amount, to which Mr. Manuel Lisa, the only one of the above partners, refused as far as concerned his portion of interest in said partnership. However Mr. Manuel Lisa should know as well as any one else, that a merchant who has accepted a simple obligation, payable to bearer at a certain time without any reservation or especial condition, can present no reasons which will exempt him from fulfilling his written promises. For if it was otherwise, what would become of the safety and confidence that one should possess in such actions, which alone form the foundations and support of commerce. For these reasons your petitioner prays it may please you to direct Mr. Manuel Lisa, Benoit and Company to pay at once and without delay, the above named sum of fifteen hundred dollars, without excepting any portion which Mr. Manuel Lisa pretends he should refuse to pay, on pain of seeing himself constrained for all losses, delay, claims and interest, and so do justice

" AUGUSTE CHOUTEAU.

" ST. LOUIS OF ILLINOIS, April 30, 1803."

"Mr. Josef Horttiz will notify Messrs. Manuel Lisa, Francis M. Benoit, Gregoire Sarpy and Charles Sanguinet, partners in the 'Trade of the Osage Nation,' to pay in one amount the said obligation.

"DELASSUS."

"*To Mr. Charles Dehault de Lassus, Lieut. Col. Commandant, and Lieutenant Governor of Upper Louisiana, Sir,*

"The undersigned have the honor to represent to you that Mr. Chouteau presented the petition against them April 30th last, to collect the amount of an obligation of fifteen hundred dollars, signed 'Manuel Lisa, Benoit & Company.' The undersigned did not refuse its payment, they expect to pay each one his portion separately, recognizing between themselves no title of a partnership, and having no contract whatever. It is true they explored together the posts of the Osages, each one furnishing his individual part, but assuming no responsibility; they had no style or title authorizing them to enter into obligations in the name of the association, as it is true none ever existed, and the payments were always made individually. They have decided to pay each his portion.

"The petitioners hope you will do justice to their request.

"ST. LOUIS, May 2, 1803.

"GREGOIRE SARPY.
"CHARLES SANGUINET.
"FRANS. M. BENOIT.

"*To Don Charles Dehault de Lassus Lieut. Governor &c.,* substance.

"Acknowledges the receipt of the Governor's order to pay Mr. Chouteau 375 dollars his proportion of the 1500 dollars claimed by Mr. Chouteau, amount of the note of 'Manuel Lisa, Benoit and Company.' protested by Chouteau, the protest sent by C. to the Superior Tribunal of this province at New Orleans, with power amply sufficient to Sir Knight Register, Don John de Castanado, to establish the nullity of other notes for this same debt.

"He humbly replies to Mr. Chouteau's petition his firm determination to postpone for the present any further steps in the matter, until the Superior Tribunal shall deliberate, and justly decide the merits of the case, and give a final decree thereon.

"His course in the matter does not proceed from malicious motives, but from necessity.

"With all due respect &c.

"ST. LOUIS, May 2, 1803.

"MANUEL DE LISA."

"*To Mr. Charles Dehault de Lassus, Lieut. Col. of the Army, and Lieut. Governor of Upper Louisiana:*

"SIR—Your petitioner has the honor to represent to you, that he has been notified by Mr. Manuel Lisa of his formal refusal to pay the sum of three hundred and seventy five dollars, for his proportion of the obligation consented to by him in the name of those interested in the trade of the Osage Nation. Since that refusal Messrs. Charles Sanguinet, Gregoire Sarpy and Frans. M Benoit notified the holder that they were ready each to pay his part, amounting together to eleven hundred and twenty five dollars—owing to which and the refusal of the fourth party in interested, your petitioner requests your justice to direct Messrs. Greg'e Sarpy, Chas. Sanguinet and Frans. M. Benoit depositories of the funds of all interested, to withhold in their hands the sum of three hundred and seventy five dollars, which is due by Mr. Lisa, to release it at once from the hands of your petitioner, so that with the sum of eleven hundred and twenty five from the three other interested parties in said trade, for whose operations, the above payment is claimed and do justice.

"AUGUST CHOUTEAU."

"ST. LOUIS, May 3, 1803.

"On the same day, May 3rd, the Governor by his notary, decreed to Mr. De Lisa to pay his proportion as the others, and at same time to the three others, Sarpy, Sanguinet and Benoit to withhold from the funds of the association the amount due by Lisa, with the costs &c.

The bill for which made out by Horttiz is as follows:

To the Judge (Governor) 5 decrees and signatures,		4 Reals	20 R	$2.50,
" " Notary	8 notifications	4 "	32	4.00,
	13	4	52	$6.50,

Received Payment of this bill of costs, St. Louis, May 4, 1803.

JOSEPH HORTTIZ.

NICHOLAS ST. ANDRE.

"In the town of St. Louis of Illinois, May 11th, 1803, I, Joseph Horttiz, Notary public in this town, by order of Don Carlos Dehault Delassus, Lieut. Col. and Lieut. Governor, went to the residence of Nicholas André in this same village, accompanied by Francis Valois and Francis A. Horttiz witnesses, to take an exact note of a Pirogue that the said Nicholas St. André met adrift in the middle of the Mississippi with no one in it, filled with water, and the following articles,—One deer skin, one shaved deer skin, two large beaver pelts, to do. middling size, and eight others small, all wet, which after being dryed, were weighed and marked, and I the Notary took possession of said peltries, until the Government should dispose of them, and the pirogue was left with the said Nicholas St. André, until disposed of in like manner, and finding nothing more, the said St. André certified that it was all the contents of the pirogue, which was signed by all but the exponent who made his cross after being read to him, the same day, month and year as above. FRANCIS VALOIS,
"FRANCIS HORTIZ,
"JOSEPH HORTTIZ.

INQUEST ON A MOSCOU INDIAN.

"In the town of St. Louis of Illinois January third, eighteen hundred and four, I, Joseph Horttiz in virtue of orders from Don Carlos Dehault Delassus, Lieut. Col. and Lieutenant Governor of this Upper Louisiana, that in one of the cross streets of the town, a dead body was lying. I, said Notary repaired with the necessary witnesses Juan Robayna and Pedro Castaneda to examine into the affair, and having reached the place, we found the body to be that of an Indian rolled up in a blanket, with a white handkerchief in the cavity, and immediately came and reported the same to the Governor.

"At once and by his orders to obtain all the necessary information concerning the body, and how he came by his death, we went again to the place, and met there Batiste Thibeau, opposite whose house the dead body lay, who appeared to be a Mascou Indian, and learnt that he and three or four others in company of the same nation, had been visiting the place several times that same morning. We sent the body to the quarters of the soldiers, to be interred according to the usual custom in similar cases, put the body in a coffin, buried it and enclosed the grave with a fence of stakes and a white banderita, and with the witnesses certified to the same, and made our report to the Governor.

"JUAN ROBAYNA.
"JOSEPH HORTTIZ, PEDRO CASTANEDA."

TREATY OF PURCHASE OF LOUISIANA, BY THE UNITED STATES OF AMERICA FROM THE REPUBLIC OF FRANCE, APRIL 30, 1803.

"The President of the United States of America, and the first Consul of the French Republic, in the name of the French people, always animated with the desire to remove all misunderstandings in relation to the subjects of discussion mentioned in the second and fifteenth articles of the convention of the 8th Vendemiaire, year 9, (Sept. 30, 1800), in relation to the claims of the United States, in virtue of the treaty concluded at Madrid, the 27th of October, 1795, between his Catholic Majesty and the said United States: wishing to maintain the union and friendship which at the period of the aforesaid convention was happily re-established between the two nations, have named respectively their plenipotentiaries as follows: —

"The President of the United States of America, with the advice and consent of the Senate of said States, names as his minister plenipotentiary Robert R. Livingston, and James Monroe, minister plenipotentiary, and envoy extraordinary of the United States to the government of the French Republic — and the first Consul in the name of the French people, names the citizen Francis Barbe Marbois, minister of the public Treasury, who after having exchanged their respective powers have agreed upon the following articles: —

"ARTICLE 1ST.

"In virtue of article 3rd, of the treaty concluded at St. Ildefonso, the 9th Vendemiaire year 9 (October 1, 1800) between the First Consul of the French Republic and his Catholic Majesty, it was stipulated as follows: His Catholic Majesty promises and binds himself on his part, to cede to the French Republic, six months after the full and complete execution of the conditions and agreements of the said article in relation to his Royal Highness, the Duke of Parma; the colony and Province of Louisiana, in all its extent as now actually possessed by Spain and other States.

"In consequence of said treaty, and particularly of the third article, the French Republic enjoying the incontestible right of domain and possession of the said territory, the First Consul desirous of giving to the United States, incontestible proofs of his friendship, cedes to them by these presents, in the name of the French Republic forever, and in full sovereignty, the said Territory, with all its rights and dependencies, as fully and in the same manner as he acquired it, in virtue of the above cited treaty concluded with his Catholic Majesty.

"ARTICLE 2ND.

"In the cession made by the preceding article, there is included all the Islands adjacent and belonging to Louisiana, all the lots and public places, the vacant levees, the buildings, fortifications, Barracks, and other buildings that have no owners; the archives, papers, and instructions relating to the domain and Sovereignty of Louisiana, will be placed into the possession of the commissioners of the United States, and copies of the same in good and due form will be furnished to the magistrates and municipal officers that may be necessary to them.

"ARTICLE 3RD.

"The inhabitants of the ceded territory, will be incorporated into the Union of the States and admitted, as soon as possible, conformably to the requirements of the Federal Constitution, to enjoy all the rights, advantages and immunities of the citizens of the United States, and during this time they will be upheld and protected in the enjoyment of their liberty, property, and religion they profess.

"ARTICLE 4TH.

"The French government will send a commissioner to Louisiana, who will prepare all that is necessary; as much to receive from the officers of his Catholic Majesty the said territory with its dependencies in behalf of the French Republic, if that has not already been done; as to transmit it in the name of the French Republic to the commissioner or agent of the United States.

"ARTICLE 5TH.

"Immediately after the ratification of the present treaty on the part of the President of the United States, and of that of the First Consul if it has been done; the commissioner of the French Republic, will deliver up all the military posts of New Orleans, as of other parts of the said Territory, to the commissioner appointed by the President to receive possession; all the French and Spanish troops that may be there, will cease to occupy the said Posts, from the moment of the delivery of possession, and will be embarked, if possible, in the course of three months after the ratification of this treaty.

"ARTICLE 6TH.

"The United States engages and promises to execute all the treaties and articles, that might have been agreed on between the Indian tribes and Spain, until such time as, by mutual consent between the United States and said tribes or people, other suitable articles are agreed on.

"ARTICLE 7TH.

" As it is equally advantageous to the commerce of France and the United States to foster the intercourse of the two nations for a limited period, in the country ceded by the present treaty, until arrangements are made relative to the commerce of the two nations; the contracting parties have agreed that all the French vessels coming directly from France or her colonies, loaded exclusively with her productions, and also that those coming directly from Spain or her colonies, and loaded in like manner with her productions, will be admitted for the period of twelve years into the ports of New Orleans, as well as in all those of the ceded Territory, in the same manner as the vessels of the United States coming directly from France or Spain or their colonies; without being subject to other duties on their cargoes or other imposts than those paid by the citizens of the United States, during the period of time above specified no other nation shall partake of this privilege in the said Territory; the twelve years to commence three months after the exchange of ratifications, whether at Paris or in the United States; well understood that this article has for its object to favor the manufactures, commerce, charges and navigation of France and Spain alone, as to the importations which these two nations may make into the above said ports of the United States, without detriment to the regulations which the said United States may adopt for the exportation of the products or merchandise of their States — nor to their rights to establish others.

"ARTICLE 8TH.

" After the expiration of the twelve years, all french vessels will be treated on the same footing as the most favored nation, in the above mentioned ports.

"ARTICLE 9TH.

" The especial convention signed this day by the respective ministers, having for its object the payment of the debts due to citizens of the United States by the French Republic, prior to the 30th Sept. 1800, 8th Vendemiaire year 9, is approved; and to be put in full execution, as stipulated in the present treaty, it will be ratified at the same time, and in the same manner; so that the one will not be without the other. Another special convention, signed the same date as the present treaty, relative to the definitive law between the contracting parties, and which has been in like manner approved, will also be confirmed at the same time.

" ARTICLE 10TH.

" The present treaty will be ratified in good and proper form, and the ratifications exchanged within six months after the date of signatures of the ministers plenipotentiary, or sooner if possible; in faith of which the ministers plenipotentiary have signed these articles in French and in English, remarking however that the present treaty is primitively in the french idiom, and have thereto affixed their seals.

" Executed at Paris the tenth Floreal, eleventh year of the French Republic, the 30th April 1803.

" Signed   ROBERT R. LIVINGSTON,
" JAMES MONROE,
" F. BARBE MARBOIS."

CONVENTION BETWEEN THE UNITED STATES OF AMERICA, AND THE FRENCH REPUBLIC.

" The President of the United States of America, and the First Consul of the French Republic, in the name of the french people: In consequence of the treaty of cession of Louisiana which has been signed this day, desiring to settle definitively all matters pertaining to the said cession, have for that purpose authorized the plenipotentiaries; to wit, the President of the United States with the advice and consent of the Senate of the said States, has appointed for their plenipotentiary Robert R. Livingston minister plenipotentiary of the United States, and James Monroe, Minister plenipotentiary and Envoy extraordinary of the said States to the government of the French Republic, and the first Consul of the French Republic in the name of the french people, has appointed for plenipotentiary of the said Republic, the citizen Francis Barbe Marbois; who in virtue of their full powers, this day exchanged, have agreed upon the following articles —

" ARTICLE FIRST.

" The government of the the United States obligates itself to to pay to the french government in the manner specified in the next article, the sum of sixty million of livres, independent of that which will be fixed upon, by another convention, to pay the debts which France has contracted towards the citzens of the United States.

" ARTICLE SECOND.

" For the payment of the sixty millions of livres stipulated in the preceding article, the United States will create a stock of eleven millions two hundred and fifty thousand dollars, bearing interest at six per cent. per annum, payable half-yearly at London, Amsterdam, or at Paris, being the sum of three hundred and thirty seven thousand five hundred dollars for six months, in the proportions that the French government will determine on for these places. The principal of this fund re-imbursed at the Treasury of the United States in annual payments of not less than three millions each, the first of which will commence fifteen years after the date of the exchange of ratifications; this fund will be remitted to the French government, or to any other person who will be empowered to receive it, in three months, at the furthest, after the exchange of ratifications of the treaty, and of the possession of Louisiana on part of the United States; it is also agreed that if the French government desires to earlier realize the capital of this stock by disposing of it in Europe, they will take the proper steps, as well to augment the credit of the United States, as to give greater value to said stock.

" ARTICLE THIRD.

" It is also agreed that the dollar of the United States, specified in the present convention shall be fixed at five livres and eight sous tournois; the present convention shall be ratified in good and due form, and the ratifications exchanged in the period of six months from this day's date, or sooner if possible. In faith of which the respective plenipotentiaries have signed the said articles, in both French and English, declaring also that the present treaty was made and primitively written in the french idiom, to which they have attached their seals.

" Done at Paris the 10th Floreal, the 11th year of the French Republic, April 30, 1803.

" ROBERT R. LIVINGSTON,
" JAMES MONROE,
" FRAN'S BARBE MARBOIS."

CONVENTION BETWEEN THE FRENCH REPUBLIC AND THE UNITED STATES OF AMERICA.

" The president of the United States of America, and the First Consul of the French Republic in the name of the french people, after having, by a treaty of this date, terminated all difficulties relating to Louisiana; always desiring to establish on a solid basis, the friendship which unites the two nations; more and more animated with the desire to accomplish the 2nd and 15th articles of the Convention of the 8th Vendemiaire, year 9 of the French Republic (30th Sept.) 1800, and to assure the payment of the amount due by France to Citizens of the United States, have respectively appointed for their plenipotentiaries, namely, the President of the United States of America with the advice and consent of their Senate, has appointed Robert R. Livingston Minister plenipotentiary, and James Monroe, also minister plenipotentiary, and Envoy extraordinary of the said United States near the government of the French Republic; and the First Consul in the name of the French people has appointed the citizen Francis Barbe Marbois, minister of the public Treasury, who after exchanging their full powers, agreed upon the following articles —

" ARTICLE 1ST.

" The debts due by France to citizens of the United States, contracted prior to the 8th Vendemiaire, year 9 of the French

Republic (Sept. 30, 1800) will be paid in the following manner, with interest at six per cent from the date of the presentation of their claims by the parties interested to the French Government.

" ARTICLE 2ND.

" The claims to be paid by the preceding article, are those designated in the note annexed to the present convention, which with interest must not exceed the sum of twenty millions of livres; the claims included in said note which will be found rejected in the Articles following, cannot be admitted to the benefit of this provision.

" ARTICLE 3RD.

" The principal and interest of said debts will be paid by the United States, through orders drawn by their ministers plenipotentiary on their Treasury; these orders will be payable sixty days after the exchange of the ratifications of the treaty and conventions this day signed; and after the french commissioners shall have placed those of the United States in possession of Louisiana.

"ARTICLE 4TH.

" It is especially agreed that the foregoing articles are confined exclusively to the debts contracted to the citizens collectively who have been, or may yet be creditors of France for provisions embargoed and taken on the high seas, and for which the claim was duly made within the time specified in said convention of 8th Vendemiaire, year 9 (Sept. 30, 1800).

"ARTICLE 5TH.

" The preceding articles will be only applicable (I. O.): *first*, to prizes which the prize court have ordered to be restored, well understood that the claimant can have no relief from the United States, otherwise than he could have had from the French government. *Second*, to the claims specified in the above-mentioned, 2nd article of the convention, contracted prior to the 8th Vendemiaire, year 9 (Sept. 30, 1800) the payment of which has heretofore been demanded from the actual government of France, and for which the creditors have the right to demand the protection of the United States.

ARTICLE 6TH.

" For the purpose of amicably clearing up the various questions that may arise from the preceding article; the ministers plenipotentiary of the United States will appoint three persons, who will act provisionally at this time, having full power to examine without delay all the statements of the various claims already liquidated by the offices established for that purpose by the French Republic, and to satisfy themselves if they are admissible into the classes of claims designated in the present convention, and based upon the regulations there found, or if they are included in some one of the exceptions. And declaring by their certificates, that the debt is due to American citizens, or their representatives, and existing before the 8th Vendemiaire year 9 (Sept. 30, 1800) the debtor (creditor?) will receive an order on the Treasury of the United States in the manner prescribed in the third article.

ARTICLE 7TH.

" The same agents will also possess the authority to examine the claims presented for examination, and to certify those that should be allowed, in marking them, to shew that they are not to be shut out with those excluded by the present convention.

ARTICLE 8TH.

" The same agents will also examine the claims which may not have been presented for liquidation, and will certify that they decide them admissible for liquidation.

" ARTICLE 9TH.

" According as the debts designated in these articles will be admitted; they will be paid with interest at six per cent by the Treasury of the United States.

" ARTICLE 10TH.

" To remove all doubt on the above mentioned conditions and to reject all unjust and exorbitant demands ; the commercial agent of the United States at Paris, in his capacity as minister plenipotentiary of the United States, will appoint if he thinks proper, an agent to assist in the operation of the offices, and examine the claims preferred. If he thinks the debt is not sufficiently proven, or that it is perhaps comprised in the rules of the 15th article above mentioned ; and if notwithstanding his opinion, the offices established by the French government should decide that the debt should be settled, he will pass his observations thereon to the judicial courts of the United States, which will at once examine into it, and give the result to the minister of the United States, who will transmit his observations in like manner to the minister of the Treasury of the French Republic, and the French government will then decide definitively on the case.

" ARTICLE 11TH.

" All decisions must be made within the period of one year, from the exchange of the ratifications, after which period no claim will be considered.

" ARTICLE 12TH.

" In cases where the claims for debts contracted by the French government with citizens of the United States, since the 8th Vendemiaire year 9 (Sept. 30, 1800), are not included in this convention ; the payment of the same can be claimed and prosecuetd as if no convention had been agreed on.

" ARTICLE 13TH.

"This convention will be ratified in good and due form, and the ratifications exchanged within six months from the date of the signatures of the ministers plenipotentiaries, or sooner if possible.

" In faith of which the ministers plenipotentiaries respectively, have signed the foregoing articles in French and in English, declaring that the present treaty was first made and written in the French idiom, to which they have affixed their seals.

Done at Paris the 10th Floreal, year 11th of the French Republic.
"APRIL 30, 1803.
"ROBERT R. LIVINGSTON,
"JAMES MONROE,
"FRANCIS BARBE MARBOIS."

Ratified July 1803.[1]

PURCHASE OF LOUISIANA.

The principal causes that led to the acquisition of Louisiana by the United States are these: After the achievement of our independence, and our territory bordering on the Ohio and Mississippi Rivers became gradually settled with new comers, our people in that region of country were not long in discovering that it was very essential for their future advance and prosperity that they should have an outlet to the ocean through the lower Mississippi, the country being then owned on both sides for some distance up from the Gulf of Mexico by Spain. For this purpose a treaty was concluded in October 1795, between Spain and the United States, which provided for the settlement of their respective boundaries, and the joint navigation of the lower Mississippi River by the people of the two countries.

After several gross infractions of this treaty in the course of the next five succeeding years by the

---

[1] From a copy printed at Paris in 1804.

Spanish authorities at New Orleans, Mr. Jefferson, on his elevation to the Presidency in 1801, commenced the incipient measures to negotiate for the acquisition of the country by the United States, by its purchase, which he eventually accomplished.

In the year 1797, Don Manuel Gayoso de Lemos was appointed governor-general of Louisiana as successor to the Baron de Carondelet. Governor De Lemos died on July 18, 1799, and the Marquis of Casa Calvo was sent over from Havana as provisional governor until

In June, 1801, Don Juan Manuel de Salcedo arrived at New Orleans as governor-general to succeed the deceased governor Gayoso.

In meantime, by the treaty of St. Ildefonso, October 1, 1800, Spain retroceded to France the province of Louisiana, retaining possession of it, however, during the next three years, until sold by France to the United States.

March 26, 1803.— Pierre Clement de Laussat, the new French colonial prefect appointed by the First Consul, arrived at New Orleans, and on the succeeding day, March 27th, issued his proclamation, announcing to the inhabitants the retrocession to France.

While awaiting the arrival of General Victor, the new French governor-general, with his troops, to take possession, news arrived of the sale of the country to the United States, at Paris, on the 30th of April.

The treaties were ratified in July.

On November 30, 1803, Lower Louisiana was formally transferred to France at New Orleans, and on Monday December 20, following, it was transferred by Laussat to Governor Claiborne and General James Wilkinson, U. S. Army, commissioners of the United States appointed to receive it.

The following documents having relation to the transfer at St. Louis of Upper Louisiana are now presented seriatim : —

DOCUMENT NO. 1.

" The King, our Sovereign, having determined to retrocede this province of Louisiana to the French Republic, according to the announcement in the royal order issued at Barcelona on the 15th of October 1802, to that effect; and having also commissioned us to carry the same into effect, by his subsequent royal order dated at Madrid on the 18th of January, 1803, we have put in execution the intentions of the Sovereign, by delivering up the government of this place, and the command of the province to the Colonial Prefect Pedro Clement Laussat, Commissioner of the French republic, on the 30th day of November of the present year, and you are hereby requested to deliver up to the agent or officer of the said prefect who may be authorized by him to receive from you the command of the post and its dependencies, now under the orders of your excellency, as soon as he shall present himself before you, under the formalities of an inventory and valuations to be made by skilful persons in that post, upon oath to act with due impartiality, of the buildings which belong to the King, not including the artillery and other munitions of war, which must be remitted entire to this place.

"Under the same formalities of an inventory, the archives with the papers and documents which concern only the inhabitants of the district and their property shall be delivered, taking for the whole a receipt, in order that there always may be evidence of what has been delivered upon our part to the French republic, and cause the same to appear on the general inventory.

"We particularly enjoin upon your excellency the punctual execution of the foregoing, for which you are authorized to avail yourself of all the means that may be found in the district under your charge.

"NEW ORLEANS, 30th December, 1803.
"MANUEL DE SALCEDO,
"THE MARQUIS OF CASA CALVO.
"To DON CARLOS DE LASSUS,
 "Commander of Illinois.

DOCUMENT NO. 2.

"NEW ORLEANS, 21 Nivose, year 12 (Jan'y 12, 1804).
"*The Colonial Prefect com. of the French government, to Mr. Dehault de la Suze, Lieut. Governor of Illinois at St. Louis.*

"I have this day forwarded to Mr. Stoddard, captain of artillery in the United States army, and who is authorized to take possession of the territory and the establishments where you command for his Catholic Majesty, the following documents, viz.:

First. A letter, unsealed, from M. de Salcedo, and marquis of Casa Calvo, commissioners of his C. M. dated the 31st of December last, which authorizes you to give possession of the post where you now command, to the officer or agent that may be sent by me to receive it, in virtue of the treaty of St. Ildefonso, by which Louisiana was retroceded to the French republic.

Second. A letter written by me to Mr. Stoddard, which was approved by the commissioners of the United States, who were sent here for the execution of the treaty of Paris, by which France has ceded Louisiana to the United States. By said letter bearing date this day, I transferred to said officer my power to receive from you, in the name of the French republic, the military and civil possession of that part of Louisiana over which you command, and I authorize him at the same time to keep possession for the United States.

"*third.* Also another letter written by me this day to Mr. Pierre Chouteau by which I give him all the necessary power to make, in concert with you, and for the republic of France, an inventory and appraisement of the buildings and houses (except, however, the fortifications and works of defence) which belong to his C. M. in the country under your command, and possession of which must also be given to us.

"*fourth.* Letters from the commissioners of his C. M., dated 21st December, also unsealed, and addressed to:

" Don Pedro Dehault Delassus, commandant at New Bourbon.
" Don Francisco Vallé, commandant at Ste. Genevieve.
" Don Louis Lorimier, commandant at Cape Girardeau.
" Don John Lavallée, commandant at New Madrid.

"These letters are nearly similar to the letter that was sent to you by the same commissioner.

" I am ignorant whether your authority over these commandants is such that it would have been sufficient if I had transmitted you alone my dispositions, and that they would have conformed to these, but the distances are so great, and mistakes would be too vexatious, that I concluded to write to them also.

"*fifth.* I sent then, also, to Capt. Stoddard a separate circular for each of these commandants.

·" I pray you, sir, in all these changes of governments, to accept the different powers which I have announced to you, so far as they concern the French republic, and I hope that you will graciously receive the persons who will present them to you.

" I have the honor to salute you. LAUSSAT."

NO. 3. CAPT. STODDARD, KAS., TO GOV'R DELASSUS AT ST. LOUIS.

"KASKASKIA, 18th Feb., 1804.

" SIR, I have just received by express from New Orleans a variety of dispatches relative to the late retrocession of Louisiana.

" Those addressed to you and entrusted to my care by the French and Spanish commissioners, I do myself the honor to forward by a sergeant of our army, who is bound on business to Capt. Lewis.

"In a few days the troops under my command will ascend the Mississippi in public boats. I shall proceed before them by land and concert with you the necessary arrangements before their arrival at St. Louis. The inclosed letter to Mr. Chouteau I would thank you to deliver him.

"Please accept the assurances of my respectful consideration.

"AMOS STODDARD,
"*Capt. U. S. Artillerists,*
"*Agent and Commissioner for the
French Republic.*"

to CHAS. DEHAULT DELASSUS,
"Lieut Govr., Upper Louis'a."

NO. 4. GOV'R DELASSUS' REPLY TO THE FOREGOING.

"ST. LOUIS, 20th February, 1804.

"SIR, I received yesterday your letter of the 18th of this month, with those entrusted to your care, and which you had the kindness to send to me, and which contained the orders of the brigadiers and commissioners of his C. M. for the retrocession of this colony to the French Republic, and the disposition of the French prefect, which authorize you to receive possession of this part of Louisiana.

"I hasten to reply to you by the same sergeant of the U. S. army by whom you had forwarded to me your dispatches, and notify you that Mr. Louis Lorimier, Jr., is bearer of the necessary orders for each one of the commandants of the posts of this province, and which joined with those delivered to them by the said commissioners, will sufficiently authorize them to receive the commissioners that you may deem proper to send, to receive from them possessions of the said posts, and as Mr. Laussat, prefect, advises me that he has written to them also upon the same subject, and if those letters are addressed to you, and if you wish to avail yourself of the opportunity of Mr. Louis Lorimier to send said letters to them you can hand them over to him with confidence, and he is hereby directed to present himself to you for that object.

"I am also informed by your letter that troops under your orders are about to march for this post, and that you come ahead of them so that we may understand ourselves before their arrival. I shall have the honor to receive you, offering to you in advance the most gracious reception which will be possible to bestow upon you in the name of the King, my Sovereign.

"I have handed to Mr. Pierre Chouteau the letter that you had recommended to me. I shall be obliged to you, if you make known to me, in advance, the day of your arrival, and if you are coming by land or water.

"I write you in French, being informed that the Spanish language is not understood by you.   I have the honor, etc.
" CHARLES DEHAULT DELASSUS.
"AMOS STODDARD, Capt. U. S. A.,
" and Agent and Commissioner for the French Republic."

CAPT. LORIMIER TO COL. DELASSUS.

By the present I have the honor to inform you of the receipt of your official letter of the 20th Inst. which was delivered to me in the night of the 22nd, by your messenger, with the instructions from Messrs. the Brigadiers of the Armies, and Commissioners of his Catholic M. to deliver up my Post to the Commissioners of the French Republic.

I received by the same messenger the letter of Citizen P. C. Laussat, Colonial prefect and commissioner of the French Republic, in which he tells me that he appoints Mr. Stoddard Capt. of the Artillery of the United States, to receive from me on behalf of the French Republic possession of my command, either by himself in person, or by any other officer he may appoint for the purpose; apprising me also that the said Capt. Stoddard, or his appointees, after receiving the country on behalf of the French Republic, is authorized to retain the same for his own Nation.

Conformable to these orders, I will deliver up possession of my command to such American Officer as may present himself duly authorized by said Capt. Stoddard to receive it.

God have you in his holy keeping.
CAPE GIRARDEAU, FEB'Y 24 1804.   L. LORIMIER.

A few days after this Capt. Stoddard arrived at St. Louis, and addressed the following to Govr. Delassus: —

"DOCUMENT NO. 5.

"ST. LOUIS, 25th February, 1804.

"SIR, The colonial prefect, Mr. Lausat, agent and commissioner on the part of the French Republic, by an instrument under his hand, directed to me, bearing date at New Orleans, the 12th day of January, 1804, has been pleased, in consequence of the authority with which he is invested, to appoint me sole agent and commissioner on the part of the said republic, with plenary powers, to demand and receive in the name of his nation the quiet and peaceable possession of Upper Louisiana, together with all the military posts at St. Louis and its dependencies, from his Catholic Majesty's lieutenant-governor and commandants, agreeably to the late treaty of retrocession; and I do by these presents demand the quiet and peaceable delivery in due form, of the said territory, posts and dependencies, accordingly.

"Accept the assurances of respectful consideration.

"AMOS STODDARD,
" *Capt. of U. S. Artillerists,*
"*Agent and Commissioner for the French Republic."*

" to Col. CHARLES DEHAULT DELASSUS,
" Lieut. Governor, Upper Louisiana."

GOVERNOR DELASSUS' REPLY.

ST. LOUIS OF ILLINOIS, Feby. 25, 1804.

" Sir, As the terms of the letter which I have the honor to receive from you accord entirely with those of the brigadiers of his C. M. dated New Orleans, Decr. 31, 1803, and are also in accordance with the requisition of Mr. Pierre Clement Lausat, dated New Orleans, January 12, 1804, and which contained the documents that had been sent to you, and which you had the kindness to forward to me from Kaskaskia on the 18th, and which I received on the 19th of the present month.

DOCUMENTS REGARDING THE TRANSFER. 357

"In virtue of their contents, I have made the necessary arrangements to give you possession of Upper Louisiana.

"I am ready to give you possession of this province on the day and hour you may name, in the most authentic form, as the circumstances and nature of the country will permit.

"I have the honor to be, etc.

"CHARLES DEHAULT DELASSUS."

to MR. AMOS STODDARD, St. Louis.

In the meantime, while awaiting the day to be designated for the transfer, Col. Delassus, a veteran of over twenty years' service in the royal armies of Spain, there and in France, deeming it but proper that so important an event as the transfer of the country should be accompanied by some public display and *eclat* appropiate to such an occasion, had issued the following order to the troops composing his garrison on the hill.

"*Regiment of Infantry of Louisiana, Post of St. Louis.*

(order of the 23rd of February, 1804.)

"This day henceforth all the men of this department including the guard, will keep themselves in full uniform, and with strict regard to personal neatness, &c. So that all the garrison may be in readiness to take arms at the first verbal order made through first Sergeant Juan Robayna, to evacuate the Fort, with arms at a shoulder and knapsack on the back.

"Pursuant to this order, no one will absent himself from the quarters, either by day or night, except those necessarily so, such as water-carriers, hostlers, &c., until the day of the delivery of these fortifications to the United States.

"As all this detachment is composed of individuals, the larger portion of whom have been long in the Service and know how to comport themselves in a praiseworthy manner, the commander expects that from the day of the transfer, and afterwards, until we take up the line of march to embody ourselves with our country men, each man will so comport himself as to uphold the reputation of the Spanish troops so justly acquired and extolled for ages past; and I flatter myself that during the time they may remain at this post their conduct will be such as to earn for themselves the respect and esteem of the American troops.

"At the moment when the United States commandant will enter this government house to receive possession, a salute will be fired from the Fort by a salvo from all the cannon that are mounted and in battery. This will be carried into execution by a signal from a soldier stationed for the purpose at the corner of the gallery of the house, by waving his hat to the sentinel at the fort, when the firing will commence, taking good care that there will be a regular interval of time between each successive discharge.

CHARLES DEHAULT DELASSUS.

Upon the arrival of the boats from Kaskaskia, with Capt. Stoddard's troops, they landed at Cahokia, on the American side, where they were cantoned for some days, awaiting the final arrangements for the transfer.

FRIDAY MARCH 9, 1804.

When the eventful day at length arrived, to wit, Friday, March 9, 1804, the American troops were brought over to this side under the command of Lieut. Worrall of the United States Army, acting as Adjutant to Capt Stoddard, who, accompanied by Capt. Meriwether Lewis of the United States infantry (then in St. Louis on his expedition to the Pacific Ocean) and others, repaired to the government house at the southeast corner of our present Main and

Walnut Streets, here he was formally received and welcomed by Governor Delassus, in presence of his officials and some of the most prominent citizens of the place, the largest portion of the inhabitants of the village being assembled in the street in front.

Governor Delassus then addressed the people in the following brief

PROCLAMATION.

" March 9, 1804.

" *Inhabitants of Upper Louisiana:*

" By the King's command, I am about to deliver up this post and its dependencies.

" The flag under which you have been protected for a period of nearly thirty-six years is to be withdrawn. From this moment you are released from the oath of fidelity you took to support it.

" The fidelity and courage with which you have guarded and defended it, will never be forgotten; and in my character of representative, I entertain the most sincere wishes for your perfect prosperity."

Governor Delassus then in a brief address to Capt. Stoddard, placed him in possession of the governmental residence, to which Capt. Stoddard made an appropriate reply, at the conclusion of which, the pre-arranged signal being given by the soldier placed at the northwest corner of the gallery for that purpose, the Spanish troops at the fort on the hill commenced to fire the salute ordered by Gov. Delassus, and which was continued at regular intervals until completed.

Pending these proceedings, the official document testifying to the transfer, which had been previously prepared for the purpose, was duly executed in triplicate by the representatives of the two governments, parties to the act, in the following terms: —

"In consequence of a letter sent from New Orleans, of the 31st December of last year (1803), by the Marquis de Casa Calvo and Don Juan Manuel de Salcedo, brigadier general of the royal armies and commissaries for his Catholic Majesty, for the transfer of the colony and province of Louisiana, to the French Republic, addressed to Don Chas. D. Delassus, Col. in the same armies, Lieutenant Governor of Upper Louisiana, and commissioner, appointed by the said Casa Calvo and Salcedo, for its transfer, according to the contents of said letter requiring him to give full and entire possession of said Upper Louisiana, including the military post of St. Louis, and its dependencies, to wit, Clement Lausat, appointed by the French Republic, to take possession of the said colony and province of Louisiana, or any other person which may have been named to that effect, according to the treaty of cession, and as by letter also sent from New Orleans, dated 12th of January of the current year, the said commissary of the French Republic appoints, constitutes and nominates as sole agent and commissary in behalf of his nation, Amos Stoddard, Captain of Artillery of the United States of America, for the purpose of demanding and receiving the said Upper Louisiana, comprehending the said aforesaid military posts of St. Louis, and its dependencies, in virtue of the respective powers which are explained above.

"Now, be it known by these presents, that I, the above Don Carlos D. Delassus, in quality of lieutenant governor of the same, at the requirements duly made to me by the said Amos Stoddard, agent and commissary of the French Republic, have delivered the full possession, sovereignty and government of the said Upper Louisiana, with all the military posts, quarters and fortifications thereto belonging or dependent thereof, and I, Amos Stoddard, commissary as such, do acknowledge to have received the said possession on the same terms already mentioned, of which I acknowledge myself satisfied as possessed of on this day.

In testimony whereof the aforesaid lieutenant governor and myself have respectively signed these presents, sealed with the seal of our arms, being attested with the witnesses signed below, of which proceedings six copies have been made out to wit, three in the Spanish and the other three in the English languages.

Given in the town of St. Louis of Illinois,
9th March, 1804.

CARLOS DEHAULT DELASSUS (Seal).
AMOS STODDARD (Seal).

In presence of
MERIWETHER LEWIS, Capt. 1st U. S. Regt. Infty.
ANTOINE SOULARD, Surveyor General, &c.
CHARLES GRATIOT.[1]

Upon the conclusion of the proceedings at the government house, the American troops were marched up to the Fort on the hill, where they were received by the Spanish troops under arms, and after an exchange of salutes, received possession, and were quartered therein, the stars and stripes being displayed on the staff in place of the standard of Spain.

The Spanish troops after the evacuation of the Fort were marched down the hill to a large old French house of logs at the southwest corner of Third and Elm streets, the property of Manuel Lisa, from whom it had been rented by Governor Delassus,

---

[1] We bought the country from France, its real owner, to whom it had been retroceded by Spain, and would only receive it from her, hence the necessity of the double transfer.

for quarters for the Spanish troops, until they could depart for New Orleans.

After the transfer Col. Delassus remained in St. Louis, until the month of October, of the same year, closing up the affairs of the Spanish government, and awaiting further orders, and finally left with his soldiers, and the cannons and munitions of war which were not included in the sale of the country, and on his arrival in New Orleans was ordered to Pensacola, Florida, the headquarters of his Spanish Regiment.

On Monday following the transfer, March 12, 1804, Col. Delassus, at the request of Capt. Stoddard, delivered to certain Indian tribes, then in and about St. Louis, in the presence of Captains Stoddard and Lewis, Lieuts. Worral and others, the following speech, announcing to them the change of Government.

" *Delawares, Abenakis, Saquis, and others:*

"Your old fathers, the Spaniard and the Frenchman, who grasp by the hand your new father, the head chief of the United States, by an act of their good will, and in virtue of their last treaty, I have delivered up to them all these lands. They will keep and defend them, and protect all the white and red skins who live thereon. You will live as happily as if the Spaniard was still here.

"I have informed your new father, who here takes my place, that since I have been here the Delawares, Shawnees and Sakis have always conducted themselves well, that I have always received them kindly; that the chiefs have always restrained their young men as much as it was possible. I have recommended thee Takinonsa, as chief of the natives, that thou hast always labored much and well to maintain a sincere friendship with the whites and that in consequence of thy good services, I recently presented thee a medal with the portrait of thy great father the Spaniard, and letters patent reciting thy good and loyal services. For several days past we have fired off cannon shots to announce to all the nations that your father the Spaniard is going, his heart happy to know that you will be protected and sustained by your new father, and that the smoke of the powder may ascend to the master of life, praying him to shower on you all a happy destiny and prosperity in always living in good union with the whites."

Col. Delassus also on the same day, addressed the following official circular to the several commandants in his jurisdiction, apprising them of the change:—

To M. Baptiste Vallé, Ste. Genevieve.
" "   Deluziere, New Bourbon.
" "   Louis Lorimier, Cape Girardeau.
" "   Jean Lavallée, New Madrid.
" "   Pierre De Treget, Carondelet.
" "   James Mackay, St. Andrew.
" "   Francis Dunegant, St. Ferdinand.
" "   Charles Tayon, St. Charles.
" "   Francis Saucier, Portage des Sioux.
" "   Pierre Lajoie, Sindic at Maramek.
" "   Edmond Hodges, post at Missouri.

"On the ninth day of the present month, I relinquished the command of this place and of all upper Louisiana to Mr. Amos Stoddard, captain of artillery of the United States and commissioner for the French Republic, who since has retained it in the name of the said states.

I apprise you of this for your guidance, according to orders I issued to you of date February 20th, last past, notifying you to communicate the same to the Sindics of your dependency.

God have you in his holy keeping.

CHARLES DEHAULT DELASSUS.

ST. LOUIS OF ILLINOIS.

DELASSUS' SUBORDINATES.

President Jefferson in selecting Capt. Amos Stoddard, of the United States Army, as commissioner to receive possession of Upper Louisiana, and to remain in charge of the same as civil and military commandant until Congress should assemble in the fall and enact such laws for the government of our new acquisition as to them might seem suitable and proper, instructed him particularly that "inasmuch as the largest portion of the old inhabitants were strenuously opposed to the change of government, it would go far to conciliate them, and they would much sooner become reconciled to the new order of things, by making little, if any change in the *modus operandi* of the government, at least for a time." And so careful was Capt. Stoddard to carry out, to the letter, the instructions of the President, that his seven months' administration of affairs in our new purchase was simply a prolongation of the Spanish *regime*, he occupying the same building for offices and quarters, using the same archives and records, and continuing in the public employment the same subordinates as his immediate predecessor, the only visible change being the substitution of the English language in lieu of the Spanish.

At his request Col. Delassus furnished him a list

of those then in his employ, with remarks as to their *"personels."*

"1. *Anthony Soulard*, St. Louis, is a former officer of the French Navy, emigrated since the revolution. Since his arrival in the country, he has been in the employ of the Government and has discharged his duties with zeal and accuracy; he would have received a salary as assistant to the Lieut. Governor, who designed to raise his rank, had it not been for the change of government. So that for over two years he has done nothing of this kind for the Spanish Service.

"He was recommended to the King to be appointed a captain with the pay of Lieutenant, and lately withdrew his application which I have favored anew. In his character of Surveyor of this Upper Louisiana, he can furnish you the most reliable information in regard to all the titles of grants, including therein New Madrid, the last post in Upper Louisiana where grants of lands have been made, he is an officer of much merit.

"2. *Don Benito Basquez*, a former officer, father of a numerous family, poor, who does not succeed in business, and whose age makes him at present of but little force for the Service.

"3. *James De St. Vrain*, officer of the French navy, emigrated to the country with his family since 1795. He commands his majesty's galliot the Phebé — he serves with zeal and exactness, he has made several voyages or campaigns with his galliot, in which he always carried out his instructions with sagacity and prudence. In his last campaign to Prairie du Chien he obtained a little paraclete (comfort or consolation) of forty dollars pay, forty-five of bounty, and $1\frac{1}{2}$ reals a day rations, together ninety dollars the month.

"He is my brother and I confine myself to expressing his desire to be useful to the new government under which he is to live.

"4. *Mr. Antoine Dubreuil*, a young officer, very zealous in all he is commanded to execute, he was employed in the expeditions of the Galliots under De St. Vrain, who was satisfied with his conduct.

"5. *Mr. Joseph Robidou*, an infirm old man, almost blind.

" 6. *Mr. Pierre Chouteau,* a very zealous officer, he was commandant of Fort Carondelet, at the Osage Nation, whose trade it pleased his Majesty's Governor Salcedo to grant exclusively to Messrs. Manuel Lisa, Sanguinet, Greg'e Sarpy, and Benoit — So long as this officer had the trade of this nation, he so managed them, and his authority was such as to induce them whenever they killed any one, to bring in the ring-leaders He is respected and feared, and I believe loved by this nation. In the year 180– I saw him here with a party of 200 Indians, make himself respected and obeyed, and manage them with firmness and mildness. I think he is the most suitable officer of this post, to be employed in that nation and others of the Missouri.

" 7. *Mr. Vincent Bouis* — I am unacquainted with his services, he is an honest man in business affairs, but entirely given to drink since I have been here.

" 8. *Mr. Pascal Cerré,* 2nd Lieut., a very zealous officer, speaks and writes English.

" 9. *Mr. Benito Basquez, Jr.,* I believe him very zealous, although I have not had occasion to employ him.

" 10. *Mr. Francis Dunegant,* commandant at St. Ferdinand, a perfectly honest man, brave officer who has filled positions, and who was made commandant at the commencement of the settlement, but his capacity is such that he is now often embarrassed in view of the growth of his district, and that he can neither read or write.

" 11. *Mr. Francis Delorier,* of the same genus as Dunegant preceeding.

" 12. *Mr. Charles Tayon,* commandant at St. Charles, a brave officer and zealous in obeying orders he receives when he can comprehend them. He received a brevet from the King of 2nd Lieut. and pay of eleven or twelve dollars a month, for having distinguished himself in an action, I think with the English — for some time past he gives himself to drink; he recently committed an injustice towards the inhabitants of his post, which is already too important for his capacity to enable him to regulate as it should be — he neither reads nor writes.

" 13. *Mr. Antoine Gauthier,* a good man, without knowledge, but zealous in the service.

" 14. *Mr. Pierre Trogé* about the same stamp as the preceding one.

" 15. *Mr. James Mackay*, an officer of knowledge, zealous and punctual, he formed the settlement of St. Andrew (Bonhomme bottom along the Missouri above St. Charles), he caused roads and bridges to be constructed by the inhabitants to communicate with the chief place — he is not litigious, and has adjusted dissensions between the people as much as lay in his power, and he keeps them in good order with judgment. I think him a recommendable officer with many good qualities — he reads and writes french.

" 16. *M. Edmond Hodges*, Sindic at Columbia bottom, since I appointed him, I have always found him very correct, and devoted to the public service.

" 17. *Mr. Amos Richerson*, I think him a proper man for public business, and since his appointment he has always borne himself earnestly in the matters which required his attention.

" 18. *Mr. Boone*, a respectable old man, just and impartial, he has already, since I appointed him, offered his resignation owing to his infirmities — believing I know his probity, I have induced him to remain, in view of my confidence in him for the public good.

" 19. *Mr. Mat. McKonel*, I have not had the opportunity of knowing personally, but since I have appointed him, the reports I hear of his conduct, are not advantageous for the public.

" 20. *Mr. Francis Saucier*, at Portage des Sioux, a former French Officer in the colony, father of a numerous family, an honest man, zealous and friend of good order.

" 21. *Mr. Pierre De Treget*, Sindic of Carondelet, a good man with no capacity, he neither reads nor writes, he was appointed Capt. Commandant for want of others, the post is so near here, that the least affair of that post is done here, nevertheless it should have its Archives, which are not important.

" 22. *Pierre Lapie* at Maramek, a bad fellow, but the best I could find there, where a Sindic was absolutely necessary when I appointed him, he speaks English and is a determined man.

" 23. *M. Francois Vallé*, St. Genevieve — the fidelity of the family of these officers under all the administrations where they found themselves, the much good service of this one since his employment, the universal esteem of all the inhabitants that he so justly merited, cannot but cause to be regretted so useful a man at the moment when he is about to depart this life; and recommend his family, which has always been zealous in the public service, and have given proofs of it under all circumstances.

"24. *M. John B. Vallé*, brother of Don Francis, a very zealous officer, he has been employed under several circumstances, he always conducted himself well, and commands at present temporarily the post of St. Genevieve, since the illness of his brother.

"25. *M. Joseph Pratte*, a zealous officer when employed, speaks English.

"26. *M. Francis Vallé*, Jr., son of the dying commandant. He resembles his father in disposition; in an expedition I commanded last year, composed of a detachment of militia I conducted to New Madrid, I noticed his zeal, alacrity and correctness in the service.

"27. *M. Jno. B. Janis*, St. Genevieve, a zealous officer.

"28. *M. Camille Delassus*, this officer is at present on duty at New Bourbon, where he acts as interpreter, without pay, for the English language — he has been employed several times in the service, he commanded the post at New Bourbon, in the absence of his father. He discharged the duty of Adjutant of the detachment I conducted last year to New Madrid.

"He is my brother, the desire I entertain to see him obtain promotion under the new government where he is to remain, forbids my saying anything further of him, but I think I may add without compromising, that he will always be highly flattered at being employed.

"29. *Pierre Delassus Deluziére*, New Bourbon, entirely devoted to public affairs, gained him the approbation of the Governor General of Louisiana, he is my father, I can only recommend him as a zealous servant.

"30. *M. Louis Lorimier*, Cape Girardeau — this officer can neither read nor write, but he has natural genius; since he has had the command at the Cape, he has always had the judgment to have some one near him able to assist him, in regard to his correspondence, he signs nothing without having it read to him two or three times until he comprehends it, or it must be read again. He has maintained order in his post, with incredible firmness against some inhabitants who designed to mutiny against him with out cause. He is extremely zealous when employed. Although supposed to be interested, I have known him to neglect all his business to execute a commission which would produce him, instead of profit but expense. He is much experienced in regard to Indians, particularly the Shawnees and Loups, it was through his influence with the latter tribe, that the Delaware Indian who had killed a citizen of the United States on the road to post Vincennes, was taken by his nation to Kaskaskia.

"I had an incontestable proof of his talent with the Indians last year at New Madrid, where without his mediation, I would have been obliged to employ force to execute the Mascou Indian, it was he who eventually persuaded them to attend the council. The subjoined copy of the letter of the Governor General is a testimonial of his services. He is brave and extremely well posted in the Indian method of war — feared and respected by the savages; I think I should recommend him especially for these matters, which he knows thoroughly.

"31. *M. John Lavalee*, a skilful and zealous officer, recommended for a long time for Captain, the change of government has restrained these expeditions. I appointed him commandant *ad interim* of New Madrid, he was recognized by the government, and I think would have been retained but for the changes; every time I employed him, he gave me great satisfaction in the manner he acquitted himself of his commissions of service; he speaks and writes Spanish, French, and English, and is a firm, brave and prudent man. I recommend him as an officer to be employed.

"32. *M. Rich'd J. Waters*, zealous officer of extensive knowledge, but of a somewhat extravagant disposition and very quarrelsome.

"33. *M. Francois Riche Dupin*, a zealous officer.

"34. *M. Robert McKoy*, a brave officer, extremely zealous, he was a long time in command of a Galley of his Majesty, stationed at New Madrid and always served well and actively employed. He was severely wounded lately by the Mascou brigand, while bringing him up from Orleans to Natchez, and crippled for life.

" 35. *M. Peter Antoine Laforge*, New Madrid, a very zealous officer, performing the duties of Adjutant of the militia, and justice of the peace and notary public. He performs these various duties with correctness and precision — he records all that is done, either of customary or unusual services, etc. I can do no less than recommend him as a man very active, correct, and useful in public service in every respect, but he does not write English.

" 36. *M. Francis Lesieur*, a zealous officer, settled at the little Prairie, where, although not appointed Sindic, yet it is to him in that capacity that the people of this new settlement look to for information and advice — he does not read nor write.

" 37. *There* is also at New Madrid, *M. Charpentier*, interpreter of the English language, appointed by the government, who receives at present twenty dollars a month.

" 38. *Samuel Dorsey*, Surgeon of the Fort, receives thirty dollars a month.

NOTE.

"There are in the districts of St. Genevieve, New Bourbon, Cape Girardeau and New Madrid, Sindics of whom each commander of these posts may obtain information.

" All the Sindics I mention were appointed by me the year we were threatened with an attack by the Indians from the English side, for the purpose of placing themselves at the head of the inhabitants of their district to be in readiness to lead them to the place where they would have been ordered. Since then I have retained them with the approval of the Government to settle small misunderstandings between the inhabitants with a view to do justice.

" All the commandants named and appointed by the government who are not on regular pay as military, receive a bounty of 100 dollars per annum, and their Post expenses.

SOME OTHER EMPLOYEES PAID BY THE GOVERNMENT.

" 39. *Hypolite Bolon*, speaks several languages of the Mississippi tribes. I have always been satisfied with him, and know no other here to interpret for these nations — in that capacity he receives 200 dollars a year and his firewood.

"40. *Nic. Leconte*, St. Louis, gunsmith for the Indians, receives 140 dollars a year — this office is indispensable for the Indians, accustomed to have their fire-arms repaired when they come to the place — they make the trip expressly to bring them.

"41. Mr. ——, the curate of this parish, receives a salary of

"42. Mr. ——, the curate of St. Charles and St. Ferdinand receives

"43. Doctor Saugrain, Surgeon of the hospital, receives thirty dollars per month.

"The presents made to the Indians cost the Spanish government for Upper Louisiana, including provisions, liquors, etc., for St. Louis, St. Genevieve and New Madrid, about from twelve to thirteen thousand dollars, more or less, per annum.

"St. Louis of Illinois, March 6, 1804.

"Charles Dehault Delassus.

"To Capt. Amos Stoddard."

As connected with our purchase of Louisiana from France, in view of the current rumor on the American side that a former Spanish official had been engaged in fraudulent concessions to certain parties of large grants of lands, Capt. Stoddard, then posted at Kaskaskia, awaiting the period for the transfer of Upper Louisiana to the United States, addressed the following to the Secretary of War from that place: —

CAPT. AMOS STODDARD TO THE SECRETARY OF WAR ABOUT THE SPURIOUS GRANTS OF LAND IN UPPER LOUISIANA.

Kaskaskia, Jan'y 10, 1804.

Sir: The Attorney-General of the Indian Territory, who, a

few days since, visited the Louisiana side, has given me some information which I think my duty to communicate:

Attempts are now making to defraud the United States. As nearly as can be estimated, two hundred thousand acres of land, including all the best mines, have been surveyed by various individuals in the course of a few weeks past. All the official papers relative to these lands, bear the signature of M. — the predecessor of the present lieutenant-governor. He now commands a Spanish garrison in the neighborhood of New Orleans. To understand the nature of this fraudulent transaction, it will be necessary to state the mode of arranging titles. The settler applies to the Commandant by way of petition, and prays a grant of certain lands described by him. At the bottom, or on the back of the same petition, the commandant accedes to the prayer, and directs the surveyor to run out the lands prayed for. This petition and order, together with the proceedings of the surveyor, entitles actual settlers to grants on application to the proper officer at New Orleans. But the fact seems to be, that the great body of the people have no other title to their lands than what results from their original petitions, orders and surveys. Very few of them have taken the trouble to procure grants. Under these circumstances, they seem to have an equitable claim to their lands, and really expect a confirmation of them by the United States.

This state of things has suggested the possibility of a successful fraud; and the progress of it will probably turn to be this: Mr. —— (who, when commandant, was certainly authorized to cause surveys of land to be made to settlers) has been prevailed on to put his signature to blank papers; to suffer some persons in this quarter to insert the necessary petition and order of survey over it, and to fix the necessary dates. The persons concerned in this transaction probably expect that, as the dates of the spurious papers are confounded with those of a just nature, our Government cannot, or will not, attempt to distinguish the one from the other.

It is now about five years since M—— was commandant of Upper Louisiana, to which time the papers appear to be antedated. Extensive surveys have been made, and are now making, under his orders, and many of them to persons who have not resided two years in the country.

It is also understood that each purchaser gives forty dollars for every one hundred or four hundred acres, and that this sum is divided between three persons, the projectors of this speculation.

I am, with sentiments of high respect,

Your Obedient Servant,

AMOS STODDARD,

THE SECRETARY OF WAR.   *Capt. Corps of Artillery.*

President Jefferson communicated to Congress the above which might require legislative action, February 29, 1804.

COL. DELASSUS TO CAPT. STODDARD CONCERNING THE MASCOU INDIANS, ETC.

"ST. LOUIS OF THE ILLINOIS,
"March 30, 1804.

"*Mr. Amos Stoddard, Capt. of Artillery and first Civil Commandant of Upper Louisiana.*

"SIR: I think it essential for the measures you may probably take for the safety and tranquility of these inhabitants, to inform you that there exists in these parts since nearly ten years, a party of vagabond robbers of the Mashcoux nation, or self-styled Talapoosa Creeks, expelled from their tribe, and not daring to return on account of the crimes they there committed, and who since that time have been about on both the east and west banks of the river, scattered along this side from New Madrid to the upper waters of the Maramec, and constantly committing barbarities, in stealing, killing, violating, or burning houses.

In the year 1802, they carried their audacity to the extent of killing an inhabitant of New Madrid named David Trotter, and afterwards burnt his house. Some time thereafter this same party, to the number of five, were captured through the watchfulness and vigilance of Mr. Louis Lorimier, commandant of Cape Girardeau, who went with a detachment of the Militia of his Post and took them in custody, since which time I had them taken to New Madrid, where they were detained as prisoners, guarded by the

Militia of that Post, until the decision of the Governor-General, who subsequently sent me his orders to execute, by shooting the principal culprit named Tewanayé, with all the necessary care and preparation, as an example, usual in similar cases — and which orders I executed in January of the past year 1803, in presence of the four other culprits and one of their chiefs named Aypaletchy, and another of consideration called Kaskaloua; this sentence, after some representations of these two chiefs, without bitterness, was finally put in execution with their own consent, and after they had again admitted in full council that it was but an act of well merited Justice, and that their principal chiefs would be satisfied with it, as it is stated in the copy of the sentence of execution, which I transmit you herewith, and which is verified by a party of their nation who came to accompany the chiefs of said nation, to collect the balance of this gang of vagabonds, as you will see by the official statement appended hereto, of the council held by the commandant of New Madrid Mr. John Lavallée, in which the chief very clearly says, to '*run after and chastise them and cut off their ears, and if they cannot be caught to fire on them as deer.*'

But the above cited execution and arrangement with their nation has not put an end to their barbarities; for last autumn I received notice that one Gabriel Bolon and his two nephews were beaten and killed by a party of Osages on the grand glaize river — it was a Delaware woman who was with them and who escaped, that came and reported this to me, but a few days afterwards.

" I learnt that a party of seven or eight Mashcoux's came into the Village of Ste. Genevieve singing the war song and dance, and danced the scalp dance, and when questioned as to whose scalp they had, they denied it and said that they had met with the Osages, that they had fired on them, but they had no man wounded *who was of the Band;* shortly afterwards, their falsehood was discovered, in that they were in possession of the spoils of the unfortunate persons they had murdered, that is, the blanket-coat of one of the nephews of Hypolite Bolon, his rifle and his horse. They also had the insolence some days afterwards to come to the post of St. Louis with the said rifle. I was about to have them arrested to ascertain the facts, but in the interval some imprudent persons who went to see them, wanted to take this rifle from them, they resisted and made their escape. Since then Hypolite Bolon came and brought me these two gun-barrels, which I send you, with this was a tomahawk; and which he told me were found near the corpses of his brother and his two children, and which he says were arms of these Mascoux's, and the tomahawk left as a signal of war, and added that the man who found them would come here this spring. I awaited this period to proceed and demand reparation from the chiefs of that nation, in the event of not being enabled to take the guilty parties, and on the second of January I was informed that these same barbarians were in the village, that they went drunk from house to house. I found it impossible to discover them by a heavy rain, and one of the darkest of nights, I could only warn the various houses, for the inmates to remain quiet, and to keep their doors fastened, and in case of insult or attack from them to defend themselves if they had not the time to apprise me. The next day January 3, I was informed early that there was a dead Indian in the street opposite the house of one Thibault, and that he was supposed to be a Mashcoux, because two others of that nation had passed the body which they had looked at, one weeping, another singing the war song, and that they had started off immediately.

"After a proper examination of the body, it was taken up and interred, as is verified and stated in a document now on file in the archives, which I have delivered over to you. I immediately notified the commandants and sindics of the lower posts, including New Madrid, to be on the alert, and to bear with nothing from those Brigands, and to be ready to protect themselves if insulted by them.

"Five Indians of that nation came to talk with me, and brought me the subjoined letter. I held a talk with them; they said they had no head man, and they would go and seek him — they left, and I did not see them again.

"The 19th day of the month of February, the Sindic of Marameck came to bring me his report, that there were five of that band that were killed by the inhabitants of the two banks of the river who gave chase to them to recover a canoe or pirogue that they had stolen from the salt works on the Maramek, and which was afterwards confirmed by a paragraph subjoined, from a letter of the deceased Don Francisco Vallé, commandant of Ste. Genevieve. I also made known this affair to all the commandants and Sindics including New Madrid, in reiterating to them to be on the lookout.

"All this I communicate for your information, so that it may be of use to you in the steps you may judge proper to take.

"I have the honor to be
"With the highest consideration,
"Sir, Yours, &c.,
"CHARLES DEHAULT DELASSUS."

"ST. LOUIS OF ILLINOIS, March 30, 1804.
"To M. Amos Stoddard, Capt. of Artillery of the U. S., First Civil Commandant of Upper Louisiana:

"SIR: On the 17th of last month I received from his C. M.'s captain commandant, *par interim* of the Post of Ste. Genevieve, M. Jno. Bap. Valle, an official letter with a petition from Mr. Madden, appointed assistant surveyor for the said Post and its dependencies, by the surveyor of this Upper Louisiana, Mr. Antoine Soulard. The said letter and petition were a complaint on the part of the said Madden against certain inhabitants of Mine à Breton, who presented themselves armed against him, and opposed in the name of the United States, his surveying the land of Mr. Pascal Detchemendy, which he had been authorized to do by one of my orders, and making use of offensive and injurious expressions, carrying their audacity even so far as to threaten the said Madden, and the said Pascal, who was there to be present at the survey of his land.

"After having attentively considered the contents of these papers, there remained no doubt on my part, that it constituted a mutinous opposition against the rights of the territory and authority of his C. M., and a contempt of the orders of the officers under whose authority the inhabitants then were, and I have every reason to believe that they were instigated to the commission of this act of violence in armed force; and I am more confirmed in this view, by the complaint brought me by said M. Antoine Soulard, who added thereto a paragraph from the letter written him by his said assistant on this affair, and requesting me to verify the fact and sustain his operations in virtue of his appointment of Surveyor of this Upper Louisiana by the Government. In view of these charges and petitions, I found myself obliged to prepare myself to adopt the most effectual means to substantiate the fact and inflict punishment on the principal movers and most culpable of this sedition, but I was delayed the nineteenth of the month by the arrival of your courier from Kaskaskia at the moment I was about to send an express to said commandant Jean Bap. Vallé to obtain the proper information, and if necessary to arm the force to inflict punishment on the guilty and compel them to respect the territory and rights of his Majesty, by sending the said assistant Surveyor escorted by a detachment of militia to verify his operations and be regarded as a public officer on duty — when, on the said day the 19th of the month of February your dispatches with those of Messrs., the commissioners of his C. M., enjoining me to deliver over those posts to the commissioner of the prefect Francois Pierre Clement Laussat, so soon as he would present himself; and as you notified me by your letter that you would arrive as soon as possible with your soldiers, I thought, therefore, that my duty obliged me to suspend this act of justice, that would not suffer by the delay, to devote myself entirely to the cares necessary to be ready to receive you, and transfer to you this Territory without delay and in a state of tranquility; in consequence I simply wrote to said commandant Vallé of date 20th in returning him his papers, that in view of the circumstances he had only to send some one to the Mine a Breton to take the declarations necessary to identify the principal movers in the seditious movement, to the end that the violence done his majesty's territory should not go unpunished, notwithstanding the change of government; proposing to appeal to the representative authority as I do this day.

"But it seems these seditious persons were so determined, that the said commandant was not able to have my above cited order carried into execution. To not expose the person he would have sent, in view of the fact that I did not instruct him to send a detachment of militia for his protection, he simply ordered the comissary of Police of the said Mines to signify, in presence of two witnesses, to all the parties named in Madden's report, to appear before him within eight days, under penalty of being prosecuted under the laws, etc., as the said commandant informed me by his official letter of February 25th.

"Following this, I awaited the result of these investigations to apply to you, as I have already stated, and make known to you the guilty ones, but the said commandant, whom you have retained in his office, by a letter of the 19th of this month, tells me that those people instead of complying with the summons made them to appear before him, have sent him a petition that he forwarded to you, and of which he sent me a copy. As the contents of this copy are of an incendiary nature, and a characteristic sequel of their sedition against the Spanish government under which these same inhabitants had received but favors, and had they had any grievances to complain of at this time? they should have presented them and never have revolted, above all in specifying the limits to which they were willing that the lands should be surveyed, and probably reserve for themselves, without title, those within their said limits, which they think probably they may possess through this act of violence.

"After the exposition of the facts of the case, I leave it to your knowledge and sagacity to pursue the course you may deem proper to take on this outrage committed against the rights of sovereignty of the King my master; and I pray you to take the steps that are in your power that the person interested Mr. Paschal Detchemendy be not wronged by the delay occasioned him by the interference of these seditious persons, by having surveyed the land which was granted him. I add hereto copies of the papers referred to in the present — as follows: —

"From Mr. B. Vallé marked A. and the papers there cited with the official note of A. Soulard in possession of said commandant, if he has not recently sent them to you, with the petition of the inhabitants of the Mine á Breton.

"Copy of the Paragraph of Mr. Madden's letter marked B
"Also my official note to said Vallé " C
"Also M. B. Vallé's reply to my above " D
"Also from same with copy of the petition above cited " E

"The good feeling that has always subsisted between the Officers of his C. M. and the United States, and particularly, under present circumstances, between you and myself, for the accomplishment of the duties of our respective commissions, leaves me no room to doubt that you will find nothing but what is just and reasonable in the request that I have the honor to address to you. I will be obliged to you to forward your reply, that I may transmit the same to the commissioners of his C. M.

"I have the honor to be with the highest consideration
Sir, your very humble and Obd't. Servant,
"CHAS. DEHAULT DELASSUS.

"ST. LOUIS, 3rd April, 1804.

"SIR: I have received your letter of the 30th ultimo, as also the several papers accompanying it relative to the conduct of the people at Belleview in preventing the surveys of the lands at that place.

"As this transaction happened under the Spanish Government, I have my doubts, whether the United States can take cognizance of it. A crime of this nature committed against one government, seems not to be punishable by another; tho' if any private injury be involved in it, perhaps a reparation in damages may be legally obtained.

To prevent such excesses for the future, as well as to save unnecessary expenses, I have conceived advisable to suspend all surveys under Spanish Grants and concessions, and orders to this effect have been given to the Surveyor-General. These two points, however, I shall reserve for the consideration of the acting Governor-General and Intendant, to whom I will write on the subject, and, at the same time, transmit him the necessary Documents by the first safe conveyance by water.

"I am, sir, with sentiments of respect,
"Your very humble Servant,
"AMOS STODDARD,
"Capt & first Civil Comd't, Upper Louisiana.
"To COL. DELASSUS."

"*To Capt. Amos Stoddard, first civil command't of St. Louis district:*

"Complains James Culbertson against Michael Mackey, for that said Mackey at St. Louis in said U. Louisiana, on the twenty-seventh day of April last past, with force and arms, did take, steal, and carry away, the following articles of clothing the property of your complainant, viz., one silver watch, valued at fifteen Dollars, one great coat, valued at ten Dollars, one roundabout jacket, valued at ten Dollars, one vest, valued at five Dollars, one pair of blue pantaloons, valued at ten Dollars, and one pair of buckskin leather pantaloons, valued at fifteen Dollars. Wherefore your complainant prays that said Mackey may be apprehended and held to answer to the above complaint, and further to be dealt with as to law and justice shall appertain.

St. Louis, May 4, 1804.

JAMES CULBERTSON.

"Daniel Fralee and Calvin Adams are authorized to apprehend the body of the said Michael Mackey and have him before us.
"ST. LOUIS, 4 MAY, 1804.

"A. STODDARD."

"We now present the body of the said Mackey to the commandant.
"MAY 4, 1804.

"DANIEL FRALEE
"CALVIN ADAMS."

"And now Michael Mackey is arraigned on the complaint of James Culbertson, in which he is charged with stealing sundry articles of wearing apparel belonging to said Culbertson — to which said complaint the said Mackey pleaded Guilty. It is, therefore, considered and decreed by us, that the said Michael Mackey pay to the said James Culbertson the sum of fifteen Dollars, which with some of the articles of wearing apparel returned, amounts to the value of the goods stolen, and also that the said Mackey pay the further sum of thirty Dollars, being the costs of prosecution; and if the said Mackey does not pay the aforesaid sums, amounting in the whole to forty-five Dollars by 12 o'clock at noon to-morrow, the said Culbertson shall have full power and authority to sell and dispose of said Mackey for the term of four calendar months from this date, to any person whomsoever, for the purpose of paying the aforesaid sum of forty-five Dollars.

" Due to Culbertson $15,   A. STODDARD, *Capt.*
"   to Calvin Adams   4,   *and first C. Comd't. U. Louisiana.*
"   to Danl. Fralee,   24,
"   to the Commandant 2, for warrant and tryal."

$45

" To Mr. *John Bapt. Vallé*, Civil Commandant of the Post of St. Genevieve :

" In the superior orders which I have received from the commissioners of his Catholic Majesty, dated Dec. 30th of the last year, to deliver up this post, and which were also sent to you; it is there expressly ordered to also deliver the archives with such papers and documents as would appear to have connection with the inhabitants of the district and their property, taking a receipt for everything, and a statement of those papers not delivered. So that it may be known what has been delivered up to the French Republic, and specify the same in the general inventory, &c., &c.

"And by another order which I received from the Marquis of Casa Calvo, June 24th, I am *enjoined to bring with me the government correspondence now in all the posts of Upper Louisiana, that has no relation to suits, deeds, grants of land, &c., or with the individual fortunes and interests of the inhabitants, &c.*

" As up to this day, you have as yet sent me no inventory of the papers that you have passed over to the United States, or of those which you have retained in their name, nor of those above cited that I must take with me, I beg of you to at once busy yourself with that matter, and send it to me as soon as you have finished it; that is to say, you will send me a list of those you keep, and a copy of the list of those passed over to the United States. And, also, the papers of government correspondence, of the Lieutenants-Governors, and others of public matters, relating to War, Political dispositions, &c., having no relation with your inhabitants and the colony — with a list appended in your handwriting, and which it is important to the old Government to retain, according to the stipulations of the treaty. As for example, an order of the Governor Baron de Carondelet, of date June 22, 1792, speaking of the measures for the relief of New Madrid, &c., &c.

" It is proven by an official letter of the Baron de Carondelet, dated January 27, 1795, in reply to Don Zenon Trudeau, that the Fort at Ste. Genevieve was mounted by four cannons of the King, and one of a private estate. By a letter of the same Governor, of the 29th, same month and year, the commandant at Ste. Genevieve is ordered to turn over to the care of the estate of Charles Peyroux, the small cannon or swivel which was in the new Fort, and which was thought useless, of course there remains no doubt that the cannons of which we speak lastly belong to the King, consequently you will have them together, so that I may take them with me on my passage by your post, about the close of the month of September, or commencement of October.

" God have you in his holy keeping.
"St. Louis, August 10, 1804.
" Charles Dehault Delassus.

MISCELLANEOUS LETTERS.

" My Dear Sir: I had the honor this moment to receive your note of the present day, together with your very acceptable present for Mrs. Harrison and myself.

"Believe me, my dear sir, that I esteem my visit to St. Louis as an event the most fortunate — it has produced an intimacy with a family which I shall continue to love and honor as long as I have life.

" Inclosed you have a copy of my notification respecting the wood. I have taken care to have it made as public as possible.

"Be pleased to present me in terms of the warmest respect to Mr. and Mrs. De Louis Siere.

"I have the honor to be with sincere Respect and attachment,
"My Dear Sir.
"Your most humble Servant,
"WILLIAM HENRY HARRISON.

CAHOKIA, 6TH NOV., 1802.
"The HON'BLE CHAS. DEHAULT DELASSUS, &c., &c.

"ST. LOUIS, 26th Sept., 1804.

"DEAR SIR: In consequence of your letter of this date, I am led to suspect that I have been guilty of a breach of *etiquette*, if not of duty. It never before occurred to me, that it was necessary and proper on my part to acquaint you of the arrival of Major Bruff and of the consequent military command of Upper Louisiana which has devolved on him.

"I now do myself the honor to enclose you an extract of a letter from the Secretary of War to me on the subject; and permit me to add, that Major Bruff quarters in the same house with me, and that he assumed the *military* command of Upper Louisiana on the first day of July last.

"With sentiments of respect,
"I am, Sir, your hum. ser't,
"AMOS STODDARD, *Capt. Art'y Corps.*
"COL. CHAS. D. DELASSUS."

"WAR DEPARTMENT, May 4, 1804.

"Major Bruff will probably arrive soon after this reaches you; he will have the command of Upper Louisiana and its vicinity, and to whom you will communicate all instructions you may have received from me, General Wilkinson or the commissioners at New Orleans; and you will afford Major Bruff every aid in your power in all matters appertaining to the interest of the country, or the good of the service.
"HENRY DEARBORN.
"CAPT. AMOS STODDARD."

CAPT. MERIWETHER LEWIS

passed the winter of 1803–4 in St. Louis, preparing for his expedition over the Rocky Mountains to the Pacific Ocean.

He addressed the following note to Col. Auguste Chouteau, translated for him into French: —

"St. Louis, Jan'y 4, 1804.

"Sir: I have taken the liberty to add to this, additional questions of a mixed nature relating to Upper Louisiana, your answers to which will be extremely gratifying, and very gratefully acknowledged.

"Your friend and Ob't Servant,
"Meriwether Lewis, *Capt.*
"*1st U. S. Regt. Infy.*

"Mr. Aug's. Chouteau,

MIXED QUESTIONS RELATING TO UPPER LOUISIANA.

" 1. What is the present population?

" 2. What is the number of Emigrants from the United States into this country since the last year, ending Oct. 31, 1803, and what is the proportion of this kind of people, to the other free white population of Upper Louisiana?

" 3. What number of slaves and other people of colour?

" 4. What is the quantity of land granted, or which is claimed by individuals? The nature of the right, or pretensions by which the present possessors hold these lands? and the probable proportions of the whole amount which is separately held by these respective titles?

" 5. What is the condition of the inhabitants in general in regard to wealth? and what kind of property generally constitutes that wealth?

" 6. What is the situation and extent of the several settlements? and what is the prospect of each to become the most peopled?

CHARLES DEHAULT DELASSUS. 385

that is to say (allowing as a rule a family for each mile square) what proportion does the remaining population of each settlement bear to the remaining number of square miles she contains.

"7. What is the condition of Agriculture? and what improvements, and to what extent, have been made on newly inhabited lands?

"8. What is the probable amount in dollars of goods annually brought into Upper Louisiana? What proportion of them is intended for the consumption of her people, and what proportion for her Indian Trade? What proportion of all her entries arrives by water from Canada, New Orleans, or the United States?

"9. What is the amount in dollars of the annual exports of Upper Louisiana? Of what articles do they consist in, and what proportion goes out by each of the routes, Canada, New Orleans, or the United States?

"10. What are the names and nick-names of all the villages of Upper Louisiana? Where are they situated? When established, and the number of houses and people they contain at present?

"11. What are your mines and minerals? Have you lead, iron, copper, pewter, gypsum, salts, salines, or other mineral waters, nitre, stone-coal, marble, lime-stone, or any other mineral substance? Where are they situated, and in what quantities found?

"12. Which of those mines or salt springs are worked? and what quantity of metal or salt is annually produced?

"13. What are the animals, birds and fish of Louisiana? and what their form, appearance, habits, dispositions, of those especially that are not abundant in the inhabited parts of the country?

"M. L."

GOV. CHARLES DEHAULT DELASSUS.

The ancestors of this gentlemen were of the old nobility of France, of the town of Bouchaine, Hainault, old French Flanders (now the Department of the North, the chief city of which being Lille), of which they were hereditary mayors, and filled other important positions. In that city he was born in April, 1764.

In 1782, at the age of 18 years, he entered the Spanish service as a cadet in the royal regiment of guards, of which the King himself was the Colonel. In 1793, at the age of 29 years, he was promoted to the rank of Lieutenant-Colonel, for distinguished services in leading his company as captain of Grenadiers to the assault and capture of Fort St. Elmo, in the Pyrenees, and in several other battles in that campaign. In 1794 he was promoted and ordered to the command of a battalion of the King's "body guard," at Madrid, the capital.

Receiving here a letter from his father, who had been driven from France with his family by the Revolution, and had taken refuge in Louisiana, Col. Delassus abandoned his advantageous position at Madrid, and on his application to the King, was transferred as Lieutenant-Colonel to the "Louisiana Regiment," so that he might be useful to his father's family, and yet continue in the Spanish service. He arrived in New Orleans in the latter part of the year 1794. In 1796 the Governor-General, the Baron de Carondelet, appointed him civil and military commander (3rd) of the post of New Madrid. In 1799, by orders from Spain, he was appointed by Governor-General don Manuel Gayoso de Lemos, ieutenant-governor and commander-in-chief of Upper Louisiana at St. Louis. In 1802, he received the king's commission as full Colonel of the Louisiana regiment, in 1804, March 9th, transferred this Upper Louisiana to Capt. Amos Stoddard, U. S. A., as agent of France.

After the transfer, Col. Delassus remained here until October of that year, when he descended the river to New Orleans, with his few remaining Spanish troops, being ordered to Pensacola, Florida, the headquarters of his regiment, to assume command as its Colonel. Subsequently he was ordered to Baton Rouge to relieve Governor de Grand Pré, and remained here in command until 1810, when he resigned his position and closed his military career of nearly thirty years at the age of forty-six.

Col. Delassus married at Baton Rouge, in 1811, a daughter of don Gilberto Leonardo, the Spanish Contador (auditor). Their only child, Augustus, was born in New Orleans, July 4, 1813.

Madame Delassus died in the South, in 1816. Mr. De L. then came up to St. Louis with his son, three years of age, and purchased a place below the town (afterwards suburb St. George), where he continued to reside with us about ten years, returning to New Orleans in 1826. He paid us a brief visit in July,

1836, on which occasion he was a guest of our native born fellow-townsman, Henry G. Soulard, son of Antoine Soulard, the countryman and intimate friend of Delassus, and with whom he had been associated in the administration of public affairs.

Governor Delassus died in New Orleans, May 1, 1842, aged 78 years. His only child, Augustus, lives at his homestead at De Lassus Station, Iron Mountain Railroad, St. Francois County, and a son of this latter, son-in-law of our old fellow-citizen, Henry L. Clark, lives at home with his father.

MAJOR AMOS STODDARD

was born in Massachusetts. The first organization of the army of the United States after the adoption of the constitution was by act of Congress in 1797, providing for one regiment of artillerists and two of infantry.

Amos Stoddard was appointed by President Adams a captain in the regiment of artillery on June 4, 1798. Two years before the establishment of our Military Academy at West Point.

After our purchase of Louisiana, Capt. Stoddard was appointed by President Jefferson the commissioner to receive this upper portion, and to remain in charge of the same, as civil and military commandant, until further instructed.

On July 1, 1804, he was relieved in his *military* command of the post by his senior officer, Major James Bruff, but still continued to exercise the functions of *civil* chief magistrate until Sept. 30 following, when he was relieved altogether by Gen'l. Harrison, governor of Indiana Territory, to which we were attached for a brief period.

After Capt. Stoddard was relieved of the command at St. Louis, he was ordered to the South, where he remained on duty at various places in Lower Louisiana for about five years. There he gathered his materials for his "Sketches of Louisiana," published by Matthew Carey, in Philadelphia, in 1812.

While in the South he was promoted to the rank of Major, June 30, 1807 — and after our declaration of war against England, in June, 1812, being on active service in the field, he was mortally wounded in the action at the sortie of Fort Meigs, in Ohio, on May 5, 1813, and died a few days after the action. Major Stoddard had never married.

THE PHYSICIANS OF THE EARLY FRENCH AND SPANISH DAYS OF ST. LOUIS.

DOCTOR ANDRÉ AUGUST CONDÉ

is the first physician whose name is found in our early archives. A native of Aunis, France, he was post surgeon in the French service at Fort Chartres prior to the cession to England, and removed over to this side with the few soldiers brought over by St. Ange de Bellerive, after he had placed the British Captain Sterling in possession of the other, on Oct. 20, 1765. Doctor Condé had married Marie Anne Bardet de Laferne, July 16, 1763, whom, with his infant daughter, Marie Anne, he brought over with him to the new post. He received from Governor St. Ange, June 2, 1766, a concession, the fifth recorded in the "Livres Terriens" — the land-grant books — of two adjoining lots in the village, fronting two hundred and forty feet on Second Street, by one hundred and fifty deep, being the east half of the block next south of the Catholic church block (now No. 58). On this lot he built for his residence a house of upright posts, with a barn and other conveniences, where he resided for some ten years, until his death, Nov. 28, 1776.

Doct. Condé was a gentleman of fine education, wrote a beautiful hand, and a prominent man in the village in his day. He had an extensive professional practice, as well on the west as on the east side of the river, being for a time alone in his profession at this point. Having died intestate, the governor appointed his relative, Louis Dubreuil, merchant, guardian to his two minor daughters, the eldest Marianne, mentioned above, the second, Constance, born in St. Louis in 1768. An inventory of his estate, taken a few days after his death, includes the names (numbering two hundred and thirty-three), of all those indebted to him on both sides of the river for professional services rendered, comprising nearly all the inhabitants of the two places, and might almost serve for a directory, had such a thing then been needed. His widow married a second husband, Gaspard Roubieu, also a European, Sept. 19, 1777. They subsequently removed to St. Charles, where they both died.

Doct. Condé's eldest daughter, Marianne, was married to Charles Sanguinet, Sr., Aug. 1, 1779, and the second, Constance, first to Bonaventura Collell, a Spanish officer, in the year 1788, and secondly to Patricio Lee, in 1797. Each of these ladies left a numerous progeny. The Sanguinets of St. Louis include the Benoists, the wife of Hon. John Hogan, former postmaster and member of Congress, Wm. H. Cozens, etc. — and the Lees of St. Charles, Mrs. Thos. and Stephen Rector, Rousseaus, Benjamin O'Fallon and others.

DOCT. JNO. B. VALLEAU,

a native of France in the service of Spain, the second physician, who came to St. Louis in 1767, has already been noticed in the early part of our annals.

DOCT. ANTOINE REYNAL,

appears, from the archives, to have been the third surgeon in St. Louis, from about the year 1776. In the year 1777, he purchased from one Jean Hugé, the west half of the block (now No. 60), on the east side of Third Street, from Market to Chestnut Streets, with a house of posts at the south end, fronting on Market Street, opposite the Catholic graveyard. The north end of this lot at the southeast corner of Chestnut and Third Streets, is now occupied by the *Missouri Republican* building.

Reynal lived here for over twenty-three years, and then sold it to Eugenio Alvarez in November, 1799, removing to St. Charles, where he ended his days.

DR. BERNARD GIBKINS

was the fourth physician of St. Louis in the years 1779–1780, as we find him the possessor of a house and lot at that period, but of what nationality, where from, or whether he died here or removed from the place, is not found in the archives of the day.

DOCT. CLAUDIO MERCIER

came up to St. Louis from New Orleans early in 1784. His native place was Lavisiere, Dauphiny, France, where he was born in the year 1726. He had resided for a time in New Orleans, where he had acquired some property, and left a will there when he came up to St. Louis, which he had executed in 1784.

He added a codicil to this will at St. Louis, dated May 17, 1786, in which he re-affirms his first will, emancipates his negro woman, Francoise, gives one hundred dollars to the poor of St. Louis, and appoints Jno. B. Sarpy his executor. He died unmarried at St. Louis on January 20, 1787, aged sixty-one years. It does not appear that he practiced here.

Early in the year 1792, there was a Doct. Philip Joachim Gingembre (Ginger), in St. Louis. He purchased a small stone house at the northwest corner of Olive and Second Streets, where he lived for a few years; he then went to France, leaving his house vacant and closed, not returning after some years' absence, and the house going to ruin, it was sold by order of the governor, Trudeau, to pay his creditors.

THE ARCHIVES OF ST. LOUIS.

The term " archive " from the Latin of " depositorium " signified originally a place of deposit, for safe keeping, of official documents, including subsequently in the term the papers, etc., therein deposited

Here in St. Louis, at the present day, in speaking of the old French and Spanish archives of the early village, we apply the term to the "*books*" in which a large portion of these early documents have been placed on record since the change of government.

The documents deposited in the archives of the French and Spanish days of St. Louis comprised concession or grants of lots and lands, deeds, leases, marriage contracts, wills, inventories, powers of attorney, agreements and many miscellaneous documents pertaining to individuals. These papers were always executed in the presence of the governor, or in his absence, in the presence of his official representative, and were left for safety in the custody of the government authorities; and as far the largest portion of the inhabitants of that day could not read, much less write their names, but made their signatures with a cross, as is evidenced by an examination of them, they were deemed safer in the keeping of the government than in the possession of the parties to whom they mostly belonged. At the date of the execution of each of these papers no other record was made of it than to register it alphabetically under its proper head on a few sheets of foolscap paper loosely stitched together for the purpose, and at the close of the administration of each successive governor this alphabetical list of his official acts was certified to under his own signature, and together with the original documents themselves handed over into the possession of his successor in the government; and it was not until after the country had passed into the possession of the United States that these loose sheets were stitched together in the order of their dates, the last of the series being that of Capt. Amos Stoddard, who acted in the capacity of the civil governor for the United States until Sept. 30, 1804, and who, having been especially so instructed by the president, made no change in regard to these matters, and pursued the same course as his predecessor under the former dominations.

Of these documents there were over three thousand, many of which still remain in the Recorder's office in St. Louis to the present day. When, at the change of the government, March 10, 1804, these documents, together with such books and papers of the old French and Spanish authorities as related to concessions of lands and lots, came into the possession of the authorities of the United States, they consisted of six small books of ordinary foolscap size of about three quires each, called the "Livres Terriens" (Land books), in which were entered, very concisely, each concession or grant of lands or lots, and four smaller books in size, with leather covers, in which were recorded about one hundred and thirty of the above three thousand documents between the years 1797 and 1799. (From these it would appear that during the first thirty-five years of the village it was deemed unnecessary to record these papers in books, and these last were so recorded at the instance, perhaps, of the respective owners, who had an eye to the future.)

What are now designated as the "archives" comprise six large volumes, into which are copied the most important of the foregoing three thousand documents, particularly all those relating to real property, lands, lots and houses, and of a personal nature. These record books were commenced in November, 1816, twelve years after the change of government, when the country began to increase in population from abroad, and a consequent increase in the value of lands and lots pointed out to individuals the safety of having their titles recorded, and for some years thereafter only those were put on record whose owners were willing to pay the fees for recording the same.

The first of these old deeds put on record in volume 1st of the so-called archives was by Marie P. Leduc, on November 16, 1816.

The archives of St. Louis date from January 21, 1766, on which day they were commenced by Joseph Labusciere, in his capacity of former notary of the

---

[1] Mr. Leduc was a native of Paris, and had come to the country about the close of the last century, a notary and scrivener by profession, and after the acquisition by the United States and the organization of the new territory was appointed the first recorder of St. Louis, and opened the record books in the English language.

ARCHIVES OF ST. LOUIS.

French king in the Illinois, as per the following heading in his handwriting: —

"Statement of the deeds, contracts and other papers executed before Joseph Labusciere, former attorney of the king, and notary public under the French government in the Illinois, from April 21, one thousand seven hundred and sixty-six, to the 20th May, one thousand seven hundred and seventy."

On which day they were placed, with the government of Upper Louisiana, into the possession of Capt. Pedro Piernas, the newly appointed Lieutenant-Governor of his Catholic Majesty, the King of Spain.

After this, each successive Lieutenant-Governor, in turning over the country to his successor in office, accompanied it with a similar statement, from which the table has been compiled.

A table showing the total number of documents executed in the presence of the different governors, as detailed in their respective catalogues of the archives: —

By Gov. St. Ange, from	Jany. 21, 1766,	to May 20, 1770	197
" " Piernas,	" May 20, 1770,	" May 19, 1775	387
" " Cruzat,	" May 20, 1775,	" June 17, 1778	209
" " De Leyba,	" June 18, 1778,	" June 28, 1780	176
" " Cruzat,	" Sept. 24, 1780,	" Nov. 25, 1787	454
" " Perez,	" Nov. 25, 1787,	" July 24, 1792	304
" " Trudeau,	" July 21, 1792,	" Aug. 28, 1799	471
" " De Lassus,	" Aug. 29, 1799,	" Mar. 9, 1804	585
" " Stoddard,	" Mar. 10, 1804,	" Sept. 30, 1804	75
Also four small books of Gov. Trudeau, each 33–45, 31 & 27			136
Total			2,985

These documents were deeds and conveyances for houses, lots and lands, slaves, merchandise, personal property, etc., sold at public and private sale, also bonds and mortgages, leases, powers of attorney, wills, inventories, marriage contracts, agreements, contracts, bargains, partitions, donations, indentures, emancipation of slaves, suits, civil and criminal, and many other miscellaneous papers, multifarious in their nature, etc.

FIRST AMERICANS IN ST. LOUIS.

Until Clark's surprise of Kaskaskia in 1778, no American, as far as known, had ever visited St. Louis. The first one that settled in St. Louis was Philip Fine, born in Virginia about the year 1751, son of Thomas Fine and Agnes Merchant. He came to St. Louis in 1781 when about thirty years of age, and on Nov. 26, 1782, was married to Mary Gaignon, an elderly lady with a handsome property, who had been twice a widow, he a young man of thirty-one.

(Mary Newby Cleburne, born in London, daughter of John Newby and Ann Spratt, and widow of John Cleburne, was married in St. Louis, Dec. 26, 1769, to Philibert Gaignon, son of Antoine Gaignon, and Claudine Sebrin, born in St. Laurent, Beaujolais, diocese of Lyons, in France, a French soldier; they became acquainted in coming together from Canada. She died childless, Oct. 25, 1791.) Philip Fine, age 43, married his second wife Celeste (Sarah) Boly, age 17, daughter of John Boly and Sophia Shaeffer, born in Pittsburgh, Pennsylvania, Sept. 4, 1794. Fine died 1824-25, aged 74 years, at Fine's Ferry, across the Meramec River at its month, which he had established and where he had lived for many years, leaving his widow and nine children: Melsor, Joseph, Viza, Benjamin, Joshua, Elizabeth, Charles, Elisha and Catherine. A number of his posterity reside about St. Louis.

JOHN COONS, A CARPENTER AND JOINER,

our second American resident was here in 1786, and lived for nearly six years at the northeast corner of Main and Spruce, which property he sold in 1792 to Philip Fine, his neighbor, then across the street at the northwest corner. In 1804 Coons purchased the south half of block 80, then open ground west of the village, 300 feet in length from Third to Fourth, by 120 feet front on each of those streets. On this lot he built in 1810 a large frame house, which he sold to James Baird, a blacksmith, in 1811. He then purchased the David Hilderbrand tract of 640 acres on the Meramec, eighteen miles southwest of St. Louis, at the Fishpot Creek, and removed there. Here he lived for over 20 years, and sold the tract in 1831 to R. M. Dougherty, afterwards a justice of the county court. The place afterwards became well known as Dougherty's ferry and bridge over the Meramec.

After this we lose sight of old John Coons and his wife, they had lived with us in village and county over forty-five years, and were well up in years.

JOHN BOLY, SENIOR,

came here in 1794 from Pittsburgh, and lived for some years in St. Louis, and then settled on the Meramec, on a tract he had purchased in 1798 from Jesse Keyne, here he died.

His widow, Sophia Shaffer, born in Germantown, Philadelphia, about 1743, died in St. Louis, Oct. 24, 1801, aged 58 years. They left three sons, John, Henry and William, and three daughters, Elizabeth, Maria and Sarah, wife of Philip Fine, with children.

Their place on the Meramec, which became Jno. Boly, Junior's, was long well known as Boly's ford and ferry, being on the main road to the salt works. He and wife were living in Carondelet in October, 1823.

JOHN GATES,

from Quebec, counted with the Americans, came to St. Louis in 1796, and was married to Genevieve

Morin, by Governor Trudeau, June 18, 1797. He died somewhere up the Mississippi River, I think at Fort Madison, Iowa.

They lived for many years at the southwest corner of Third and Poplar, where his widow and family were still living in 1821.

CALVIN ADAMS

came here from Connecticut at the close of the century with a wife and sons.

In 1801 he lived in a small house, built by Pierre Roy, blacksmith, at the northwest corner of Main and Plum.

About the year 1814, he went with others to Old Mexico, leaving his family here, from which he never returned, being killed in the revolution in that country.

WILLIAM SULLIVAN

came here in the Spanish days.

In June, 1804, purchased from M. Lisa the old Barrere bakery, then occupied temporarily by Delassus' soldiers before going to New Orleans. He then occupied the house for some years until he sold it to Col. Easton in 1808.

In December, 1804, appointed by Gen. W. H.

Harrison, constable and coroner of St. Louis — for a number of years jailer of the prison in the old tower on the hill. In 1816 when Chouteau laid out the first addition, Sullivan purchased the half block, south side of Walnut from Fourth to Fifth (site of the Southern Hotel), for $750. On this he built a small frame in which he died Dec. 4, 1821, a justice of the peace under the State laws, office northwest corner Main and Locust.

JAMES RANKIN

came here about 1802–3. Purchased in March, 1803, the old Mainville house, southeast corner of Main and Locust, where he lived for a couple of years and then removed to Jefferson County. He was the first sheriff of St. Louis, appointed in Dec., 1804.

DAVID ROHRER,

a salt manufacturer at the works on the Meramec, bought in Feb., 1804, a small log house at the northwest corner of Third and Elm, where he lived a short time and then went to his salt works. The property, after several transfers, became Doct. Robert Simpson's in 1812, and still belongs to his estate, now 74 years.

A JOHN BIGGS

purchased in May, 1804, from Joseph Hebert, a small frame house at the northeast corner of Main and Almond, where he lived for about 18 months and then sold it to Col. Sam'l Hammond in November, 1805.

These comprise all the Americans that had become residents of St. Louis prior to the transfer of 1804.

PLACES BELOW THE VILLAGE.

In the Spanish days of St. Louis there were several habitations immediately below the village, lying between the road to Carondelet and the river, which then ran along much nearer to the road than at present, the new shore line in extending it south for the formation of the levee or Front Street, reclaiming in places, much land that was previously in the river. These places, although outside the village itself, yet as they originated with and belonged to parties in daily intercourse with it, should not be overlooked in our annals.

THE SOULARD PLACE.

The first of these was the Soulard place adjoined the village just below the Mill Creek. This was a concession to Gabriel Cerré shortly after his removal to St. Louis from Kaskaskia, about the year 1780, of a tract of 76 arpents. In his lifetime, while residing on his town block, No. 13, he made it his country seat, built a house, etc., improved the grounds in fields, garden, orchard, etc. After the death of Mrs. Cerré, July 21, 1800, and the partition of the estate June 19, 1802, it was allotted to his daughter, Mrs. Julia Soulard, and confirmed to Antoine Soulard as survey No. 1333 for $64\frac{65}{100}$ acres.

Subsequently Mr. Soulard settled on the place, where he resided until his death March 10, 1825, and his widow and children for some years thereafter, until in 1836 they subdivided it into "Soulard's first addition." It extends on Carondelet Avenue from Park Avenue on the north, to the Duchouquette line, Lesperance Street, on the south.

THE DUCHOUQUETTE PLACE.

The second place was a concession of Governor Cruzat to Joseph Brazeau, Sr., in 1783 of 100 arpents. It was surveyed as No. 298 for $85\frac{7}{100}$ acres. Brazeau had improved it with a stone house near the river front and put it in cultivation. Brazeau had made his will as long back as May 5, 1798, in which he left all his estate to his wife, they having no children. He survived eighteen years longer, dying Nov. 23, 1816. After his death, his widow in conformity to her husband's wishes, entered into an agreement with Jno. B. Duchouquette, usually called Batiste Lami, husband of her niece, Marie Brazeau, a daughter of her husband's brother, Louis Brazeau, Sr., by which she conveyed to them all her property for the sum of $350 per annum for the remainder of her life. This agreement she survived over seventeen years, dying in February, 1834, at the age of 85 years.

Duchouquette himself died shortly after the old lady, and the tract was equally divided between his six children, since known as the Lesperance, Picotte, Papin and Duchouquette additions, from Lesperance Street, its north boundary, to below Barton Street, its south line.

The third place was well known in former years as the

DELASSUS HOMESTEAD,

was a concession by Gov. Cruzat to Benito Vasquez in 1786 of a piece two arpents front on the river, by ten back to the Carondelet Road, 20 arpents, surveyed as No. 332 for 17.01 acres.

This, after several transfers, became, in 1811, the property of Jos. Brazeau, Jr., a nephew of old Jos. B., who built a good frame house and otherwise improved it, and sold it to Theodore Hunt in 1815, and he to our old Governor Delassus in 1816, on his return to our place from the south after an absence of twelve years. Mr. Delassus resided in this house for eleven years, leaving St. Louis finally in 1827. In 1831, the place was purchased by Wm. T. Phillips, who converted the buildings into a powder mill.

Adjoining this tract on the south was another concession of Cruzat to Vasquez of same date, 1786, for 50 arpents, survey No. 1836 as 42.17 acres. This piece remained unimproved for many years, after several conveyances from one to another, these two pieces, together 59.08 acres, were purchased by Doct. W. Carr Lane in 1836, who the same year laid out on them Lane's Suburb St. George from above Victor to below Anna Street.

THE BENT PLACE.

The next, the fourth place below St. Louis on this side was well known to the people of Cahokia from the earliest day of that village, long before St. Louis was ever conceived or dreamt of. It was here they used to land from their canoes whenever they came over to this side fishing or hunting, and that was all there was to bring them over at that early day. It was here also Laclede first landed a half century later when seeking a suitable location for his future home, which, having selected and established, the intervening space soon became a beaten path, the only one between the places for many years.

Eugene Pouré, (Beau Soleil) appears as the first owner; we find no concessions; he died April 30, 1783.

His widow, née Josepha Godeau, sold it to Jno. J. Motard, Oct. 12, 1785, with a house of posts, ground enclosed, for 200 dollars.

J. Motard to Jno. B. Hubert Lacroix, May 10, 1790, with a barn, etc., for 600 dollars.

Hubert Lacroix to Jno. Rice Jones, of Kaskaskia, March 17, 1796, for $2,000, dollars, *$1,000* cash, *$1,000* in three years, 1,000 lbs. good flour, and 500 lbs. of bacon. Eight arpents front on Mississippi, running back to the Catalan road, house 40 feet long, another 30 feet long, bake-house and oven, dairy and hen-house, another building of 50 feet, a barn 40 feet, and lime-kiln.

Jones, finding it a hard bargain did not pay the second $1,000, preferring to lose his first *$1,000*. At the request of Lacroix, the governor appointed Charles Gratiot and Charles Sanguinet to appraise the property, which having done, they reported that "they could not conscientiously appraise the property at more than $200" (oh! what a falling off was there, my countrymen). It was then sold at public sale to the highest bidder, Manuel Lisa, for $201, Sept. 9, 1799.

M. Lisa sold it to Pat Collins and Jos. Berry, June 19, 1804, for 800 silver dollars, or 800 lbs. good powder at $1.00 per pound, called 67 arpents.

Patrick Cullen and James Berry sold it to Silas Bent, Aug. 10, 1807, for 300 dollars, 67 arpents, survey No. 99,— 56.53 acres.

Judge Bent put up a new stone house and many improvements on the place and lived there some twenty years until his death Nov. 20, 1827, and his family for long years afterwards.

This place fronted the river and road from below Anna Street to the Arsenal grounds.

ARSENAL TRACT, FIFTH PLACE.

The land next south of the Bent tract was in former years, how far back is not known, occupied by the half civilized remnant of the Delaware and Shawnee tribes of Indians united as one band.

Part of this land, eight arpents front on river running back to the road, was conceded by Governor Cruzat to Jos. M. Papin, March 30, 1787, about 68 arpents, survey 334, — 57.64 acres. Papin (in 1812) and wife (in 1817) died still owning the land unimproved. It was sold by the executor to Sil. V. Papin, Oct. 17, 1817. After several conveyances of portions of it between the Papins and other parties, the United

States became the owners by purchase of a piece containing 43.19 arpents, the northeast portion on the river front, on which they erected the Arsenal buildings, enclosed with a stone wall, on the ground formerly occupied by the Indian Village. This fronts from Arsenal to Utah Streets.

JOHN MULLANPHY'S.

The sixth place was a concession to Joseph Taillon by the Governor, of 6 arpents front on the river by 10 west to the Catalan road.

Joseph Taillon to Manuel Lisa, July 11, 1799, the above 60 arpents, with an old cabin and some fruit trees and corn, for $50.

Manuel Lisa to Francis Chatillon, September 5, 1799, the same with a house 20 by 15 feet, for $200.[1]

Francis Chatillon to P. Martin Ladouceur, June 16, 1802, for $255.

Pierre Martin to John Mullanphy, April 10, 1805, for $500.

About 48 arpents, survey No. 286, — 40.83 acres.

On this piece of land was the old original ferry to Cahokia. Mullanphy built a small stone house here in 1805 to strengthen his title, the walls of which are still standing (1886).

---

[1] To President Street.

LOUIS DUBREUIL'S.

The seventh place was a concession by Governor Cruzat to Silvestre Sarpy of 4 arpents front on river by 8 arpents deep to the road to Catalan's ford.

Sarpy sold this to Louis Dubreuil November 22, 1790, with a house of posts 20 by 15 feet, and some other improvements, for ——.

Estate of Susanne Dubreuil to Louis Debreuil and Louis A. Labeaume, December 2, 1838, for $680.50. 32 arpents. Survey No. 374, for 27.20 acres.

APPENDIX.

BEING BRIEF NOTICES OF SOME OF THE MOST PROMINENT OF THE EARLY FAMILIES OF ST. LOUIS; PARTICULARLY OF THOSE WHOSE NAMES HAVE BEEN CONTINUED, THROUGH MALE DESCENDANTS, TO THE PRESENT TIME.

PIERRE LACLEDE.

But little of his personal history is known.

Pierre Margry, of the French Naval Bureau, fixes his birth about 1724 in the "Parish of Bedons, in the valley of the Aspre, diocese of Oleron in Bearne, about fifteen leagues from Pau, capital of ancient Navarre," now Department of the Lower Pyrenees.[1]

This would confirm the statement of Jno. B. Ortes, who died here in 1814 — "that he was born in Bion (Bedons) Bearne, France, near the Pyrenees, in the same place as Laclede; that he came with him to America, and to St. Louis in 1765."

In 1755 when Laclede came to New Orleans he was thirty-one years of age, and Ortes about eighteen.

---

[1] Margry says he was a younger brother of M. Laclede, chief circuit justice of the province of Bearne.

The French universal dictionary of the nineteenth century, mentions a Laclede, a young French historian, who died young in 1736, who had written a general history of Portugal, published at Paris, in two volumes quarto, in 1735 — afterwards translated into Portuguese at Lisbon in 1781–1797.

The name Liguest is no where found in the French authorities and is doubtless an appendage.

(411)

MARIE THERESE CHOUTEAU,

maiden name Bourgeois, was born in New Orleans in the year 1733, and in 1749, at the age of sixteen years was married to Auguste René Chouteau of that place. The only child of this marriage, Auguste, was born on September 26, 1750.

This union continued but for a brief period, as in the following year Mrs. C. left her husband and returned to her friends.

The family tradition regarding the cause of her separation from Chouteau, and her subsequent connection with Laclede, is this: —

"She had not long been married to Chouteau, who was much older than herself, and of a jealous disposition and violent temper; than he commenced a system of abuse, which culminated in personal violence on his part, in which he inflicted a wound on her face the scar of which she carried to her grave. After this she left him and returned to her friends, which step on her part, they claim, met the approval, not only of all her friends, but of the Catholic clergy with the bishop at their head, who advised them in future to live apart from each other, and sanctioned their separation as far as he consistently could, and which they chose to consider as final and complete.

"Laclede came to New Orleans in 1755, and after becoming acquainted with each other, a mutual attachment ensued, which resulted in what they chose to consider their *legal* union, although not strictly in conformity to the usages of the church, which met the approval, not only of their personal friends, but of the community at large — for New Orleans was then but a very small place, hardly more than a village, its population according to Gayarré, not ex-

APPENDIX. 413

ceeding 2,000 souls, of whom fully one-third were African slaves. This was in the year 1757."

By this second union she was the mother of John Pierre, born in 1758, Victoire in 1760, Pelagie in 1762, and Marie Louise in 1764.

On the 3rd of August, 1763, Mrs. Chouteau left New Orleans in a boat with her second husband, Peter Laclede Liguest, and her children, for Upper Louisiana, and landed at Fort Chartres, on the Illinois side, on November 3d, after a voyage up of three months. Spending the winter of 1763-64 at this place, she proceeded on to Cahokia in March 1764, where she remained six months, during the erection of the first house in St. Louis, and on its completion in the month of September of that year, she came over to the new post, the first white female inhabitant of the west bank of this upper Louisiana, and here she passed the balance of her days.

After the death of Laclede on June 20, 1778, Mrs. C., who was a thrifty, industrious woman, carried on business on a small scale on her own account, and in the thirty-six years that she survived him had accumulated a very handsome estate in property, money and slaves. Thirty-one years of age on her arrival here, Mrs. C. spent the balance of her long life in this place, residing in the same house,[1] for just half a century. She died in it on Aug. 14, 1814, at the venerable age of eighty-one years, leaving a numerous progeny and respected and esteemed by all.

Her children were,

1. Augustus, born Sept. 26, 1750; he married Therese Cerre, Sept. 21, 1786, and died Feb. 24, 1829, in his seventy-ninth year.

2. John Pierre, born Oct. 10, 1758, died July 10, 1849,

---

[1] Southwest corner of Main and Chestnut Streets.

aged ninety years, nine months. Married first Pelagie Kiersereau, July 26, 1783, who died Feb. 9, 1793;

And secondly, Brigitte Saucier, Feb. 14, 1794, who died May 18, 1829.

3. Victoire, born 1760, married to Charles Gratiot, June 25, 1781, she died June 15, 1825, at sixty-five. G. had died April 20, 1817, at sixty-five.

4. Pelagie, born 1762, married to Sylvester Labbadie, July 27, 1776. She died June 5, 1812, at fifty. Labbadie had died June 19, 1794.

5. Marie Louise, born in 1764, married to Joseph M. Papin, Jan. 9, 1779. She died Feb. 27, 1817 at fifty-three and Papin had died Sept. 18, 1811.

JOSEPH MICHEL (HIS CORRECT NAME) DIT TAILLON,

was born in Canada in the year 1715. He came to St. Louis 1764, and died there in 1807, at the age of ninety-two years, his wife *née* Marie Louise Bossett, born in 1728, also died in St. Louis in 1797 aged sixty-nine years. They had lived for a number of years at Fort Chartres, where some of their oldest children were born. They were the parents of a numerous family of children of whom the following attained maturity:—

1. Marie Louise, married to Jacques Chauvin at Fort Chartres.

2. Marie Josepha, born in 1748, was married to Paul Gregory Kiersereau May 10, 1766 (the second marriage in St. Louis) at eighteen years, and died in 1767 a short year after marriage, at nineteen, leaving a daughter, Pelagie, who became the first wife of Peter Chouteau, Sr.

3. Marie Anne, widow of Etienne Daigle, in 1777.

4. Joseph, Jr., married to Marie Berger, May 1, 1781.

5. Charles, married to Cecile Deschamps, in 1780.

6. John.

7. Francis, to Pelagie Chauvin Charleville, June 8, 1795.

8. Helene, to Louis Chevallier, in 1799. He died June, 1801.

Old Joseph Tayon, from his long residence in the place,[1] the respectability of his family and connections, became an important and influential man in the village, being one of the sindics or overseers of the place.

His son Charles was a lieutenant in the militia, and the first commandant at St. Charles.

NICHOLAS BEAUGENOU, SR.,

with his family, came over from Fort Chartres, where they had lived for a number of years, with the first comers, accompanied by Mrs. Beaugenou's two brothers, Charles and Francis Henrion, both single men.

Nicholas Beaugenou, Sr., born in Canada, died in St. Louis, in 1770. Mrs. Beaugenou, *née* Henrion, born in Canada, died in St. Louis Sept., 1769. Their children, born in Canada and Fort Chartres, were then all minors except the oldest of them, Nicholas, Jr.

1. Nicholas Jr. (Fifi), born in Canada in 1741, married Catherine Gravelle in 1775; she died in St. Louis, 1795, and he in 1826, aged eighty-five years.

2. Charles.

3. Maria Josepha, born 1748, married to Toussaint Hunaut in 1766, at eighteen (the first marriage recorded in the archives); she died in 1799.

4. Helen, born in 1751, married to James Brunel, La Sabloniere, in 1771, at twenty years.

5. Therese, first married to Joachim D'eau, from Canada, in 1777, and secondly to Jacques Noise in 1781; she died in Cahokia in 183–.

---

[1] The northwest corner of Main and Market streets.

6. Agnes Frances, to Joseph Hugé, from France, in 1776, died in 1797.

7. Elizabeth to Alexis Loise, 1773.

NICHOLAS BEAUGENOU, JR., CALLED FIFI.

Born in Canada, 1741, came with his father, first to Fort Chartres and then to St. Louis in 1764.

He married here Catharine Gravelle in 1775, who died in 1795; they raised three children.

1. Julie, born 1775–76, married to Francois Valois, February 4, 1794, at eighteen.
2. Nicholas (No. 3).
3. Vital.

This second Nicholas Beaugenou lived here and about from the origin of St. Louis, 1764, to his death at St. Ferdinand in 1826, a period of over sixty years; he lived in various parts of the village and surroundings, was much on horseback, made and traded off several farms. Fee Fee creek in our county, received its cognomen from his juvenile nick-name of Fifi. He died in St. Ferdinand in 1826, aged eighty-five years.

FRANCIS HENRION,

brother of Mrs. Beaugenou, died unmarried in 1781, leaving his property to his nephew Nicholas B., Jr., and wife, in trust for their children.

CHARLES HENRION,

the oldest brother of Mrs. B., died in 1783, at the residence of his nephew Fifi Beaugenou, on Second Street. Some time before his death he had purchased from Louis Barada, his illegitimate mulatto child Marianne, nine years of age, to emancipate her (which, he did at once), and make her

APPENDIX. 417

his heir. This he neglected to do, and dying not long after without a will, his property fell to his heirs, the Beaugenous. The matter was left to the decision of Gov.-General Miro at New Orleans, who placed her as one of the heirs with the seven Beaugenous, all of them then yet living in 1787.

ALEXIS LOISE, SR.,

and Elizabeth Beaugenou were married in 1773. Their children: —
1. Victoire, baptized May 8, 1774.
2. Alexis, Jr., baptized Nov. 14, 1776; married to Marie J. Calvé.
3. Helene, baptized May 26, 1779.
4. Paul.
5. Therese, married to Pierre Vial dit Manitou, Florisant.
6. Catherine, married to Charles Martineau.
7. Joseph, married to Marie.
8. Marie Irene, married to Antoine Senecal.

MARCHETEAU DIT DENOYER.

Among the first that came over from the east side to settle here, was the very numerous family of the Marcheteaus, alias Denoyers.[1]

The three old ones of these Marcheteaus were brothers; Louis, Sr., Joseph and Francis originally from Canada, with each a family.

LOUIS MARCHETEAU, SR.'S

first wife was Francoise Leduc, their children were two sons, Basil and Louis, Jr.,[2] and three daughters, Veronique

---

[1] Chouteau wrote them Marcereau.
[2] This son Louis (Kiery) was married Nov., 1766, to Veronica Panissé, widow of John Prunet, alias La Giroflee.

the first wife of Louis Ride, then a married woman with several children, and two others whose names are not given.

His wife died about 1770–71, not on record. They were then living on the north half of block 3,[1] his original grant from Laclede, which he had well improved with two houses, barn, stable, etc. Being about to marry a second wife an inventory of their property was taken, as the law required on June 23, 1772, in presence of his son Louis (Kiery), and his sons-in-law, Ride and the others. Besides their homestead, they had a vacant lot on the back street, 120 arpents in the Cul de Sac, and abandoned lands at Fort Chartres.

The old gentleman then married his second wife Angelique Metivier, the widow of Dequirigoust Filip, July 3, 1772. She had but one child, a daughter, and lived in her house, the next one north in block No. 4. Louis Marcheteau died Nov. 19, 1773, eighteen months after his second marriage.

LOUIS RIDE, SR.,

farmer, who also came in the boat with Chouteau in 1764, was born in Canada; his first wife whom he married at Fort Chartres, was Veronica, a daughter of Louis Marcheteau, Sr.; their children were four sons:—

1. Louis, Jr., born 1762, died February, 1794. Deaf and dumb.
2. Laurent, born 1764.
3. Claude, born 1766.
4. Francois, born 1768.

---

[1] The two houses and lot in block No. 3 above, and the vacant lot on the back street, were sold to Eugene Pouré, by the son, Louis Marcheteau, Jr. Eugene Poure himself died in 1783, and the property was then purchased by Charles Gratiot, who lived on it a number of years, and some of his first children were born in this house.

APPENDIX. 419

Mrs. Veronica Ride died January 2, 1773, at their residence, northeast corner of Main and Elm, where Ride had built his house in 1765.

(He married his second wife, Charlotte Hyacinthe, the widow of Louis Hunaud, of St. Genevieve, in 1776, who had three sons, Antoine, Louis and Toussaint Hunaud who came up to St. Louis, and two married daughters in Ste. Genevieve.)

This second Mrs. Ride, Sr., died in 1784–5, and
Louis Ride, Sr., Nov. 6, 1787.

THE RIVIERES, DIT BACCANNET.

Antoine, Sr., born in 1706 in Canada, married at Kaskaskia in 1744 at thirty-eight years, and died at St. Ferdinand in 1816, aged one hundred and ten — his wife Mary Barbara Eloy, born in New Orleans in 1726, died in St. Louis in 1786, aged sixty, leaving five sons and three daughters, viz: —

1. Antoine, Jr., born 1745, married first Adelaide Lefebvre in 1784, and secondly, Charlotte Roque in 1795; he died in 1823 at seventy-eight years.

2. John Bap., born 1752 married to Margaret Vial in 1786 at thirty-four.

3. Philip, born 1757, married to Marie Pinot in 1784, his first wife, at twenty-seven, and Marie Leberge, his second wife in 1802; he died in 1812 at fifty-five.

4. Pelagie, married to Auguste Dodier in 1787.

5. Marie Jeanne, married to Louis Hunaud in 1782 first, and secondly to Jno. B. Greza dit Capitaine in 1802.

6. Francois, born 1772, was living in July, 1820.

7. Julia, born 1775.

Old Antoine Riviere drove the cart in which Laclede brought up his family from Fort Chartres to Cahokia in

1764, and then brought up his own family to St. Louis in 1765.

He was eighty years of age when his wife died in 1786, and survived her thirty years, dying at the house of his son, John B., in the village of St. Ferdinand, at the age of one hundred and ten years.

His will: —

"In the year thousand eight hundred and seven, December second, I, Antoine Riviere, Sr., under my ordinary mark, in presence of Francis Cottard, Louis Cottin and Louis Ouvré, give and bequeath after my death and my debts paid, all that may belong to me at present and since the death of my wife. I make this gift to Margaret Vial, my son John Baptiste Riviere's wife, for the care she took of me in the sicknesses I had, and also for the care and trouble she had while in health.

I make this gift to the above named while in health and full knowledge, by the above named witnesses.

Done at St. Ferdinand the day and year above.

         his
      ANTOINE X RIVIERE, SR.
         mark

"COTTARD, C. COTTIN,
  his
"LOUIS X OUVRÉ, *Witnesses*."
  mark.

He was in its strictest sense the patriarch of our early settlers, one of the first to come here, and living to attain the greatest age.

JOSEPH MAINVILLE, DIT DESCHENES,

a carpenter, came in the first boat with Chouteau; he was born in Canada. He was an active business man and prominent in the affairs of the village, being for a number of years one of the sindics. He married Anne Chancellier, sister of Joseph and Louis Chancellier, February 9, 1770. They lived for many years at the southeast corner of Main and Locust Streets, where his wife died in August, 1787, at the age of fifty, and Mainville in April, 1795, leaving seven children: —

1. Theresa, married to Joseph Desautelle in 1787, and to Louis Lemonde in 1797.
2. Helen, married to Pierre Gagnon in 1789, to P. D. Joliboix in 1801, and to Charles Cardinal in 1813.
3. Julie, married to Joseph Hubert in 1794.
4. Pelagie, married to Joseph Lagrave, 1795.
5. Marie Anne, married to Auguste Filteau in 1797,
And two sons Joseph, Jr., and Charles Mainville.

JOSEPH CHANCELLIER.

The two Chancelliers, Joseph and Louis, brothers of Mrs. Mainville, were born in the little village of Ste. Phillippe, and came also in the same boat with Chouteau and Mainville from Fort Chartres; they were young lads, the oldest, Joseph, but fourteen years of age. He married in June, 1772, at the age of twenty-two, Elizabeth Becquet, daughter of Jno. B. Becquet, the miller, aged nineteen, and died in 1784, at the age of thirty-four, leaving three little girls, the oldest eleven years of age.

His widow married Antoine Gauthier of St. Charles in February, 1786.

LOUIS CHANCELLIER.

Louis Chancellier married Marie Louise Deschamps in September, 1782; he was then thirty, living in his stone house at the southeast corner of Main and Vine Streets. He died in June, 1785, six months after the death of his brother, leaving an infant son. His widow following the example set her by her sister-in-law, married her second husband, Joseph Beauchamp, also of St. Charles.

JNO. B. GAMACHE,

farmer, one of the thirty that came on the first boat with Chouteau in 1764, was born near Quebec, Canada, in 1733.

He married Charlotte D'Amours, May 3, 1767, he then being thirty-four years of age and she twenty-one.

He built his house at the northwest corner of Main and Pine Streets, where he lived some eighteen years, until the death [of his wife, August 23, 1781, at the age of thirty-five, after which he sold his house and removed to Carondelet where he died in 1805, aged seventy-two years. Their children were: —

1. Jno. Batiste, born in 1768, married Catherine Constant.
2. Auguste, born in 1774, married Genevieve Courtois.
3. Marie Therese, born in 1776.
4. Louis, born in 1778, and several others died young.

LOUIS TESSON HONORÉ, SR.,

tailor, was born in Canada in the year 1734, and died in St. Louis in 1807, at the age of seventy-three years.

Magdalena Peterson, his wife, was born in 1739, and died here in 1812, also at the age of seventy-three. They came here from Kaskaskia. Their children were —

1. Louis Tesson Honoré, Jr., who married, first, Marie Duchouquette in the year 1782 in St. Louis, who died in 1784; and secondly, Therese Creely in 1788, who died in 1821.
2. Francis T. H., who married Susan Liberge in 1787.
3. Marie Euphrosine to Louis Baudoin in 1789.

4. Elizabeth T. H. to Antoine Barada, Jr., in 1796.

5. Michael T. H. to Genevieve Menard in 1796, who died in 1807, and then to Maria Glenn in Carondelet in 1812–13.

6. Victoire T. H. to George Schultz in 1797.

7. Jno. B. T. H. to Mary Bolly in 1802.

8. Noel T. H. to Mary Sipp in 1802.

Louis Tesson Honoré No. 3 was the son of Louis T. Honoré No. 2, and his second wife Therese Creely. He was born about 1790 in St. Louis.

In 1812, with Jno. B. D. Belcour, they purchased the southwest quarter of block No. 27, which was the northeast corner of Second and Washington Avenue; this they divided, Honoré getting the south portion at the corner. He lived here for fifteen years, until his death, August 20, 1827. His wife was Aramanthe, one of the daughters of Jno. B. Dumoulin, the old stone mason, for many years at the southwest corner of Chestnut and Second.

His will was very brief, in substance as follows, viz.:—

"I, Louis Tesson Honoré, in very feeble health, although sound in mind and understanding, I leave to my wife, Amaranthe Honoré, in the event of the death of our only child, all my worldly goods, house, furniture, clothing, beds and bedding, money, etc., St. Louis, Aug. 20, 1827."

His widow afterwards married for a second husband Louis Leduc.

GREGORY KIERSEREAU, SR.,

was born at Port Louis, Brittany, France, ——. He was married about the year 1720 to Gilette Lebourg, a widow Pothier. They were at Cahokia in 1740, and he died before 1770, the widow then living. Their children were three —

1. *René H.*, dit Renaud, born in France in 1723, was married to Marie M. Robillard, who died in St. Louis

December 15, 1783, and he at St. Ferdinand in 1798, aged seventy-five years. In the early years of St. Louis he was the chanter or chorister at the church, and in the absence of the curate frequently officiated at interments. Their children were —

1. Gregory, Jr., born at Fort Chartres 1752, married Magdalen St. Francois 1774.
2. Rosalind, married Francois Faustin, dit Parent, 1781.
3. Marie Josephine, married to Pierre Choret, 1786.
4. Julie, married to Gabriel Latreille, 1800.
5. Marguerite, married to Louis Aubuchon, 1804.

2. *Paul Kiersereau*, born in New Orleans, married Marie Josepha Michel Tayon May 10, 1766, the second marriage in St. Louis. Their only child, Pelagie, born in 1767, married Pierre Chouteau, Sr., in 1783. She died in 1793, aged twenty-six years, leaving four children: Aug. P., Pierre, Jr., and Paul L. Chouteau, three sons; and Pelagie, one daughter, afterwards Mrs. B. Berthold.

3. *Marie*, born in 1735, married to Antoine Deshetres in 1788. Deshetres died in 1798, aged sixty years, and she in 1815, aged eighty.

Gregory Kiersereau, Jr., aged twenty-two, and Madelaine St. Francois, aged eighteen, daughter of Antoine St. Francois and Carlotta Larche, were married August 26, 1774. Their children —

1. Gregory, No. 3, married to Caroline Dodier 1801.
2. Adrienne, married to Joseph Beauchamp 1837.
3. Louis Gregory, married to Catherine Tayon 1833.
4. Catherine, married to Francis Tayon 1820.
5. Marie Louise, married to Pierre Tayon 1823.
6. Marie Louise, married to Ignace Tayon 1833.

JULIEN LEROY,

was also one of those who came in the first boat in 1764, with Aug. Chouteau, he and his wife *née* Marie Barbara

Saucier were married in Mobile, Alabama, in the year 1755, and their first child, Charles, was born in that place.

1. Charles, born in Mobile, 1756, married Susanne Dodier 1779 at twenty-three.

2. Madelaine, Fort Chartres, 1758, to Francis Hebert, 1774, at sixteen.

3. Julien, Jr., Fort Chartres, 1760, to Marie Louise Cotte, in 1784. She died in 1793, and he married the widow of Pierre A. Marie in 1797.

4. Pierre Patrick, St. Louis, married to Victoire Stark.

5. Henri Francois, St. Louis, 1767, married to Jeanne Montardy, 1793.

6. Louis, St. Louis, 1773.

7. Etienne, St. Louis, 1776.

Julien LeRoy was a well informed, enterprising man, and a useful citizen, having built several houses in the village, by obtaining a lot, building on it, and then selling it to some one who needed a house at once. Several of his sons removed to Carondelet where their posterity still reside, having dropped the " Le " from their name and calling themselves simply " Roy."

As the death of LeRoy is not on the church register, he perhaps died elsewhere.

THE MARTIGNY BROTHERS, JNO. B. AND JOS. L.,

were also of those who came in the first boat with Chouteau, 1764.

Jno. Bap. Martigny, born in 1712, at Varenne, Quebec, Canada, married to Helene Hebert at Fort Chartres. She was born in 1732 at Fort Chartres, was sister of Ignace and Joseph Hebert, Sr.

J. B. Martigny was a prominent and well to do man, he built, in 1768, the stone house at the southeast corner of Main and Walnut, which in after years became noted in the early history of the village and town as appears in another article. He was for a long time captain of the militia of the village, died September 22, 1792, aged eighty, and Mrs. M., February 25, 1802, at seventy, having no children, they left their property to Mrs. M.'s niece, Helene Hebert, the wife of Hyacinthe St. Cir.

Joseph Lemoine Martigny built his house of posts in 1765-6, on the west side of Main, between Plum and Cedar, where he lived about a year, and then sold it to Nicholas Royer, dit Sansquartier, a soldier, He was engaged in the Indian trade as late as July 3, 1789, when his name is last found in the archives.

JEAN SALLÉ, DIT LAJOIE,

was born in Saintes, Saintous, France, about the year 1741. He came to St. Louis in 1764 in the boat with Chouteau from Fort Chartres, and was married to Marie Rose Vidalpano, born in Taos, New Mexico, July 3, 1770, by Father Valentin, curate of the parish of St. Louis.

Their daughter, Helen Sallé Lajoie, was married to Benjamin Lerou, merchant, January 17, 1792, whose children were one son, Watkins Lerou, and two daughters, Marie Angelique, who was married to Peter Primm, from Virginia, on January 18, 1809, and

Helene Lerou, who married Capt. Jas. Lafferty, in 1827, Aug. 27.

The old lady, Marie Rose V. Sallé, died on July 27, 1830, at the house of her daughter, Mrs. Lerou, on Elm Street, between Fourth and Fifth, at the remarkable age of one one hundred and seven years, and Mrs. Lerou in 1854 at the age of eighty-one.

OLD JOSEPH MARCHETEAU DENOYER,

the second brother, a cabinet maker, had been twice married before coming over to St. Louis, and three married daughters with their husbands and children came over with him, viz. : —

1. Marie Jeanne and husband, Charles Routier, stone mason, daughter of his first wife, Madeline Robert.

2. Elizabeth, and husband, Jno. B. Becquet, a miller, and —

3. Catherine and husband, Francis Bissonet, farmer, were daughters by his second wife, Elizabeth Leduc, a sister of the first wife of his elder brother, Louis, Sr.

CHARLES ROUTIER,

stone mason, born in 1703, married on the other side, died in St. Louis March 10, 1777, at northeast corner of Main and Pine, aged seventy-four, and his widow February 20, 1800, aged seventy-two.

JNO. B. BECQUET,

miller, born 1723, married also at Fort Chartres, removed to Ste. Genevieve.

FRANCIS BISSONNET,

farmer, born in 1741, married in 1772 at Kaskaskia, died at St. Louis January 1, 1787, aged forty-six.

LOUIS BISSONNET,

an older brother of Francis B., born in 1731, married Genevieve Routier, only child of Chas. Routier above, April 30, 1771; he forty; she twenty-two.

He died April 20, 1786, aged fifty-five, at the corner of Main and Pine, and his widow in May, 1804, also aged fifty-five years, leaving seven children, Louis, thirty-five; Charles, thirty-three; Joseph, thirty-one; Pascal, twenty-nine.

Angelica Ladouceur had died, Pelagie, wife of Paul Primo, and Helene, wife of Henry Delaurier.

Her will is dated May 24, 1804, by Capt. Stoddard.

She died northwest corner Main and Olive.

OLD FRANCIS MARCHETEAU, DENOYER,

the third brother, a carpenter, came over with his two brothers in 1765, and built himself a small house. We have but few particulars of this Marcheteau.

His wife was Marie Josepha Noiselle.

A son, Joseph Marcheteau, Jr., married, in 1779, Ursula Cardinal.

A daughter, Marie Josette, was married to John B. Durand in 1768. She died in 1769-70, leaving an infant daughter, Theotiste, and Jno. B. Durand died in 1773 at the age of thirty-one.

When this child grew up to be a young woman she was married in 1783 to Emilien Yosti, an Italian from Novarra, in Piedmont. He was for many years a prominent man in our place, and died in his house, southwest corner of Main and Locust, in 1818, aged seventy-eight years, and his widow six years thereafter in 1824, at the age of fifty-five years.

They raised to maturity five children.

1. Pelagie, married to Alfred Crutsinger, from Virginia, in 1809.

2. Marie, married to John C. Potter in 1816.

3. Joseph, born in 1791, died single in 1820, at twenty-nine years.

4. Louis, born 1796, died on his farm, St. Louis County in 1853 at fifty-seven.

5. Francis, born 1798, died at St. Charles, August 19, 1879, aged eighty-one.

NICHOLAS MARECHAL, SR.,

a native of Verdun, France, had been a soldier in the French service and married his wife, Marie Jeanne Isleret, a half-breed Indian, at Fort Chartres, previous to 1753. They came over to St Louis in 1765, with a family of eight children, five sons and three daughters and received from Laclede a verbal grant of the northwest corner of Main and Chestnut, upon which he built a house, etc. Here he died in September, 1770. Their children were: —

1. Marie, married to Joseph Calvé, Sr. She died in 1791, and Calvé in 1792.
2. Francis, who married Marie Therese Riviere, in 1770.
3. Catherine, to Joseph Francis Moreau, in 1767.
4. Marie Elizabeth, to Antoine Martin Ladouceur, in 1774, and after his death, to Jno. B. Primeau, in 1791.
5. Jacques, married Genevieve Cardinal, widow of J. B. Vifvarenne.
6. Antoine, to Catherine Tabeau, 1777.
7. Joseph.
8. Nicholas, Jr.

GABRIEL DODIER, SR.,

was a blacksmith at Fort Chartres, where he had been established for some years, his wife was Marie Francoise Millet. He had been industrious and prosperous and had accumulated quite a handsome property for the times.

He died over there August 1, 1763, leaving five children, one son and four daughters, viz.: —

1. Gabriel, Jr., born in 1740, was twenty-three years of age, and had been married to Miss Becquet about a year.
2. Marie Francoise, married to Jno. B. Becquet about a year.
3. Jeanne.

4. Elizabeth.
5. Marie Therese, three daughters, all minors.

An inventory of his estate was taken on August 4, 1763, by John V. Bobé, Desclausau, orderer and judge of Illinois, consisting in his house and lot, slaves, shop and tools, money, furniture, horses and cattle, etc., to the amount of 29,214 livres; deducting expenses, debts, etc., 2,104 livres, the estate netted 27,110 livres; the widow's half 13,555 livres and the five children 13,555 livres.

The family came to this side in 1765, comprising the widow of Gabriel, Sr., she died February 10, 1783, aged about sixty.

1. Gabriel Dodier, Jr., who died in 1805, aged sixty-five years.
2. Marie Francoise Becquet, died in 1785, aged forty-one years.
3. Jeanne.
4. Elizabeth, wife of Alexis Cotté.
5. Marie Therese, wife of Simon Coussot, died in 1782, at twenty-five.

JOHN BATISTE [1] BECQUET.

There were two of this name that came over with the first crowd in 1765. One was Jno. B. B., the *blacksmith*, whose wife was Francoise Dodier, and who received a verbal grant from Laclede, of the northwest corner of Main and Myrtle, upon which he built his house and shop, and where he lived during the whole of his residence in St. Louis, of thirty-two years, from 1765, dying in it October 21, 1797, aged seventy-four years. His wife had died there twelve years previously, April 19, 1785.

The other, Jno. B. B., was a *miller*, whose wife was

---

[1] The John Batistes were very numerous here in those early days, almost every family of several sons, having one in the number.

Elizabeth, a daughter of Joseph Marchetau, dit Desnoyer. This Becquet had built a small house, likewise on a verbal grant from Laclede, on the southwest corner of Main and Olive, where he lived until 1772, when he exchanged it with Pierre Gagnon for the southeast quarter of block No. 26, corner of Main and Green; here he lived until 1776-77, when he removed to Ste. Genevieve, selling it to Jno. M. Cardinal, who was occupying it when killed by Indians in 1780.

THE HEBERTS.

Helene Danis, widow of Ignace Hebert, Sr., received a concession of the south half of Block No. 38, from Gov. St. Ange, July 18, 1769. She, or her husband Hebert (as there is no record of the date of his death or where he died), had built on this lot in 1765 with the then usual verbal permission of Laclede, and had occupied it about twenty years at the date of her death, November 28, 1784.

Inventory and sale of her effects in January, 1785, by Chas Sanguinet, executor, and partition between the representatives of the seven heirs in July 1786, as follows:—

1. Ignace Hebert, Jr., born 1730, then dead, with three heirs.
2. Helene Hebert, wife of Jno. B. Martigny, 1732, then fifty-four years of age.
3. Joseph Hebert.
4. Auguste Hebert.
5. Pelagie Carpentier, a grand-child, parents deceased.
6. Francois Hebert, born 1750, killed by Indians in 1780, his widow living.
7. Marie Hebert Berger, deceased, with a son, Pierre, grand-child. These were all born in Illinois, and lived there, the only two of them who came over to this place were Mrs. Martigny, and Francois, deceased.

JOSEPH HEBERT, SR.,

born at Fort Chartres in 1741, came over in 1765.

He died in St. Louis January 28, 1801, aged sixty years. His wife, Agnes Michel Philipe, born in 1744, died March 21, 1814, at seventy; their children, all born in St. Louis, were,—

1. Helene, born 1767, May.
2. Joseph, Jr., September, 1771, married to Victoire A. Hortiz, May 2, 1801: he twenty-six, she sixteen.
3. Constance, 1774, July.
4. Marie, October, 1776.

AMABLE GUION, JR.,

the only son of Amable Guion, Sr., and wife, Margaret Blondeau, born at Fort Chartres in 1763, came over with his parents in 1765.

He was married in 1783, at the age of twenty years, to Irene Felicité Robert, and settled in Carondelet.

Their children were: —

1. Clara Margaret, born 1787, married to Antoine Dangen, from Marseilles, France, July 22, 1807. Dangen died April 12, 1827, and Mrs. D. July 8th, less than three months after her husband leaving several children.
2. Hubert, 1789, married Josephine Didier from Beçancon, France, May 7, 1811; he died at Jefferson Barracks, May 23, 1833, aged 44.
3. Vincent, 1791, married Eulalie Derouin, 1813, who died January 5, 1817; and secondly, Genevieve Bouvet.
4. Louis, 1793, to Clarissa Delisle, 1818, and Catherine Mackay, 1832.
5. Joseph, 1797, to Monica Boudon, 1818, and Theodosia Chouquet, 1836.

APPENDIX. 433

6. Irene Felicite, 1800, to Richard Milligen, 1822, and then to Jno. B. Delisle.

7. Bartholomew, 1803, to Margaret Barada, 1828.

8. Antoine, 1807, to Adelaide Delor, 1830.

Amable Guion, Jr., above, died in Carondelet, Sept. 18, 1813, aged 50 years.

JOHN M. PEPIN, DIT LACHANSE,

a stone mason, came from Quebec, Canada, in 1765, bringing with him a sister, Marie Christine, then a young woman of eighteen. In January, 1774, she was married to Charles Bissette, a young man of her own age, they being respectively twenty-seven years of age. Bissette was killed by the Indians, May 26, 1780, and on Sept. 1, 1781, the widow married Jno. B. Provencher, a wheelwright, living on the northeast corner of Second and Pine Streets, where he had built his house on the lot granted him by Laclede in 1765. In this house Provencher died early in the year 1816, having lived in it the whole of his fifty-one years he passed in St. Louis. His widow survived him but three years dying January 22, 1819, aged seventy-two. They left an only son, Jno. Louis Provencher, a married daughter, Margaret Provencher Tournat, having previously died. Pepin Lachanse lived here some 20 years, a single man, and built a number of the early stone houses. Having married a Catherine Lalumandiere of Ste. Genevieve, he removed to that place about 1787.

PIERRE ALEXIS MARIE,

with wife, Reine Gilgaud, and little son came over from the other side in 1765; he was an enterprising business man, built several houses in the village on lots granted him at various times, and died January 10, 1797, in good circumstances, in his house at the northeast corner of Main and Market Streets.

After his death his widow and only child, Michel Alexis Marie, then a married man with a family of several children, sold the property to Bernard Pratte, Sr., the father of our present Bernard Pratte, in whose family the property is still held.

The widow Marie subsequently married a second husband, Julien Leroy, Jr., and the son M. A. Marie, removed with his family to Carondelet, where he died.

LOUIS C. DUBREUIL,

a prominent and influential merchant for thirty years in our early village, died on July 16, 1794, leaving nine children, all at the time minors.

1. Joseph C. Dubreuil, born July 19, 1773, died June 7, 1775, at two years.

2. Marie Adelaide, born January 4, 1775, died, single, Nov. 6, 1800, at twenty-five.

3. Marie Felicite, born March 19, 1776; married to James Ceran De St. Vrain, from France, April 30, 1796.

4. Antoine, born Oct. 16, 1778; went a young man to St. Genevieve, married and lived there a number of years, and about 1826 returned to St. Louis with his family, several grown daughters. He died about 1840, leaving several married daughters.

5. Susanne, born in 1780, married to Louis Tarteron De Lebeaume, from France, June 8, 1797.

6. Celeste, born in 1782; was married to Chas. Aug't Fremon Delaurier, from France, May 21, 1799.

7. Louis C., born about 1785; went south a young man, and settled in Baton Rouge, Louisiana, where he married and lived for several years; after his death his two sons,

Louis and Charles, came up and settled in St. Louis, where they married and died, leaving each a family.

8. Eleonore, born 178–; was married to William Tharp, of St. Louis County, about the year 1810. They had four children: —

Caroline, who was married to Hezekiah C. Simmons, June 17, 1829.

Clarisse, to Jno. R. Shaw, St. Genevieve.

And two sons, Thomas and James.

9. Clarissa, born in 1790; married first to Edward Hempstead, from Connecticut, on January 13, 1808; he was our first delegate in Congress, and died Aug. 9, 1817, having lost their children; and secondly to Louis Detheirs, from Liege in Belgium, in 1818–19. She died July 7, 1825, at the age of thirty-five years, leaving some young children by her second husband.

10. Constance, born 1793, to Paul Liguest Chouteau, son of Peter Chouteau, Sr., Feb. 11, 1813, his first wife. She died January 3, 1824, at the age of thirty, leaving three boys, Edward, August and Liguest.

11. Caroline, a posthumous child, born April 6, 1795, died in October same year, 1795, aged 6 months.

Mrs. Louis C. Dubreuil survived her husband over thirty-one years, living to see all her children, minors at the death of their father, grown to maturity and all married but one, her first daughter, Adelaide, who died single at twenty-five years.

She died Oct. 25, 1825, having attained her seventieth year.

PIERRE FRANCIS DE VOLSAY,

knight of the Royal Order of St. Louis, and a captain in he French service, was born in or near Paris about the year 1730.

He married Elizabeth Coulon De Villiers, daughter of

Neyon De Villiers, the last French governor on the Illinois side, at Fort Chartres, in the year 1758, and at the date of the transfer of that side to England in 1765, was the French commandant at Cahokia and crossed to this side at the time St. Ange came over, and for some years was captain of the French company at St. Louis.

In the year 1772, his wife, under the pretext of visiting her father, in New Orleans, went only as far as St. Genevieve, where she remained about nine months, leading a dissolute life, which so scandalized the good people of St. Genevieve, that Mr. Carpentier, a prominent man in the place, brought her up to St. Louis, where De Volsay for a long time refused to receive her. Finally through the persuasions of Governor and Madame Piernas, and Father Valentin, the Catholic curate of the place, a reconciliation was effected, and he consented to take her back, being a kind-hearted man. For a time she conducted herself in a proper manner. In 1774, De Volsay had a furlough and went to France. He was absent about two years on business matters, leaving her in his house on Main Street, the only one on the block, well provided with everything in abundance sufficient for the time of his contemplated absence. He had been gone but a short time when she broke out again in her evil course, receiving at her house daily and nightly the visits of one Renaud, to the disgust and scandal of all her near neighbors, and in a short time ran through all that her husband had provided her with, through her dissipation and debauchery, and finally, previous to De Volsay's return in 1776, the guilty parties fled to the Illinois side, carrying off with them what little was left of the ample provision De Volsay had left her, leaving nothing more than the vacant house.

So soon as De Volsay had returned from France, he commenced proceedings before Governor Cruzat, who had succeeded De Piernas as governor, for a dissolution of his marriage ties, which were only terminated under the administration of Governor De Leyba, August 21, 1779. This Kiersereau, dit Renaud, had come over to this side from Fort Chartres in 1765. This Mrs. De Volsay was a niece of Governor St. Ange, her mother being his sister. Picoté de Belestre was a lieutenant in the regular French service, and a brother-in-law of De Volsay, their wives being sisters.

De Volsay was a hard drinker in his latter years. He died on September 28, 1795, at the age of sixty-five. Nothing more is said of his wife, but it appears he remembered her in his will by leaving her three coats, an embroidered waistcoat, and five pairs of breeches.

DUCHOUQUETTE AND LAMY.

Francois Lafleur Duchouquette, a trader of New Chartres, Illinois, and Celeste Barrois, who was born in Montreal in 1737, were married in Kaskaskia in 1757, where they continued to reside for a number of years, and where their children were born.

1. John Baptist, about 1760, who married Mary Brazeau, daughter of Louis Brazeau, Sr., in St. Louis in 1798. She died in July, 1818, and he in May, 1834, at seventy-four.

2. Henry Lafleur, 1761, he married Feliciana Quirigoust Philip, in February, 1786. She died in January, 1789, and he after, Feb. 14, 1835, at seventy-five years.

3. Marie, 1763, married to Louis Tesson Honoré in Kaskaskia in 1782, and died in St. Louis March 19, 1784, at twenty-two years of age with a child of four months, but two months after the death of her stepfather, Michael Lamy.

4. Pierre, 1764, married Genevieve Charleville. She died in 1822 at forty-eight, and Pierre Duchouquette after August, 1835. No children.

5. Francois, 1766, never married; his will is dated August 15, 1834, died in 1836 (these three last brothers all died without families, the children of their sister, Mrs. Bompart, becoming their heirs; the whole four died within a year or two of each other, and all of them between seventy and eighty).

6. Celeste, born 1770, was married to Louis Bompart in Oct. 1790, who died in July, 1801, and the widow married Henry Delaurier in 180–.

Francis L. Duchouquette, Sr., removed with his family from Kaskaskia across to Ste. Genevieve, where he died.

MICHAEL LAMY,

born in Montreal, Canada, came to St. Louis with the first in 1765. He received a concession of a lot in block No. 43, on which he built a house in 1766. In 1774, he bought Buet's stone house in block No. 50, and then married the widow of Francois Duchouquette, Sr., at Ste. Genevieve, April 30, 1776, and brought the family up to St. Louis. Lamy died January 3, 1784, leaving but one child, Theresa Lamy, who was married to Pascal Leon Cerré, the only son of Gabriel Cerré, on Feb. 13, 1797.

Madame Therese Celeste Barrois, the widow of both Duchouquette and Lamy, died on Dec. 28, 1820, at the age of eighty-three years, surviving her first husband some fifty years, and her second about thirty-seven.

The three children of Mr. and Mrs. Pascal L. Cerré and wife were:—

1. Pascal L. Cerré, Jr.;
2. Michael Lamy Cerré, and
3. Catherine Cerré, who became the wife of Peter D. Papin.

APPENDIX.

RENE BUET

came here from Cahokia in 1766-67; he had a concession of two lots, being a half block of 120 feet front by 300 deep, upon which he procured to be built by his friend, Laclede, a large stone house for the day, of forty by thirty feet, which, when completed, he occupied for a few years. Upon his death on Nov. 30, 1773, being a single man, he bequeathed this house and other property to a daughter of his brother residing in Cahokia.

This house was for many years the southwesternmost one of the village, and from its ample well cultivated grounds, and the social position of the different families that successively owned and occupied it, it had acquired a history. Michael Lamy purchased it after the death of Buet in 1773, and with the Duchouquette family, occupied it for twenty-seven years, he dying in it January 3, 1784, and they remaining in it sixteen years longer, when they disposed of the property in October, 1800, to Doctor Saugrain, who had but recently arrived here, and whose family occupied it for almost sixty years, the doctor himself dying in it on May 19, 1820, and his widow July 13, 1860.[1]

WILLIAM BISSETTE

was born in Montreal, Canada, and was in business in Fort Chartres, prior to the establishment of St. Louis, where he had acquired a handsome property before coming over to this side, which he did amongst the first.

He purchased the Beaugenou House[2] in 1769, after the death of Mrs. B., and resided in it a little over a couple of

---

[1] A somewhat singular coincidence that the three first owners should all have ended their days in it.

[2] Southwest corner Main and Almond.

years dying in it himself, a single man, in June, 1772, leaving a large estate for the period, to be divided between his nine surviving brothers and sisters, seven of them married ladies, all but one living in their native city of Montreal, and the seventh in St. Louis, and two brothers Charles and Jno. B., young men in his employment, whom he had brought over with him from Fort Chartres, another brother Paul having died over there, they being eleven in all. His will, May 30, 1772. Substance: —

1. Debts to be paid.
2. Five hundred livres for masses in the church for two years.
3. Five hundred livres for ornaments for the church.[1]
4. Five hundred livres to his god-daughter Pelagie, wife of Charles Vallé of Ste. Genevieve.
5. Five hundred livres to Francoise B., wife of Batiste Charleville, daughter of Charles Brazeau, of Fort Chartres.
6. One thousand livres to Juan La Montagne, his clerk.
7. Three hundred livres to Marie Berger, seven years of age.
8. All his other property, peltries, silverware, slaves, animals, houses, buildings, lands, debts due him, etc., etc., to his brother Charles, now on his way up from New Orleans, his heir and executor, on condition that he first pay all the above, and to carry on the business in partnership with La Montagne for two years, then to divide the profits equally, to give La Montagne a chance to establish himself in business.

After the two years, all his property to be divided equally between his brothers and sisters, and appoints Laclede his executor for that purpose.

(Signed) BIZET, M. DURALDE, P. PERIT, N. CHABOT, *Witnesses.*
LABUSCIERE, *Notary*, P. PIERNAS, *Gov'r.*

---

[1] They had a small one June 24, 1770.

The brothers and sisters were: —
1. Angelina, wife of Joseph Tessier,
2. Margaret, widow of Antoine Lemer,
3. Marie Anne, wife of James Leduc, } Of Montreal.
4. Catherine, wife of John Biron,
5. Marie Louise, wife of Jno. Bap. Flavard,
6. Isabella, wife of Louis Vachard, } Of Illinois.
7. Marie Anne, wife of Claude Marechal,
8. Charles Bissette, } Of St. Louis.
9. Jno. B. Bissette,

Laclede settled up the estate June 7, 1776.

CHARLES SARPY AND WIFE, SUSANNE TRENTY,

were residents of Fumel, near Agen, in the province of Gascony, France, and were the parents of a large family of ten children.

1. John B. Sarpy, No. 1, the eldest son, was in business in New Orleans, before the commencement of St. Louis, he came up in 1766, and carried on business here as a merchant for over twenty years, when he returned to New Orleans, and died there, in 1798, single.

2. Silvester Delor Sarpy, came here some years after his brother above, remained here but a few years, went back to New Orleans, married and died there in 1799, leaving several children; two of his daughters married the two brothers Burthe, from Paris.

3. Pierre L' Estang Sarpy came here in 1786-87, and died in the year 1788 at thirty-three years of age.

4. Gregoire Berald Sarpy, born in 1764, came here in 1786, at the age of twenty-two, and married here in 1797 at thirty-three years of age, and died May 15, 1824, at sixty years of age.

5. Jno. B. Lille Sarpy, was in New Orleans in 1809.

6. Pierre St. Marc Sarpy.

7. Susanne Mad'e D'Alverny.
8. Therese Mad'e Noirit.
9. Helene Mad'e Lanausse.
10. Marie Mad'e Laporte, spent their lives in France.

Gregoire B. Sarpy was married to Pelagie, daughter of Mr. Silvester Labbadie, on May 1, 1797 — their children were,—

1. John B. Sarpy No. 2, born January 12, 1798.
2. Susanne, born Oct. 22, 1800.
3. Pierre Abadie, born in 1805.
4. Thos. Lestang, in 1810, and several that died young.

CLEMENT DELOR DE TREGET,

born in Quercy, Cahors, south of France, had been an officer in the French navy, and with his wife, Catherine Marin, also born in France, came up with one or more young children in 1767 from Ste. Genevieve to settle themselves in St. Louis. Passing up by water, being persons of refined tastes, they were particularly struck with the romantic beauty of a particular point on the river bank some five miles below the then infant village. On his arrival he made application to St. Ange for a grant, upon which he erected a stone house, and this was the first commencement of what in time became Carondelet — the precise spot is just east of the platform of the first station at the foot of Elwood Street, where, until very recently, the rubbish of the old building was still to be seen, erected over one hundred years ago.

Their children were —

1. Pierre Delor, married to Sophie Chouquet.
2. A son died young.
3. Madelaine, to Francois Cailhol, 1781, and to Lambert Lajoie in 1811.
4. Marie Rose, to M. Alexis Marie in 1784.
5. Felicité born 1775.

Mad. Catherine Marin Delor died Dec. 14, 1776, at thirty-four years of age.

Delor De Treget married his second wife, Angelique A. Martin, February 15, 1779. They had four children.
1. Angelique married Hyacinthe Pigeon.
2. Felicité to Antoine Moitier.
3. Marguerite to Jno. B. M. Chatillon.
4. Agnes to Leon Constant, Feb. 6, 1811, by Leduc.

Children of Pierre Delor, Sr. and wife, Sophia Chouquet.
1. Pierre Delor, Jr.
2. Gregory.
3. Alexis.
4. Antoine.
5. Cecile, widow of Charles Robert, Jr.
6. Adelle, widow of Antoine Guion.
7. Odille, wife of John Lux.
8. Selina, wife of Charles Vallé.

JOHN BAP'T ORTES,

carpenter, was born in Bearne, France, near the Pyrenees, in 1737, the same place as Laclede, and came with him to America, and to St. Louis in 1765. In the year 1782 he married Elizabeth Barada, born in Vincennes, September 27, 1764, and who came to St. Louis in 1768, at the age of four years. He died November 25, 1814, at the age of seventy-seven years, and his widow, who survived him fifty-four years, in the year 1868, at the remarkable age of one hundred and four years, having lived a full century in the place.

They were the parents of three daughters: —

Florence, born in 1784, married to Joseph Philibert in 1803.

Marie, born in 1786, married to Joseph Laprise in 1802, and after his death again twice.

Felicité, born in 1787, married to Charles Le Guerrier about 1810.

JOSEPH PHILIBERT, SR.,

born in Canada, came to St. Louis about the year 1801, and was married to Florence Ortes in 1803.

He died in 1866, and Mrs. Philibert in 18—.

Their nine children were Joseph, Jno. Bap't, Augustus, Henry, Benjamin, Adolph and Edward, seven sons, and Mrs. Aug. Guelberth and Mrs. Barada, two daughters; most of them yet live.

JOSEPH ROBIDOU, SR.,

shoemaker, was born in Montreal about the year 1720. He came to St. Louis in the year 1770 with his only son, a young man just of age, born also in Montreal, of the same name as his father, Joseph.

The father died September 12, 1771, at the house of Kiery Denoyer, southwest corner of Main and Elm, an inventory of his effects taken, and they placed by the Governor in the possession of his son.

This Joseph No. 2 was married to Catharine Rollet, dit Laderoute, September 21, 1782. He had embarked in the fur business, which he prosecuted for over thirty years quite successfully and prosperously, having acquired a handsome property.

He died on March 17, 1809, at the age of 60 years, leaving a widow and half a dozen sons, all grown to manhood, and appointing Col. Auguste Chouteau his executor, who closed up his estate.

His widow married Victor Lagoterie in 1811, and removed from this place.

APPENDIX. 445

His children were: —

1. Joseph No. 3, born 1784, who married, first, a Miss Delisle, and for his second wife, Angelique Vaudry, of Cahokia; and

3. Francois, born 1788. These two brothers were associated here in business for some twenty years, when Joseph established himself at and was the founder of the city of St. Joseph.

2. Lewis, born 1786, between Joseph and Francois, died 1788.

4. Margaret, born 1790.
5. Isidore, born 1791.
6. Antoine, born 1794.
7. Louis, born 1796.
8. Michel, born 1798.
9. Eulalie, born 1800.
10. Pelagie, born 1802.

Joseph Robidou's first wife and the wife of his brother Francis were sisters, Desliles.

BENITO VASQUEZ, SR.

Born in Gallicia, Spain, in the year 1750, came to St. Louis in the Spanish service with Gov. Piernas in 1770, then twenty years of age, holding a subordinate position in the military service.

He was married Nov. 27, 1774, then twenty-four, to Miss Julie Papin, born in Canada, daughter of Pierre Papin and Catherine Richard, called sixteen years; they were parents of twelve children.

1. Felicité, born 1775, married to Antoine Roy 1792, died in 1803.

2. Julia, born 1777, married to Louis Coignard, 1797.

3. Benito, Jr., born 1780, married to Clarissa Lefebvre 1814.

4. Francis Xavier, born 1781, died 1782 at one year.

5. A. F. Baronet, born 1783, married to Emily Faustin Parent in 1810, a lieutenant in the United States Army.

6. Joseph Pepé, born 1786, married to Marie L. Hebert Lecompte in 1816.

7. Victoire, born 1787, married to Isaac Septlivres in 1814.

8 Marie Anne, born 1790, died 1791.

9. Hypolite Guillory, born 1792, married first, to Mary Lajeunesse 1817; second, to H. L. Tison 1837.

10. Celeste, born 1794, married to Antoine Vincent Bouis 1812.

11. Eulalie, born 1795, married, first, to John Stotts; and second, to Jacques Martin.

12. Pierre Louis, born 1798.

Benito Vasquez, Sr., died in 1810 at sixty years of age, and Mrs. B. Vasquez in 1825, aged sixty-seven years.

JOSEPH ALVAREZ HORTIZ,

son of Francis Alvarez and Bernarda Hortiz, born in Lienira, Estremadura, Spain, in 1753, came to St. Louis a young soldier with the first Spaniards, having taken his mother's name of Hortiz when he enlisted.

In January, 1780 he married Marguerite Marianne Becquet, daughter of Jno. B. Becquet and Marie Francoise Dodier, born at New Chartres, Ill., in 1763; he being twenty-seven and she seventeen years of age.

Their children were John B., Francis, Andrew, Benjamin, Joseph sons, and Eulalie, wife of Laberge, Leonora wife of Bergeron, the wife of Jos. Morin and Jno. Bap. Lebeau's wife.

He was of a good family and well educated, and became the secretary of Governors Trudeau and Delassus.

Hortiz died in 1808, aged fifty-five years.

EUGENIO ALVAREZ,

born in Madrid, Spain, about 1736, was a Spanish soldier and came to St. Louis with Piernas in 1770.

He married in 1782 Josepha Crepeau, born in Post Vincennes; their children were two sons and one daughter.
1. Manuel Alvarez, who married Aspasie ———.
2. Auguste, who married Brigitte Latresse.
3. Eugenie, wife of Francis Creley.

Alvarez in his old age was the king's military store keeper; he died in June, 1816, at the age of eighty years, and his widow survived him a number of years.

MARTIN MILONY DURALDE,

born in Biscaya, Spain, son of Pierre Duralde and Marie di Elizaga, came here with Piernas; he was a well educated gentleman, of good family and abilities, and raised to business; he was the first surveyor of the place, appointed by Gov. Piernas. He married here in 1776, Marie Josepha Perrault, born in Quebec, daughter of Louis Perrault, merchant of that place, and wife Josepha Bobé, deceased.

Duralde remained but a few years in the place, returning to New Orleans, where his wife's connections resided.

These last four comprise all the Spaniards that married here during its occupancy of thirty-five years by that nation; they all married French wives, who with their children spoke only the French language, converting their husbands into very good Frenchmen.

One other Spaniard, Manuel Lisa, who came up from below but a few years before the transfer to the United States, brought a wife with him, but I think an American lady, as she was the widow of one Chew.

JOSEPH PAPIN, SR.,

a fur trader, the first of the name in St. Louis, and his wife Margaret Laforce, were born and married in Montreal, Canada, where the lady died leaving but a son. He then came to St. Louis, where his name first appears in our archives in April, 1769, although there is no doubt that he had arrived there some years previously. He died April 18, 1772, at the house of Francis Bissonet, Main Street, his son Joseph M. then absent in Canada.

His will of April 9, 1772, leaves all his property to his son, J. M. Papin, who on his return from Canada was placed in immediate possession of it.

JOSEPH MARIE PAPIN,

supposed to be about twenty-eight years, was married to Marie Louise Chouteau on January 9, 1779, called by her mother in the contract a minor of fourteen and a half years, their children were —

1. Joseph Papin, born in 1780, married a widow Bradshaw, in 1820.
2. Marguerite, in 1781, to M. P. Leduc, 1802. She died April 1, 1808.
3. Alexander, in 1782, to Julie Brazeau, 1814.
4. Marie Therese, in 1784, to Antoine Chenie, 1806.
5. Marie Louise, in 1785, to Antoine Roy, 1812, and to H. Renard, 1818.
6. Hypolite, in 1787, to Josephine Loisel, 1815.
7. Pelagie, in 1789.
8. Sophie, in 1791, died April 22, 1808.
9. Pierre Millecour, 1793.
10. Silvestre V., 1794, to Clementine Loisel, 1817.
11. Emilie, 1796, to Francois Chauvin, 1816.

APPENDIX. 449

12. Pierre Didier, 1798, to Catherine L. Cerré, 1826, Sept. 10.
13. Theodore, 1799, to Marie Celeste Duchouquet, 1820.
14. Joseph, died an infant in 1802.

Mr. Jos. M. Papin, died Sept. 18, 1811, called about sixty years of age, and Mrs. Papin, Feb. 27, 1817, about fifty-three years.

JOHN B. TRUDEAU,

village schoolmaster, was born in Canada, in 1748, and came to St. Louis in 1774, when twenty-six years of age. He married in 1781, Madeleine Leroy, widow of Francis Hebert, and daughter of Julien Le Roy and Barbara Saucier. Their children were: —

1. John B., born 1782, died in 1783.
2. A child in 1785.
3. Euphrosine, in 1787, married to Louis Bissette in 1803; secondly, to Jos. Leblond in 1812; and 3rdly, to Jno. B. Bercier, 1829.
4. Louis, born in 1794, married Archange Dumouchel, in 1814.
5. Jno. Batiste, born in 1800.
6. Aspasia, born in 1803, died in 1804.
7. Adrienne, who married Antoine Citoleur, in 1813.

Mr. T. was the only schoolmaster of the Spanish days, and continued to teach for over twenty years after the transfer, a period of exceeding a half century.

He died in 1827, at the age of seventy-nine.

ANTOINE BARADA,

and his wife, Marguerite Derosier, were married at the post of Vincennes on October 2, 1759, where their first child, Louis, was born in 1760; they came to St. Louis with the early comers to the place, having several children born to them between their arrival here and the death of Mr. A. Barada.

1. Francis, baptized June 26, 1775.
2. Jeannette, April 6, 1777.
3. Marie Therese, Nov. 22, 1778.

Antoine Barada, Sr., died at the northeast corner of Main and Myrtle Streets in 1780, and his widow, married Joseph Sorin, dit La Rochelle, April 30, 1782.

LOUIS BARADA,

son of Antoine Barada, deceased, born at Vincennes, and Marie Becquet, daughter of Jno. B. Becquet and Marie Dodier, and widow of Ignace Laroche, born in St. Louis, were married on February 24, 1781.

In the year 1800, Louis Barada, having disposed of his house and lot on the south side of Plum Street, from Second to Third, to Francois Duchouquette, removed to St. Charles.

In our territorial days we had here the following Baradas, viz.: Antoine, Honoré, Isidore, Louis, Pierre and Silvestre, and perhaps others.

CHARLES SANGUINET, SR.,

was born in Quebec, Canada, in the year 1740. He was the son of Simon Sanguinet, a notary of the city, his mother's maiden name was Angelique Duchouquette; he had been married in that place; his first wife's name was Veronica Cardin, and he was a widower without children when he came to St. Louis in 1775, at the age of thirty-five years.

He was married on April 12, 1779, to Marie Anne Condé,

APPENDIX. 451

the eldest of the two daughters of Doc. Aug't A. Condé deceased, the former post-surgeon at Fort Chartres.

Chas. Sanguinet, Sr., died Oct. 18, 1818, aged seventy-eight years, and Mrs. S., in 1822, aged fifty-nine; they raised a large family of children: —

1. Marie Catherine, born Feb. 23, 1781, married to Frans. M. Benoit Nov. 22, 1798; raised five children; died in 1866, aged eighty-five years.

2. Charles, Jr., born Dec. 9, 1783; married to Cecile Brazeau, Oct. 19, 1816; he died in 1876, aged ninety-two years.

3. Simon, born Aug. 1, 1785; married first to Mary Greaer, St. Ferdinand, March 5, 1822, who died Nov. 19, 1823, aged eighteen years; and secondly to Mrs. Mary Poupart, *née* Thouin, July, 1824, who died Jan. 25, 1835; Simon Sanguinet died Oct. 14, 1857, in his seventy-third year.

4. Celeste, born Sept. 23, 1787, married to Jno. B. Lemoine, Despin, April 16, 1811; she died Sept. 15, 1812, aged twenty-five years, without children.

5. Marie, born Feb. 2, 1790, married to Joseph V. Garnier, April 30, 1812; died Feb. 3, 1885, at ninety-five years of age; one daughter, Mrs. John Hogan.

6. Constance, born March 27, 1792, married to Aug't A. Chouteau, June 10, 1810; she died in 1834, aged about forty-two.

7. Christopher, born March 8, 1794; died unmarried.

8. Eulalie Angelique, born May 14, 1796, married to Josiah Bright in 1814; she died Feb. 14, 1817, at twenty-one, leaving a son and daughter.

9. Adelaide, born Feb. 7, 1798, married to Jno. E. Tholozan, Jan. 5, 1819; she died April 2, 1877, at the age of seventy-nine without children.

10. Anne Caroline, born March 25, 1800, married to Horatio Cozens Nov. 24, 1818; died Jan. 1, 1884, in eighty-fourth year; a son and daughter.

GABRIEL CERRÉ,

merchant, was born in Montreal, Canada, in the year 1733, and came to Kaskaskia a young man of twenty-two, about the year 1755. He married there Miss Catherine Girard, a young lady of the place, daughter of Antoine Girard and Maria Lafontaine, in 1865, and here their four children were born.

Mr. Cerré was a resident of Kaskaskia about twenty-six years, engaged in active business until the year 1781, when, with his wife and three children (the eldest then a married lady of Montreal) he removed to St. Louis, where he still continued in business for twenty-four additional years, until his death, April 4, 1805, having attained the age of seventy-two years. Mr. Cerré had pursued a successful business for fifty years and left a handsome fortune.

His wife, Mrs. Cerré, had died in St. Louis, July 31, 1800, five years before him, at the age of fifty years.

Their children were: —

1. Marie Anne, born in 1766, was married at the age of fifteen years, on August 13, 1781, to Pierre Louis Panet, a young man of twenty, of Quebec, Canada, where and at Montreal she resided during her life.

2. Marie Therese, born November 26, 1769, was married on September 21, 1786, at the age of seventeen years, to Augst. Chouteau, of St. Louis, he then thirty-six years of age. She died August 14, 1842, aged seventy-two years and nine months.

3. Pascal Leon (the only son), born in 1771, married in St. Louis, February 13, 1797, to Marie Therese Lamy, only child of Michael Lamy. He died May 9, 1849, aged seventy-seven years. Mrs. Cerré, August 12, 1833.

4. Julia Cerré, born August 10, 1775, married November 16, 1795, at twenty, to Antoine Pierre Soulard, born in

APPENDIX. 453

Rochefort, Aunis, France, in 1766, aged twenty-nine years, formerly of the French navy, now the king's surveyor, in Louisiana. Ant. P. Soulard died November 9, 1825, at fifty-nine years. Mrs. Soulard, May 9, 1845, at sixty-nine years.

JOHN P. POURCELLI,

was born in Provence, France, in 1749, and was married to Margaret Barada, at Vincennes, in the year 1780, and came to St. Louis about 1784. Their children were: —

1. Jno. Louis, born in 1780.
2. Margaret Pascale, 1782, married Joseph Lafrenaye in 1796.
3. John, in 1784, to Angelique Laperche, in 1815.
4. Marie Rose, in 1786, to Dominique Hugé, in 1803.
5. Antoine, in 1788.

Pourcelli, died October 15, 1789, at 40 years of age.

LOUIS VACHARD, DIT LARDOISE,

and wife, Isabelle Bissette, one of the sisters and heirs of Wm. Bissette, came here from Montreal and purchased their house from Laclede early in 1775 and then moved into it.

They had four sons, Louis, Joseph, Charles, and Antoine, all born in Montreal, and all then unmarried.

Louis Vachard died in 1787, and his widow, Isabella Bissette, ten years later in 1797. The house was then thirty-two years old, having been built by Beaugenou in 1765, and all the previous owners and their wives had died in it. The next owner was one of the sons, Antoine Vachard.

ANTOINE VINCENT BOUIS, SR.,

born in Genoa, Italy, about the year 1752, and Marie Madeleine Robert, born in Carondelet in 1768, were married in that village in the year 1782. They raised six sons and four daughters: —

1. Ant'e V. Bouis, Jr., born 1783, married Celeste Vasquez, in 1812; he died in 181–. (His only son, Ant'e R. Bouis, married Mary Forsythe.)
2. André V. Bouis, born 1785, married first Angelique Noise in 1807, who died November 10, 1812, and secondly, Polly Roddy, in 1813. He died in 1833–34.
3. Pascal V. Bouis, born in 1787, graduated at West Point in 1806, and was killed in a duel in 1812, leaving a widow, Celeste B.
4. Francis V. Bouis, who married Helene Croizet.
5. John Baptist Bouis, who died single.
6. Pierre Expedient Bouis, who died in the South.
1. Marie Teresa, married to Richard Dillon.
2. Eulalie Bouis, married to Charles D. St. Vrain.
3. Julia O. Bouis, married to Lucien Dumaine.
4. Elizabeth Bouis, married to Samuel English.

A. V. Bouis, Sr., died April 23, 1812, aged over sixty years, and Mrs. A. V. Bouis July 30, 1834, aged sixty-six, at the northeast corner of Main and Pine, where she had lived near half a century.

JOSEPH BRAZEAU, SR.,

the first of the name we have found, is mentioned in the archives of Kaskaskia as an early comer to the Illinois country from Canada, who was killed by Indians on the Kaskaskia River in the year 1779, aged 78 years, of course born in the year 1701.

APPENDIX. 455

His widow, old Madame Francoise Brazeau No. 1, was born in Canada in 1719, and was sixty years of age when her husband was killed.

She came to St. Louis with her children about the year 1787, where she died March 13, 1793, aged seventy-four years, their children were —

First. Joseph Brazeau No. 2, born in Kaskaskia in 1742, and died in St. Louis, Nov. 23, 1816, aged seventy-four years; he had married —

Marie Therese Delisle, born in Kaskaskia in 1749, and died in St. Louis, Feb., 1834, at eighty-five years. This Brazeau came first to St. Louis in 1781, and had no children.

Second. Louis Brazeau, Sr., born about 1745, died Dec. 5, 1828, aged eighty-three, his wife, Marie Francoise Delisle, born 1750 at Kaskaskia, died Nov. 26, 1810, at sixty years.

Third. Francoise Brazeau No. 2 born about 1757, died April, 1826, aged sixty-nine, was the widow of Jno. B. Chauvin dit Charleville, who had died at Kaskaskia.

Children of Louis Brazeau, Sr., called "Caioua:" —

1. Joseph, Jr., married to Julia Phisbac, July 24, 1810, he died August, 1825.
2. Louis, Jr., to Miss Dumoulin.
3. Augustus to Melanie St. Cir.
4. Marie to Jno. B. Duchouquette, July 2, 1798. She died July, 1818, and he May, 1834.
5. Therese to Charles Bosseron, July 28, 1805.
6. Julia to Alexander Papin, July 24, 1810.
7. Cecile to Chas. Sanguinet, Jr., Oct. 19, 1816.
8. Aurora to Louis Bompart, Jr., July 24, 1821.

Children of Mad'e Francoise Brazeau Charleville: —

1. Genevieve, born 1774, to Pierre Duchouquette, died 1822, at forty-eight.

2. Joseph C, born 1776, to Victoire Verdon, July 15, 1797.

3. Pelagie, born 1778, to F. Tayon, June 8, 1795.

4. John B., born 1780.

5. Louis, born 1782.

HYACINTHE ST. CIR, SR.,

born near Quebec, Canada, son of Francis St. Cir, and Francesca Proto, and Helene Hebert, born in Illinois, daughter of Joseph Hebert, Sr., and Agnes Michel were married in St. Louis, Feb. 25, 1783.

St. Cir was one of the few prominent men of the early times in St. Louis, and one of the most energetic and enterprising, having built several stone houses in different parts of the village, a mill, etc., and received from the government several grants of land northwest and contiguous to St. Louis, on one of which, seven miles north in St. Ferdinand Township, he died Nov. 26, 1826, aged eighty years, and was interred there.

They were the parents of fifteen children, and left a numerous progeny of descendants.

1. Hyacinthe, Jr., born 1784.

2. Marie Constance, 1785, married to Wm. Christy, of St. Charles.

3. Leon Narcissus, 1787, supposed drowned.

4. Marie Helen, 1789, died 1820, aged thirty-one.

5. Frances Agnes, 1792, married to Lewellyn Hickman.

6. Melanie, 1793, married to Auguste Brazeau.

7. Therese, 1795, died 1806, aged eleven.

8. Francis, 1797, to Mary Ann Bellew, 1825; he died 1839.

9. Brigitte, 1799, died 1801, aged one year.

10. Brigitte P., 1801, to Samuel Abbott.

APPENDIX. 457

11. Pascal Hebert, 1803, to Maria Taylor.
12. Helene to Nicholas Boilvin.
13. Emilie.
14. Benjamin C., living in Galena a few years back.
15. Stephen

ALEXANDRE BELLISIME,

born in Toulon, France, in 1747, came over to America, during the revolutionary struggle, with the French troops, and served under Lafayette at Yorktown and elsewhere.

After the close of the Revolution the old soldier, as did many others, came out West and found his way to St. Louis, where he concluded to take up his permanent residence.

August 9, 1796, he married Maria Josepha Robidou, widow of Pierre Morrisseau. This lady died January 13, 1797, about five months after marriage, at the age of thirty years.

On December 27, 1806, he married again,— Mary, daughter of John W. and Mary Waters, born at the River des Moines,— the parties and witneses all signed with their crosses.

Old Alexie, as he was usually called, kept for many years a tavern on Second Street, between Myrtle and Spruce, opposite the old "Green Tree," patronized mostly by French river boatmen with whom he was a great favorite.

On the occasion of the visit of General Lafayette to our city, April 29, 1825, Bellisime arrayed himself in his old uniform, which he religiously preserved for especial occasions, and hurried to greet the old commander of his youthful years. The General, not expecting to meet with one of his old soldiers after a lapse of nearly half a century, and at such a remote point as this then was, was not only surprised and delighted, but visibly affected at the event. The General embraced the old soldier warmly, to his great pride and infinite satisfaction.

Bellisime died August 23, 1833, in his eighty-seventh year, and was buried by the St. Louis Grays, Captain Easton, at North St. Louis Cemetery.

CHAUVINS AND CHARLEVILLES.

The surname Chauvin is quite common in certain parts of France, particularly in the northwest portion. The first of the name in Canada was a sea captain of Dieppe in Normandy, who came there in 1599 with a grant for the monopoly of the fur trade of the country, on the condition of establishing and maintaining a colony on the St. Lawrence.

His flotilla of five vessels landed at Tadoussac. After establishing his colony and trading off his goods, he returned to France with a rich return; he made a second voyage equally successful, and was preparing for a third, when he died at Dieppe towards the end of the year 1600. His death ruined the colony.[1]

Gayarré tells us that the name first appeared in Louisiana in 1722, when three brothers Chauvin, Nicholas, John B., and Joseph, arrived there from Canada. We find in the church register of interments in St. Louis that of a John B. Chauvin, born in Canada in 1703, who died here June 27, 1789, aged eighty-six years, doubtless one of these three.

The first, in fact the only Chauvin, found in our St. Louis archives was Jacques (James) Chauvin, born in Illinois in 1743.

We find him at Fort Chartres, a well educated young officer in the French service, prior to the cession of that

---

[1] He must have been the progenitor of the Canadian Chauvins, who are quite numerous.

APPENDIX. 459

side to the English in 1763, and married to a daughter of Joseph Michel dit Tayon, with whose family he came over to this side in 1764-65, a half pay officer, having been retired from the service at the transfer to Spain and England.

After living in the village exceeding thirty-five years, he received a concession from Governor Delassus in 1799 of a large tract of land in the west part of our county opposite St. Charles, to which he removed, and where he died suddenly on May 8, 1826, at the age of eighty-three years, his widow surviving him but a short period.

Their children were —

Jacques, Lafreniere J., Joseph, Francois D., Silvestre, and John, six sons, and Jeanne, Marie Louise, Eulalie, the wife of Pierre Beland, and Helene, wife of Loisel and Lebeau.

Now Charleville, as a family name, is nowhere found in any old French encyclopedias, or any other works of that nature. We can only trace the name back to old Joseph Chauvin dit Charleville, who died in Kaskaskia about 1783-84, quite an aged man with a large family of married sons and daughters, some of whom called themselves Chauvins *alias* Charleville, while others of the family had dropped the Chauvin, their real name, and thereafter were called by the *alias* of Charleville only. This old Joseph Chauvin was very probably one of the three mentioned by Gayaré, as it was said by others, that originating from Charleville, a large town in northern France, it was to distinguish him from the others that they had appended it to his name, as many others were called by the names of the places they came from.

He married in Kaskaskia about the year 1740, a Genevieve Bon acceuil, and died in the place about the year 1785.

Among his sons were: —

1. Jean Bap. Chauvin *alias* Charleville, whose wife was Francoise Brazeau of Kaskaskia.

2. Louis Chauvin Charleville, whose wife was Therese Lemoine Despins, daughter of Renaud Despins and Marie Louise Beauvais, of Ste. Genevieve.

3. Charles Chauvin Charleville, his wife Marie Louise Lemoine-Despins, the two brothers Chauvin marrying the two sisters Lemoine–Despins.

4. Daniel Blouin, a prominent merchant of Kaskaskia, at the period, was a son-in-law of this Joseph Chauvin Charleville.

5. John B. St. Gem Beauvais of Ste. Genevieve, was also a son-in-law and closed up his affairs December 27, 1787.

6. Francois was another son.

MADAME FRANCOISE BRAZEAU CHARLEVILLE,

widow of the above Jno. B., with her five children, in company with the family of her brother Louis Brazeau, Sr., removed up to St. Louis in 1787.

1. Genevieve, born 1774, to Pierre Duchouquette. She died November 14, 1822, at forty-eight.
2. Joseph C., 1776, to Vic. Verdon, July 15, 1797.
3. Pelagie 1778, to Fr's Tayon, June 8, 1795, — one son Francis Tayon, Jr.
4. John B., 1780.
5. Louis, 1782.

JOSEPH CHARLEVILLE'S CHILDREN.

1. Jno. B. Charleville.
2. Pelagie, Mrs. Boyer.
3. Joseph.
4. Athenaise, Mrs. Farris.
5. Henrietta, Mrs. Hunt.
6. Louis.

APPENDIX. 461

7. Virginia, first Mrs. Duchouquette, now Mrs. Henry Lynch.

8. Alexander, from his will, October 31, 1838.

These last are the only Charlevilles identified with St. Louis.

THE CAMP FAMILY,

previously mentioned very briefly in the Annals, were originally from the parish of Nazing, Essex, England, where for many generations the name is found in the parish records, and in New England, as early as 1639, where Nicholas Camp was one of the first settlers of Milford, Conn't., and John Camp, Sr., one of the first proprietors of Hartford, in 1649.

John Camp, of Durham, the father of the Rev. Dr. Ichabod Camp, our subject, moved to Durham, that place being settled principally by Milford people. The baptism of Ichabod Camp, son of John, on February 20, 1726, is found in the Durham records.

Ichabod Camp, was born February 15, 1726, at Durham. In September, 1739, at thirteen years, entered Yale College, received the degree of B. A. September, 1743; and M. A. September, 1746, at the age of twenty, and was licensed to read prayers in the Episcopal Church.

On March 22nd, 1752, received the office of deacon, in London, Eng'd., and on March 26th, 1752, ordained a Priest by the Bishop of Lincoln, at Berwick Street Chapel, Parish of St. James, Westminster, London, and his license as same from the Bishop of London, March 27, 1752; he commenced his duties at Christ Church, Middletown, July 19, and at North Haven, August 2, 1752.

He was twice married, first to Content Ward, in Connecticut, November 26, 1749, who died in Middletown, December 29, 1754, leaving a son and daughter who attained maturity; and secondly, Anne Oliver, of Boston, June 6, 1757, who survived him, and bore him eight children, of whom two or three died young, and the others attained maturity.

In 1760, desirous of removing to a more genial climate, he left Middletown on his way to Virginia, and spent the following winter in Wilmington, Delaware, and the next one at Cornwall Parish, Lunenburg County, Va. In the spring of 1762, he removed to Amherst County and parish to which he had been appointed. He officiated in this parish for sixteen years; here his last six children were born, all girls, — his last one Caroline born in 1770, died early in 1778. This was an eventful period in the history of Virginia. She had just become a State, the eyes of her people were turned on Kentucky, as the garden spot of our country, to which a goodly number of her people had already gone, and others were preparing to follow in increased numbers, not strange then that even a clergyman should catch the mania, and move with the crowd.

The family tradition says "that Mr. Camp having a great many negroes, sent some of them ahead under 'Uncle Billy,' an old negro genius, to build on the Monongahela, the flat bottomed boats for the family and stock to descend the river; two other families started in company with them from Amherst, these with others left Pittsburg with Clark's expedition in June, 1778. There were eleven boats in the party, each with a cabin, with their furniture and plenty of clothing — each boat had a swivel that they fired off at morning and at night to keep off the Indians, who were so terrified on the lower river that they reported at New Orleans that an army was coming down." [1]

Whether it was Mr. Camp's design, or an afterthought

---

[1] So far the diary is in the handwriting of Mr. Camp, afterwards continued by Mrs. Camp.

does not appear, but he did not stop at the Falls of the Ohio as most of the movers west did, but kept on down the Mississippi to Natchez, where they passed the winter. Here his oldest daughter, Mary Ann, died, on February 23, 1779, at the age of sixteen years. They then returned up the Mississippi to Kaskaskia where they landed May 1, 1779, and settled themselves.

Mr. Camp soon became well and favorably known to all the prominent personages of the day, as well on this as on the other side of the river, and he and his family were treated with much consideration.

In October, 1781, Mr. Camp being very ill executed his will, drawn up by another but signed by himself, and witnessed by Shadrach Bond, Joseph Hunter and James Willey, three of the most prominent of the early Americans there in the Territorial days.

Shadrach Bond was afterwards the first Governor of the State of Illinois. Mr. Camp was a little over sixty years of age on April 20th, 1786, the date of his sudden and violent death.

After the widow Camp came over to St. Louis, she purchased a house at the southeast corner of Second and Spruce Streets with the quarter block of ground upon which it stood. In this house she resided during the seventeen years she lived in St. Louis, and here she died on October 27, 1803, highly respected by all the French inhabitants of the place (for we were yet French), as this proves:

1. A concession by Gov. Manuel Perez to Ann Camp, March 12, 1791, of a lot of 120 by 150 feet, for a barn lot (southeast corner of Fourth and Almond).

2. A concession by Gov. Zenon Trudeau to Ann Camp and Antoine Reilhe, her son-in-law, December 6, 1797, of a tract of land on the River Des Peres, of 2,900 arpents.

The three daughters who came with her from Kaskaskia, were all married in St. Louis.

Mackey Wherry from Pennsylvania, married Louise, the youngest, on March 19, 1800. They had seven children, of whom they raised the three eldest, Joseph A. Wherry, who succeeded his father, Mackey, as City Register, in 1827, Doct M. Wherry, of this county, and Dan'l B. Wherry, who died in Central Missouri.

The Wherrys of the present day are their descendants.

Catherine Camp, the widow of Jno. B. Guion, was married January 18, 1804, to Israel Dodge, from Connecticut, then residing at New Bourbon, Ste. Genevieve County, he settling on her "a house and grounds in New Bourbon, one thousand silver dollars, two young slaves, and one thousand arpents of land."

The remaining daughter, Charlotte, was married to Moses Bates, then of Ste. Genevieve, in the year 1805 in St. Louis; subsequently they removed to St. Charles. She died in April, 1818, at the age of fifty-one years.

The eldest of the four, Estella, the wife of Antoine Reilhe, had died in St. Louis April 24, 1793, in her thirtieth year, and Reilhe himself March 3, 1802, aged sixty-seven. They left three children —

1. Antoine, Jr., who subsequently removed to Portage des Sioux, St. Charles County.

2. Margaret, born January 29, 1787, married to Alexander McNair March, 1805. Ten children.

3. Stella, born January 1, 1789, married to David Harvey January, 1806. Seven children.

The descendants of Ichabod and Mrs. Ann Camp are very numerous, including the names of McNair, Wherry, Reilhe, Dodge, Harvey and others. On the 9th of April, 1804, the Camp heirs, to save costs and trouble, petitioned Gov. Stoddard for permission to make an amicable partition of the estate without the process of court; this permission he granted them, dated April 15th. It is the first official act of Stoddard on record.

JOHN PIERRE DIDIER, WATCHMAKER,

came from Besancon, Franche Comté, France, his native place, with his wife and only child, an infant danghter, about the year 1793, in company with other refugees during the French Revolution.

He came first to Galliopolis, Ohio, and then to this place (St. Louis), where he spent the rest of his life.

On March 29, 1796, he purchased the south half of block No. 54 with a stone house at the northwest corner of Second and Poplar Streets, in which he resided until his death, August 25, 1823, at the age of about sixty years, after a residence of thirty years in the place.

He filled the position of Territorial Treasurer for a number of years. His only daughter, Josephine, was married in May, 1811, to Mr. Hubert Guion, a native of the place, who died at Jefferson Barracks May 23, 1833, where he was the clerk of the sutler, Capt. Geo. H. Kennerly.

Mr. Guion left a son and two daughters, who became the first wives of Judge Wilson Primm and Moses Lamoureux, merchant, all now deceased.

REGISTRE LOISEL, MERCHANT,

was born in the parish of Assumption, Lower Canada, son of Registre Loisel and Manette Massin, both deceased. He came to St. Louis in 1793, and on May 7th, 1800, was married to Helene, minor daughter of Jacques Chauvin and Marie Louise Taillon.

Their children were : —

1. Josephine, born in 1801, and married to Hypolite Papin, July 4, 1815.

2. Clementine, born 1803, and married to Silvestre V. Papin, July 18, 1817.

3. Regis, Jr., born in 1805, a posthumous son.

R. Loisel, Sr., died in New Orleans in October, 1804, and his widow was afterwards married to Francois Lebeau, of this place, The son Regis became a priest and removed across to Cahokia.

Mr. and Mrs. Hypolite Papin were the parents of a numerous progeny. Of the sons there were Hypolite, Jr., Joseph L., Theodore, Raymond, Henry, Millecour, Eugene, etc., and the daughters were Mesdames Dupré, Ed. Tracy, Jas. Waugh and Greer.

Mr. Silvestre V. Papin, Sr., died August 3, 1828, father of Silvestre V., Doct. Timothy L., and Theophile Papin, and one daughter, Mrs. C. Carriere.

BERNARD PRATTE, SR., MERCHANT,

son of John B. Pratte and Marie Anne Lalumandière, was born in Ste. Genevieve about 1772, and came a young man to St. Louis, where he embarked in business in 1793.

On May 12, 1794, he was married to Emilie Sauveur, minor daughter of Silvester Labbadie and Pelagie Chouteau.

Their children were: —

1. Silvestre, born September 22, 1799, married June 5, 1822, to Odille Delassus, of Ste. Genevieve, and died June 1828, on the Platte River.

2. Bernard, Jr., born December 17, 1803, married to Louise Chenié July 20, 1824.

3. Emilie, married to Ramsey Crooks, of New York, March 10, 1825, deceased.

4. Therese, married first to Walter B. Alexander, March 21, 1824, who died July 15, 1826, and secondly to L. D. Peugnet, of New York, February, 1830.

5. Celeste, married to Stephen F. Nidelet, of Philadelphia, August 12, 1826.

APPENDIX. 467

6. Pelagie, married to Louis V. Bogy of St. Louis, both deceased.

7. Aimeé, married to Mr. Blaine, of France.

Bernard Pratte, Sr., died on Friday, April 1, 1836, aged sixty-four years, and his widow November 23d, 1844. His will, executed March 30th, two days before his death.

LOUIS AUGUSTUS TARTERON DE LABEAUME,

was born in Vigan, province of Languedoc, France, about the year 1766, and was married when a young man to Adelaide Dutemple, about the year 1787, who bore him three children, and died in France, a young woman. About the year 1792, after France had adopted her Republican constitution, Mr. Labeaume left France with his two young children, Marie Louise Lucille, born about 1788, and Pierre Auguste, about 1790, leaving the third, an infant, and came to St. Louis, where he spent the balance of his life.

On June 8, 1797, Mr. Labeaume married his second wife, Susanne, the third daughter of Louis Chauvet Dubreuil, deceased, by whom he had four sons: Louis Alexandre, Theodore, Louis Tarteron and Charles Edmond, and three daughters, Eleanor Olympe, who died young from an accident, Susan Clarrissa, and Eugenie.

On May 8, 1804, Mr. Labeaume purchased from a Jno. B. Paquet a piece of land of 4 by 40 arpents 160, lying about five miles north of the village, on the road to old Fort Bellefontaine, and now forming a part of Bellefontaine Cemetery. On this land he built a house of logs (which has only been removed within these last few years); here he resided until his death, January 4, 1821, leaving eight children, and here his youngest children were born.

At that early period in our history the country around about this region of our Baden of the present day, was called the White-Ox prairie. While living here, a few years prior to his death, Mr. Labeaume wrote his will, dated November 22, 1817, which is found of Record in Book G3, 244. In this will he says : —

"There are left of my first wife, Adelaide Dutemple, two children, Pierre Auguste, and Marie Lucille, and perhaps a third named Theodore, that circumstances compelled me to leave in France, of whom I never could learn any thing, and whom I have reason to believe is dead." He then goes on to name his five children at that day by his second wife, of whom they subsequently lost the eldest daughter, Eleanor, by a casualty, and prior to his death three years later, two more were born to them, a son and daughter, making eight in all.

Mr. Labeaume's children were, by his first wife, Adelaide Dutemple : —

1. Marie Louise Lucille, born in France in 1788 ; married to Albert Tison, also from France, on May 1, 1806, in St. Louis.

2. Pierre Auguste, born in France in 1790 ; was married first to Elizabeth A. McPherson, in St. Louis, January 9, 1827 ; and secondly,—

And by his second wife, Susanne Dubreuil, all born in St. Louis : —

3. Louis Alexander, who married in France Miss Melanie Lapierre.

4. Theodore, married in St. Louis, Miss Eliza A. Hammond.

5. Louis Tarteron, married Miss Mary —

6. Susan, married, May 1, 1824, Mr. Jonas Newman, merchant from Kentucky.

7. Charles Edmond, married Isadora Shaw, of Vincennes.

8. Eugenia, married Peter E. Blow, merchant of St. Louis.

ALBERT TISON,

born in France, came to St. Louis in 1793. He lived for several years in the family of Governor Trudeau, and was attached to his administration during the whole time.

He married on May 1, 1806, Marie Louise Lucille, the eldest child of Louis Labeaume, born in France. They were the parents of: —

Adele, married to Theo. L. McGill, of St. Louis and New Orleans, August 9, 1823.

Rosalie, unmarried.

Lucille, married to Thos. S. Rutherford, December 18, 1840.

Caroline, married to John Birkenbine, June 14, 1838.

Hypolite, whose wife was Miss Miller.

Augustus.

PIERRE CHARLES DEHAULT DELASSUS ET DE DELUZIERE,

Knight of the Grand Cross of the Royal Order of St. Michael, with his wife, Madame Domitille Josepha Dumont Danzin de Beaufort, of the ancient nobility of the town of Bouchaine, in Hainault, French Flanders, northern part of France, came away from their native place, where their ancestors had lived from time immemorial, during the early period of the French Revolution. They arrived at New Orleans about the year 1794 and after a time they came up to Ste. Genevieve, and established and located themselves at New Bourbon, contiguous to Ste. Genevieve. Their children were at the time, Chas. Dehault Delassus, a colonel in the service of Spain, their oldest son; another James M. C. Delassus, already mentioned in these annals, and a third Camillus Delassus, then a young man. If there were other sons or daughters their names are not found in our St. Louis archives. Governor Trudeau made them a concession of land for the support of the family, and the old gentleman was appointed civil magistrate of the place, which position he filled until the transfer of the country to the United States in 1804.[1]

Camillus Delassus married in due time and raised a family. A daughter, Odille, was married June 5, 1822, at Ste. Genevieve, to Silvestre S. Pratte, the oldest son of Gen. B. Pratte, Sr., of St. Louis. He died, without children, in the mountains at the head waters of the Platte in June, 1828, and his widow afterwards married Louis Vallé, of Ste. Genevieve, who died September 24, 1833, and she herself about the year 1864, without children by either husband.

The two sons of Camille D. Delassus, Leon and Paul, had each a large family of children.

Old Deluziere and his lady both died at New Bourbon, before Frank Vallé's day, from whom I obtain these particulars, now over fifty years since.

JAMES MARCELLIN CERAN DEHAULT DELASSUS DE ST. VRAIN,

was the second son of Delassus de Luziere, born at at Bouchaine in Hainault, French Flanders, in the year 1770. He came to Louisiana with his father's family in 1794, and settled with them at New Bourbon, near St. Genevieve. He had been in the French naval service prior to their revolution, and for a time had command of a Spanish galliot on the upper Mississippi.

April 30, 1796, he married Marie Felicité Chauvet Dubreuil, a daughter of Louis Chauvet Dubreuil, deceased, of St. Louis, and established his home at the Spanish Pond,

---

[1] The two oldest sons are noticed elsewhere in the Annals.

APPENDIX. 471

twelve miles north of the city on the road to the old Bellefontaine Fort, then a noted point in our ancient annals, which he handsomely improved.

He died here on June 22, 1818, aged forty-eight years; his sons were Charles, Savary, Felix, Ceran, Domitille, etc., with several daughters.

AUGUSTIN, CHARLES FREMON, DELAURIERE,

Lord of Bouffay and Des Croix, born in the parish of St. Pere Curet, Nantes, Republic of France, came to St. Louis in 1796, and lived in Ste. Genevieve from that time until 1802, as Greffier (Recorder). He then gave up the position to enable him to attend to his business as a manufacturer of salt.

May 21, 1799, he married Josephine Celeste Chauvet Dubreuil, daughter of Louis Chauvet Dubreuil, deceased, of St. Louis. They raised a number of children.

Geo. Y. Bright, from Lexington, Ky., married their eldest daughter, Miss Susan C. A. Fremon, Dec. 10th, 1818, and six weeks afterwards, Jan. 21, 1819, their second daughter, Miss C. O. Fremon, was married to Richard M. Duval, from Cincinnati, Ohio, by Bishop Dubourg.

Another daughter married Lucius Phipps.

Their sons were, Du Bouffay Fremon, Auguste, Leon and some other sons and daughters. They had dropped the Delauriere, and were afterwards called simply " Fremon."

ANTOINE PIERRE SOULARD,

son of Henry Francois Soulard and Marie Francoise Leroux, was born in Rochefort, province of Aunis, France, in the year 1766. His father had been a lieutenant in the French navy, and he himself had adopted the same profession, and had attained the grade of sub-lieutenant when he left the French service and came to the United States in 1794, coming out to St. Louis the same year, where he received the appointment of "King's Surveyor" for upper Louisiana, which office he held until the transfer to the United States in 1804.

Mr. Soulard was married on Nov. 16, 1795, to Miss Marie Julie Cerré, the youngest daughter of Gabriel Cerré, merchant of St. Louis.

He died Nov. 9, 1825, aged fifty-nine years, and Mrs. Soulard, May 9, 1845, in her seventieth year.

Their children were: —

1. James G., born in 1797, married March 20, 1820, to Miss Eliza N., daughter of the late Col. Thos. Hunt, United States army.

2. Henry G., born May, 1801, to Miss Lane, daughter of Doctor Harvey Lane, formerly of St. Genevieve.

3. Eliza, born ———, died Feb. 3, 1845, unmarried.

4. Benjamin A., ——— born ——— married Miss Closey, Pittsburg.

FRANCIS M. BENOIT, SR.,

a fur merchant, son of Louis Antoine Benoit and Marie Rouse Sumande, born in Quebec, in 1768, married Marie Catherine Sanguinet in St. Louis, Nov. 22, 1798. He died Oct. 21, 1819. Aged fifty-one years, leaving three sons and two daughters, and his widow Dec. 8, 1859, in her seventy-ninth year.

1. Francis, Jr., born 1799, died in Louisiana.

2. Louis A. (Condé), Aug. 13, 1803, and died Jan. 17, 1867, at sixty-four; first wife Miss Barton, two children; second, Miss Hackney, five children; third, Miss Wilson, eight children, fifteen in all.

3. Sanguinet, 1805, to Miss Dubois; separated.

APPENDIX. 473

4. Adeline, 1807, to Jas. M. Riley at Liberty, Sept. 20, 1831.

5. Amanda, 1809, to Cyrus Curtis, March 27, 1827.

FRANCIS BARROUSEL,

born in Cape Francois, Island of St. Domingo, a refugee from that island at the negro insurrection of 1793, came to Baltimore, and established himself in business there with Nicholas Lesconflaires. In 1796-97 he came to St. Louis on business. He executed his will before Governor Trudeau, dated April 18, 1797, in which he names his friend, Charles Gratiot, of St. Louis, his executor, directs him to pay his debts in Philadelphia, to John West, $354, and to John Mallett, $455; and being unmarried, and no family, he leaves his partner the balance of his interest in the store; and to his brothers and sisters his claims for indemnity on St. Domingo and his property in France. He died at Ste. Genevieve, July 31, 1797.

This Mr. Barrousel was the grand uncle of the late Edward P. Tesson, of St. Louis, whose mother was a niece of Barrousel.

JOHN P. CABANNÉ,

Merchant, son of Jean Cabanné and Jeanne Dutilh, his wife, was born in the city of Pau, Bearne, France, October 18, 1773, and came a young man to New Orleans, where he remained for a time, and then came up to St. Louis, in the year 1798.

He married Julia, the eldest daughter of Charles Gratiot, merchant, born July 24, 1782, on April 8, 1799.

He died June 27, 1841, aged sixty-eight years, and Mrs. Cabanné, April 14, 1852, in her seventieth year. Their children were:—

1. Batiste Gregoire, born February 8, 1800, died in 1801.

2. Jeanne Victoire, born November 16, 1803, also died young.

3. Adelle, born in 1805, was married to John B. Sarpy, No. 2, on September 14, 1820, and died March 27, 1832, aged twenty-seven.

4. John Charles, born November 4, 1806, married to Virginia, second daughter of Judge Wm. C. Carr, February 12, 1835. He died on July 17, 1854, leaving three sons; the eldest, John Pierre, died, unmarried, April 18, 1863, aged twenty-six years; the two others, J. C. and S. C. Cabanné, both married, with families, and their mother, the widow, are living.

5. Augustus Eneas, born March 28, 1808, died January 23, 1825, aged seventeen years.

6. Julia A., born July 8, 1809, married to Lieut. James W. Kingsbury, U. S. A., May 25, 1830. She died in 1836, and Capt. K. in 1854, and their only son, Julius, was killed by lightning in 1868, at the age of thirty-two. Their two daughters, Mrs. Giverville and Mrs. A. M. Waterman, both widows, are living.

7. Louisa, born August 12, 1811, was married to Lieut. Albert G. Edwards, U. S. A., April 28, 1835. She died August 4, 1841, at the age of thirty years, her infant son in his third year, having preceded her about twenty days.

8. Lucien Dutilh, born July 28, 1814, married Miss Susan Shepard. He died April 10, 1875, in his sixty-first year, leaving but one son, Dr. Shepard Cabanné.

9. Francis, born January 1, 1816, died, unmarried, November 9, 1876, in his sixty-first year.

10. Louis Julius, born February 22, 1818, was married to Stella McNair, November 24, 1846, and died up the Mississippi, leaving several children.

11. Isabella, born in 1820, died an infant.

Mr. John P. Cabanné, Sr., was prominent in the fur trade of St. Louis for exceeding forty years.

MARIE PHILLIPPE LEDUC,

was born in St. Denis, Paris, in 1772. When a young man he came over to Louisiana with his mother and two brothers and remained for some time at New Orleans, and then came up to New Madrid in 1793.

When Governor Delassus relieved Portell in the command at New Madrid, in 1796, he employed Leduc as his private secretary, and in 1799, when appointed lieutenant-governor of this upper Louisiana, Leduc came with him to St. Louis as secretary of the province, and continued to serve in various civil positions for the balance of his protracted life of seventy years.

On August 30, 1802, he was married to Marguerite, the eldest daughter of Jos. M. Papin. She died April 1, 1808, after a brief married life of less than six years, having lost two infant sons, and leaving a third child, a daughter, Zoe, born in 1807, who lived to become a young lady of sixteen years, completing her education, and then died on May 6, 1823, thus leaving the sorely afflicted old gentleman without kinsmen, — his last brother, Joseph Leduc, had died in St. Louis, May 21, 1810, at the age of forty-two.

He devoted the balance of his life to public usefulness, filling the various positions of recorder, alderman, justice of the peace, notary, clerk of the circuit and county courts, judge of probate, member of the legislature, etc., discharging all his duties with ability and to the general satisfaction.

Judge Leduc died at the residence of his brother-in-law, Hypolite Papin, at Cote Brilliante, Monday, August 15, 1842, having reached the age of seventy years.

DOCT. ANTOINE FRANCOIS SAUGRAIN,

was born in the center of Paris, called Isle de la Cité in February, 1763. His paternal ancestors were book-sellers for nearly two centuries. He was a chemist and mineralogist, and when a young man of age, about 1784–85, he went in the service of the king of Spain, to examine into the mines and mineral productions of Mexico, from which he returned to France the same year, 1785. In 1786, he went again to Mexico and returned to France. In 1787, he went to the United States, accompanied by two young Parisian friends, M. Pique, a botanist, and M. Raguet, bearing a letter of introduction to Doct. Franklin, from Mr. Le Veillard, an old Parisian friend of the doctor, as per the doctor's reply: —

"Philadelphia, February 17, 1788.

"*To M. Le Veillard:*

"My Dear Friend — I received your kind letter of June 23d, by Mr. Saugrain, and it is the last of yours that is come to my hands. I find Mr. Saugrain to answer well the good character you give of him, and shall with pleasure render him any services in my power. He is now gone down the Ohio to reconnoitre that country, &c., &c.

"Benj. Franklin."

After remaining a time in Philadelphia, he, in the winter of 1787–88, being then twenty-four years of age, proceeded with his two young French companions, Messrs. Pique and Raguet, to Pittsburg. Early in the spring of 1788, having been joined there by an American, a Mr. Pierce, the four left Pittsburg in a flat boat, or broad horn, then so called, with their horses and baggage, to descend to the falls of the Ohio, now Louisville. "We got along very well for some days, but about March 24th, when opposite the Big Miami

River, we were suddenly fired into by a party of Indians, hidden behind an old flat boat that lay aground on the north shore. This first discharge wounded Mr. Pique severely in the head, killed one of our horses, wounded another, which in falling, fell upon Mr. Saugrain's left hand, crushing his forefinger, and yelling to us to land, but hoping to escape them we continued on our course pursued by the Indians in their canoes. Seeing we must be overtaken, we jumped overboard, hoping to reach the Kentucky shore and escape to the woods. Mr. Pique, badly wounded, was drowned in the attempt. Mr. Raguet, on reaching shore, encountered two on the watch for us, who soon despatched and scalped him. Mr. Pierce and myself escaped to land, but were pursued and captured by the two who had killed M. Raguet, who bound our hands and started after our boat which the others had taken. During the next night I contrived to loosen my hands while our captors were sound asleep, we stole away quietly, keeping in the woods down the river, in hopes of being overtaken by a descending boat. After three days' severe suffering, nearly famished, barefoot, frosted feet, left hand disabled, a slight gun-shot wound in the neck which bled profusely. On the third day, the 27th, to our great delight, we were overtaken by two boats, the hands of which waded ashore, carried us on board, and did all they could to relieve us. In two more days, March 29th in the evening, we were landed at Louisville.

"On the next day, March 30th, I was taken over the river to the American fort at Clarksville for better care, where I was cordially welcomed by Major Willis and his officers of the garrison and placed in the care of the surgeon of the post. I remained here till May 11th, six weeks, by which time I was pretty well restored, except my disabled finger, and one of my feet, small portions of which had been amputated from the effects of the frost."

In the summer of 1788 Doct. Saugrain returned to Philadelphia and to France.

Remaining in France the eventful year 1789, Doct. Saugrain sailed again for the United States in April, 1790, on the same vessel with a number of the French emigrants destined for the new settlement of Galliopolis, Gallia County, Ohio. They landed at Alexandria, on the Potomac, July 6th, came by Winchester, Virginia, and Redstone (Brownsville), to the Monongahela, and descended that river and the Alleghany to their destination, where they arrived in the fall.

Doct. Saugrain resided for six years in Galliopolis where he married his wife in 1793, in Kanawha County, Virginia, just opposite, removed to Lexington, Kentucky, in 1796, where his two eldest daughters were born, and in the year 1800, accompanied by the family of his father-in-law, John Michau, Sr., they came to St. Louis. Doct. Antoine F. Saugrain, born at Paris, February, 1763, and Genevieve Rosalie Michau, born at Paris, July 23, 1776, were married in Kanawha County, Virginia, opposite Galliopolis, Ohio, on March 20, 1793.

Their children were: —

1. Rosalie Saugrain, born in Lexington, Kentucky, June 22, 1797, married to Henry Von Phul, in St. Louis, June 10, 1816.

2. Eliza Maria, born in Lexington, Kentucky, October 12, 1799, married to James Kennerly, St. Louis, June 10, 1817.

3. Alphonse Alfred, born in St. Louis, February 3, 1803.

4. Frederic, born March 24, 1806.

5. Henrietta Theresa, November 27, 1808, married to Thomas Noel, June 14, 1827.

6. Eugenie, born October 9, 1813, married to John W. Reel.

Doct. Antoine F. Saugrain died in St. Louis, May 19, 1820, aged fifty-seven, and his widow, Mrs. Saugrain, July 13, 1860, aged eighty-four.

JOHN MICHAU, SR.,

son of Andrew Michau, master saddler, and wife, Marie Louise Bailleul, born in Cross Street, of Little Fields, Paris, Friday, March 27, 1739, and

Jeanne Genevieve Rosalie, daughter of Jean Francois Chevallier, master painter, and wife Genevieve Francoise Chavard, born in Bailleul Street, Paris, Sunday, July 16, 1752, were married in that city in 1775, where they continued to reside for the next fifteen years, and where all their children but one were born.

In the year 1790 Mr. Michau, with his family of wife, two sons and three daughters, came over to the United States with the emigration from that city to establish themselves at Galliopolis, Ohio, where they arrived in the fall of that year and located themselves. Here they resided for the next ten years, during which a third son was born to them, and the eldest daughter, Rosalie, was married.

In May, 1791, Mr. Michau, being a well educated man, was appointed by Winthrop Sargeant, the secretary and acting governor of the Northwest Territory, a justice of the peace. His commission is dated at Galliopolis May 7 of that year. In the year 1800 the two families, Michau and Saugrain, came together to St. Louis and became permanent residents of the place. Their children were: —

1. Genevieve Rosalie, born July 23, 1776; married March 20, 1793, at Galliopolis, to Doct. Antoine F. Saugrain.

2. Marie Eleonore, born November 20, 1777; died September 1, 1818, at St. Louis.

5. Sophia Mary, born February 22, 1786; married De-

cember 24, 1805, at St. Louis, to Dr. John Hamilton Robinson;

3. John Alexander, born July 4, 1781.
4. Melchior Amand Fidele, born July 4, 1783.
6. Antoine Aristide, born July 17, 1792.

Mr. John Michau, Sr., died in St. Louis, June 29, 1819, aged eighty-one years. His wife, Mrs. John Michau, Sr., had died at Galliopolis, date not preserved.

PIERRE PROVENCHÉRE, SR.

Among those who fled from France during the reign of terror, to seek safety in foreign climes, and who found his final home in the city of Philadelphia, where he spent the ablance of his days, was Pierre Provenchère. He was born as we have it from the best authority; (Relf's Philadelphia Gazette, Jan'y 26, 1831) in the City of Orleans, France, on February 29 1740, "held a position in the household of "the brother of Louis XVI. the Compte D'Artois, after- "wards Charles the X, as preceptor to his second son the "Duke of Berri, when a youth," and had always been held by the royal family of France in proper respect and consideration. He died in Philadelphia where he resided for more than thirty years on January 19, 1831, in the ninety-first year of his age. His son,

ANTOINE NICHOLAS PIERRE,

I believe the only one, was born in France on September, 13, 1769, and came to St. Louis a few years before the transfer of the country to the United States. He was married here on July 9, 1803, to Miss Mary Jeronima Rutgers, daughter of Arend Rutgers, from Dortrecht, Holland, a merchant of St. Louis.

APPENDIX. 481

Mr. Provenchère died at his residence, South Second Street, below Chouteau Avenue, on September 8, 1824, in his fifty-fifth year — leaving three daughters and a son. Mrs. Provenchère survived her husband forty-five years, and died on June 11, 1869, in her eighty-sixth year, in the same house.

1. Amelia Mary, was married to George Maguire Ex-Mayor, November 26, 1833, both now deceased. They had but one daughter, Mary, the first wife of Charles W. Francis, Health Commissioner.

2. Eliza, married to Frederick Saugrain, November 2, 1835. She died March 25, 1868, leaving one son, Anthony Pierre, who died a young man May 1, 1882, and two daughters the wives respectively of Wm. H. H. Pettus and John Waddell.

3. Eulalie, the first wife of Saugrain Robinson. She died in 1840, leaving but one daughter, Mary.

4. The son, Ferdinand Provenchère, born March 3, 1808, married the widow of Alfred Saugrain and died Sept. 23, 1878, in his seventy-first year, leaving a number of sons and daughters.

MR. AREND RUTGERS

came here from Dortrecht Holland at the commencement of the present century, with a wife and two daughters, the Mrs. Provenchère, above, and Miss Sally, who never married. He was a noted man in his day, acquired property, and Rutgers Street was named for him, running through his property.

CHARLES GRATIOT, SR.,

the only son of David Gratiot and Marie Bernard, was born at Lausanne, Canton of Vaud, Switzerland, in the year 1752; his paternal ancestors were French Protestants, who had taken refuge there from the persecutions of the Catholics, consequent upon the revocation of the edict of Nantz by Louis XIV. in 1685.

He received his early education at that place, and when yet a youth in his teens, was sent by his parents to an uncle Bernard in London, a brother of his mother, established in that city in business, with his uncle he remained some years. In the year 1769, at the age of seventeen years, he came over to Canada to be employed in the house of his Montreal uncle, Bernard, another brother of his mother, engaged largely there in trade with the Indians of the Northwest.

1769, April 2nd, he sailed from London on the ship Layton, and arrived at Quebec, Canada, on May 30th, after a tolerably favorable voyage of 60 days. Here he met his uncle Bernard, of Montreal, expecting the arrival of the ship.

June 9. — After ten days at Quebec, loading his uncle's goods on a boat, he went up to Montreal by water, then about seventeen years of age.

He remained in Montreal about five years, most of the time with his uncle as a clerk learning the Indian trade, he being yet a minor under the laws of France, and under the control of his uncle.

When he came to America in 1769, he was an only child; in his second letter to his parents from Montreal in August, 1770, after he had been there fourteen months, he expresses his great joy at the receipt of the first letter from them of March 9th preceding, 1770, in which they inform him of the birth of a sister, his first and only one, a difference of seventeen years in their ages; and in all his subsequent letters to his parents he never failed to expresss his brotherly affection for her. This sister, Isabella, he saw for the first time, when he revisited his native place in the winter of 1791–92, when she had become a young woman of twenty-two years, and he in his fortieth year.

1774. — He spent this summer in a business trip for his uncle to the "upper country" (at that day this meant all the country north and west of Kingston at the foot of Lake Ontario, including all the lakes and rivers to the Mississippi), as far as Michilimackinac, the uppermost trading post, and the Illinois country on the Mississippi, returning to Montreal September 30th, then twenty-two years of age.

1775. — About May 1st, he left Montreal on his first trading adventure for himself, associated with a partner whose name is not given, with an outfit of goods furnished them by his uncle Bernard and another merchant of that place (then 23). They wintered 1775-76 among the tribes with whom they traded, and got back to Montreal at the end of August, 1776, absent sixteen months.

This first adventure was unsuccessful from his partner's extravagant expenditures and heavy losses, leaving them largely in debt, resulting in an open rupture with his uncle Bernard.

1776. — He spent another year in Montreal endeavoring to settle up this first adventure, and effecting preparations for a second one.

1777. — He left Montreal in August for the Illinois country, where he had been very successful for his uncle in 1774. He had formed a trading connection in Montreal with three others, all experienced in the Indian trade, John Kay and David McCrae, two Scotchmen, and — Barthe and himself, two Swiss. They had procured the largest portion of their goods through the house of William Kay, elder brother of John, an established merchant of Montreal. They reached Mackinac in September, where his first entry is made in his ledger on September 24th as "David McCrae & Co.," passing up to Green Bay in October, by the portage and Prairie du Chien in November, he arrived in Cahokia at the close of November, where he opened his store early in December. His partners, being Indian traders, had stopped at various places on the route to pursue the trade (then 25); shortly afterward they opened another store at Kaskaskia.

1778. — His first spring and summer in Cahokia, Mr. Gratiot devoted his leisure time in instructing a number of persons how to prepare leaf tobacco into carrots as it is imported into Montreal, and induced a number to embark in its cultivation as very profitable.

July 4. — Mr. Gratiot had been seven months located at Cahokia, when on this day Geo. Rogers Clark surprised Kaskaskia.

At the close of this year, Gratiot wrote a long letter to his father, and his first one to his little sister, Isabella, then nine years old.

Mr. Barthe, his Swiss partner, was killed by the Indians with whom he was trading in the winter of 1778-79.

1779. — In this year Mr. G. had a trading station on the Illinois river at the Indian village of Ouyatanon, at or near the present site of Peoria. After Clark's occupation of the country, Gratiot, from his knowledge of the English and French languages, and his influence with the people of the district, and near the same age, became very intimate with him, and although holding no official position, yet from his influence and knowledge, had much to do with the affairs of the time, and was usually consulted on important matters of a public nature.

In December there was an alarm at Cahokia concerning some Indians encamped at the Cantine, about ten miles northeast of the village, supposed to be Wabash Indians and hostile. On December 16th Mr. Gratiot wrote to Col. Montgomery, the American commandant at Kaskaskia, in relation to this alarm.

1780. — In April, the inhabitants of the village having received an intimation that a large force of Indians, led by British officers, were on their way to endeavor to surprise and recapture the place, held a meeting and requested Mr. Gratiot to go in search of Col. Clark, then at Fort Jefferson, at the iron banks in Kentucky, below the mouth of the Ohio, to request him to come to their assistance. This Mr. Gratiot undertook, but returned from his mission unsuccessful, Clark having gone to Louisville by order of the governor of Virginia.

The surprise of the British side of the Illinois country, and the immediate establishment of the authority of the State of Virginia over the same, with the death of Mr. Barthe, one of the partners, seems to have put an end to the firm of David McCrae & Co., as we see nothing more of it, and find Mr. Gratiot operating alone after this date.

1781.—Early in this year Mr. Gratiot removed over to St. Louis and became a Spanish subject to enable him to participate in the Indian trade of both the Spanish and English sides of the country, which he could not do as an English subject.

Early in the summer of 1783, Mr. Gratiot for himself, his late firm of McCrae & Co., and one Godfrey Linctot, with whom he had been interested in several speculations, having claims to a considerable amount against the State of Virginia, which he had been unsuccessful in his efforts to collect through other parties, concluded to go himself to Richmond and Williamsburg, hoping to meet with more success than those he had previously employed. On this trip Mr. G. was absent for over a year, extending it as far as Philadelphia, the first one from St. Louis to visit that then far distant city, and got back to his home in St. Louis late in June, 1784, the trip having been made on horseback. After this trip he appears to have remained at home in the pursuit of his business with varying success, until his first voyage to Europe, in 1791.

Mr. Gratiot had long been ambitious to establish a house in New Orleans in connection with one in Europe, through which to import from Europe the articles necessary for the Indian trade, and to send back through the same channel the returns from that trade.

In 1791, having gathered together his little capital in money and peltries, he sailed from New Orleans in the fall of this year for Bordeaux, with letters to parties in that city. From Bordeaux he went in October to Havre de Grace, with letters to the house of Amet, Ronus & Co., who suggested to him that "London being the largest fur market in the world," he had better go there, and gave him a letter of introduction to Mr. John H. Schneider, a merchant of that city, who had amassed a handsome fortune from his business, principally in the fur market; here he spent about a month in various interviews with Mr. S. relating to his contemplated enterprise.

At the end of November he went to Switzerland, to revisit his native place and relatives, from whom he had been absent exceeding twenty-five years.

After remaining a couple of months with his mother and sister, and relatives, his father being dead, he left Geneva January 27th, 1792, in the "diligence," reached Poligny next day, 28th, and on February 4th reached Paris, where he remained some days, and London toward the close of February, bringing with him his cousin Frederic (Fritz), a young lad, son of Charles Bugnion, whom his father had intrusted to his care to bring to America, and qualify him for the Indian trade. (Mr. G. brought him to St. Louis, and placed him with Mr. Aug'te Chouteau.) Mr. Gratiot remained a couple of months in London, arranging a plan of operations with Mr. Schneider, who acquired a great ascendancy over him, procured for him a partner in one Solomon Abraham, a protegé of Schneider, and furnished them an outfit of goods. They sailed from London in April and arrived at Montreal in June, and in July went on up to Mackinac, where, after remaining some time, Mr.

Gratiot got back to his home in St. Louis in November, 1792, after an absence of fourteen months. (This partnership resulted in a miserable failure from various causes, producing great loss to all the parties.)

1793. — Mr. Gratiot, having induced his brothers-in-law, Auguste and Pierre Chouteau, then associated in Indian trading, Papin & Tabeau, and Benito & Roy, to place in his charge their peltries to dispose of, and to fill their orders for goods in London, left St. Louis late in May for Montreal, from which place he sailed, at the close of October on the ship Eureta, and arrived at London on December 15th.

Here he remained for more than six months, listening and agreeing to the various schemes and projects suggested by Schneider to Gratiot, by which G. would accumulate a rapid fortune, — to furnish him the capital to establish a house in New York, or St. Petersburg, or Ostend, etc. Gratiot, who from his great desire to acquire wealth, had become completely infatuated with the fancied generosity of Schneider, listened eagerly to the various plans and propositions of S., who resorted to these steps to detain Gratiot in London until the arrival of Abraham from Canada to learn the true state of his affairs there. Finally Gratiot began to suspect the sincerity of S. in these various schemes, and to open his eyes to his own foolish credulity, when they come to an open rupture on May 7, 1794, and Gratiot determined to return at once to his home in America. Yet such an ascendancy had Schneider acquired over him by his plausibility and renewed offers of capital, that he contrived to yet detain Gratiot there until June 21, 1794, on which day he sailed from London, and after a passage of sixty-three days arrived at New York August 23d. On the next day, September 24th, 1794, he wrote from New York to his quondam friend a long letter in which he narrates all these occurrences. After remaining a couple of months in

New York, he left for home by Baltimore and Pittsburg, and making a quick trip of but eighteen days by boat from Pittsburg to St. Louis, he reached his home in January, 1795, about twenty months from May, 1793, to January, 1795, and immediately gave notice in the Montreal paper of the dissolution of the firm of Abraham & Gratiot.

1795. — In May he went down to New Orleans, on his way around to New York. He sailed from New Orleans about the middle of June on the brigatine Hanna, Capt. W. Westcott, arrived in New York in July, where he remained about three months until October, the year in which the yellow fever was so fatal in that and other Atlantic cities. He left New York for Baltimore early in October; there to Pittsburg with his goods, where he loaded them on a boat he had had built there, and reached St. Louis with them in January, 1796.

1796. — As his stock of goods were only gotten home in January of this year, and could not be disposed of and returns received from sales until 1797, he had no occasion to leave his home this year. He had become the possessor, some years previously, of a tract of land of a league square, four miles back from the village on the waters of the River des Peres, upon which he had improved a small farm, a house, orchard, garden, etc., he devoted his leisure in further improving, putting up a mill, distillery, etc.

He also received a proposition this year from a friend, Mr. Collignon, a merchant of London, who made consignments of goods to New York and New Orleans, to give him two hundred pounds sterling ($1,000) per annum, to act as his agent, in visiting these houses once a year to see after his interests — which Mr. Gratiot, who was fond of roaming about, accepted in a letter of June 6, 1776, too late to receive a reply thereto this same year. This proposition, however, was not effected, as we find from his ledger No. 4, that for the years 1797 to 1800, he was at home carrying on his store in St. Louis, and besides his mill and distillery on his farm near the village, he was also operating a tannery and salt works on the Meramec River.

In 1798, Mr. Gratiot obtained from Governor-General Don Manuel Gayoso de Lemos, at New Orleans, a concession for his league square near St. Louis, on which he had improved his farm some years previously.

After his return from his second voyage to London in 1795, Mr. Gratiot being in a great measure cured of his early desire to accumulate a rapid fortune, settled himself down to the enjoyment of his home comforts, content to prosecute a moderate business. In this he was successful, having a good custom in his retail store from the Americans, who began to come into the country from the Ohio River and Kentucky, and made the new settlements of Bonhomme, Gravois, and along the Meramec, besides acquiring at times a number of tracts of land in various parts of the St. Louis district, by concessions, purchases, and other speculations, eventually becoming the possessor of the handsome competency he had long sought, enabling him to give his numerous family of sons and daughters the best education the country could furnish.

1804.—After the transfer of the country to the United States, and the establishment of the first Court of Quarter Sessions in St. Louis, in December, 1804, Mr. Gratiot was appointed by Governor Harrison, the first presiding justice of that Court, his two associates being Augustus Chouteau and David Delaunay, which position he filled for three years 1805, 1806, and 1807, after this he was appointed a justice of the peace.

1809.—At the incorporation of the "Town of St. Louis," he was elected a trustee, and filled the office of chairman of the board for the years 1811, 1812, and 1813—this was his last public office.

On the 25th June, 1781, Mr. Gratiot was united in marriage to Miss Victoire the eldest daughter of Madame Therese Bourgeois Chouteau.

They were the parents of thirteen children, nine of whom, four sons and five daughters grew to maturity, married and left families.

Mr. Chas. Gratiot died of paralysis on April 20, 1817, at the age of sixty-five years. His widow survived him eight years and died June 15, 1825, at the same age of sixty-five years.

Their children were: —

1. Julie, born July 24, 1782; married to John P. Cabanné, from France, April 8, 1799.

2. Victoire, born March 25, 1785, married to Sylvestre Labbadie, August 16, 1806.

3. Charles, born August 29, 1786, married to Ann Belin, Philadelphia, April 22, 1819.

4. Marie Therese, born February 20, 1788, married to John Nicholas Macklot from France, August 16, 1806.

5. Henry, born April 25, 1789, married to Susan Hempstead, Connecticut, February, 1813.

6. Emily Anne, born October 5, 1793, married to Peter Chouteau, Jr., June 15, 1813.

7. Louise Isabella, born October 15, 1796, married to Jules Demun, St. Dom, from May 31, 1812.

8. Marie Brigitte born January 6, 1798, died September 7, 1803; aet. 5 years, 8 months.

9. John Pierre, born February 19, 1799, married to Marie Antoinette Adele Perdreauville from Paris, Nov. 18, 1819.

10. Paul Benjamin, born March 13, 1800, married to Virginia Billon, from Philadelphia, June 6, 1825, and three infants, died young in 1801, 1803, 1804.

PERSONAL CHARACTERISTICS OF CHARLES GRATIOT, SR.

He was a man of more than ordinary capacity and ability, and from his early business education had grown to manhood with the idea that the chief aim of man was, to learn how to keep books properly, and to acquire wealth. In his school-boy days at home with his parents, and his youth and early manhood with his uncles in London and Canada, he does not seem to have been any more than ordinarily active in the pursuit of business knowledge, and while with his Montreal uncle Bernard, a period of some five years, and with whom he does not appear to have got along very agreeably, his uncle frequently chiding him — he seems from the tenor of his letters to his father at home, to be somewhat under the influence of depressed spirits, frequently lamenting his unfortunate condition, doubtless from home-sickness. But after leaving the service of this Montreal uncle, and starting out for himself, he soon displayed great energy and perseverance in his pursuit of wealth, which continued with him through life.

A prominent trait in his character was his disposition for controversial argument; nature had cut him out for the legal profession, he was a special pleader, and possessed the faculty of presenting his case so favorably that he never failed to carry his point, as is evidenced by the fact that in every instance in which we find him as a litigant, he came off winner of his case, his written arguments being always prepared by himself, possessing the advantages of familiarity with both the French and English languages.

Nothing can better furnish an insight into the disposition and character of any one whom we never personally knew, than a careful perusal of his letters; more especially of those written to his kinsmen and personal friends, when policy and reserve are usually cast aside, and a man is apt to lay open his inmost thoughts with the candor and frankness inherent in his nature, and from these we are enabled, not only to correctly estimate his mental calibre, but to arrive in a great measure at a correct appreciation of the predominant traits in his temper and disposition.

It is from a careful study of his letters solely, that I have formed my estimate of Charles Gratiot, Sr., a man I never knew, he being laid in his grave some eighteen months previously to my arrival in the place.

FRED. L. BILLON.

INDEX.

	PAGE
Adams, Calvin	401
Alvarez, E.	447
Arsenal Tract	408
Aubry, Captain, takes command	23
Barada, A.	449
Barada, Louis	450
Barelas, Jos., inquiry into conduct of	56
Acquittal of	57
Barrousel, F.	473
Barjas, Dominic	135
Beaugenou, N., Sr.	415
Beaugenou, N., Jr.	416
Becquet, John B.	427, 430
Bellisime, A.	457
Benoit, F. M., Sr.	472
Bent Place	406
Beynal, Dr. A.	392
Biggs, John	403
Bissette, Wm.	439
Bissonet, Francis	427
Bissonet, Louis	427
Blouin, Daniel	40
Bouise, A. V., Sr.	454
Boly, John, Sr.	400
Brazeau, Jos., Sr.,	454
Buet, Rene	439
Cabanne, John P.	473
Cahokia	45
Camp Family	461

	PAGE
Camp, Mrs. Ann .	231
Cartabona, De Don S. F., acting governor	206
Cerre, Gabriel	452
Cession from France to Spain. Remarks on	22
Chancellier, Jos. .	421
Chancellier, Louis	421
Charleville, Jos. .	458
Charleville, Mme. F. B.	460
Charleville, Joseph	460
Chauvin	458
Chouteau, Auguste	146
Chouteau, Mrs. .	243
Chouteau, Marie Thérèsé Bourgeois,	412
Chouteau *vs.* Lisa	334
Chronology, Introductory	1–15
Clark, G. R. Col.	142
Conde, Dr. A. A.	389
Coons, John	399
Cruzat, Francis, governor	129
Administration	131
Second term	207
D'Abadie, death of	23
Debruisseau, J. L. D'I., granted exclusive privilege to trade	30
Death of his son	31
DeLabeaume, L. A. T.	467
Delassus, Col. C. D., succeeds Gov. Trudeau	295
Official notes to	316
Military orders of	319
Names of subordinates	364
Ancestors of	385
Account of Homestead	405
P. C. D. .	469
(De St. Vrain) .	470
DeLeyba, Don F., administration of	142
Will of	203
Interment of	205
Denoyer, J. M. .	426

INDEX. 495

	PAGE
Denoyer, Francis	428
DeTreget, C. D.	442
DeVolsay, P. F.	435
Didier, John P.	465
Dodier, G., Sr.	429
Dubreuil, L. C.	262, 434
Dubreuil, Louis	410
Duchouquette Place	404
Duchouquette & Lamy	437
Duralde, M. M.	447
Early agreement	63
Flood of 1784, account of	225
Florisant Village	273
Fort Chartres, first arrivals from	24
Debruisseau first judge	23
And Mme. St. Ange	42
Fremon, A. C.	471
French merchants, names of early	75
Fur traders and merchants	132
Gamache, John B.	422
Gates, John	400
Gibkins, Dr. B.	392
Gratiot, Chas., Sr.	481
Guion, A., Jr.	432
Heberts, The	431
Henrion, Francis and Charles	416
Honore, L. Tesson, Sr.	~~442~~ 42-
Hortiz, Jos. A.	446
Indians, Attack on St. Louis May 26, 1780	191
List of killed	199
Keer and family killed by	248
The Mascou	373
Inventory, Early	33
Kaskaskia	44
Kiersereau, G., Sr.	423
Labbadie, Sylvester	260

	PAGE
Labusciere, Jos., Acting Secretary	25
Biography of	29
Laclede and Companions	17
Arrival at St. Louis	18
Considered legal proprietor	25
Verbal grants by	36
Capture trading boat	50
Prison constructed by	124
Supposed wealth	143
Death of	145
Aug. Chouteau administers estate	147
Sale of his house	149
Laclede, Pierre	411
Lamy, Michael	438
Leduc, M. P.	475
Leroy, Julien	424
Lewis, M., Capt.	384
Livre Terriens	30
Loise, A., Sr.	417
Loisel, R.	465
Louisiana Treaty	339
Purchase	349
Documents regarding transfer	351
Transfer of	359
Mainville, Jos.	420
Manumission, The first	39
Marechal, N., Sr.	429
Marcheteau dit Denoyer	417
Marcheteau, Louis	417
Marie, P. A.	433
Martigny Bros.	425
Maxent, Laclede & Co.	50
Mercier, Dr. C.	392
Michan, J., Sr.	479
Michel, Jos. (dit Taillon)	414
Mine à Breton	377
Mullanphy, John	409

INDEX.

	PAGE
New Madrid, Early history	263
New Orleans, Ordinances of	275
Ortes, John B.	443
Papin, Jos., Sr.	448
Papin, Jos. M.	448
Peltier, Isidor	41
Pepin, J. M.	433
Perez, Emanuel, administration	246
Peyroux, Mme., Will of	247
Philibert, Jos., Sr.	444
Physicians, Early list of	389
Piernas, Capt. Jos., St. Ange delivers possession to him	97
Piernas, Capt. Pedro	30, 66, 129
Pierre, A. N.	480
Pitman, Capt.	46
Pourcelli, John P.	453
Prairie du Rocher	45
Pratte, Bernard, Sr.	466
Provenchere, Pierre, Sr.	480
Rankin, Jas.	402
Ride, Louis, Sr.	418
Rios, Francisco, Capt., arrives at St. Louis	52
Erects "Fort Prince Charles"	53
List of officers and soldiers	54
Departure	65
Rivieres, The (dit Baccannet)	419
Robidou, Jos., Sr.	444
Rohrer, David	402
Routier, Chas.	427
Rutgers, A.	481
St. Ange, Capt., Acting Governor, delivers possession to Capt. Sterling	24
Biography of	27
Will of	125
Death of	128
St. Cir Hyacinthe, Sr.	456
Ste. Genevieve	41, 258

498　ANNALS OF ST. LOUIS.

	PAGE
St. Louis, families arrive from Ste. Genevieve and New Orleans	20
Called " Laclede's Village "	22
Government in operation April, 1766	28
First documents recorded	32
Public property inventory	47
Military matters	66
Number of houses in 1770	75
Names of the early priests	76
First parish register	79
Early houses	81
Early furniture	82
Water supply	83
Fuel and agriculture	84
Amusements	86
Public sales	87
Marriage contracts	88
Commons and common fields	91
Naming of	93
Dachurut and Diard's agreement	100
Emancipation by Villars	102
Detailly's inventory	107
First auction sale	108
Delage's Will	113
Masse and Valle lawsuit	136
Father de Limpach arrives	138
Denoyer *vs.* Tinon	151
Petit *vs.* Menard	154
Maha's trial	156
Complaint of Mrs. Montardy	173
Conspiracy of Robidou	174
Gratiot *vs.* Sanguinet	177
La Fleur et al. *vs.* Gratiot.	209
Village laws	216
Suit *vs.* Vachard	227
Killing of Batiste	233
Separation of Barrere and wife	251
Lapiere absconds	253

INDEX. 499

	PAGE
St. Louis, Trudeau's gift to sons of John B. Trudeau	279
Murder of House	298
Edwards *vs.* Kishler	299
Action *vs.* Moodey	301
Colgin *vs.* Lyons	303
Bell *vs.* Colgin	305
Sarpy *vs.* Saffray	311
Inquests	312, 313
Salle, Jean	426
Saugrain, A. F., Dr.	476
Sanguinet, Chas., Sr.	450
Sarpy, Chas. and wife	441
Soulard, A. P.	471
Place	403
Spain, the King's scheme to replenish his treasury	289-294
Spanish domination	97
Sterling, Capt., takes possession	24
Report of	43
Stoddard, Amos, letter to Secretary of War	371
Reply to Delassus	379
Biography of	388
Sullivan, William	401
Tison, Albert	469
Trille, Michael, trial of	55-56
Trudeau, Don Zenow, administration of	257
Trudeau, John B.	449
Ulloa, Count	23
Vachard, dit Hardoise	453
Valleau, Dr. John B., arrival in St. Louis	58
Death of	59
Will of	60-62
Biography	391
Vasquez, B., Sr.	445

ILLUSTRATIONS.

Portrait of F. L. Billon.

Portrait of Madame Chouteau.

St. Louis in 1770.

Plat of St. Louis in 1770.

Beaugenou House, 1765.

Chouteau Mansion.

Church and Parish Residence.

Government House, 1765.

Fort on the Hill, 1794.

LIST OF SUBSCRIBERS.

ALEXANDER, BASIL W.
ALEXANDER, M. W.
ALEXIAN BROTHERS,
ALLEN, GERARD B.
ALLEN, N. D.
ALLEYNE, J. S. B. — M. D.
ALOE, A. S.
ANDERSON, HARRY, New York,
ANDERSON, MRS. JNO. J., New York,
ANDERSON, WM. B., Chicago,
ANHEUSER-BUSCH BREWERY CO.,
ARMSTRONG, COL. D. H., 2 copies
AUFDERHEIDE, F. W.

BABCOCK, LIECESTER
BACON, FREDERICK H.
BAIN, GEORGE
BALMER, CHARLES
BAMBERGER, PHILIP A.
BARADA, FRANCIS X.
BARBER, S. W.
BARCLAY, D. ROBERT
BARCLAY, HON. S. W.
BARLOW, STEPHEN D.
BARNARD, GEO. D.
BARNES, ROBERT A., 5 copies
BARNETT, GEO. I.
BARNEY, CHAS. E.
BAUER, ALFRED G.
BAUMAN, L., JEWELRY CO., 2 copies
BEAUVAIS, F. A.
BELL, LEVERETT
BENOIST, CONDE L., 2 copies
BENOIST, EUGENE H.
BENOIST, THEODORE
BENOIST, SANGUINET
BENT, SILAS

BERNAYS, A. le — M. D.
BERTHOLD, AUGUSTUS
BERTHOLD, BARTHOLOMEW
BERTHOLD, PIERRE A.
BIEBINGER, FRED'K W.
BLAND, JOHN H.
BLANK, ALOIS
BLAIR, FRANK P.
BLATTNER, JACOB
BLISS, WM. W.
BLOCK, JNO. C. H. D.
BLOSSOM, H. M.
BLYTHE, JAMES E.
BOBB, CHARLES
BOECK, ADAM
BOECKLER, A.
BOEDICKER, L.
BOFINGER, JNO. N.
BOLAND, JOHN L.
BOYLE, WILBUR F.
BRADY, V. REV'D PHILIP P.
BRANCH, JOSEPH W.
BRAZEAU, AUGUSTUS G.
BRECKENRIDGE, HON. S. M.
BREDELL, EDWARD
BROADHEAD, HON. JAMES O.
BROOKMEIR, JAMES H.
BRUENEMANN, ERNST
BULL, JNO. C.
BUCK, MYRON M.
BURR, WM. E.
BUSH, ISIDOR
BYRNE, JOHN

CABANNÉ, J. SHEPARD — M. D., 3 copies
CABANNÉ, JOS. C.

(501)

CABANNÉ, SARPY C.
CADY, HON. CHAS. F.
CAMPBELL, ROB'T A. (No. 1),
CAMPBELL, ROB'T A. (No. 2),
CAMPBELL, W. D.
CAPEN, GEO. D.
CARPENTER, JAS. M.
CARR, ALFRED
CARR, CHARLES BENT
CARR, JAMES
CARR, LUCIEN, Cambridge, Mass.
CARRIÈRE, Mrs. C.
CATLIN, DANIEL
CATLIN, EPHRAIM
CENTRAL TYPE FOUNDRY
CHADBOURNE, G. W.
CHAPMAN, JOSEPH G.
CHARLOT, C. S.
CHASE, EDWARD
CHOUTEAU, CHAS. P., 5 copies
CHOUTEAU, J. GILMAN
CHRISTIAN BROTHERS, 3 copies
CHURCH, ALONZO C.
CLAIBORNE, JAS. R.
CLARK, HENRY L.
CLARK, HINMAN H.
CLARK, JEFFERSON K.
CLARK, WM. G.
CLEMENS, B. M.
CLEMENS, JERE W.
CLENDENIN, WM. A.
CLOVER, HON. H. A.
COBB, SETH W.
COLBURN, FRED. M.
COLE, HON. NATHAN
COLLINS, L. E.
COLLINS, MARTIN
COMPTON, RICH'D J.
COMSTOCK, T. G. — M. D.
COPP, SAMUEL
CORNET, FRANCIS
COSTE, FELIX
COUZINS, JNO. E. D.
COX, MRS. CHAS. A.
CRAWFORD, DAVID

CRUNDEN, F. M.
CRUTTENDEN, R. W.

DAENZER, CARL
DAVIS AND DAVIS
DAVIS, JOHN T.
DELAFIELD, WALLACE
DELANY, JOHN O'FALLON
DELASSUS, AUGUSTUS
DESLOGE, JULES
DEYONG, A.
DILLON, JOHN A
DIMMOCK, MRS. THOMAS, 2 copies
DITTMANN, GEORGE F.
DODD, S. M.
DODSWORTH, REV'D C.
DOERR, P. J.
DONALDSON, ANDREW
DONALDSON, JOHN W.
DONALDSON, WM. R.
DONAVAN, FRANK J.
DOWLING, RICHARD
DOWNING, EDWIN
DRAKE, GEO. S.
DREW, FRANCIS A.
DRUMMOND, J. T.
DUESTROW, LOUIS
DURKEE, DWIGHT
DYER, JOHN N., 2 copies
DYER, TRUSTEN P.

EASTON, ALTON R.
EDGAR, T. B.
EDWARDS, ALBERT G.
EHLERMANN, CHAS.
EISENHARDT, HERMAN
ELIOT, REV'D WM. G.
ENGELMANN, GEO. S. — M. D.
ERSKINE, GREENE
ESSEX, JAMES C.
ESSEX, WM. T.
EWALD, PHILIP — M. D.
EWING, AUGUSTUS B.

FAERBER, REV'D. WM.
FARIS, CHARLES A., 2 copies

LIST OF SUBSCRIBERS. 503

Farish, Edward T.
Farmer, James B.
Farrar, James S.
Farrelly, Thos. F.
Fath, Conrad
Faust, Anthony
Ferguson, D. K.
Filley, Giles F.
Finney, Bernard
Fisse, John H.
Fitzgerald, Miss M.
Flad, Col. Henry
Fletcher, Hon. Thos. C.
Foster, Benj. R.
Fox, Patrick
Foy, Mrs. P. L.
Francis, Hon. D. R.
Franklin, Joseph
Frost, Gen'l. D. M.
Fruin, Jeremiah
Fusz, Louis

Gales, Sigismund, J.
Gantt, Thos. T.
Gardner, A. M.
Garesche, A. J. P.
Garland, Nathan
Garrison, Danl. R.
Gaylord, Saml. A.
Gehner, Augustus
Gibson, Charles, 2 copies
Gibson, James H.
Gilfillan, John A.
Gilkeson, John W., 2 copies
Gill, George H.
Gilmore, Col. P. S., New York
Glasgow, Edward J.
Glasgow, Wm. Jr.
Goddard, E.
Goode, Robt. W.
Goodin, John
Gore, Stephen A.
Gould, David B.
Grand Lodge Mo., A. F. and A. M.
Gratiot, Adolph

Gratiot, Charles B. — M. D.
Gratiot, Paul B.
Gray, Melvin L.
Greeley, Carlos S.
Green, Charles
Gregory, G. H. — M. D.
Grether, John
Grissom, D. M.
Gugerty, Thomas
Guibor, Henri

Haarstick, Henry C.
Haeusler, Herman A.
Harney, John M.
Harrington, Henry F.
Harris, James A.
Hart, Oliver A.
Hauck's, Brothers — M. D.
Hayward, G. A.
Helfenstein, John P.
Hennessy, Rev'd John J.
Henry, Rev'd James
Hill, Britton A.
Hirschberg, F. D.
Hirschberg, Louis C.
Hitchcock, Henry
Hoblitzelle, C. L.
Hogan, Mrs. John
Hogan, Mrs. Lizzie W., California
Homes, Charles R.
Homes, Fred'k B., 2 copies
Hospes, Richard
Hough, Henry W.
Hough, Warwick
Houser, D. M.
How, James F.
Howard, Francis A.
Hubbard, R. M.
Humphrey, F. H.
Hurlburt, Geo. F. — M. D.
Hyde, William

Irwin, Charles W.
Isaacs, J. L.
Ittner, Anthony

JACCARD, EUGENE
JACOBS, ABR'M S.
JEWETT, DAN'L T.
JOHNSON, CHAS. P.
JOHNSON, JOHN B. — M. D.
JONAS, REV'D J. F.
JONES, WM. C.

KARST, EMILE
KARST, EUGENE
KAUFFMAN, J. W.
KEEVIL, WM. H.
KEHR, EDWARD C.
KEILTY, REV'D F. M.
KEISER, JOHN P.
KELLEY, MRS. A. M., Stamford, Connt.
KELLOGG NEWSPAPER CO.
KEMPLAND, ARTHUR
KENNARD, SAM'L L.
KENRICK, M. REV'D PETER R.
KERSHAW, J. M.
KIMBALL, BENJ.
KLEIN, JACOB
KNAPP, ANDREW J.
KNAPP, COL. JOHN
KNAPP, THOS. M.
KOEHLER, C.
KRIECKHAUS, AUGUSTUS
KRUM, CHESTER H.

LACKLAND, RUFUS J.
LADD, JOHN A.
LAMMERT, MARTIN
LAMOTTE, J. SOULARD
LANCASTER, R. J.
LANE, FRANCIS A.
LEEDS, ELLIS N.
LEFFINGWELL, HIRAM W.
LEIGHTON, COL. GEO. E., 2 copies,
LEMP, WM. J.
LEONARD, NICHOLAS
LEWIS, HON. E. A.
LEWIS, JOHN
LEWIS, MARTROM D.

LIGHTNER, JOHN H.
LINDLEY, HON. JAS. J.
LIPPMAN, MORRIS J.
LODGE, JOSEPH G.
LOUDERMAN, JOHN H., 2 copies
LUBKE, HON. GEO. W.
LUCAS, JOHN B. C.
LUCAS, ROBT. J.
LUDLOW, R. C.
LUEDEKING, ROBT. — M. D.
LUNGSTRASS COMPANY,
LUYTIES, H. C. G.
LYNCH, GEO. N.

McCABE, FRAN'S. X.
McCLUNEY, J. H.
McCOY, JOHN T.
McDONALD, ALEX'R.
McKINLEY, ANDREW
McKISSOCK, THOS.
McREE, WM. T.
MADILL, HON. GEO. A.
MAFFITT, CHAS. C.
MAFFITT, P. CHOUTEAU
MAFFITT, WM. C.
MAGUIRE, JOHN
MALLINCKRODT, EDW'D
MARTIN, ALEX.
MARTIN, JOHN G.
MASTBROOK, ALEX.
MAUNTEL, JOHN G.
MAYO, WM. H.
MEAD, EDWARD H.
MECHIN, AUGS. V. R.
MEIER, ADOLPHUS
MEIER, E. F. W.
MEYER, C. F. G.
MEYER, REV'D R. J.
MEYERSON, MRS. L. G.
MINCKE, GEO. H.
MISSOURI HISTORICAL SOCIETY,
MISSOURI LODGE, No. 1, of A. F. and A. M.
MOLL, ADOLPH
MORRISON, J. L. DON

LIST OF SUBSCRIBERS. 505

Moses, G. A. — M. D.
Mott, Fred'k W.

Nagel, Charles
Nasse, August
Neun, John
Neun, Philip
Newman, Socrates, 2 copies
Nicholson, Peter
Nidelet, James C. — M. D.
Norwood, Jos. G. — M. D., Columbia, Mo.
Nugent, Danl. C.

O'Brien, John
O'Fallon, John J.
O'Neil, Frank R.
O'Reilly, Philip S. — M. D.
Obear, Ephraim G.
Orthwein — Brothers
Overstolz, Henry

Paddock, Orville
Page, J. C. — M. D.
Page, Wm. M.
Pallen, Mrs. A. E.
Papin, Theophile.
Papin, Timothy — M. D.
Parker, Geo. W.
Parsons, Charles
Patterson, Robt. D.
Peck, Chas. H.
Percy, J. T.
Pettus, Wm. H. H.
Peugnet, Ernst
Peugnet, Mrs. V. S., Paris, France
Peyinghaus, Robert
Phelan, Rev'd D. S.
Philibert, Wm. B., 2 copies
Picot, Louis D.
Pierce, N. G.
Pitzman, Julius
Polkowski, E. S.
Powell, R. W.
Power, Rev'd G. D.

Prather, Col. John G.
Pratte, Gen'l Bernard, Sr., Jonesburg
Preetorius, Emil
Price, Celsus
Priest, John G.
Primm, Hubert
Provenchere, P. Wm.
Pullis, Augustus
Pullis, Thos. R.

Randall, John F.
Ranken, David
Ranken, Hugh L.
Rassieur, Leo
Rebstock, Charles
Renshaw, Morrison
Renshaw, William
Rex, John
Reyburn, Mrs. Julia V.
Richardson, Jack P.
Richeson, Thos.
Robbins, E. C.
Robidoux, Chas. E.
Roemer, Bernard — M. D.
Rogers, Henry L.
Rolfmeyer, Joseph
Rombauer, Hon. Rod'k E.
Roos, Leonard
Rowse, E. S.
Russell, Chas. S.
Rutherfurd, Thos. S., 2 copies
Ryan, M. Rev'd P. J.

Sampson, Clarke H.
Samuel, Webster M.
Sander, Enno
Sander, M. E.
Saugrain, Frederick
Saunders, V. O.
Scanlan, Mrs. Mary F.
Schadé, Frederick — M. D.
Schaffer Bros. and Powell,
Scherpé, John F.
Schmieding, Frederick
Schnaider, Joseph M.

SCHULENBERG, OTTO G.
SCOTT, ROBERT R.
SELLERS, JOHN M., 2 copies
SELLS, MILES
SESSINGHAUS, THEODORE
SEXTON, HENRY C.
SHAPLEIGH, A. F.
SHAPLEIGH, FRANK
SHATTINGER, ADAM
SHAW, HENRY
SHICKLE, FREDERICK
SIMMONS, C. C.
SIMMONS, ED. C.
SIMMONS, SAMUEL
SIMON, HENRY T.
SKINKER, THOMAS
SKINKER, T. K.
SKRAINKA, WILLIAM
SMITH, ANDREW J.
SMITH, REV'D CONS'E P.
SMITH, PERCY F.
SMITHERS, JOHN A.
SPAUNHORST, HENRY J.
SPECHT, JOSEPH, 2 copies
SPECK, CHARLES
SONNESCHEIN, REV'D S. H.
SOULARD, MRS. H'Y G.
ST. LOUIS STAMPING CO., 2 copies
STEINBERG, MRS. M. J.
STEVENS, CHAS. D. — M. D.
STEVENSON, GEN'L JNO. D.
STEWART, A. W.
STICKNEY, BENJAMIN
STIFEL, CHAS. G.
STILES, HENRY A., Philadelphia.
STIPPICH, JOSEPH
STODDART, T. A.
STUMPF, JACOB
SUTTON, HENRY L.

TALLON, REV'D P. W.
TAMM, JACOB
TANSEY, ROB'T P.
TAUSSIG, CHARLES
TAUSSIG, JOHN J.

TEICHMANN, CHAS. H.
TESSON, EDWARD M.
THOMAS, WM. L.
THOMPSON, HON. S. D.
THOMSON, WM. H.
THONSSEN, G. H.
TIEMEYER, JOHN C.
TIERNAN, JAMES, 2 copies
TIERNAN, JOS. H., 3 copies
TITTMAN, EUGENE C.
TODD, CHARLES
TOENSFELDT, J.
TOMPKINS, CORNELIUS
TRACY, DAN'L O'CONNELL
TREAT, SAMUEL
TRIPLETT, JOHN R.
TRORLICHT, J. H.
TUNSTALL, R. J.
TURNER, CHARLES H.
TURNER, JOHN W.
TURNER, J. LUCAS

VALLÉ, MRS. AGLAE
VAN STUDDIFORD, HENRY — M. D.
VASQUEZ, ANTOINE B.
VINCIL, JOHN D.
VOGEL, CHARLES F., 10 copies
VON PHUL, BENJAMIN

WACHTER, EMILE
WAGNER, WM. E.
WAGONER, HENRY H.
WAHL, JOHN
WAINWRIGHT, MRS. C. D.
WALDAUER, AUGUSTE
WALLIS, A. H.
WALSH, JULIUS S.
WALSH, REV'D WM.
WAMSGANZ, JOHN
WATERHOUSE, SILVESTER
WATERS, W. H.
WATERWORTH, JAS. A.
WASH, MILTON H.
WASHBURNE, MRS. A. G., Chicago
WEHRHEIM, A. G.

WEIGEL, EUGENE F.
WEISER, MARTIN
WELLS, ROLLA
WEST, WASHINGTON
WESSELER, F. W.—M. D.
WHERRY, MISS MARGARET
WICKHAM, HON. JOHN
WIEBUSH, HENRY
WIGGANS, J. F.
WILLIAMS, HENRY W.
WINKELMEIER, C., Brewery
WINTHROP, JOHN S. Tallahassee, Florida

WITT, THOMAS D.
WOERNER, HON. J. G.
WOLFF, MARCUS A.
WULFING, CHARLES

XAUPI, ED. J.

YEATMAN, JAMES E.
YOUNG, JOHN

ZEIGLER, REV'D CHARLES